D1632106

WEATHER
IN THE
GARDEN

Jane Taylor

JOHN MURRAY
Albemarle Street, London

(M)635. 952T.

A catalogue record for this book is available from the British Library

ISBN 0-7195-5267-2

Typeset in 12½/13 pt Bembo by Colset Pte Ltd, Singapore
Printed and bound in Great Britain by The University Press, Cambridge

Contents

Maps and Diagrams

Introduction

Half-way through writing this book, at the end of a mild, overcoat-free, central London winter, I was due to go to Washington, DC. On the day I was booked to fly, snowstorms muffled the east coast from Miami northwards in deep drifts, closing all the airports. I finally made it to Washington three days late, moving straight from an English spring to the depths of a continental winter. Then, three months later, a combination of temperatures in the low thirties centigrade (around 80 °F) and very high humidity made London feel more like Miami in summer. The television news showed clips of ceiling-high floods in towns and villages in the west of England, while here we had had only a sprinkling, barely enough to lay the dust. So much for Britain's equable climate.

At other times, I have shivered in San Francisco in May in temperatures not much different from a grey-skied London winter's day; yet there were palm trees overhead, melaleucas were flowering in the streets, and across the Bay in Sausalito it was brilliantly sunny and hot. Flamboyant or gul mohr (*Delonix regia*) and bougainvillea seem equally at home in steamy Florida amid the gardenias and frangipanis and in desert Karachi with its neem trees and thorny acacias in wasteland corners.

This book aims to explain some of these apparent contradictions and, in showing how weather and climate have affected plant evolution and how plants react to climatic influences, to indicate how gardeners can

1

turn that information to practical use in choosing plants most likely to succeed with them, or in giving the best chance to those that might seem unlikely to survive but are too tempting to forgo.

Both adventurous and timid gardeners are apt to ask similiar questions about the plants they would like to grow, though not for the same reasons. Cautious gardeners want to be reassured that they have chosen plants which will thrive, and not leave a gaping hole after the first hard winter or challenging drought; bolder souls are more likely to succumb to a possibly tender plant first, and speculate later where to put it so as to give it the best chance of survival.

Each garden has its own characteristics – it is more or less sheltered, more or less sunny, more or less of a frost-pocket, more or less exposed to cold or to blustery winds – the sum of which constitutes its microclimate. But even that is over-simplified: the smallest garden may have within it several further microclimates, from cool and shady to hot and sunny, from a tranquil corner where even a breeze does not penetrate and fragrance hangs in the air, to one where the wind buffets fragile foliage and wet washing is dry in no time.

Some people have green fingers and seem able to grow almost anything. Partly this is because they seem to know instinctively where a given species will be happiest, and how to contrive congenial conditions for plants with subtly different preferences. Most of the gardeners I know who have this gift do not rely only on instinct, however: they also spend time studying their plants, not just in the sense of observing them as they grow – though this is very important, as success often depends on spotting quickly that a plant is in need of water or shelter or other remedial treatment – but actually learning about them. Few of the plants we grow in our gardens today are native to where we live, and the gardeners who are most consistently successful with the widest range of plants find out where the plants originally came from, what the climate is like in that region, what habitat they favour in the wild, where else they grow well.

This kind of information is surprisingly difficult to find. Even quite substantial reference works often give little more than the country of origin of the plants; details of the climate, altitude and habitat are rarely available, unless you have access to the original collector's field notes. Of course, even with that sort of information, there are pitfalls; the object of your desire may dwell in damp places, say, but in its native land experience a milder climate or one with a different seasonal pattern of rainfall, so that to give it wet feet in your garden would be to condemn it to death. Such is the case with kniphofias (red hot pokers, torch lilies) in Britain; though most species grow beside streams in their native southern Africa, they greatly resent the cold, soggy winters of much of Britain and here must be given a well-drained soil, dry rather than wet.

Being of an adventurous and acquisitive turn of mind, and having, over the years, gardened in a variety of climates, I have grown a huge variety of plants from almost every part of the globe; I have certainly tested to the full the dictum that you cannot consider a plant too tender to grow in your garden until you have personally killed it three times. Endeavouring to do better, I have spent hours in libraries, progressing from the standard works of reference to ancient floras in a variety of languages, as I sought to discover just where this plant or that is to be found in the wild: at what altitude, in the company of which other species, in what kind of habitat. It is some of that knowledge that I share with you in this book, which concludes by inviting you to join me on a tour of eight different climatic regions to look at a great many – though still only a tiny selection – of the plants that are grown in gardens somewhere, by someone, as well as others that could or should be. If you are of a prudent turn of mind, you can choose to grow plants native to regions with a climate as close as possible to your own; as you grow more ambitious, you can balance a knowledge of your own garden against what you have learned about a given plant's habitat and the climate that has shaped its evolution, to judge whether you are more likely to succeed with it, or kill it.

First of all, however, I will look at how plants have evolved in response to local climatic conditions; at what we might do to make plants from other regions and habitats feel more at home in alien conditions; and at some of the reasons for the weather experienced in these eight climatic regions, and at what it means for plants and for gardeners. There are maps and diagrams, but no colour pictures, nor even any descriptions; and you will almost certainly need an atlas at your side as you read. At the very least, I hope that reading about where plants come from and their relationship with climate and weather will add a further dimension to your enjoyment of those you grow, or see on your travels.

1

Weather, climate and the gardener

Gardening in different climates

Gardeners have long grown plants from other lands, and in consequence from other climates. The impulse to try something new or to meet the challenge of growing a plant that has no business to succeed in your climate is often strong. Holidays in the Mediterranean or California tempt British gardeners to grow mimosa or agaves, and to bemoan the frost-tenderness of the bougainvillea that gardeners in climates more suited to it tend to despise for its ease and ubiquity. With often surprising success, they grow Californian or Australian plants side by side with Chilean rain-forest evergreens and rhododendrons from the cool, mist-wreathed Himalayan forests. Conversely, migrants to other lands often pine for the gardens of their youth; the British in particular, who have settled in so many different regions, are notorious for their attempts to recreate an English country garden in climates where subtleties of colour that look well under the grey-washed skies of 'home' simply do not work in the relentless clarity of a southerly sun, and most of the plants will hardly grow satisfactorily anyway.

CONTINENTAL CLIMATES
Continental climates, with their cold winters and warm or hot summers, are a challenge to plants from those less extreme. Frost is

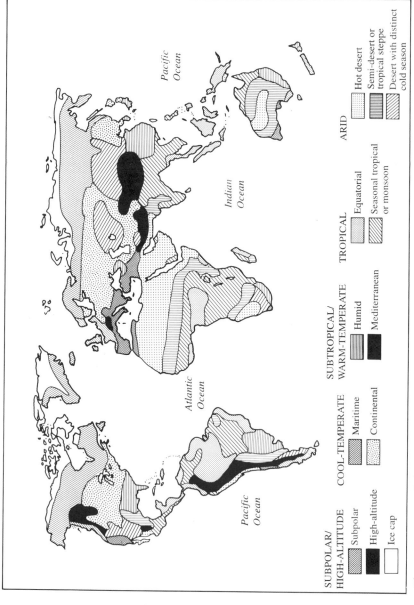

SUBPOLAR/
HIGH-ALTITUDE

Subpolar

High-altitude

Ice cap

COOL-TEMPERATE

Maritime

Continental

SUBTROPICAL/
WARM-TEMPERATE

Humid

Mediterranean

TROPICAL

Equatorial

Seasonal tropical
or monsoon

ARID

Hot desert

Semi-desert or
tropical steppe

Desert with distinct
cold season

Pacific
Ocean

Indian
Ocean

Atlantic
Ocean

Pacific
Ocean

Climatic regions of the world

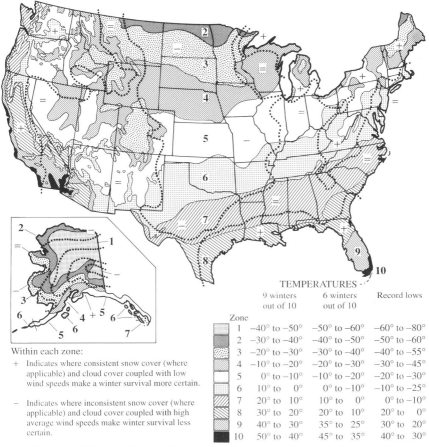

TEMPERATURES

Zone	9 winters out of 10	6 winters out of 10	Record lows
1	−40° to −50°	−50° to −60°	−60° to −80°
2	−30° to −40°	−40° to −50°	−50° to −60°
3	−20° to −30°	−30° to −40°	−40° to −55°
4	−10° to −20°	−20° to −30°	−30° to −45°
5	0° to −10°	−10° to −20°	−20° to −30°
6	10° to 0°	0° to −10°	−10° to −25°
7	20° to 10°	10° to 0°	0° to −10°
8	30° to 20°	20° to 10°	20° to 0°
9	40° to 30°	35° to 25°	30° to 20°
10	50° to 40°	45° to 35°	40° to 30°

Within each zone:

+ Indicates where consistent snow cover (where applicable) and cloud cover coupled with low wind speeds make a winter survival more certain.

− Indicates where inconsistent snow cover (where applicable) and cloud cover coupled with high average wind speeds make winter survival less certain.

= Indicates the middle range of these conditions.

Source: Compiled by John J. Sabuco and The White Oak Group Inc.

John Sabuco's Floradapt plant hardiness zone map

primarily the limiting factor but, as we shall see, snowfall, wind and cloud cover, aspect and elevation, all play their part in determining just what is likely to survive in your garden. Gardeners in North America are used to judging a plant's hardiness by its zone number, but the zones ordinarily in use are based on temperature only and are of limited helpfulness – as anyone trying to use them to predict a given plant's hardiness outside the US can testify.

John Sabuco, in *The Best of the Hardiest*, has produced what he calls the Floradapt map, which uses not only temperature records but data for snowfall, monthly average wind speeds from December to March, and the number of cloudy, partly cloudy and foggy days for the months of December through March. As well as the average daily low for the coldest month, the factor for temperature takes into account the record low; after all, it is not averages which kill plants, but extremes, including sudden extreme falls in temperature.

If snow falls before the ground has become frozen hard, and reasonable snow cover remains throughout winter, this will provide effective protection against severe cold; on the other hand, if snow cover alternates with thaws that leave the soil bare, or if continuous snow cover is slow to thaw in spring, the winter will be more challenging to plants, while little or no snow, or limited snow cover with frequent thaws alternating with freezes, are worse still. The stronger and more persistent the winds of winter, the more severe their drying effect and the more plants will suffer. Winter sun can also be stressful: the greater the winter cloud cover (however depressing for humans), the kinder the winter to plants.

Spring and autumn are shorter in continental than in island or maritime climates. Hardly has the snow of New England's winter melted before the heat of summer has arrived; the planting season (necessarily spring, given the extremely cold winters) is short and frenetic. At the approach of winter, leaf colours flare for a moment of intensity unequalled in a more moderate climate.

The hot summers compensate for cold winters in many ways, not least by ripening and baking plants to ensure prolific flowering and mature, frost-resistant wood. Many shrubs and trees which prove costive in more temperate climates or are exhausted in frost-free zones by the absence of a period of dormancy are at their best in the clear-cut seasons of continental climates. There are trees such as maples and sweet gum (*Liquidambar styraciflua*) for autumn tints, golden rain tree (*Koelreuteria paniculata*) and pink locusts (*Robinia* species) for flower, and a range of noble conifers for a dark backdrop. Kalmias flower with abandon, the moutan or tree peony (*Paeonia suffruticosa*) seldom gets caught out by stop–start spring weather, and trumpet vines are a mass of orange blooms.

MARITIME CLIMATES

Maritime climates are usually windy climates, in which a windbreak may be necessary even inland. Given shelter, a surprising number of Mediterranean and Californian plants do well in these, and in the island climates of western Europe, adapting to summer rain and winter chill. Once protected from salty gales, the coastal gardens of south-western

Britain and of Brittany in north-western France are, if wetter, scarcely colder in winter than the Mediterranean, though much less sunny and dry in summer.

With good drainage, a sunny position and shelter from biting winds, many plants will survive quite severe frosts. In our Swiss garden, which is in a region where the almost continental climate is tempered by Lake Léman but still experiences sharp cold spells, tough Mediterraneans such as rosemary and lavender do well because of our fast-draining sandy soil, the sunny summers which ripen the wood, and shelter from the cutting north wind.

The 'English' garden of smooth lawns and herbaceous borders is widely admired, but another type of gardening that the British have brought to near-perfection is the 'woodland as Eden', with Himalayan rhododendrons – species for the purist, hardy hybrids for the tyro – camellias and magnolias. The western coastal regions – again, once sheltered from wind – are ideal for these moisture-demanding plants, many of which thrive even in north-western Scotland, where the summers are shorter and the skies greyer (though the winters are not significantly colder) than in the south-west. The same gardens offer congenial quarters to southern-hemisphere evergreens from the temperate Chilean and New Zealand rain forests.

A frequent concern of gardeners in cool maritime climates is to ensure that plants are well ripened so as to flower freely; those from regions with hotter summers need to be given maximum sun and heat, by setting them against a wall that faces the midday, or at least the afternoon, sun. The effect of grey skies can be judged by comparing the flowering of trumpet creepers, *Campsis*, in southern Britain and in France. Nerines and other bulbs from warmer regions need a good baking, too. A short growing season and cool summers also affect the ability of woody plants to withstand low temperatures – British gardeners are familiar with the frustration of losing plants to winters much less severe than those of their native lands; a woody plant adapted to long, hot summers may be unable to ripen its wood sufficiently to withstand even mild winters, when they follow a short, comparatively cool growing season.

British gardeners also soon discover the limitations of the USDA hardiness zones (based upon average minimum winter temperatures) when applied to a different continent. In maritime, high-latitude climates, where the winters are characteristically alternately mild and frosty, a mean monthly temperature reveals nothing of the false starts and checks which will damage plants accustomed to a steadier progress from

11

winter to summer and back again. The drawn-out British spring, with its treacherous sudden frosts after a mild spell, its brief untimely heat waves or icy, desiccating winds from the east, is quite unlike the fleeting spring of continental climates. Plants from less unpredictable climates are easily lured into growth by a spell of mild weather, only to be damaged, perhaps killed, when frost returns. Other plants may be prompted to flower too early, so that the display is spoiled or lost entirely; the great tree magnolias are of this kind, and are often in consequence thought of as suitable only for milder climates, but if you are willing to accept a ruined display in, say, three years out of every four, by all means plant a *Magnolia sargentiana* or *M. campbellii* even if you garden away from favoured areas.

MEDITERRANEAN CLIMATES
In garden after garden on the Riviera, the Costa Brava and the Costa del Sol, and in California, plants from many lands, not all of them regions with Mediterranean climates, grow in a colourful assembly: antipodean mimosas and eucalypts, melaleucas and bottlebrushes, the Norfolk Island pine (*Araucaria heterophylla*), tropical cassias, the South American pepper tree (*Schinus molle*), tree tobacco (*Nicotiana glauca*), poinsettias, jacarandas and lantanas, aloes from Africa and agaves from the American deserts, Atlantic island echiums and Hottentot figs (*Carpobrotus edulis*) native to South Africa, grow alongside olives and pomegranates and citrus trees.

Creepers and climbers add an important dimension to these gardens. On whitewashed walls, *Tecomaria capensis* and *Podranea ricasoliana* clash with bougainvillea in many colours. The fragrance of *Jasminum grandiflorum* fills the air, succeeding in summer the spring-flowering primrose jasmine, *J. mesnyi*; and for months there is the perfume of honeysuckles, native or introduced. Spring is the season too of *Rosa banksiae*, a Chinese native which grows freely in southern European gardens. In summer, morning glories drape themselves like weeds over hedges and reach high into pines, rivalling the sea and sky in the intensity of their colour, and hibiscus flaunt their huge blooms.

A completely different style, appealing to gardeners who value native plants, uses the maquis as the model for dry-garden plantings of Jerusalem sage, lavender and rosemary in which close-knit groups of silver-leaved and waxy-glaucous plants contrast with the dark glittering foliage of kermes oak or myrtle, enlivened in due season by the flowers of cistus or oleander. The wide canopy of an umbrella pine, the gnarled branches and grey leaves of olives or a Judas tree, may cast welcome shade in the hottest months, a *primavera* of bulbs spread beneath in spring before summer's sun turns the landscape to a shimmering heat haze. In California, tree poppy and ceanothus, native oak and sumac, mariposa lily and California poppy play a similar role.

Yet another style of gardening in Mediterranean climates aims to recreate a desert atmosphere, with succulents and drought-tolerant plants such as agaves, aloes, Hottentot fig and cacti. *Opuntia*, the prickly pears and chollas, extend into cooler zones in North America and are planted in many countries of the world, so that species such as the blue-blade or dollar cactus, *Opuntia macrocentra* (*O. violacea santa-rita*), have become as characteristic of the Mediterranean and Australian landscapes as of their native lands. Some opuntias, native to high altitudes or to regions where the winters can be cold, are even resistant to quite long periods of frost. One of the most spectacular agaves, *A. franzosinii*, which forms bold rosettes of silver-blue, curving leaves, is used to great effect in a California garden, Lotusland in Santa Barbara, with the lowly blue grass *Festuca ovina* var. *glauca*, the succulent *Dudleya brittonii*, the Mexican blue fan palm *Brahea armata*, and blue Atlas cedar (*Cedrus libani* var. *atlantica* 'Glauca') in a scheme of harmonizing colour and contrasting form. Some agaves can even be grown in south-western Britain, where *A. americana* has been known to produce its massive, 10 m/33ft flowering stem.

THE SUBTROPICS

In climates where the summers are steamy and the winters warm and dry, the rare frost that does descend wreaks havoc; nothing is acclimatized, all the growth is soft and lush. Every so often the citrus crop in Florida is thus devastated, but in the intervening years there are ample compensations. The flowering trees are wonderfully colourful: the flamboyant or gul mohr (*Delonix regia*), jacarandas, *Lagerstroemia indica*, bauhinias, flame trees (*Brachychiton* [*Sterculia*] *acerifolius*), Mexican and South American *Tabebuia* species, kapok trees (*Chorisia speciosa*) and *Tibouchina*. Poinsettias, cherished as house plants in colder climates, grow into muscular garden shrubs. Hedges are of hibiscus or oleander or *Pittosporum tobira*. The air is heady with the fragrance of orange blossom, frangipani, jasmine, gardenias, and angel's trumpets (*Brugmansia* species). Climbing allamandas in yellow or pink, purple *Petraea volubilis*, pink *Mandevilla splendens*, the orange sweetheart vine (*Pyrostegia venusta*) from South America, and the Himalayan *Beaumontia grandiflora*, deck walls and trees. As relief from all that colour, *Ficus* species make solid dark trees, climbing aroids, sometimes variegated, add their bold foliage, and avenues of palms grace the streets.

In place of the border flowers of colder climates, the ground plantings are composed of bulbous plants and a handful of perennials – blood lilies (*Scadoxus multiflorus*), *Hippeastrum*, with cannas, caladiums, torch gingers, busy Lizzies, *Agapanthus*, peacock moraeas, gladioli, and the shrubby shrimp plant (*Justicia brandegeeana* [*Beloperone guttata*]) in copper or yellow.

Unlike the Mediterranean type of climate where the very dry summers induce dormancy, the subtropical allows for no resting season. Everything grows like mad in the hot and humid summers, and though the winters are drier, they are not dry enough, or cold enough, to impose dormancy: few plants from regions with cold winters can cope with this uninterrupted growing season.

ARID LANDS

For centuries, the chief aim of people living in arid regions has been to create green oases. Persian gardens, which gave us the word 'paradise' and inspired the great Mughal gardens of the Indian subcontinent, were enclosed and tranquil, a place where water cooled the air and delighted the ear, where trees provided graceful shade against the searing summer sun. The Arabs who made the gardens of the Generalife and the Alhambra in Granada, Spain, drew upon the same traditions.

Until recently, people making gardens in desert areas would use water without stint to create a modern style of oasis, aiming to deny rather than acknowledge the limitations of climate. Now, as water resources become more and more precious, the new orthodoxy is to use plants that need minimal irrigation; water-demanding plants are confined to areas near the house, where they can be efficiently irrigated using submerged drip-lines. Elsewhere, drought-tolerant plants form screens and provide ground-cover and shade trees. A tapestry of dwarf coyote brush (*Baccharis pilularis*) and saltbush (*Atriplex* species), spangled in season with the flowers of Hottentot fig, trailing lantana and the annual California poppy, will survive with barely any water beyond what falls in the brief wet season. The shade of drought-resistant trees, or of bougainvillea or queen's wreath (*Antigonon leptopus*) on a trellis or pergola, brings relief from the hot sun.

As in the Mediterranean, some gardeners prefer to accentuate the desert ambience. The American West is evoked by the use of spiky yuccas and dasylirions, the flat pads of prickly pear, the rosettes of massive, spiny agaves and small, succulent echeverias, amid the feathery outline of trees such as tamarisk or mesquite (*Prosopis* species), making full use of contrasting texture and form. Rather than green lawns, these plants look well with stone, raked sand or gravel paths. The Australian desert is quite different, with its wattles and eucalypts, casuarinas, heath myrtles and desert fuchsias, and the water-storing Queensland bottle tree.

THE TROPICS

For a gardener from the cool temperate regions, a visit to the tropics means an encounter with plants hitherto seen only in hothouses – and here they are growing outside. Orchids of a beauty rivalling anything from the specialist shows grow as freely as weeds. There are spathi-phyllums, anthuriums and heliconias, dappled marantas and caladiums, and the colourful leaves of *Acalypha wilkesiana*, red dracaenas (*Cordyline*), *Graptophyllum*, *Pseuderanthemum*, *Polyscias*, *Sanchezia*, *Pedilanthus* and *Codiaeum variegatum*, burgundy-red and silver-grey *Noeregelia* and *Aechmea* bromeliads.

In the tropics, fruits that command high prices as exotics in high-latitude supermarkets are everyday items. Originally from the Indo-Malayan region come breadfruit (*Artocarpus altilis*) and jackfruit (*A. heterophyllus*); the carambola (*Averrhoa carambola*); the wood apple (*Feronia limonia*) from the dry plains of India and Sri Lanka; the bignay (*Antidesma bunius*); the emblic (*Phyllanthes emblica*); the litchi (*Litchi chinensis* [*Nephelium litchi*]) and the rambutan (*Nephelium lappaceum* [*Euphoria nephelium, Dimocarpus crinita*]); the phalsa (*Grewia subinae-qualis*); the durian (*Durio zibethinus*); the mangosteen (*Garcinia mango-stana*); the jambhool (*Syzygium cumini* [*S. jambolana, Eugenia cumini, E. jambolana*]), *S. malaccense* and the rose apple (*S. jambos* [*Eugenia jambos, Jambosa jambos*]); and, of course, the mango (*Mangifera indica*) and the banana (*Musa acuminata*).

Tropical America has contributed the cherimoya (*Annona cherimola*), sugar apple (*A. squamosa*), soursop (*A. muricata*) and bullock's heart (*A. reticulata*); the pineapple (*Ananas comosus*); the papaya (*Carica papaya*); the guava (*Psidium guajava*) and the strawberry guava (*P. cattleyanum*); the strawberry pear, fruit of the night-blooming cereus (*Hylocereus undatus*); the sapodilla or chikoo (*Manilkara zapota*) which also produces chicle, the basis of chewing-gum; the star apple (*Chrysophyllum cainito*); the purple mombin (*Spondias purpurea*) and the yellow mombin or hog plum (*S. mombin*); the Jamaica cherry (*Muntingia calabura*) and the Barbados cherry (*Malpighia punicifolia*); the white sapote (*Casimiroa edulis*); and from subtropical regions, the avocado (*Persea americana*), the feijoa (*Acca sellowiana*), the giant granadilla (*Passiflora quadrangularis*), the passion fruit (*P. edulis*) and the banana passion fruit (*P. mollissima*) from the Andean valleys of Colombia, Bolivia and Peru. Among the fruits of Africa are the tamarind (*Tamarindus indica*), the kei apple (*Dovyalis caffra*), the amatungula or Natal plum (*Carissa grandiflora*) and, from the coastal forests of tropical West Africa, the akee (*Blighia sapida*). The ambarella (*Spondias dulcis*) is a native of Melanesia and Polynesia, and the date palm (*Phoenix dactylifera*) of the oases of North Africa. Some of these have been so long cultivated and have become so widespread that it is no longer possible to be sure of their origins.

For gardeners wishing to create something approximating to a temperate garden, there are a number of problems. Plants, like people, can suffer from too much sun, and the hot, dry afternoon air can be especially damaging, drying or even killing soft growths. Trees or climbers to provide shade are a practical necessity. People who live in hill stations, where it is cooler, may succeed with plants such as autumn-flowering chrysanthemums and Michaelmas daisies, which require a short day-length to flower, but anything that needs a long day will not succeed. The flowering trees and climbers that grow in the humid subtropics also thrive in the tropics; with so much to choose from, it seems perverse to struggle with roses or daffodils.

2

How plants adapt

Whether 'is it hardy' means 'will it stand my winters?', or 'will it cope with parched summers and saline soils?', it is a difficult question to answer: there are so many imponderables. That great English gardener Collingwood ('Cherry') Ingram wrote, in *A Garden of Memories*:

> Despite my forty years' experience of collecting plants in many parts of the world, I still find it almost impossible to predict with any degree of certainty whether an unfamiliar species will turn out to be hardy or not. But during that time I have learnt to recognize at least *some* of the meteorological and other factors which will almost certainly inhibit a plant's survival in England.

What is true of England, indeed of the whole of Britain, with its temperate but fickle climate that yet suits an amazing range of plants, is no less true elsewhere. The only alteration I am tempted to make to the quotation is to add the words 'familiar or' before 'unfamiliar'; even in one's own garden, with its known climate and microclimates, the hardiness (or lack of it) of both well-known and unfamiliar plants can result in unexpected losses and successes. Hardiness encompasses the ability to resist all vagaries of climate. Fortunately for gardeners, many species are able to tolerate a much wider range of environmental conditions than they experience in their natural habitats.

17

Factors for growth and hardiness

The ecologist Victor Shelford proposed a theory of tolerance which was later elaborated by the plant geographer Ronald Good to include principles such as: 'each and every plant species is able to exist and reproduce successfully only within a definite range of environmental conditions'; and, 'in order of importance, the environmental conditions are climatic, edaphic [pertaining to soil], and biotic [pertaining to life processes]'. Good recognized not only that these factors are interdependent, but that competition has its own effect on tolerance ranges. Fortunately for those of us who want to grow as wide a range of species as possible in our gardens, plants reared in what are effectively alien environments often show a tolerance of conditions they would never encounter in their natural habitats, so that we need not be reduced to growing only native plants or those from regions with nearly identical climates. Clearly, however, the greater the difference between the weather conditions of a species' native habitat and what it is called upon to survive in our gardens, the more important it is, if we hope to succeed with it, that we understand how its native climate differs from what we can offer.

Every species, every specialized form or variant within a species, appears to have a critical minimum temperature below which it cannot survive. This may range from 5 °C/40 °F for many tropical species to well below freezing for arctic or high-alpine species, and may be modified by other factors. For individual species, as well as for vegetation types, the amount and, especially, the distribution of rainfall are important: different plants vary in their tolerance of drought, of atmospheric and soil moisture or its lack, and of the relationship between temperature and moisture.

The intensity and number of hours of sunlight each day also play a part. In high latitudes the lower light levels and shorter summers, especially in maritime climates with their frequent cloud cover, are unfavourable for the ripening of woody tissues. Plants that have evolved in regions of hotter and sunnier summers may be damaged or killed, in maritime climates, by frosts they would disdain in their native lands. If they are undamaged by frost, they may not flower freely, or at all, either because their wood is insufficiently ripened or because the summers are too short for them to develop and open their flower buds before the first frosts of autumn.

Wind exacerbates both frosty and dry conditions. Plants from regions where severe cold usually occurs only in still conditions may be unable to adapt to windier though no colder winters elsewhere; this is true of many evergreens from windy New Zealand, where such frosts as occur generally do so in still weather. On the other hand, some quite frost-hardy plants which are barely affected by icy winds coming from overland will succumb to warmer but fierce salt- and sand-laden winds blowing off the ocean.

The processes of evolution have resulted in many different plant-distribution patterns. The most limited distribution is that of endemics – genera or species found naturally in one specific region – of which there are about 10,000. Some are very rare, or are restricted to a very small range, suggesting a plant that is not very adaptable; and indeed many, having evolved in response to particular environment factors that cannot easily be duplicated elsewhere, are among the most difficult to satisfy in the garden. On the other hand, plants with a very limited distribution may simply be unable to cope with the competition found in more favourable habitats; cossetted in the garden, they may thrive as they seldom do in the more or less hostile habitats to which they retreat in the wild.

Biorhythms and survival mechanisms

Despite the surprising adaptability of many plants, the specific responses they have evolved to cope with particular environmental influences sometimes prove their downfall under different conditions. Plants accustomed to the clear-cut seasons of continental climates are often tricked by the stop–go winters of maritime regions into untimely spring growth, prey to damage or death from frosts that would have left them unscathed in the deeper dormancy induced by their native winters; monsoon-habited plants tend to grow late in the season and in temperate climates may fail to ripen enough to withstand early autumn frosts or winter cold.

Plants adapted to spend part of each year dormant underground may need a hot, dry season to induce flowering; such species are said to need 'a good baking' to thrive and flower. However, it is a drop in temperature that prompts the wind flower or rain lily, *Zephyranthes candida*, into flower: the bulbs grow in wet meadows on the banks of the River Plate in Argentina, and flower after the fall in temperature that follows heavy rain.

Plants adapted to a hot summer may survive in regions where the summers are cooler or greyer, but fail to flower or fruit. The trumpet creepers, *Campsis*, which are such a glory in much of the United States and southern continental Europe, need the hottest possible position against a sunny wall to produce ripe, flowering growths in Britain. Where the summer is short, plants adapted to a longer growing season may not reach flowering maturity before autumn frosts bring them to a standstill. The hardy *Hibiscus syriacus*, for example, can withstand lower winter temperatures than those commonly experienced in most of Britain, but because it needs long, hot summers it is very late leafing in spring, does not flower before late summer in the south, and in the north of Britain may simply not flower at all. Other such species may flower, but fail to set viable seed, or the seed that is set may be damaged by cold or excessive damp.

A short growing season also reduces the ability of woody plants to withstand winter temperatures much less severe than those of their native lands. Gardeners in Britain are accustomed to casualties among plants which, adapted to long, hot summers, are unable to ripen their wood sufficiently during a short, cool growing season to withstand even mild, Gulf Stream winters.

Deciduous broad-leaved woody plants are generally more frost-resistant than evergreen broad-leaves. Some are adaptable enough to shed their leaves in cold winters while retaining them, at least in part, in milder years or milder regions. Others, drought-deciduous in summer by nature, may be adaptable enough to become winter-deciduous where the summers are damp and the winters colder, even if not drier, than in their native habitats.

Leaf-shedding is not merely a response to such adverse conditions as cold and drought, nor is it confined to deciduous plants. Evergreens in dry areas shed their leaves progressively, producing a steady supply of nutrients which helps to minimize nutrient loss through leaching. Nutrients are less easily leached from needle litter than from broad-leaf litter, so coniferous forests conserve nutrients more efficiently than evergreen broadleaf forests.

TREES FROM THE TROPICS
Tropical trees have many different patterns of growth, in contrast to the simple division of temperate woody plants into evergreen, winter-deciduous, and those semi-evergreens which retain their leaves in mild winters but shed some or all in colder ones. Most tropical and rain-forest trees renew their leaves in periodic flushes rather than at a constant rate through the year; the interval may be regular or irregular. Examples of regular leaf production include *Parkia roxburghii, Cratoxylon*

polyanthum, Tamarindus indica (every 12 months); *Terminalia catappa, Ficus variegata* and *Peltophorum ferrugineum* (every 6 months); *Breynia cernua* (every 5½ months); a tree of *Delonix regia* at Singapore (9 months) and one of *Heritiera macrophylla* (2 years and 8 months). The rubber tree, *Hevea brasiliensis*, and the mango, *Mangifera indica*, both produce new leaves at very irregular intervals. In the case of the rubber tree, the intervals differ on different individuals and alter with the age of the individual – except in more seasonal climates, which appear to impose greater regularity. The mango produces new leaves on different branches of the same individual at different times; this is also the pattern of *Ceiba pentandra*, some specimens of which will show some branches entirely bare and others in full leaf at the same time, while others are regularly and evenly deciduous. *Pterocarpus indicus* is irregularly deciduous at Singapore, but completely deciduous in northern Malaya.

In some species, all or most of the old leaves fall well before the new ones unfurl, so the tree is bare for some time: *Bombax malabaricum, Toona australis, Hymenaea courbaril, Terminalia superba*, and others. More commonly, in rain-forest trees, the old leaves fall and the new unfurl at more or less the same time, so the tree may be bare for only a few days. In some species leaf fall is very rapid (*Ficus variegata* takes only a few days), but more often it takes much longer.

Deciduous trees (those which shed all their leaves to become entirely bare, if only for a few days) are common in the tropical rain forest, even in areas that are almost completely non-seasonal, but are found mainly in the upper storey. The drier the climate, the higher the proportion of deciduous species, at first in the upper and then in the lower storey. Curiously, new leaves do not necessarily expand after the rains; in the evergreen forests of West Africa, for example, many deciduous trees unfurl new leaves long before the end of the dry season, even during the very dry harmattan which blows from the Sahara south-westwards to the Guinea Coast, when the risk of desiccation is high. A similar pattern is seen in Sri Lanka and the east-monsoon region of Java.

Environmental factors and genetic make-up may play their part, and one or the other may be more important, depending upon the climate and the species. Leaf fall may be prompted by the soil drying out, or by the exhaustion of available nutrients. In non-seasonal climates, genetic factors appear to be important; some families such as Sterculiaceae and Bombacaceae have many deciduous members, but others like Lauraceae are almost wholly evergreen. In very seasonal climates teak, *Tectona grandis*, like *Bombax malabaricum*, has a long leafless period during the dry season, but in a largely non-seasonal climate, such as that of Singapore or West Java, teak is evergreen while the *Bombax* still loses all its leaves for a long time.

Tropical trees flower as erratically as they leaf. Flowering in most rain-forest climates peaks at the end of the dry season, especially in the upper storey, where the tree crowns are more exposed to variations in humidity and temperature than are denizens of the equable micro-climate below the canopy. Some trees flower almost continuously, carrying flowers and fruit at the same time, while others flower once or twice a year, still others at even longer intervals. Some flower only when they are bare of leaves, or only on individual branches that are bare; among these is *Ceiba pentandra*. Some trees flower intermittently, at regular intervals of 7 to 10 months, with different individuals flowering at different times: the poinciana (*Delonix regia*), *Lagerstroemia speciosa*. Gregarious flowering is the very opposite, when all the individuals of a given species, perhaps over a very large area, burst into flower at once; this is common in the Amazonian Myrtaceae, for example, and is also seen in certain Malayan orchids, such as the pigeon orchid, *Dendrobium crumenatum*, in which flowering nearly always follows a thunder-shower after a dry spell and the resulting sudden fall in temperature.

Adapting to different climatic rhythms

Some plants which start into growth with the onset of rain and cease as the dry season begins are unable to adapt to a different climate. Plants from the western Cape region of South Africa, where dry summers and wet winters impose summer dormancy on winter growth, are less well able to stand the cool climate of, say, Britain than are those from the much warmer areas of Natal and Transvaal (particularly from higher altitudes), where summer rain and dry winters have accustomed them to winter dormancy.

Xerophilous plants – those that are adapted to more or less permanently dry conditions – may be unable to cope with very moist air or soil, especially in cold weather, while if kept dry they may survive quite low temperatures, even frost. For such plants in particular, free-draining soil is essential, while one that lies wet and cold in winter means almost certain death. Even very frost-resistant plants can suffer if grown too 'soft': for example, the dyer's greenweed, *Genista tinctoria*, stands severe frost when grown in dry, poor soil, but is killed by less extreme cold where a moist, rich soil induces rapid, soft growth. By contrast, *Ilex glabra*, the inkberry, needs a moist, even wet soil to survive cold winters; in normal, well-drained garden soil its evergreen leaves burn in winter. There are cultivars of the inkberry which do not suffer in this way, however; and it is possible that by selection a greater resistance to specific climatic factors might be developed in species from many genera. The desirability of maintaining such genetic diversity is just one of the arguments in favour of plant conservation, of both species and cultivated varieties.

The suffering during dry spells of plants adapted to high atmospheric humidity and to permanently moist soils will be exacerbated by dry air, wind, and hot sun, to which their often large, soft leaves, having no mechanism for reducing transpiration, will be very vulnerable.

The age of an individual plant may also affect its ability to withstand adverse environmental conditions. As a general rule, plants required to survive temperatures lower than they would experience in their native habitat will prove hardier once they have developed some mature wood than while they are still immature and soft. However, some genera, such as the *Cistus* of the Mediterranean region or the *Ceanothus* of the California chaparral, are hardier as young plants than when they become old and woody.

Coping with frost

Plants from regions where they occur cope with frosts by entering dormancy, their life processes, reduced to a minimum, resuming when warmth returns in the spring.

ARCTIC PLANTS
The tundra flora of the Arctic represents a small percentage only of the world's species. Adapted to a very short growing season of only fifty to sixty very long days, and to soil that is permanently frozen below a surface layer which thaws in summer, they are mainly non-woody perennials with over-wintering buds just at the soil surface. Even in full summer growth they are not tall; many are cushion plants, with foliage similar in its characteristics to that of some plants of dry regions – small leaves, often downy, often light in colour, sometimes succulent. Although tundra plants break their winter dormancy even while still covered with snow in the spring, their seeds require surprisingly high temperature – close to 20 °C/68 °F – to germinate; flower

buds, formed one or more seasons previously, open in response to the lengthening days; seed, set in abundance, has a long life. In late summer, dormancy is triggered by shortening days, lowering temperatures, and a consequent decrease in the moisture available in the soil; it may also be related to the lowering angle of the sun in these very high latitudes.

HIGH-ALPINE PLANTS

The similarities between tundra and alpine plants are clear, though the latter are adapted to less extreme seasonal variations in day length, and to brighter light and greater extremes of temperature in summer. Like some in the tundra, there are alpine and subalpine plants which awaken to spring before the snow has melted; in *Mertensia ciliata*, a North American subalpine snow bank plant, activity begins even before the leaves have expanded, within the stems.

Some alpine plants are covered with woolly hairs; one of the best known is edelweiss, *Leontopodium alpinum*, with leaves like white flannel protecting it against water loss under the fierce mountain sun. The evergreen mats of foliage belonging to other species are protected by a blanket of snow, beneath which they may pass the months of dormancy at temperatures just above freezing; like tundra plants they too have a very short season in which to flower and seed. As the energy this requires leaves little over for vegetative growth, both types are commonly slow-growing and relatively long-lived. Alpine plants often have woody rootstocks that penetrate far into the rocky soil in search of moisture and nutrients, and also store the food reserves manufactured during the summer.

THE TREE LINE AND THE TAIGA

The coniferous trees of the taiga – that vast region of subpolar North America and Eurasia with a cold, wet climate and a short growing season of one to three months, where the annual temperature range is very wide, especially in the continental interior – form the dominating part of a two-tier community, above a ground layer of dwarf shrubs, ferns, mosses and lichens; taller shrubs are uncommon. A similar type of vegetation is found at the highest altitudes at which trees will survive in mountainous regions. Being evergreen, the trees are able to take full advantage of the short growing season by resuming photosynthesis as soon as the temperature rises above freezing in spring; narrow needles covered with a hard cuticle withstand cold and frost-induced desiccation. The larch, *Larix*, an exception to the generally evergreen nature of conifers, loses its needles completely in winter and shows other adaptations to extreme climatic conditions, such as very tough timber, and an ability to regenerate readily if broken by gales, avalanches or exceptionally heavy snow.

PLANTS OF THE COOL TEMPERATE REGIONS

At lower latitudes and altitudes, though still in regions where the winters are more or less frost-bound, deciduous broad-leaved trees make an appearance. Some of the most cold-resistant, in the northern hemisphere, are the birches, a genus found throughout the polar regions, and the North American quaking aspen, *Populus tremuloïdes*. Where winters are less severe, beech and oak, maple and rowan, cherry and crab – the trees of the northern cool temperate landscape – make their appearance.

Although there is comparatively much less land mass in the southern hemisphere at cool temperate latitudes, it exhibits parallel species of broad-leaved trees; for example, in southern South America deciduous species of *Nothofagus* or southern beech echo the *Fagus* of the northern hemisphere. These and other frost-tolerant high-latitude trees from both hemispheres enter dormancy by shedding their leaves. After a spell of cold, rising temperatures and lengthening days trigger renewed activity; the sap rises, new leaves unfurl from dormant buds, and photosynthesis resumes.

In these cool temperate regions of less extreme annual temperature ranges are also many herbaceous perennials, which grow fresh foliage each spring; during the cold weather they are leafless, the crown from which the new spring growth will emerge protected by the dead stems and leaves of the previous season's growth. Some plants will be permanently leafy or woody in mild climates, but can regenerate from shoots at or below ground level if the top growth is killed by frost in winter.

PLANTS FROM THE SUBTROPICS AND TROPICS

Many of the plants from the seasonally dry Mediterranean and the constantly humid subtropical climates, which straddle the frost line, are able to withstand light frost, though most would be killed if it were prolonged or sharp. Although it is often said that the incidence of frost is the single most important environmental factor affecting species distribution, the fact that a species originates in a frost-free climate does not necessarily mean that it will be unable to survive freezing temperatures; as always, the relationship between temperature and other climatic factors, especially rainfall, has to be considered. Many species from the frost-free Atlantic islands of Madeira and the Canaries, for example, survive remarkably well in southern England, where frosts are not unknown. And while many tropical species are so intolerant of cold that they may be killed by temperatures a few degrees above freezing, a few trees, for example *Eucalyptus deglupta*, are able to tolerate mild frost.

Surviving drought

In regions where frost is not prevalent, the availability of moisture may take its place as a limiting factor. Dormancy, an adaptation to cold, is also one way in which plants cope with stress in climates marked by regular dry spells; 'going to ground' is a familiar form of response in plants from such regions. A great many plant species of the Mediterranean, central Asia and South Africa form bulbs, corms or tubers in which to store the food reserves accumulated while they are in leaf. They emerge and flower in a great burst of activity after the rains, and as soon as the leaves have returned nourishment to the underground storage organ they wither and die and the plant is seen no more above ground until the next rainy season. Bulbs originating where a Mediterranean-type climate merges into desert – the Sahara, the Syrian desert, the California deserts, the Karoo in South Africa and the Atacama in Chile – are particularly intolerant of excess damp, especially when it is combined with cold.

A different kind of drought-induced dormancy is that of many succulent plant families, such as Agavaceae, Crassulaceae and Cactaceae, which fix carbon dioxide during the night, in contrast to the norm of fixing it during the day. Indeed, some succulent desert plants, such as the giant saguaro cactus, *Carnegiea gigantea*, will enter a long period of dormancy during the hottest, driest season, storing both carbon dioxide and water and metabolizing internally until the rains; plants of this type are slow-growing but long-lived. Other succulents store water in their fleshy leaves, stems or caudex to survive periods of drought: the Queensland bottle tree, *Brachychiton rupestris*, actually has a bottle-shaped trunk, which stores a jelly-like liquid with a high water content; agaves, echeverias and aloes all store water in their thick leaves; cacti and succulent euphorbias have stout, fleshy stems and a tough, waxy skin.

Some conifers, notably the huge trees of the Pacific north-west of North America, store large quantities of water in their sapwood; if transpiration exceeds the water supply from the roots, this reserve is available to the plant. It has been calculated that a typical specimen of Douglas fir, *Pseudotsuga menziesii*, 80 m/265 ft tall, stores 4,000 litres of water, of which 75 per cent is available during times of drought. This ability to use stored water is why, unlike broad-leaved trees, few conifers shed their leaves as a response to drought.

Water is also stored in the fleshy roots of plants such as the cat's-claw vine (*Macfadyena unguis-cati*), the asparagus fern and the queen's wreath, *Antigonon leptopus*. Other responses are to develop massive, spreading root systems or very deep tap roots, which search for moisture beyond the reach of other plants: eucalypts, mesquite (*Prosopis* species) and the desert hackberry, *Celtis pallida*, are plants of this type. They are able to take advantage of ground water when it is present, but can tolerate periods of drought. Some other plants from arid zones are confined to habitats where there is permanent underground water; among them are trees such as cottonwood (*Populus fremontii*), willow (*Salix* species), *Platanus racemosa*, salt cedar (*Tamarix* species) and fan palm (*Washingtonia filifera*). Despite the harsh environment, they may develop into very large trees.

LEAF ADAPTATIONS TO DROUGHT

The Mexican palo verde, *Parkinsonia aculeata*, has no fewer than three adaptations to drought: a shallow, fibrous root system which spreads widely just below the surface to take advantage of every drop of rain; a deep-tap root; and the ability to shed its tiny leaves, its midribs, and even small twigs, in response to continuing drought – its green bark contains chlorophyll, enabling it to continue photosynthesis even without leaves. The ocotillo, *Fouquieria splendens*, a desert plant, loses its leaves in response to drought and grows new ones each time moisture becomes available, perhaps as often as five times a year. Other drought-deciduous desert plants include the brittle bush, *Encelia farinosa*, and the burro bush, *Ambrosia dumosa*.

Some plants native to Mediterranean climates are also drought-deciduous and thus dormant during the heat of summer, even though the total annual rainfall is higher than in desert regions. The maquis of the Mediterranean, the chaparral of California and Chile, and parts of Australia, all contain a mixture of evergreen and drought-deciduous shrubs. The California buckeye, *Aesculus californica*, is a drought-deciduous broad-leaved tree, leafless during summer; in wetter regions,

27

however, for example when grown in England, it retains its leaves in summer and sheds them in winter, in response to the cold.

Very small leaves, like the needles of conifers, also help plants to conserve moisture. Many brooms from the Mediterranean region (species of *Cytisus, Genista* and *Spartium*) have green stems (to add to their photosynthesizing capacity) and very small leaves; the broom baccharis or desert broom, *Baccharis sarothroïdes*, copes with dry conditions by means of its vestigial leaves and green stems. Both the casuarinas of Australia and the tamarisks of North Africa and the Middle East have adapted to drought, hot winds and poor soil by developing deep roots and almost leafless stems; what look like needle-fine leaves are in fact tiny jointed branchlets, on which the true leaves are minutely small. Among the tamarisks are the athel tree or athel salt cedar, *Tamarix aphylla*, and the salt cedar, *T. africana*. The narrow, spiky leaves of some yuccas, such as *Y. glauca*, are hard-textured and lose little moisture through transpiration. Some species of hakea, and cacti such as the barrel cactus (*Ferocactus acanthoïdes*), have leaves reduced to spines.

Broader leaves may have a hard pellicle (cuticle or membrane) to protect them against moisture loss. Many of the evergreen shrubs and trees native to regions with a Mediterranean climate are sclerophyllous – that is, they have stiff, thick, hard leaves – and as a further protection the leaf pores close during the dry season, so that the plants are semi-dormant. The coating of fine hairs on the leaf surface of many plants is effective in reducing transpiration, reflecting back light to reduce temperature within the leaf tissue and protecting against the desiccating effects of wind. It is these hairs which give a silvery finish to so many favourite garden plants for dry places: *Calocephalus brownii* with its stems like platinum wire, silky *Convolvulus cneorum*, woolly *Stachys byzantina* or felted *Brachyglottis compacta*. A waxy coating, such as that which gives the bluish cast to the California mahonias or to many eucalypts, also helps to reduce moisture loss.

Other plants protect themselves by turning their leaves edge-on to the sun, in the way of several manzanitas (*Arctostaphylos* species), *Dendromecon rigida*, and some desert plants. In the manzanitas the leaf angle increases with aridity; in *Heteromeles arbutifolia*, leaves in the sun are held at steeper angles than those in the shade. Yet another method is to fold the leaves during the hottest hours. Light-reflecting surfaces also help to reduce the temperature within the leaf tissues; the desert plant *Leucophyllum frutescens* has small, silvery leaves which during rainy spells become green and semi-succulent; in extreme drought, all the leaves are shed except for those at the branch tips. *Atriplex* species, the salt bushes and desert hollies, have evergreen leaves that are silver-white in very dry conditions, from salts deposited on the leaf surface, which helps to reflect light. As a further protection, the leaves of desert holly (*A. hymenelytra*) are held at a steep angle to the sun's rays; this reduces their exposure to heat and makes them most receptive to light during the early morning and late afternoon, when the air is at its most humid. With ample moisture the desert holly leaves become grey-green, and those produced during the cool season are nearly twice the size of summer leaves.

OTHER DROUGHT ADAPTATIONS
The jojoba, *Simmondsia chinensis*, is an evergreen shrub with cell tissues that are able to resist unusual desiccation. Other arid-region plants produce a toxic substance to deter competition for the available moisture, a technique known as allelopathy. This is the way of *Larrea tridentata*, the creosote bush, which dominates the warm deserts of North America; and of coastal sage, *Salvia leucophylla*, which thus keeps annual grasses and herbs at a distance of a metre or two. The dense, scrubby vegetation known as California hard chaparral, dominated by chamise (*Adenostoma fasciculatum*), typically has bare ground beneath the shrubs. Another way of keeping potential competitors at bay is adopted by some of the tamarisks, which shed salt-rich leaves.

Some plants have evolved a structure which captures the maximum available moisture. The rosette form of some agaves and bromeliads is such an adaptation, as are the corrugated ribs which run vertically along the stems of some succulent cacti and euphorbias; both formations tend to guide every drop of available moisture down towards the roots.

Some desert plants, such as saguaro cactus (*Carnegiea gigantea*), make use of nurse plants; almost all successful saguaro seedlings will be found to grow close to a shade-producing object, most often a perennial plant. The shading reduces both temperature and the rate of soil drying, and offers some protection from frost. Some desert annuals, too, profit from nurse plants; *Malacothrix* and *Chaenactis* are associated in this way with burro bush (*Ambrosia dumosa*) and turpentine bush (*Thamnosma montana*). It is possible that these shrubs, in trapping wind-blown organic debris, provide a more congenial soil for the annuals than that of the open ground.

Dew and fog both provide some relief from drought, although few plants are able to absorb more than a small proportion of their water needs from the moisture that condenses on their leaf surfaces. There are exceptions, however. Air plants (*Tillandsia*) are so called because they are able to gather enough moisture from the air alone, through tiny hairs on the leaves; they can be seen growing on telephone cables and power lines, as well as on living hosts. However, Spanish moss (*T. usneoïdes*) cannot fulfil all its water needs from the air, even at the 80 per cent humidity which it prefers, but requires occasional rain as well; it is limited to areas with an average annual humidity of 64 per cent or more, but its distribution is also closely related to the storm paths which occur east and north from Mexico.

Surviving as seeds

So far we have considered only perennial plants. Annuals spend their period of dormancy as seed, in which state they are able to survive extremes of temperature and drought, for perhaps years or even centuries, until the conditions they need for germination recur. This is the technique adopted by some common weeds, such as shepherd's purse and chickweed, as well as by many desert ephemerals.

A variety of mechanisms have evolved which ensure that germination does not occur when environmental conditions are unsuitable for the resultant seedlings to survive. Some seeds have a very hard or woody coat which must be breached by fire (or abrasion) before germination will take place; the fire having burnt off other undergrowth, adequate light levels for the seedlings are assured. *Canna indica* is one such, known as Indian shot because its seeds are so hard and bullet-like (an effective way for the gardener to breach such a seed coat is to whizz the dry seed in a kitchen blender for some seconds; larger seeds can be individually filed with a nail file or emery paper). Many acacias also have very hard seeds, and these can be primed for germination by pouring boiling water over them and leaving them overnight. In extreme cases, soaking in concentrated sulphuric acid may be needed to break down the seed coat.

The seed of some species contains germination inhibitors which are water-soluble in rain, thus ensuring that the seeds only germinate in moistened soil – an effective mechanism in climates where rainfall is unpredictable, or severe seasonal drought is the norm.

The annual habit is unsuited to very cold climates because the growing season is too short to allow for a full life cycle in a single season; so the typical arctic or high altitude plant is perennial. The seeds of most plants native to higher latitudes and altitudes – even some from such comparatively equable climates as that of the Australian mountains – remain dormant until a period of cold combined with moisture, followed by rising temperatures, increased moisture, lengthening days, and perhaps the physical or chemical disruption of the seed coat, leads to germination; in some species, two cold periods, with a spell of warmth between, are required to break dormancy. In cultivation, the treatment given such seeds, in imitation of nature, is known as stratification; seeds are planted in a moist medium and kept at a low temperature, around 4 or 5 °C/41 °F – exposure to frost is not necessarily implied, and it could kill seeds from frost-free climates. Some plants from warm regions are winter growers, programmed *not* to germinate at high temperatures; others, such as *Hibiscus trionum*, need a regime of wide daily temperature fluctuations.

A cold spell is needed by some plants to ensure flowering, too: seeds planted in autumn and exposed to winter cold, or kept at low temperatures during germination in spring, produce plants that flower much earlier than if the seeds were sown in spring without exposure to cold. The application of this process in cultivation – known as vernalization – is seen in, for example, the preparation of hyacinth bulbs for indoor forcing, but its widest commercial application is in cereal production.

In the deserts of North America much of the vegetation consists of annuals, which fall into two categories: those that germinate in autumn or winter and flower in late spring, and those that germinate in midsummer to flower in the autumn. Their requirements, not surprisingly, are quite different. In the Mojave desert the seeds of summer annuals, shed in autumn, remain dormant until a period of dry heat (50 °C/122 °F) is followed by the heavy rains of late summer; while the soil temperature is still above 26 °C/79 °F they germinate, and then mature within weeks, before the onset of autumn frosts. Mojave winter annuals germinate after autumn or winter rains in excess of 15 mm/0.6 in, when the soil temperature is below 18 °C/65 °F; they grow slowly through the winter, to flower rapidly in spring as temperatures rise.

Diurnal temperature variations and day length

Many plants require a particular day–night temperature difference for optimal growth: both red fir, *Abies magnifica*, and *Pinus jeffreyi*, for example, grow best with a diurnal difference of 13 °C/23.5 °F; by contrast, the coast redwood, *Sequoia sempervirens*, appears to be equally happy in constant temperatures and a difference of 4 °C/17 °F. These differing responses (known as thermoperiodism) would appear to be adaptations to particular climatic circumstances, since the coast redwood is found in an area with a small diurnal temperature range, while the uplands where the red fir and Jeffrey pine occur experience a wide diurnal temperature range. Some plants simply cannot live without such variations in temperature: the daisy, *Bellis perennis*, dies in a constant warm temperature, needing cold nights to flower freely. Such temperature variations are also needed by some plants for seed germination.

The energy received from the sun is one of the most important elements of the environment, providing not only heat but light, essential to most organisms. Green plants need light to transform carbon dioxide and water into nutrients through the process of photosynthesis; and they respond in different ways to it, especially to the length of light and dark periods, a phenomenon known as photoperiodism. Photoperiodism is evident in various responses, one of which is dormancy; this may be induced by short autumn days, to prepare the plant's defences against extreme winter cold – or it may be induced by long days, as a defence against seasonal drought.

In high latitudes, where the days of spring and autumn are of similiar length, bud dormancy as a winter defence is triggered by the shortening days of autumn which follow a period of warmth, rather than by the lengthening days of spring which follow a period of intense cold.

In some temperate deciduous tree species (among them *Rhus glabra* and *Liriodendron tulipifera*), leaf fall is induced by short days; in most, however, it is the result of falling temperatures. The relationship between temperature and day length also gives the signal for growth to cease. In some plants from temperate regions dormancy is induced by short days and prevented by long days; among such are flowering dogwood (*Cornus florida*), beech (*Fagus sylvatica*), larch (*Larix europaea*), *Weigela florida, Acer palmatum, Berberis thunbergii, Cercidiphyllum japonicum*, redbud (*Cercis canadensis*), tulip tree (*Liriodendron tulipifera*), stag's-horn sumac (*Rhus hirta* [*R. typhina*]), and black locust (*Robinia pseudoacacia*). In the robinia, dormancy is triggered either by day lengths of less than 12 hours, or by falling temperatures. In some plants the response is less positive; dormancy is merely accelerated, rather than induced, by short days and delayed, rather than prevented, by long days; such are sycamore (*Acer pseudoplatanus*), horse chestnut (*Aesculus hippocastanum*), sweet gum (*Liquidambar styraciflua*), *Paulownia tomentosa*, and *Phellodendron amurense*. In other plants, while dormancy is unaffected by day length, exposure to short days appears to increase winter hardiness: ash (*Fraxinus excelsior*), *Malus, Rosa*, rowan (*Sorbus aucuparia*).

As well as ensuring that flowering or dormancy occur at an appropriate time of year, photoperiodism is important in determining the latitudes in which a species will grow. A plant which requires long days in order to flower cannot do so (and therefore cannot reproduce) in the tropics, even if all the other environmental factors are suitable. Conversely, a plant such as poinsettia which requires short days to flower may, at higher latitudes, be killed by autumn frosts before it is able to do so. Frost-hardiness may also be related to day length: if the short days of autumn do not induce frost resistance early enough, some species of trees may not survive.

PHOTOPERIODISM AND FLOWERING
Flowering is influenced by the amount of light received, and more so by temperature, but one of the most important triggers, controlling the time of year when plants flower, is day length. Different strains within individual species may have different responses to day length: the vegetation of the prairies of North America is composed of comparatively few species, but in the north, varieties which take full advantage of the long summer days dominate, while in the south the dominant strains are short-day, or day-neutral (that is, unaffected by day length). Woodland plants from high latitudes are often short-day plants, flowering and seeding in the brief period between the first warmth of spring and the development of a dense leaf canopy which reduces light levels so much as to prevent photosynthesis in understorey plants.

Long-day plants may fail to flower in equatorial or in tropical regions, even in hill stations where the temperatures are lower. Similarly, many equatorial plants will not flower during the long summer days of high latitudes, even if they are given artificial heat. On the other hand, autumn-flowering plants of temperate regions, such as chrysanthemums and Michaelmas daisies, often flower well at altitude in tropical and equatorial regions, where they find the shorter days of their natural flowering time combined with not dissimilar temperatures.

The matter of long- or short-day response is not, however, entirely straightforward. Some plants are absolute long- or short-day plants – a particular day length is essential to them; others are facultative short- or long-day plants – a particular day length promotes or accelerates, but is not essential to, flowering; both of these may also be dependent on temperature. Dual day-length plants require exposure to both short and long days in a particular order to induce flowering; intermediate-day plants flower only within a quite narrow range of day lengths; and yet others are day-neutral.

Absolute long-day plants familiar in gardens in temperate zones include *Hibiscus syriacus*, herbaceous plants such as *Phlox paniculata*, black-eyed Susan (*Rudbeckia fulgida* var. *speciosa*), the Shasta daisy (*Leucanthemum* × *maximum* [*Chrysanthemum maximum*]) and *Sedum spectabile*, also *Nicotiana sylvestris*, usually grown as an annual in cold-winter areas. Some need a preceding period of low temperature vernalization (below 8 °C/47 °F) for several weeks; these include the Cheddar pink, *Dianthus gratianopolitanus* (*D. caesius*) and the evening primrose, *Oenothera biennis*. Others require long days in order to flower at high temperatures, but become day-neutral at low temperatures – among these is the familiar 'nasturtium', *Tropaeolum majus*, and such other familiar garden denizens as petunias, snapdragons (*Antirrhinum majus*), cornflowers (*Centaurea cyaneus*), and *Begonia semperflorens*. The reverse may also be true: at low temperatures delphiniums and annual rudbeckias, for example, are long-day plants, but at high temperatures they are day-neutral.

Facultative long-day plants familiar in gardens include *Camellia japonica*, the sweet William (*Dianthus barbatus*) and love-in-a-mist (*Nigella damascena*). Plants of this kind which also respond to low temperature vernalization include the corncockle (*Agrostemma githago*) and the dusty miller (*Lychnis coronaria*), wallflowers, foxgloves (*Digitalis purpurea*), and *Campanula persicifolia*.

Absolute short-day plants include the coffee plant, *Coffea arabica*, the familiar house plant of cooler regions *Kalanchoë blossfeldiana*, and sweet-corn, *Zea mays*. The blue dawn flower, *Ipomoea nil*, is a short-day plant at high temperatures, but is day-neutral at low temperatures; and so, probably, is the scarlet salvia (*Salvia splendens*). Sometimes there is a complete reversal, according to temperature. The poinsettia, *Euphorbia pulcherrima*, is a short-day plant at high temperatures and a long-day plant at low temperatures; to induce a poinsettia to flower in the centrally-heated midwinter warmth of homes in high latitudes in the northern hemisphere in time for Christmas it is necessary to keep it in the dark from late afternoon until well past dawn during the long days of summer. Experiments have shown not only that the aptly-named morning glory, *Ipomoea purpurea* 'Heavenly Blue', is, like the poinsettia, a short-day plant at high temperatures but a long-day plant at low temperatures, but also that, in short-day plants, the trigger is in fact a long dark period, rather than a short day; short day plants can be induced to flower with longer day-lengths, provided that these are followed by a long period of dark, whereas short days followed by short nights fail to induce flowering. Short-day plants might therefore more accurately be called long-night plants.

Facultative short-day plants, those that are not dependent upon but whose flowering will be hastened by short days, include *Cosmos bipinnatus*, the sunflower *Helianthus annuus*, zinnias, and the sweet pepper, *Capsicum frutescens*; the popular *Zygocactus truncatus* is a facultative short-day plant at high temperatures which becomes day-neutral at low temperatures.

To stimulate flowering, dual day-length plants need either a period of long days preceding short days, or a period of short days followed by long days: the queen of the night, *Cestrum nocturnum*, is an example of the first and *Echeveria harmsii* of the second. In some plants, low temperatures substitute for short days; after a spell of low temperatures *Campanula medium*, the Canterbury bells, responds as a long-day plant.

Day-neutral plants flower at about the same time under all day lengths, though their flowering may be promoted by high or low temperatures or by alterations in temperature. Such are the pot marigold (*Calendula officinalis*), *Gardenia jasminoïdes*, the common holly (*Ilex aquifolium*), and honesty (*Lunaria annua*). Day-neutral plants which need low-temperature vernalization to promote flowering include *Saxifraga rotundifolia, Geum* × *intermedium, Eryngium variifolium*, and the caper spurge, *Euphorbia lathyris*.

As if all this were not complicated enough, some plants that are very similar visually may display different photoperiodism. Thus the sprawling osteospermum with ray florets like rich purple corduroy, 'Tresco Purple', is a short-day plant which stops flowering during the long days of a high-altitude summer, but the more upright 'James Elliman', with virtually identical blooms, carries on cheerfully all through the summer.

Experiments show that in photoperiodic plants dependent upon a particular day length (whether short or long) there is usually a sharply defined critical day length which marks the transition between vegetative growth and the flowering phase, but which may vary with environmental conditions and with age. Thus the short-day plant *lpomoea nil* will, in its adult phase, flower on a longer day length than will seedlings just starting to flower.

Given that day lengths vary much less from season to season in the tropics than in higher latitudes, one might suppose tropical plants to be unaffected by day length. In fact, they are often sensitive to such extremely small differences that, in some, a difference of only fifteen minutes can determine whether they flower or not.

Just what constitutes a short or a long day varies from plant to plant, not only with the cultivar, or with the age of the plant as we have seen, but also with environmental conditions, especially temperature. In long-day plants, the photoperiodic mechanism identifies lengthening days in spring or early summer, and delays flowering until the critical day length is reached. In short-day plants, flowering occurs in late summer or early autumn, when the days have shortened to less than the critical day length.

As it is with dormancy, temperature is linked with photoperiodic responses to enable a plant to distinguish spring from autumn. Another mechanism for this distinction is the dual day-length response: a plant requiring long days followed by short days would flower in autumn, whereas one requiring short days followed by long would flower in early summer. Facultative photoperiodic plants will eventually flower even in unfavourable day lengths, other conditions being suitable.

Various other factors have been shown to affect a plant's response to day-length; for example, it must carry a certain number of leaves before flowering cells will form. This is different from juvenility, a phase in a plant's growth from seed during which flowering cannot be induced by any treatment; some plants progress automatically from juvenility to maturity, in others environmental stimuli are needed.

Reaching for the light

Many plants are adapted to a particular level of light; there are both functional and structural differences between those which grow in full sun and those that grow in shade – as there may also be between shaded and unshaded leaves on a single plant. Plants growing in shade tend to have larger, thinner, less hairy leaves, all adaptations which enable them to make the most of the available light, and to photosynthesize with less light than sun-adapted plants require.

However, below a certain light level no green plants can survive. The floor of a dense evergreen forest is likely to be more or less free of green plants, while beneath the canopy of a deciduous cool-temperate forest the ground vegetation will consist mainly of plants that grow and flower in spring, before the trees leaf up to exclude most of the sun's light. The upper storey of forests, whether tropical, subtropical or temperate, is often exploited by plants that have adapted in various ways to the habitat: climbers or lianas that reach up to the light, and epiphytes, plants which perch on host trees to be nearer to it.

CLIMBERS

Climbers attach themselves to host shrubs and trees by several different methods. Some, such as honeysuckle (*Lonicera* species), have twining stems which coil around the host stems; others attach themselves to thin branches by means of tendrils, derived from leaves or stipules (leaf-like appendages), or twining leaf stalks: *Cobaea scandens* is a tendril climber, clematis have twining leaf stalks. The tendrils of some climbers, such as Virginia creeper (*Parthenocissus quinquefolia*), have little adhesive pads at their tips so they can cling to flat surfaces; others, like those of *Macfadyena unguis-cati*, the cat's-claw vine, have little sharp hooks at the tips. Aerial roots are even more efficient at sticking to their supports; ivy is a well-known example of a root climber. Less secure, at least until they are well lodged in the host, are the climbers that hoist themselves upwards by hooked prickles on their stems (such as roses) or on the backs of their leaves or at the leaf tips (as in *Gloriosa superba*).

EPIPHYTES

These plants contrive to grow nearer the light than their stature would otherwise allow by growing on the host tree, rather than in the ground. Epiphytes may be herbaceous perennials (including orchids), ferns, bromeliads such as Spanish moss, cacti, or lower plants – true mosses, algae, or lichens. Unlike parasites, epiphytes gain no nourishment from their host; they merely use it for anchorage. Instead of particular adaptations for collecting water and nutrients, the least specialized epiphytes often have water-storing organs of one kind or another. In some species of *Peperomia* and *Dischidia* the leaves are succulent; many orchids have swellings in their stems, known as pseudobulbs; Malayan species of *Vaccinium* and *Pachycentria* have root tubers. Others, especially epiphytic orchids, have special tissue on the outside of the aerial roots, called the velamen, which fills with water after rain, but during dry weather is air-filled, forming an insulating layer against overheating and water loss.

Some epiphytes have evolved expanded leaf bases or specialized root surfaces which trap rainwater to be absorbed later. Nest epiphytes such as the fern of the eastern tropics, *Asplenium nidus*, and other ferns, aroids and orchids, have roots forming a tangled mass like a bird's nest, in which humus accumulates. Bracket epiphytes are so-called because their leaves grow out from the host like a clock or shelf bracket; the fern genus *Platycerium* has two leaf types of which one, the mantle leaves, forms brackets; in the Malayan asclepiad *Conchophyllum* all the leaves are convex, so that humus accumulates between the leaves and the bark of the host tree. *Dischidia rafflesiana* is another epiphyte with two types of leaf; one is a kind of sac, closed by a flap, in which ants make nests and soil gathers, from which the roots then gain nourishment. Tank or cistern epiphytes are all bromeliads; the leaves make a rosette, their overlapping bases forming a reservoir capable of holding large quantities of water, as well as humus, insects and so forth which all add nutrients to the water. Some of these bromeliads are able to obtain so much nourishment by this means that they grow to great size; they may also act as a congenial nursery for other epiphytes, such as *Clusia rosea*, a member of the most important genus of stranglers in the South American rain forest.

Epiphytes such as grandfather's beard (the lichen *Ramalina reticulata* of California oaks) or Spanish moss (*Tillandsia usneoïdes*) absorb much of the water they need from the atmospheric humidity. The moisture content of grandfather's beard fluctuates during the day with the humidity of the air; we have already seen that Spanish moss, on the other hand, needing more than just atmospheric humidity, grows within the storm paths which sweep up the Gulf coast from Mexico.

It is likely that it is competition for space and light with other epiphytes and with the host tree's canopy which has prompted the diverse specializations found among epiphytes. Those growing in tropical rain forest trees are of different types at different levels, ranging from small ones in the upper portion of an emergent tree to large ones in the lower, from lichens on the upper part of the trunk to bryophytes (mossy epiphytes) on the lower portion and the base. Those that live in the topmost branches, fully exposed to sun and wind, are mainly such highly-specialized flowering plants as *Tillandsia bulbosa* (a tank epiphyte which can even grow upside-down because its inner leaves meet above its reservoir), *Aechmea*, the gesneriad *Codonanthe crassifolia*, *Rhipsalis baccifera* (*R. cassytha*) and certain orchids. Those that live in the centre of the crown and along the larger branches of tall trees, known as sun epiphytes, are less exposed than those from the topmost branches and include many ferns, orchids and other flowering plants. At the lowest level, the shade epiphytes grow in an umbrageous microclimate which scarcely ever suffers from moisture deficit; they are mainly ferns, including filmy ferns (*Hymenophyllum* and *Trichomanes* species), with very few orchids or other flowering plants.

The preference of some epiphytes for certain hosts perhaps reflects the openness of the branch structure or the roughness of the bark: Spanish moss festoons cypress and some hardwoods but avoids pines which, because they shed their bark, do not provide a stable support. In Uganda the rough-barked *Entandrophragma utile* carries more epiphytes than smooth-barked trees, but some orchids prefer smooth bark. Bark characteristics may alter with age; a young, smooth-barked *Altingia excelsa*, for example, will support a community of epiphytes different from those found on older, scaly-barked altingias. Preferences may also reflect the differing chemical composition of various tree-barks, or the amount of water different bark surfaces hold.

Some potential host trees are adapted to discourage the growth of epiphytes. The kauri (*Agathis australis*) of the New Zealand rain forests shed their bark – which builds up in a great mound at their feet – as do miro (*Prumnopitys ferruginea*), matai (*P. taxifolia*) and kahikatea (*Dacrycarpus dacrydioïdes*); rimu (*Dacrydium cupressinum*) sheds its bark in strips. New Zealand trees lacking this defence mechanism, such as northern rata (*Metrosideros robusta*), are usually festooned with epiphytes.

Epiphytes can develop into parasites, or otherwise overcome their host. The strangler figs (*Ficus aurea* in Florida and other species elsewhere) and the New Zealand rata (*Metrosideros excelsa*) germinate in the canopy of a host tree and at first behave like typical epiphytes. Then they develop aerial roots which, growing towards the ground and reaching the soil, thicken to engulf the host trunk while their upper portions overtop the host and deprive it of light; eventually the host dies.

Adapting to light levels

Terrestrial plants are often adapted in various ways, including variations in leaf orientation, according to the amount of light available to them. Tree species characteristic of early stages in the growth of a plant community, such as aspens or pines, tend to be tall, thin and conical in outline, and capable of rapid growth. Their leaves are usually small, numerous and multi-layered – borne so that many leaves are shaded by others above them. Tree species characteristic of the final stages of a plant community may grow more slowly, and have fewer and larger leaves in a planar or mono-layered arrangement, so that self-shading is minimized. Examples of multi-layered trees are dawn redwood (*Metasequoia glyptostroboïdes*) and silver maple (*Acer saccharinum*); and of mono-layered trees, hemlock (*Tsuga canadensis*) and sugar maple (*Acer saccharum*).

Wind

Wind is less important as an evolutionary force affecting plants, though it affects plant growth and distribution indirectly in its influence on other climatic factors, especially temperaure and rainfall. Increased evaporation caused by wind lowers surface temperatures, and wind determines the direction of precipitation and the regions where it will fall, as is clearly seen in the monsoon of the Indian ocean.

One way in which wind and rain interact was noted by Frank Kingdon Ward in the high valleys of the Sino-Tibetan marches. Observing that trees grow at higher altitudes on valley sides than on valley floors, while the reverse is true of shrubs, he wrote:

> The reason is doubtless to be found in the fact that, towards the summit of the watershed, wind and water are both concentrated in the valley bottom, the former being inimical to trees, while at higher elevations the latter is essential to the shrub vegetation. Thus, towards their limit, trees are driven to occupy sheltered places on the mountain slopes, while towards the limit of shrubs, the dwarf vegetation which is able to withstand the wind is driven to occupy the valley floor, rhododendron giving place to willow.

Some plants have evolved to take advantage of wind, especially when it comes to seed and spore dispersal. The spores of ferns and fungi and the dust-fine seeds of, for example, members of the orchid family, can be carried far on the wind. Plumed and parachute seeds and fruits with a tuft of silky hairs at one end can travel for hundreds of miles, especially if they belong to plants which grow in open country, such as willow herb (*Epilobium*), dandelion or milkweed (*Asclepias*). Long-haired seeds and fruits, such as those of willows and poplars, cotton, and some anemones, are scarcely less effective than plumed seeds. Tumble-weeds, often natives of deserts or prairies and steppes, are plants that break off and trundle along in the wind, scattering their seeds as they go. Some trees, shrubs and woody climbers have winged seeds, such as members of the bignonia family, and pines and spruces.

Others, such as birches, maples, ash or lime, have winged or bracted fruits, which spin through the air on the wind. Bladder fruits, as in *Koelreuteria* or *Colutea*, get blown along the ground by the wind. Physical barriers eventually halt the movement of all these seeds and fruits, though those which reach the upper air may travel for very long distances; the lighter ones, spores and dust seeds and those with plumes or long hairs, may be brought to earth by rain, or even condensation.

Fire

Plants have adapted a variety of strategies to cope with fire, which dominates the history of forests, of grasslands and of such shrub communities as the chaparral of California and the maquis of the Mediterranean, the fynbos of the south-western cape of Africa and the matorral of Chile: those that develop in regions with a summer-dry climate.

Fires are of different types. Surface fires burn at relatively low temperatures and move fast, quickly reducing vegetation to ash but leaving rootstocks and underground storage organs undamaged. In forests, seedlings may be killed and the bark and needles of older trees damaged, while the heat of the fire may open cones to initiate a new cycle of germination and growth. Crown fires, which sweep through the upper levels of forests, are always accompanied by surface fire, fuelled by burning debris falling to the forest floor, and can be beneficial to certain forest communities, letting in light to stimulate seedling growth. The stands of jack pine (*Pinus banksiana*) in Canada and the Lake states often burn during hot, dry weather, as do bishop pine, *P. muricata*, and knobcone pine, *P. attenuata*, in California; in each case the result seems to be a reinvigorated community. The most damaging are ground fires, which consume not only surface vegetation but the organic matter of the soil itself down to the mineral substrate, and anything that grows in it – roots, tubers, rhizomes.

FIRE-ADAPTED PLANTS
Some plants exhibit such fire-adapted features as thick bark, basal burls or lignotubers, evanescent branches, rapid growth, early maturity, fire-induced flowering and increased seed set, bud protection with sprouting following fire, and fire-stimulated germination and seed dispersal. Plants that survive fire unharmed are known as pyrophytes; a well-known example is *Melaleuca leucadendron*, the niaouli, which grows in coastal swamps and around lagoons on the north-eastern coast

of Australia and also in New Caledonia. Here, deliberate bush fires have killed much of the original vegetation, leaving the niaouli to spread unchecked.

The mallee eucalypts of Australia, several manzanitas (*Arctostaphylos*) of the California chaparral, and chamise (*Adenostoma fasciculatum*), have a lignotuber (burl, or swelling) at the base of the trunk from which new growths are formed after the top growth is killed by fire. The buds of the lignotuber are protected by the soil, and quickly sprout after fire, drawing on stored nutrients and water in the burl. Plants with thick bark may show what is known as epicormic growth, sprouting new buds from the stem. Some South African Cape species shoot from blackened wood (*Protea arborea*) or from a fire-resistant base (*P. cynaroïdes*) or rootstock (*Erica cerinthoïdes*). There are plants that sometimes sprout and sometimes do not, among them bitterbrush (*Purshia tridentata*) and mesquite (*Prosopis velutina*).

The giant sequoia, *Sequoiadendron giganteum*, is a species with several characteristics which enable it to survive fires. The bark is thick and fibrous; the lower branches are evanescent – that is, they drop off when they become shaded by the forest canopy, rather than remaining as a 'fire ladder' that would make it easier for fire to reach the tree's crown; young saplings grow very fast, so their canopy is quickly raised above the level of surface fires. These trees also produce huge quantities of cones, many of which are green, photosynthetic and serotinous (closed). The seeds are tiny by comparison with those of the white fir, *Abies concolor*, which grows with the giant sequoia; without frequent fires the shade-tolerant white fir and incense cedar would present serious competition to the sequoias, since the larger seeds of the former, with their greater food reserves, are better able to produce a root long enough to penetrate the forest litter to reach the soil.

Though the reproduction of giant sequoia is largely fire-dependent, there is a steady slight shedding of seeds from the cones, which open once they are broken from the tree. Other conifer species bear at least a proportion of cones that need the heat of fire to open and release their seeds: among them are jack pine (*Pinus banksiana*), lodgepole pine (*P. contorta*), bishop pine (*P. muricata*), knobcone pine (*P. attenuata*) and pitch pine (*P. rigida*), black spruce (*Picea mariana*) and Monterey cypress (*Cupressus macrocarpa*). The temperature needed to open the cones may be as high as 200 °C/392 °F, as in the case of knobcone pine.

The pines of the east coast of North America – pitch pine (*Pinus rigida*) in the pine barrens of New Jersey, and further south loblolly pine (*P. taeda*), slash pine (*P. caribaea*) and longleaf pine (*P. australis*) –

are mostly rather small to medium sized trees; their dominance depends on repeated fires. Dense forest may be burned to the ground, but some of these species sprout again from below the surface; meanwhile, the fire opens cones which would otherwise remain closed on the trees for years, and the newly-released seeds germinate freely. In more open pine forest the ground is often covered by wiregrass and low herbs which become very dry in summer; ground fires in these areas do little damage to established trees.

In the forests of Australia, such as the jarrah (*Eucalyptus marginata*) and karri (*E. diversicolor*) forests of the south-west, fire has been a major environmental factor. The eucalypts cannot regenerate in the dense undergrowth because there is too little light, and too much competition for nutrients in the upper soil. Bush fires destroy much of this undergrowth, and where there are fallen logs or the stumps of dead trees, seeds of the understorey species are also destroyed; the eucalypt seeds, high on the trees, rapidly open after the fire and are shed onto the burnt ground where they germinate with the winter rains and grow fast – especially on the deep ashbeds left by burnt logs, where there is no competition from understorey seedlings.

Bulbous plants such as the mariposa lilies (*Calochortus*) exhibit enhanced flowering after a fire. The South African Cape flora is particularly well adapted to withstand natural fires by all the means already described; it seems that fire also stimulates vegetative growths into flowering (as in *Gerbera crocea*) and encourages buried bulbs to shoot and flower. An example of the latter is *Cyrtanthus ventricosus*, known as the fire lily, in which bulbs apparently dormant for years may flower within two weeks of a fire. Similar responses have been observed in *Haemanthus coccineus, Crinum, Gladiolus brevifolius, Watsonia borbonica* ssp. *ardernei* and *W. pyramidata*, and among some South African orchids, such as *Disa* species.

Some non-bulbous herbaceous plants also flower most freely after fire, such as the ubiquitous weed *Epilobium angustifolium*, better known as fireweed. The result, of course, is more abundant seed production. Many species growing in communities where fire is a regular occurrence produce seeds which will lie dormant in the soil, perhaps for many years, until another fire stimulates them into germination. This is true of many chaparral shrubs, including *Ceanothus* species such as *C. integerrimus*, the deerbrush, and of Cape species such as *Leucadendron* and *Erica pulchella*. The ubiquitous chamise, *Adenostoma fasciculatum*, is both a seeder and a sprouter; and species of *Acacia* and *Eucalyptus* also respond to burning. Some annuals and non-woody perennials are

43

fire-followers: they only appear after a burn destroys shrubby top-growth, to disappear as the shrub regrowth shades them out.

Both grassland climates – arid and semi-arid, with long periods of drought, generally at the hottest time of year – and grassland vegetation – much of which dies back above ground at least once a year, producing quantities of light, dry, combustible material – favour fire. Grassland fires are fast-moving, relatively cool, and do not greatly increase soil temperatures; they regularly kill off the woody top growth of shrubs, enabling the resistant grass and other non-woody species to dominate. Among the adaptations of grasses to fire are very hard stems with a high silica content, and a growth habit with perennating buds, often protected by persistent leaf sheaths, below the soil surface. The top growth that is burned releases minerals which, recycled into the soil, provide extra nutrients for the underground shoots that quickly regrow following fire.

Soil and vegetation

As we have seen, similar climates produce similar types of vegetation, although the specific components of these vegetation types vary from region to region. The distribution of plant species in the wild is determined, above all, by the relationship between climate and soil condition – factors which are the primary agents in plant evolution. Soil is the product of parent rock and accumulated organic debris, weathered by the action of climate and of living organisms, with topography, especially the slope of the ground, an important influence on drainage and erosion. Together, soil, climate, vegetation, animal life and the parent rock form a close relationship in which the development of the soil is influenced by the other factors.

There are four separate components of soil: parent rock weathered to mineral grains, organic matter, water and air. The weathered rock provides anchorage, pore space for air and water retention, and a source of mineral nutrients. Organic matter is composed of plant and animal residues in various stages of decomposition, and soil organisms; it enhances the cycling of nutrients and improves soil structure, pore space and water storage. Soil water is the solvent for the nutrients required by growing plants; and soil air contains oxygen for the cellular processes, carbon dioxide both to increase mineral weathering and to contribute to the decomposition of organic matter, and atmospheric nitrogen for bacteria to convert into usable nutrients.

Organic matter in the soil derives mainly from leaf and other litter. The rate at which litter decays or is removed depends upon the climate, the nature of the litter, and the frequency of fire; the activities of earth-worms and insects, bacteria and other soil organisms incorporate organic matter into the soil.

A warm, damp atmosphere hastens the disintegration and decomposition of both organic and mineral matter, for water is essential to both processes. In dry climates with limited vegetation there is little humus, and what there is decomposes slowly; the dryness also inhibits the weathering of parent rock, so soils are generally coarse. In tropical rain forest the litter layer is very thin because decomposition is rapid, and the underlying soil is quickly leached of nutrients by the high rainfall; yet the vegetation grows luxuriantly, because rain-forest trees exploit mycorrhizae (literally, root fungi) to feed directly from the litter, extracting nutrients before they can be washed away by the rains. By contrast, the cold, acidic soil of subalpine conifer forest is not conducive to decomposition, which takes between ten and twenty times longer than in the tropical rain forest.

Vegetation and climate determine what kind of soil is formed. Podzol (a Russian term, literally 'ash-soil', so-called because of its bleached ashen colour) develops beneath coniferous forests in cool, moist climates; chernozem or black earth soils develop under grasslands in temperate regions, such as the Russian steppes; and the highly-weathered iron-rich laterite soils of the tropical rain forest are very acidic as well as poor in nutrients.

THE PHYSICAL CONDITION OF SOIL

Three factors related to climatic conditions are of prime importance in determining the physical condition of soil. One is its depth. As generations of plants grow and die, the organic matter they produce is incorporated into the soil, adding to its depth and bulk, sometimes considerably. The upper layers, particularly in cool, wet climates, may come to consist of little more than organic matter – leaf mould in a beech wood, for example, or peat in a sedge or sphagnum peat bog. The depth of the soil has a marked effect on its water content; shallow soils do not hold water as effectively as deeper ones, and dry out quickly through evaporation.

Another factor is soil temperature. When soil is frozen, the water it holds is not available to plants, resulting in desiccation; in some plants even low – rather than freezing – temperatures retard the rate of water absorption to less than what is lost through transpiration.

45

Wilting plants will usually recover from the resultant physiological drought, either overnight, when the excess of transpiration over absorption is reversed, or when adequate moisture becomes otherwise available.

The third significant factor is the texture of the soil, measured by the proportions of particles of different sizes, from the largest, sand, which is often formed of irregularly-shaped grains, through medium-sized silt, to clay, which is made up of very small plate-like particles. Varying combinations of these particle sizes give different types of soil; sandy loam, for example, is approximately 60 per cent sand, 25 per cent silt and 15 per cent clay.

Because soil particles never fit together tightly, there is a certain amount of space between them; this pore space, as it is called, varies from about 30 per cent of the soil volume in sand (with comparatively large particles) to about 50 per cent in clay soils (with very small particles). It may be occupied entirely by air – as in dry soils – or entirely by water – as in saturated (waterlogged) soils – but is commonly occupied partly by air and partly by water. While clay soils clearly have a greater capacity for water retention and nutrient storage, the addition of organic matter can improve the texture of both clayey and sandy soils.

WATER AND NUTRIENT STORAGE
The quantity of moisture held in the ground and available to support plant life depends as much upon the soil texture as on the annual rainfall. Most of the water is held by capillary action in the pore spaces between soil particles, where plant roots can penetrate and absorb it. The pore spaces in clay are so small, however, that water becomes locked into them by means of surface tension, and thus unavailable to plants, while those in sand may be so large that water can drain straight through them. The most porous soils – using the term in the strict, scientific sense to mean those which hold the most moisture – are the silts. The porosity (water-holding capability) of soil and the availability of soil moisture to plants can both be dramatically increased, perhaps three- or four-fold, by the addition of organic matter, which helps to open up clogged pores and block over-large sand pores, at the same time retaining moisture in its own fibres, and providing nutrients.

Following rainfall and drainage – the extent of the latter depending upon typography and soil texture – there remain in the soil both capillary water, available to plants, and hygroscopic water, which is a surface water coating of the particles, held by molecular forces so strong that plant roots are unable to draw it off. In the upper layers of exposed soil, evaporation can remove all moisture, to leave a parched crust; evaporation is increased by high temperatures, very dry air, and surface wind.

The amount of water that a plant can take up depends upon the pattern of its roots and therefore its species, upon its condition, and upon the environmental conditions – as we have seen, at very low temperatures the process by which water and soluble nutrients are taken up into the plant may be inhibited.

Soil micro-organisms, earth worms and insects, bacteria, fungi and algae are responsible for converting organic matter into humus. A by-product of this process is organic acid, which helps to break down particles of silt into clay and (mineral) nutrients. Humus is black in colour, very fine, and decomposes eventually into soluble nutrients at a rate of about 3 per cent a year in temperate regions; the rate of 25 per cent a year in tropical regions is roughly equal to the amount of new humus formed annually. The value of a slowly-decomposing humus is that it provides a steady supply of nutrients and holds them available, dissolved in soil water, to support plant growth; excess rainfall can leach nutrients out of the soil.

THE CHEMICAL CONSTITUTION OF SOILS

Some temperate and most tropical plants seem to depend upon a particular soil structure because of its effect on the availability of moisture, but there is also a broader correlation between plant distribution and soil type: different plants grow on sandy soils, on clay, on chalk or limestone, or on soils with a very high organic content. Gardeners are accustomed to classifying plants as calcifuge (or acid-loving), and lime-tolerant; while many of the most desirable ornamentals grown in temperate gardens are calcifuge, chalk gardens also have a wide range of species to draw upon.

The level of soil acidity is indicated by the logarithmic pH scale, which measures the concentration of hydrogen present. True neutral is pH7, representing one part of hydrogen (by volume) to 10 million parts of water; pH6 is ten times stronger, being one part of hydrogen to only one million parts of water. Plants in temperate zones tend to behave as though 6.5 is neutral; a pH of 5.5 suits most of the Ericaceae, but even such calcifuge plants as these may find a pH of 4.5 or lower too acid for optimum growth.

Acid, or sour, soils are deficient in lime, either because the parent rock was acidic, or as a result of the leaching of sodium and calcium salts. Alkaline soils, on the other hand (those with a pH of more than 7), have a high sodium and calcium content; they are usually formed from calcareous parent rock such as chalk or limestone, but also occur in areas of high evaporation where there is not enough rainfall to wash away accumulated mineral salts; these are known as saline soils.

Humus is generally acidic, whereas the waters of inorganic soils are either neutral or slightly alkaline; thus the presence of ample humus, especially in neutral mineral soils, will tend to increase the acidity of a soil; acid soil can also be modified by such external factors as alkaline water draining into it from a limestone area; some gardeners even maintain that rainwater collected as run-off from a limestone-tiled roof should not be used on calcifuge plants. Extremes of acidity or alkalinity are tolerated only by plants that have evolved to cope with such conditions.

ADAPTATIONS TO SOIL TYPE

Although many plants will grow happily on a range of soil types, others are highly specialized, having evolved to exploit a particular environmental niche, perhaps as a means of avoiding competition from less specialized but more vigorous plants. For example, in the California foothills digger pine (*Pinus sabiniana*), though not endemic to them, increases in density on soils derived from a formation known as serpentine (related to marble) which are not favoured by many other species. As elevation increases rainfall increases, temperatures moderate, competition from other plants becomes more intense, and digger pine is found on a narrowing range of soils, centred on serpentine; at the upper limit of its range, the digger pine finds a refuge on sepentine outcrops.

Fresh-water swamps and marshy places support a different flora from dry and sharply drained sites, since some species are better able to tolerate waterlogged conditions. In very wet climates, soils saturated during the wet season may be adequately aerated only during the dry. In very dry climates, drainage may be impeded by a hardpan of accumulated salts, such as the cement-hard caliche or coffee rock of alkaline soils in the deserts of south-western North America.

Halophytes are plants capable of growing in saline soils; among them are mangroves, coastal salt-marsh herbs, beach plants which receive salt spray, and salt-desert plants. Again, this appears to be a tolerance, evolved because such species do not compete well in non-saline environ-

48

ments, rather than a preference; in a less specialized environment but without competition, they commonly grow better. In some areas, such as Western Australia, so many trees have been felled that the water table has risen, bringing with it dissolved mineral salts from the subsoil; salt-tolerant trees such as species of *Melaleuca* and eucalyptus are being planted in an attempt to lower the water table once more.

The more extreme the other environmental factors, the more likely it is that quite small soil differences will lead to variations in the species that form local plant communities. In the deserts of North America, for example, the gradual slopes of the lower mountains, which are known as bajadas and are composed of coarse alluvial soil eroded from the steeper slopes above, have the highest species diversity of any desert habitat; this variety decreases at the base of the slopes, where the soil is finer. In the desert, species diversity is affected more by soil texture than by rainfall: bajada soils have a very low organic content and vary from sandy loams to loamy sands; they are markedly alkaline, and often have a hardpan, caliche layer which, lying just below the surface, impedes root growth and so can also determine which species grow in a given site.

Playas, undrained basins at the base of bajadas, are composed of fine-textured soil and dissolved mineral salts carried down by run-off from the slopes; they increase in salinity from the edge to the lowest part of the basin. Soil aeration is poor, and there may be a water table close to the surface; this lack of soil oxygen is more likely than salinity to be the factor which prevents bajada species from colonizing the playas.

In southern Death Valley in California, saline soils support a saltbush scrub of desert holly (*Atriplex hymenelytra*), Parry saltbush (*A. parryi*) and honeysweet tidestromia (*Tidestromia oblongifolia*). By contrast, the alkaline soils of the desert valleys of the Great Basin in western North America support a shadscale scrub vegetation dominated by shadscale saltbush (*Atriplex confertifolia*) and bud sagebrush (*Artemisia spinescens*). The saline soils of Australia, too, are the habitat of many species of *Atriplex*, and of *Chenopodium* and such species as saline fuchsia bush (*Eremophila linearis*) and silver poverty bush (*E. pterocarpa*), bluebush (*Kochia* and *Maireana*), bindieye (*Bassia*), *Rhagodia, Acacia victoriae* and the snakewood, *A. xiphophylla*, and samphires. At the margins of Australian salt lakes grow species such as *Hakea preissii* and salt-water paperbark (*Melaleuca cuticularis*). Saline soils can be a real problem for Australian gardeners, for whom 'hardy' has nothing to do with frost, but indicates a plant that will grow in saline soil and withstand drought.

In tropical rain forest, trees growing in shallow soils or those with a high water table, where only the upper layer is well aerated, tend to have only superficial lateral roots and, lacking a tap root, often develop the buttressed trunk typical of many rain-forest species; tap-rooted trees seldom have buttressed trunks.

Differences in vegetation may also result from periodic changes – for example, different stages of recovery from destruction by fire, wind, landslip or other disturbance will exhibit different types of vegetation – or from the local topography and its associated microclimatic variations, possibly related to soil differences as well. The vegetation on south-facing slopes may differ from that on north-facing slopes, that in poorly-drained basins with fine-textured soil from that of the well-drained slopes above with coarser soil. In coastal regions the plants growing nearest to the sea, where exposure to wind, sand blast and salt spray is greatest, are different from those that grow within the shelter of the dunes. Any given region is likely to consist of a mosaic of microclimatic and soil factors influencing the plants that grow there, as we shall see in the chapters that form the final section of this book.

Adaptations within species

Climate and soil influence both vegetation and flora – the type of plant community that covers the earth in a given region, and the species that form that community. The same species may be found in different types of vegetation and in different habitats. Some species exhibit different ecotypes – races genetically adapted to cope with local conditions. The herbaceous perennial cinquefoil, *Potentilla glandulosa*, appears to have four such ecotypes: a lowland form unable to withstand severe frosts; two mid elevation forms, one from dry habitats, the other from wet meadow sites, both of which flower in late summer and are prompted into dormancy by cold temperatures; and a high-altitude form, the shortest in growth, with the earliest flowering time and very frost-tolerant foliage; the winter dormancy of this last form is apparently induced by shorter days, rather than by cold.

The experience of gardeners suggests that such variability occurs in many plants: for example, the earliest introductions of *Eucalyptus* species, reared from seed gathered at low elevations, succumbed to chilly British winters; increasingly, gardeners are finding that species collected at higher altitudes are more tolerant. The original introductions of *Metasequoia glyptostroboïdes* were from valley populations; later collections, from higher elevations, have proved resistant to far more severe frosts than the valley plants. Specimens of a given species from low latitudes may fail to adapt to the seasonal changes signalled by the different day lengths of higher latitudes: species such as *Robinia pseudoacacia* and *Populus tremula* continue to grow, only to be damaged by autumn frosts.

The wider a species' natural range, the less likely it is to be genetically homogenous. The quaking aspen, *Populus tremuloïdes*, has a wider distribution than any other North American tree (covering 110° of longitude and 47° of latitude). The red maple, *Acer rubrum*, occurs throughout the eastern deciduous forest, abundant on both sandy, dry soils and in wet bottom-land sites. *Abies lasiocarpa*, the alpine fir, extends south from sea level in the Yukon to 3,600 m/11,800 ft at the timberline near the Mexican border, and eastwards from the maritime climate of British Columbia to the severe continental climate along the Rocky Mountains range. The sweet acacia, *A. farnesiana*, which has little frost tolerance, appears to owe its wide latitudinal distribution to a broad tolerance of different day lengths. Mesquite (*Prosopis juliiflora*), with a range closely matching that of the sweet acacia, appears also to have spread by means of a variety of ecotypes adapted to different day lengths.

Looked at another way, the greater the number of ecotypes in a given species, the broader the tolerance range in the species as a whole. Some species seem better able to generate ecotypes, and thus to increase their range, than others. However, a restricted natural habitat does not necessarily imply that a species will not grow well in other regions: the Monterey cypress (*Cupressus macrocarpa*) is native only to that small area of the California coast, where it seldom forms a shapely or sizeable tree; but many good specimens can be seen on the west coast of Britain. Some plants native only to a restricted area may be so newly evolved that they have not yet had time to disperse; the live oaks of California seem to fall into this category. The California redwoods, on the other hand, may be relict populations of species that, before the Ice Age, once covered a far wider area in North America, and much of Europe as well.

The genetic diversity of species means that some seedlings in each generation are likely to exhibit greater resistance to adverse climatic or other conditions. Native plants, for example, can be killed by a winter of exceptional severity, but usually some individuals survive, and they and their descendants are more likely to be adapted to such winters in future: the 'fittest' survive, among plants as among animals.

51

Because there are certain characteristics that suggest greater cold-resistance, plant breeders can select for probable winter-hardiness without having to wait for record low temperatures. They look for melanism – the presence of darker pigment, giving the plant a maroon or bronze cast and enabling it to absorb more heat; downy or hairy leaves, in evergreens, which both retain heat and help to prevent winter sun reaching the vulnerable leaf tissues, so reducing desiccation; compactness, since a plant that grows low and compact is better protected from wind, and exposes a smaller proportion of its leaves and branches. Many gardeners know, too, that hybrids are often tougher ancl more vigorous than pure species.

3

How can we
help our plants to thrive?

Since mankind first began to forsake the way of life of the hunter-gatherer or the nomad for a more settled existence based on agriculture, human intervention has been a major factor in global plant distribution; but the best efforts of growers are still limited by climatic considerations. We cannot dominate nature wholly, and unless we learn to live in harmony with her, she may well end by dominating us, to the point of extinction.

It would take another book, one that I am not competent to write, to discuss the impact of climate on crop plants on the global scale. My concern is with the garden as pleasure ground, as a place to grow ornamental plants, and with both gardeners who respond to the challenge of climate and weather by seeking to grow as wide a range of plants as they can, and gardeners who feel more comfortable growing only what they are reasonably sure will succeed; for the more they know about their own climate, and about the climates which have moulded the garden plants they might grow, the better their chances of choosing plants that will thrive.

As we have seen, plants are more or less adaptable, and this enables keen gardeners to combine a natural acquisitiveness with the impulse to make garden pictures, resulting in the gardens of today, in which plants from many regions grow side by side. The more nearly conditions in your garden approximate to the climate and weather experienced in the regions to which you plants are native, the more easily will the plants acclimatize and grow successfully for you.

We may perhaps have to face changing climatic conditions during our lifetime, but since even highly experienced climatologists disagree on the direction of change – are we about to enter another ice age, or will global warming be the outcome of our profligacy with fossil fuels? – we can do no more than apply ourselves to knowing not just our plants and our own gardens' climate, but also the ways in which we can either make the weather our ally or protect our plants against its worst onslaughts.

Local weather and its effects are modified by many small forces to create microclimates. Gardeners quickly learn that this corner of the garden is hotter and drier than the rest, that one cold and draughty, while just here is a corner in which everything seems to thrive – through hardly a few yards away even the toughest plants struggle for life. Every garden, in short, has not just one but a whole series of microclimates, affected by exposure, aspect, air drainage and soil.

Plants themselves affect their habitat. They cast shade, drop leaves and other litter, modify temperature fluctuations, increase humidity, and by their root action alter the soil structure and chemistry. In the wild, during the succession from pioneer plant communities to forest climax, the environment becomes moister, and the effect of the prevailing climate is modified. As the forest canopy closes overhead, daily fluctuations in temperature and humidity moderate; gradually increased humus, greater soil depth, and finer soil texture enable the soil to hold more moisture, to act as a buffer against seasonal variations in precipitation. Even on the small scale of the garden, such effects can be turned to advantage to create favourable microclimates.

Since most gardeners like to grow a wide variety of plants from many different lands, it follows that variety in garden microclimates is likely to increase the range of plants that will succeed. There are some simple and obvious rules of thumb to give your plants the best chance of survival. First, play safe: choose plants from climates not too far different from your own, especially as regards temperature and humidity. Second, modify the microclimate in the appropriate direction. For example, to grow plants adapted to a continental climate in the less extreme conditions of maritime regions, in the absence of hot summers you will often need to give them full sun to encourage the ripening without which they may not be able to survive the milder maritime winters. Conversely, in continental climate regions the need is likely to be for maximum shelter from frost and from cold, desiccating winds; ripening is less likely to be a problem. To be as reasonably sure as possible of choosing the right site for a new plant, discover all you can about its origins: not just its native country, but its range and habitat in the wild.

Modifying the microclimate

If exposure, aspect, air drainage and soil are the dominant elements affecting microclimate, it follows that by modifying them we may be able to improve, at least within certain limits, the conditions we can offer our plants. Nothing short of an artificially heated glasshouse will turn a high-latitude climate into one suitable for growing tropical plants, but even without such mechanical aids it is surprising how much can be done to create a congenial environment.

Modifying the exposure of a given site may call for wind shelter, to reduce the impact of icy or buffeting winds. The amount of direct sun received each day, and when it is received, can often be altered by limbing-up trees or grubbing out shrubs, or by creating shade with artificial or living screens.

Aspect is more difficult to change; although today's heavy machinery can alter the tilt of a slope with comparative ease, its direction is another matter. Slopes facing into the sun receive more light and heat than those facing away, as is evident from the many alpine valleys where villages and their pastures are clustered on the south-facing side, leaving the north-facing slopes forested. Frank Kingdon Ward, who travelled extensively in the Himalayan regions and western China, noted that in Burma

> ... where the forest faces due north, it grows more luxuriantly than where it faces south. Aspect has great influence on the appearance of the vegetation, and even on the type of vegetation ... On north slopes there is of course less sunshine ... Where sunshine is scarce, the snow lingers long after it has disappeared from the south face, directly exposed to the warm air from the plains.

At higher elevations, he noted that

> ... the smallest rhododendrons are found on slopes fully exposed to wind and sun. At this altitude plants are very sensitive to the least change of aspect, and immediately the direction of slope changes the plants change. It is this sensitiveness to aspect – a sensitiveness

55

almost entirely controlled by water demand and supply – which produces the great diversity in the alps.

Similar variations are to be found in the quite different climate of central California, where on north-facing slopes the cover may be oak woodland (blue oak, *Quercus douglasii*) while on the south-facing slope of the same ravine the cover will be chaparral (chamise, *Adenostoma fasciculatum*), for example. Even where the same species is found on both slopes, the plants facing the sun and therefore subject to higher temperatures earlier in spring are likely to flower earlier than those on the colder, shaded slopes; these differences equate to those that would be found between plants of the same species growing at lower and higher latitudes or altitudes.

The nature of the surface, as well as its aspect, can modify the microclimate, according to the extent to which it reflects radiation. Mulching or close planting can have a small but significant effect compared with bare soil, which dries out faster and is subject to wider temperature fluctuations. Different soils, too, react with local climates in different ways, and to the extent that we can modify the soil structure and its air and moisture content, we can in a small way affect the microclimate.

In climates where frost occurs, air drainage is a very significant factor in the equation. Cold air is heavier than warm air, so its tendency is to sink, flowing downhill and collecting in hollows. At the lowest point, or sooner if there is an obstacle, the cold dense air will be arrested, to provide the makings of a frost hollow. At the bottom of deep Alpine valleys the night-time temperatures may be as much as 10 °C/18 °F lower than on adjacent slopes from which the cold

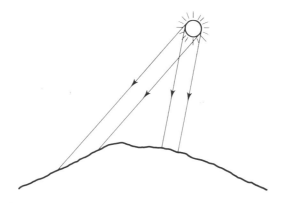

Slopes facing the sun receive more radiation than those facing away

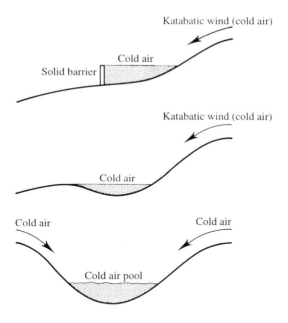

Frost pockets

air has drained. During the day heat from the sun is reflected into the valley, where there is limited movement of air, so daytime temperatures rise sharply, giving a wide diurnal (over 24 hours) range of temperature.

The effect of free air drainage may be so marked as to extend the growing season significantly in gardens on slopes compared with those in valleys below, which suffer earlier autumn and later spring frosts. If any obstacle in the garden which might impede the free movement of air, such as a hedge or fence, cannot be removed, an escape route for the cold air should at least be contrived at the lowest point, whenever possible. In the depths of winter, however, such favoured sites may experience frosts of the same severity as those lower down, or may even be colder, as the effects of altitude become more significant with falling temperatures. At high altitudes there is less atmosphere above the earth's surface and thus more direct radiation is received through clear skies, but there is also a greater loss of heat given off by the earth's surface. The result is a fall in mean temperatures, on average, of 6 °C per 1000 m (1 °F per 330 ft) of altitude.

A tree canopy helps to reduce the incidence of frost, retaining warmth beneath it. Even a tree-less hollow may benefit from densely

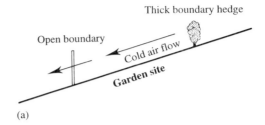

(a)

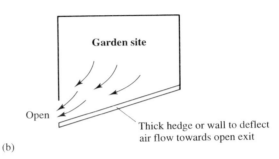

(b)

Cold air drainage

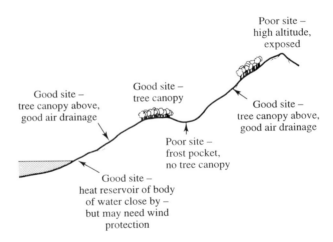

Choosing a garden site

wooded heights above (at least in spring and autumn), for as the woodland does not freeze so readily as a bare site, there is less cold air available to drain down into the valley.

URBAN HEAT ISLANDS

Man's activities can affect climate: we are nowadays aware of how the carbon dioxide balance has been altered during the past hundred years, much of the change attributable to the burning of fossil fuels. Among more localized effects, one of the most marked is the climate of an urban area, where changes occur to the chemical composition of the air, to the patterns of air flow, and to the temperature. Even in cities where certain fuels are banned because of their emissions, the air is full of alien matter from all the domestic, commercial and industrial activity that goes on: central heating and air conditioning plants, motor vehicles and factories all produce more or less noxious substances, ranging from smoke to sulphur dioxide and increased levels of carbon dioxide.

As for air flow, anyone who has visited a city of tower blocks and skyscrapers will have experienced the strong gusty winds that can build up in the canyons between them. The average speed is actually reduced because of the resistance of the buildings, but in individual streets quite violent winds can blow, not necessarily from the direction of origin.

For the gardener, another important factor is that the average temperature is higher in urban areas, especially at night, than in surrounding rural areas. Buildings and roads act like storage heaters, holding more warmth and releasing it more slowly than the open countryside. Added to this is the direct production of heat by combustion, though this may to some extent be dissipated by turbulent winds.

WIND SHELTER

In many climates the wind is the gardener's chief enemy. Wind can damage plants in a variety of ways: by twisting leaves off their stems, by snapping twigs and branchlets, and in extreme cases by breaking large limbs or felling entire trees. Young growths are especially susceptible: it is because of the destruction of growth buds on the windward side of trees growing in exposed places that these trees develop their characteristic windswept or gnarled appearance. In very windy regions it may be impossible for trees to develop at all, even if there is enough rainfall to support them, and the vegetation will be grassland or scrub; this seems to be the explanation for the absence of trees in the Falkland Islands.

Wind has a drying effect, which can add to stress in plants already suffering from lack of moisture. Anyone who has hung out wet washing on a windy day knows how much faster it dries than in still weather, cold or hot; the effect on leaves is similar, and if roots cannot make good the moisture loss because the soil is dry or frozen, the result is a flagging or wilting plant. Cold, biting winter winds damage evergreen leaves, and the tender, unfurling leaves of spring are even more vulnerable. Plants in full sail in the heat of summer, which already use a great deal of water, lose more still through their leaves in blowy weather.

A cooling breeze may be welcome during hot weather, but in winter the combination of cold, dry air and strong winds produces a phenomenon known as wind chill which can be extremely unpleasant, even dangerous; if the wind is strong enough it is possible to get frostbite when the temperature is barely below freezing. The effect of cold winds on plants can be just as dramatic, freezing their tissues and exacerbating cold-induced drought.

Creating shelter is the first priority in coastal gardens, where wind is even more of a problem because it often carries salt and sand. Salt particles can burn all but the most resistant foliage, but plants which are adapted to withstand its scorch can be used to create shelter belts; sand grains can inflict physical damage on plants, even to the extent of abrading bark; and the force of coastal gales can break off twigs or branches, or even destroy whole trees, either by wrenching them out of the ground or, in the case of grafted specimens that may not have formed a completely sound union, by snapping them off at the point of graft. Summer gales, when trees are in full sail, are especially apt to cause physical damage of this kind, while in spring, tender young growths that are just unfurling are as vulnerable to salt-laden winds as they are to untimely frost.

Cornish coastal gardens and those of the west coast of Scotland afford a striking illustration of how wind affects vegetation, and of the change that can take place once shelter has grown up. The Atlantic gales, though moisture-laden and comparatively warm, are so fierce and so salt-laden that the natural vegetation on these headlands is reduced to grass and a few stunted, distorted thorn trees. However, no sooner has a shelter belt of, say, Monterey pine (*Pinus radiata*) or bishop pine (*P. muricata*) grown to a reasonable size than such plants as rhododendrons from the rain-drenched monsoon regions of the Himalayas and Upper Burma thrive as though in their native lands.

In arid regions, shelter against hot, dry winds is no less important:

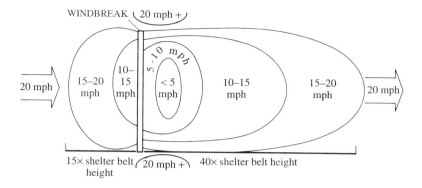

WINDBREAK 20 mph +

20 mph

15–20 mph | 10–15 mph | 5–10 mph | < 5 mph | 10–15 mph | 15–20 mph

20 mph

15× shelter belt height | 20 mph + | 40× shelter belt height

Reduction in wind speed caused by an effective windbreak (e.g., a fence of 50:50 lath and space, or a well-furnished hedge)

the drying effect of wind can kill plants already coping with low soil moisture. In the Middle West of North America, a region too dry to support forest, trees occur along rivers where the river water, percolating into the soil, is sufficient to support them, much as subterranean water in the oases of true deserts soaks up to the surface to support vegetation. However, not every type of forest tree is able to grow naturally in such areas; only species that can withstand the hot, dry air and strong winds will thrive.

A windbreak provides advantages in addition to the obvious benefit of a less windy garden, but it has drawbacks as well, and it helps to be aware of these before going to the expense and trouble of planting trees and shrubs. Windbreaks can intensify, by reflection, the amount of light and heat received, giving higher daytime temperatures; they help to retain heat from buildings within the confines of the garden; they can divert cold air; they afford privacy, and help to deaden sounds from outside; they may afford shelter for the predators that devour garden pests – and they can be decorative.

But windbreaks also take up space and need maintenance; they cast shade; they may trap cold air, resulting in lower night temperatures and frosts both earlier and later in the season; they may compete greedily for moisture and nutrients with the garden plants they are intended to protect; they may harbour pests and diseases; and the loss of one or more individuals in a shelter belt is not only unsightly, but allows wind to funnel into the garden through the gap.

Once the decision has been made to plant a windbreak, what should it consist of? The ideal, space permitting, is several rows of wind-tolerant plants which include, as well as trees, shrubs that will remain clothed with foliage to the ground; otherwise, low-level winds will cut through between the trunks of the trees as they mature and shed their lower branches. A sloping outer line of shelter which gradually increases in height leeward makes a better windbreak than a vertical planting, as it deflects the wind upwards; planting low shrubs on the windward side will achieve this, and also fill in gaps between the trees. The effective shelter from a permeable windbreak is about seven times its height in very windy sites, and up to ten or even twelve times where the winds are less fierce; there will be a reduction in wind speed even beyond this zone.

In an arid climate, the windbreak might begin on the windward side with a planting of Russian olive (*Elaeagnus angustifolia*), then a row of tamarisk or casuarina, one of Arizona cypress, and if there is space enough another of Lombardy popular and an inner, leeward row of Aleppo pine. Most of these are adaptable to a wide range of climatic zones. In smaller desert gardens two rows, a windward line of tamarisk or casuarina with one of Arizona cypress within, would provide an attractive and efficient wind-filter.

In coastal regions, the components of windbreaks need to be resistant to salt spray as well as tough enough to cope with the abrasive texture of windblown sand and the buffeting force of the wind. In regions with mild winters shelter belts should be mainly evergreen; however, some densely twiggy deciduous shrubs, such as *Fuchsia magellanica*, make effective wind sifters even when leafless.

One of the most effective low-level shrubs for coastal regions is *Brachyglottis monroi*; in full exposure to wind this silver-felted New Zealander with attractively crinkled leaf margins retains a dense, rounded outline, as does the shrubby umbellifer *Bupleurum fruticosum*. Hebes, the shiny-leaved *Euonymus japonicus*, gummy *Escallonia rubra* var. *macrantha*, *Griselinia littoralis*, *Baccharis patagonica*, *Pittosporum ralphii*, and grey-leaved *Olearia* × *haastii* and *Atriplex halimus* should all remain full of leaf to ground level, and are all suitable for mild coastal regions. Among trees, salt-resistant pines of the California coast, Monterey pine (*Pinus radiata*) and bishop pine (*P. muricata*), or the maritime pine of western Europe (*P. pinaster*) and the Corsican pine (*P. nigra* var. *maritima*), are all effective in maritime regions.

In colder seaside gardens the Scots pine (*P. sylvestris*) does well, while deciduous trees that make effective first-line defences in these conditions include the common alder (*Alnus glutinosa*), poplars such as *Populus trichocarpa* or *P. alba*, sea buckthorn (*Hippophaë rhamnoïdes*), and *Lycium chinense*. Several willows also make good, rapid shelter: *Salix*

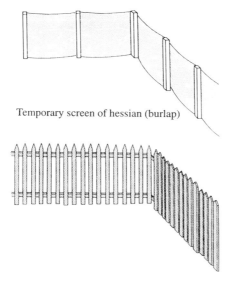

Temporary screen of hessian (burlap)

Picket fence

Artificial protection against wind and wind-blown snow

acutifolia and *S. daphnoïdes* with their bloomy stems and the goat willow, *S. caprea*.

While living windbreaks grow, or where space is too limited for even a single row of living shelter, fences and louvred baffles can be used as wind filters, as can proprietary materials such as woven plastic. Lath fences, if you can afford them, are less unsightly than plastic: use vertical 2.5 cm/1 in laths nailed parallel to cross-members, with 2.5 cm/1 in between the laths. Supporting posts should be about 5 × 7.5 cm/2 × 3 in, and set deeply in the ground, no further apart than 2 m/6½ ft for netting or 3.3 m/1 ft for laths. All timber should be treated to protect it against rot.

The least successful windbreak is a solid vertical barrier such as a wall, which creates a fierce updraft on the windward side and damaging eddies on the lee; the benefits walls offer are referred to later.

Any windbreak, whether living or artificial, helps to reduce moisture loss through transpiration by creating calm conditions and providing shade, especially valuable in latitudes where the sun's rays are very fierce. Shade and wind shelter can be helpful in winter too, reducing cold-induced desiccation.

Shelter against freak storms, hurricanes, tornadoes, and twisters – extreme manifestations of wind – is difficult to arrange. Freak storms and twisters, both violent and unpredictable, can do severe damage. In southern England in October 1987 hundreds of thousands of trees were lost to a wind that touched hurricane force, reaching speeds well in excess of the norm for the region. Like hurricanes, twisters are uncommon, though far from unknown, in Britain; it was such a wind that uprooted, even upended, some of the orchard trees in the Royal Horticultural Society's garden, while leaving others untouched.

FROST-HARDINESS AND WINTER PROTECTION
Gardeners in cool-temperate regions consider a plant is hardy if it can withstand an average winter – though a pessimist might prefer it to be able to withstand the coldest winter the region is likely to experience. Charles Eley, writing in 1939 for English gardeners (*Twentieth Century Gardening*), believed that 'the best way to grow a fine plant and to prolong its period of flowering is to put it in a *perfectly* sheltered place with a north-west aspect. Further, such a spot offers the best chance of successfully growing a tender plant if the necessary shelter is completely effective.' This may be true of plants from high-rainfall areas, but those accustomed in the wild to much hotter summers than those of Britain might not ripen their wood adequately, thus sited: a place in full sun is more likely to ensure their survival. Against this, putting plants accustomed to clear-cut seasons and easily promoted into untimely growth by a premature mild spell in a cooler site may be enough to hold them back until spring has really arrived.

A few shrubs become less able to resist winter cold as they age: cistus and ceanothus are well-known examples, both native to regions with a Mediterranean climate, comparatively short-lived, quickly reaching maturity and then senescence, when they become vulnerable to cold that would leave them unmoved as vigorous youngsters. Most woody plants, however, are more resistant to frost once they have made some mature wood. In cases of borderline hardiness, the usual rule of thumb – plant small – should therefore be weighed against the risk of frost irreparably damaging a soft young plant.

Gardeners in the south of England often achieve success with tender shrubs and trees by growing them in a cool greenhouse until they have formed some well-ripened wood; at this stage (1–1.5 m/3–5 ft or more tall) they are planted out in late spring and nurtured through their first season outside, staked against wind rock and kept moist. Artificial feeding that would encourage soft, sappy growth should be avoided; nitrogen-rich fertilizers are not for such plants, but a dusting of potash

64

after midsummer can help them to ripen their wood more effectively. They are likely to need some artificial protection against frost, at least during their first winter or two outside.

This technique is not suitable for frost-tender plants with deep, far-ranging roots adapted to search out moisture from dry soils, which need to be set out when they are still small. Eucalypts and acacias, for example, both rapidly outgrow the confines of a pot and, once potbound, their chances of becoming rootfast are slender; a eucalypt planted out too large is vulnerable to being blown over or rocked by the wind. Wind-rock is apt to chafe a crater around the base of the stem; rainwater will accumulate in this, causing the collar to rot or, if the water freezes, the bark to split.

WALLS AND OTHER STORAGE HEATERS

Gardeners have long used walls to shelter plants that might not withstand a winter fully in the open. A wall is of benefit in more than one way: its bricks or stone, warmed by the sun during the day, act as a storage heater, releasing heat by night so that plants growing against it may be spared a frost that strikes in the open garden; such plants also receive an extra dose of ripening heat during summer, enabling them to make firmer, more frost-resistant wood. Walls of course provide shelter against wind; and soil at the foot of a wall is often drier than in the open garden, which can be an advantage in winter though it may present problems during the growing season. A wall that faces into the midday sun is ideal for plants from regions with long, hot summers, ripening their wood against frost and also encouraging free flowering. In the case of late-flowering plants, wall protection in areas with a short growing season may mean the difference between flowering, or not; the extra heat reflected from the wall's surface helps to compensate for the lower intensity of the sun's rays in high latitudes, which is even more marked as summer passes into autumn.

A wall facing the afternoon sun is similarly useful. The sun's radiation is greatest after midday and, since it will continue to warm the wall until sundown, stored heat will be retained for longer into the night. Plants needing shelter in winter but for which summer ripening is less critical, or exposure to full sun may actually be damaging, may find that a wall facing away from the sun but well protected from cold winds provides a congenial environment of warm shade. The least useful wall space is that which faces the levant; not only are the sun's rays less powerful in the morning than later in the day, so that the heating effect is less, but heat will be lost all afternoon without being replenished; such a wall will be colder at night than one which receives afternoon sun.

Other structures, whether natural or artificial, can act as storage heaters and reflectors of the sun's rays. I know of more than one garden where a natural stone cliff creates in its vicinity a microclimate significantly different from that of the rest of the garden and its environs. In the Rhône Valley in Switzerland, where the winters can be quite severe, a small botanical garden illustrates the point: a banana plant is one of the unlikely survivors in the shelter of a tall, white limestone cliff, while just around the corner on the same outcrop, but fully shaded, ramondas and haberleas sow themselves on a mossy, dripping surface. Most of us are more likely to have fences than cliffs, but even large boulders can create their own tiny microclimate, and a fence will aid summer ripening to some extent and help to protect from winds, although its capacity to store heat against winter frosts is limited.

CLOSE PLANTING
Since living plants themselves give off minute amounts of heat, close planting, whether against a wall or in the open, helps to retain this heat, instead of allowing it to be dispersed by the wind. Close-set plants also support each other against wind-rock and twisting, and quickly afford each other shade at the roots. Plants that are so easily moved as to be virtually portable, such as evergreen azaleas, can be closely planted even when they are small; as they grow, they can be given more room by removing every alternate one. In the case of quick-growing plants which do not move well, such as cistus or most legumes, it may be necessary to sacrifice some of them as they grow. Plants that neither grow fast (and are consequently expensive) nor move well can be interplanted in their early years with easily-raised and dispensable plants such as tree lupins (*Lupinus arboreus*) or brooms, which can be scrapped without remorse as the permanencies begin to fill out.

Artificial frost protection

Even after exploiting the microclimate to the full, planting closely, using nurse plants, and taking care not to plant frost-tender shrubs and trees until they have formed some mature wood, gardeners who like to experiment with plants of borderline hardiness will still have to provide artificial shelter in winter for the most tender, or else accept occasional losses and the subsequent necessity (which can also be seen as an opportunity) of replanting to fill the gaps.

Late spring and early autumn frosts, though seldom very severe, cause a disproportionate amount of damage to as yet unripened growths or tender new shoots, as well as destroying flower buds, or putting paid to a late display. Even the thinnest of coverings, especially in spring, can be enough to save plants from damage; what is essential is to observe the weather, assess the risk of frost, and cover your plants unless you are sure the temperature will not fall below zero during the night.

Sheets of newspaper, inverted flower pots, straw, evergreen branch-lets, cloches and hand-lights, even wire netting or the dead, dry tops of herbaceous plants, can all be used to protect individual plants or small groups. Modern horticultural fleece and woven fabrics are lightweight, easy to handle, and effective. Whatever you use, be sure to secure it to the ground with pegs, stones or piles of soil; just because the evening is windless and frost seems to threaten, there is no assur-ance that a breeze will not get up during the night and blow your coverings all over the garden. The whole plant must be covered, so that heat released from the soil as temperatures fall is retained instead of being lost into the atmosphere. Insulation cannot provide heat, only prevent it from escaping, so temporary covers need to be in place well before sunset; remove them during the day so that the sun can warm soil and plants alike.

Whether in the form of cloches and bell-jars or of frames and houses, glass is transparent to short waves but not to long; heat received from the sun is very short-wave, whereas that subsequently given off by the earth is long-wave. Thus, the sun's heat is readily absorbed through glass, but the heat given off in return passes out only very slowly. This creates a cumulative build-up of heat under glass, which is why glass cloches and the like are an effective form of protection; the need for adequate ventilation must, however, be remembered.

Glass (or plastic) will protect plants liable to succumb to a combina-tion of winter rainfall and frost. Many, such as the grey-leaved *Helichrysum petiolare*, will barely tolerate frost in slightly moist soils, yet can survive several degrees below zero if kept bone dry.

Large-scale commercial protection against frost may take the form of overhead reed matting, or the much more advanced technology of artificially created fog, used in California by fruit growers: this is in effect a cloud at ground level, and protects against heat loss in the same way as natural cloud cover.

Technology can also help once freezing point has been reached: by

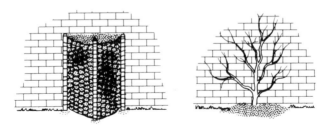

Winter protection of tender climbers against a wall: (left) a cage of chicken wire stuffed with bracken, straw or dry leaves; (right) a pile of grit over the roots

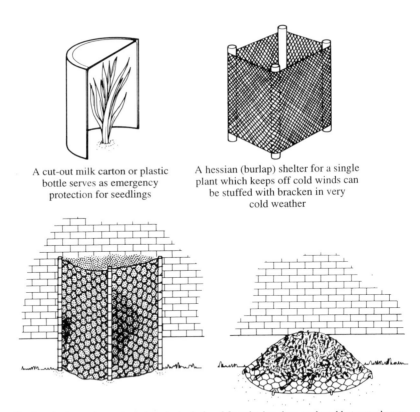

A cut-out milk carton or plastic bottle serves as emergency protection for seedlings

A hessian (burlap) shelter for a single plant which keeps off cold winds can be stuffed with bracken in very cold weather

Tender plants can be protected against wind and frost by bracken enclosed between layers of chicken wire (left). Even conifer branches can give some protection (right). However, these may need to be pinned down with chicken wire or pegs if the situation is exposed.

Protection against wind, frost and snow for shrubs and small trees

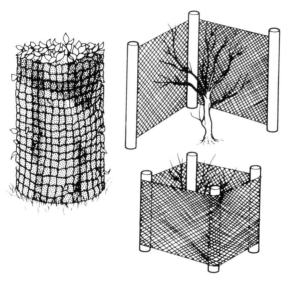

Plants can be protected by a cylinder of snow-fencing or wire mesh, loosely filled with dry leaves or straw, at left. At right are two simple structures made from hessian (burlap) and wooden stakes, to protect shrubs or young trees from wet or blown snow.

Protection devices against frost, wind and snow for small trees and shrubs

what seems like a paradox, spraying plants with a very fine jet of water which freezes and cocoons them in ice can help to protect them. The freezing process liberates minute amounts of latent heat, which may be enough to save plants from further damage; but it is important to maintain both water and ice over the plant – if only ice is present, further heat loss leads to further falls in temperature. This tricky process is not recommended for amateurs.

Protection against the deeper frosts of winter calls for more permanent arrangements. Plants that go to ground for the winter – among which I include those that, though forming a permanent woody or subshrubby top growth in their native climates, are capable of adapting to a herbaceous existence in colder regions – can be protected with a generous mound of grit, chipped bark, bracken or leaves over their crown and root spread; the mulch helps to retain warmth in the soil, so that it does not freeze. *Melianthus major* is typical of this sort of plant; shrubby in frost-free climates, it will survive quite severe frosts with the loss of its top growth only, regenerating from below ground with the return of spring. It is awarded a Z9–10 rating in the USDA hardiness zones, but in herbaceous mode would probably survive down to Z7.

With plants such as *Tropaeolum tuberosum* which quickly form clusters of tubers, the topmost tubers can be removed and overwintered in a frost-free place packed in barely moist peat or ground bark, as an insurance policy, leaving the rest in the ground beneath a thick mulch in Zones 8 and warmer. The chocolate-scented *Cosmos atrosanguineus*, a dahlia relative with tuberous roots, overwinters well with such treatment down to Z7 or perhaps even Z6, but is a very late starter in spring; mark the spot, so that you are not tempted to plant something on top of the poor cosmos in what looks like a nice empty place in the spring border.

Simply leaving their dead tops on through the winter may be enough for plants growing in regions fairly like their native climates. However, a good deal depends on the soil, and on the distribution of precipitation; while they are inactive in winter, few plants like to have their roots lie in cold, wet soil, or their crowns beset by surface water, especially if it alternately freezes and thaws.

Soils and hardiness

The provision of wind shelter, frost protection and shade is not enough; you must also consider how your soil affects the way garden plants will be able to cope with the weather. The more you are able to do to improve your soil, the better chance your plants will have of surviving the stress of cold, or drought, or downpour. Even though different soil types present different problems, a major part of the solution is almost always to add ample quantities of organic matter. Added to sandy or gravelly, fast-draining soils, organic matter helps to retain moisture; in clay soils, which often lie wet in winter only to set concrete-hard and crack open in summer drought, organic matter helps to make the soil more friable, better-drained in winter and more moisture-retentive in summer.

Most gardeners strive to maintain the fertility of their soil, yet an over-fertile one may result in excessive soft growth which, failing to ripen, may be damaged by light autumn frosts, or killed altogether by severe frost, resulting in die-back, perhaps the death of the whole plant. Nitrogen promotes soft, sappy growth, while potassium, by contributing to the formation of ripe wood, has a direct, positive effect on the frost-resistance of plants.

In high latitudes, 'hardiness' is used almost invariably to refer to the ability to withstand frost, while Australian gardeners, especially those in areas where the climate is particularly challenging, are apt to describe as 'hardy' a plant which can withstand heat, drought and saline soils – problems with which gardeners in arid regions of the south-western United States are also familiar. In such climates, deep irrigation is often carried out at intervals to leach mineral salts from the root zone; these salts would otherwise gradually accumulate in the upper levels of the soil, to the detriment of plant life.

Coping with drought

Most gardeners in temperate regions find that summer moisture deficits occur almost yearly, but the most severe difficulties, of course, are faced by gardeners in arid regions, who will perhaps be wise to choose xerophytic plants – those adapted to withstand dry climates. Desert plants such as creosote bush (*Larrea tridentata*) or *Leucophyllum frutescens* will endure very arid conditions but cannot stand cold, while for regions that are both cold and dry there are the buffalo berries (*Shepherdia* species), quaking aspen (*Populus tremuloïdes*) and some tamarisks.

IMPROVING THE WATER-HOLDING CAPACITY OF THE SOIL

Unless you are willing to accept the most limited choice of plants, it is well worth improving your soil; as well as increasing the range of plants you can grow, this will also cut down on the need to irrigate. Soils in arid regions, whether they are dense and airless clay or silt, or fast-draining sand or gravel, are usually low in organic matter. Even worse, they may be highly alkaline or saline, or both; or they may be sodic. Sodic soils, which are pasty and impervious to air and water, can be corrected by adding gypsum if the soil is naturally low in calcium, or by incorporating sulphur or sulphate of iron in high-calcium soils, including caliche.

Caliche is the name given to the hard-pan, a layer of cement-hard calcium as much as 2 m/6 ft thick, which forms beneath a thin layer of topsoil in some calcareous soils. Caliche is virtually impenetrable, so roots cannot pass through it in search of moisture and nutrients, and it impedes drainage, so that standing water accumulates and causes excess mineral salts to build up even more. Before planting in caliche soils it is vital to break up the hard-pan, or at the very least to excavate the largest planting holes you can manage, breaking the caliche enough to allow for drainage and root penetration. The alternatives are to limit yourself to plants that will tolerate caliche soils, such as palo verde (*Parkinsonia aculeata*) or mesquite (*Prosopis* species); or to build raised beds.

Chalk soils sometimes present rather similar problems. Chalk is formed from the calcium-rich shells and bodies of countless millions of tiny sea creatures which, drifting aeons ago to the ocean floor, were subsequently compressed into the dense white substance we know today. Chalk soils are often dry and hungry and, like caliche, may not drain freely, especially if, when planting, a hole large enough to take the young plant's roots, but no more, is dug. The chalk needs to be broken up around and below the planting area, so that roots can grow outwards and downwards; otherwise, the planting hole is likely to turn into a sump.

Sandy, acid soils may also have a hard-pan of accumulated mineral salts, which again must be broken up. Yet another type of hard-pan sometimes occurs in soils that have been under plough for long periods; salts build up on the unbroken subsoil, which may also have become compacted. This type of problem soil can usually be put right quite easily by means of deep cultivation, with a pickaxe or, for larger areas, a ripper plough. Deep-rooting plants will then be able to search for moisture in the lower soil levels, and the deep cultivation will help to improve the drainage. Even in droughty gardens it is essential that water – be it from rain or irrigation – can drain away freely: plants that are waterlogged will fail.

Hard-pan or no, all soils will benefit from the addition of organic material, except those (such as peat) that were actually formed from the decomposition of plant matter. The choice is wide, and includes composted forest bark, garden compost, chopped bracken, spent hops, mushroom compost, and well-rotted manure. Coarser material takes longer to decompose and is more effective to bulk up and aerate the soil. The hotter the climate, the faster organic matter decomposes; very fine materials may hardly last a year. Whatever you choose – and this will often depend on availability and cost – you should add enough to alter the soil structure; a layer 7–10 cm/3–4 in thick, incorporated into the top 20–30 cm/8–12 in of soil, would be a good quantity to start with.

MULCHING

Many gardeners believe fervently in the value of mulching to maintain soil structure, retain moisture and insulate the soil against temperature fluctuations. Certainly a good mulch helps to reduce weed growth, and hence competition for soil moisture; and mulches quite quickly become incorporated into and improve the texture of the top layers of soil – which is why they need renewing at least annually. While they do help to reduce evaporation from bare soil, they have no effect, of course, on the moisture lost by transpiration through the leaves of plants. Mulches must be applied on already moist soil; mulching dry soil simply ensures that the rains, when they do come, will take much longer to penetrate into the soil because they will have to saturate the mulch first – unless you mulch with gravel or stones, when the rain should soak through quite quickly.

If your only concern is to reduce competition from weeds, as it might be in a vegetable garden where a permanent mulch would be impractical and aesthetic considerations are of minor importance, you can use several layers of newspaper, plastic sheeting, old carpet, or slabs of straw from compressed bales; experiments in Britain have shown pieces of old carpet to be the most effective mulch, if not the most sightly. In the ornamental garden, a mulch of well-rotted compost, ground and composted bark, rotted manure, spent hops, mushroom compost or the like will both look better and help to enrich the soil and improve its structure. If it is appropriate to your climate and type of garden, an autumn mulch of fallen leaves among shrubs and trees is to be recommended. Take generous handfuls of damp leaves and pack them as tightly together as you can, taking care not to let them build up around the collars of trees and shrubs, or to smother small plants. This kind of leaf mulch is ideal for rhododendrons and other acid-soil plants, as it keeps the soil cool and reduces evaporation, but is not too dense to keep air from the fine fibrous roots. Leaves from plants grown on chalk or limestone soils may be alkaline in reaction, however, and should not be 'imported' for such use.

Even in regions where the growing season starts with the soil completely moist after winter rains a deficit may build up as, month by month, the rainfall is less than is needed to balance moisture lost through evaporation and transpiration. Plants growing in soils with a low moisture-storing capacity are the first to suffer, but adding ample quantities of organic matter may enable soil to hold three or four times as much moisture: if the average deficit during the growing season is 20 cm/8 in and the moisture storage capacity of your neighbours' soil is only equivalent to 7.5 cm/3 in of rain, their plants will quickly show signs of stress, wilting and even dying; but if you have been so generous with organic matter that the moisture storage capacity of your soil is equivalent to 15 cm/6 in of rain, you may get almost through the season before needing to irrigate – and your drought will have been much shorter than theirs.

CHOOSING AND SITING DROUGHT-RESISTANT PLANTS

The choice of plants also affects a garden's ability to withstand drought. Whatever the climate, there are plants that can survive periods of low rainfall and others that quickly show distress if they go short of water; some crops, too, require a great deal of water: cabbages, being leafy and shallow rooting, need more than tomatoes, and twining crops such as string (runner) beans need more than dwarf French beans which have less leaf exposed to the wind and sun.

Where you site your plants also affects their ability to cope with drought. Large trees with spreading root systems make heavy demands on soil moisture, so it is better to avoid planting thirsty plants or crops near trees, even if they are clear of the canopy. Wind and sun both increase transpiration, so plants that are sensitive to drought need to be sheltered and shaded, especially if the local humidity is normally low during the growing season. However, protection against excessive transpiration may have to be balanced against a plant's need for sun to ripen its growth or to flower freely or to set seed. Some plants are also apt to suffer from fungal diseases if too much sheltered; for example, rambling roses often become disfigured with mildew in dry summers if they are grown against a wall, but are unaffected if sited where the wind can blow freely through their stems.

IRRIGATION TECHNIQUES

If you do have to water to keep your plants going through a long, dry spell, it is best to water early in the morning or late in the after-noon, because less will be lost through evaporation than if you water at midday. But watering at midday is better than not being able to water all. Few but generous soakings are more effective than watering lightly; a sprinkling which merely dampens the soil surface may evapor-ate before any moisture reaches plants' roots. Furthermore, if over a longish period the surface layers only are moist, above dry soil at greater depth, the fine root hairs at lower levels may perish, leaving only the surface roots able to function: this is what gardeners mean when they say that light watering merely encourages roots to come to the surface in search of water. Allowing the water to penetrate deep into the soil and applying no more until it is absolutely necessary is especially important in arid soils, because of the high level of soil salts: long, slow waterings help to leach these from the root zone; allowing the soil to become almost dry between waterings allows air to reach the roots. Only established drought-adapted plants will stand bone-dry soil, and that not for ever; in arid regions, especially, you should watch all other plants for signs of stress. As well as wilting, such signs include changes in leaf colour to darker, greyer or bluer than normal, and curling or dropping leaves (though in some desert plants, as we have seen, shedding leaves is a natural adaptation to drought). Leaves that are dry and crisp at the margins or turning yellow are usually a sign of a severely drought-stressed plant.

Some methods of irrigation represent a more effective use of water than others. Drip or seep irrigation is the most efficient; a series of nozzles, or tiny holes along a plastic pipe, are placed to direct water at the roots of the plants that need it, and slow delivery ensures that most of the water penetrates deeply rather than running off or evaporating. Drip tubing works well even on low pressure, and is especially useful for plants in containers, or on slopes. Here, particularly, water-loss through run-off, wind deflection and evaporation is likely with other types of irrigation, especially overhead sprinklers. These are the least efficient method of irrigation, and the most prodigal with water; however, they do (if only temporarily) add to the atmospheric humidity, and moisten and cool the leaves of your plants. For individual plants that are always likely to make heavy demands on the available water, it is worth sinking a bottle in the ground beside the roots when you plant – knock the bottom out of a wine bottle and put it in neck down, or punch holes in the lower part of the sides and in the bottom of a plastic bottle and set it neck up. When you want to water the plant, fill the bottle, and the water will seep into the soil right where it is required, at the roots. A more sophisticated version of this is to sink narrow-necked, unglazed clay pots into the soil so that only the neck is visible. The pots are kept full of water, which slowly seeps through the porous clay. A good method, often used to establish individual trees and shrubs, involves hollow stakes, made for example of rigid plastic tubing with an internal diameter of about 2.5 cm/1 in, the lower end buried near the roots. The tube is filled with water, once every week or ten days. As well as delivering water efficiently to the roots, the bottle, clay pot and hollow stake techniques help to keep the soil surface dry, which cuts down on weed growth.

Any method is to be preferred that enables you to choose which plants you water. Ideally, you will have grouped your plants more or less according to their water needs, so that you will not be wasting water on a cistus because the hydrangea next to it is wilting. But even if you would never commit this solecism, there will always be times when a newly-planted shrub or tree is extra-vulnerable, compared with the mature specimens around it. Many plants that are remarkably drought-resistant once established need moderate to ample water at first, and this is where the simple watering can comes into its own. Newly-planted trees can lose moisture, through their bark as well as their leaves, at a rate they cannot replenish through their roots; in very hot or dry climates it may be helpful to wrap the trunk in hessian (burlap), which is kept damp until the tree is well established.

If you live in a climate that normally supports a year-round green lawn, never waste water on it if it starts to look miserable in summer; even if it turns brown, it will revive when the rain comes, and the water will be much better used to save plants that would die if kept too dry. In climates too dry to make good green lawns without irrigation, consider using substitutes such as hard surfaces, decking, or drought-tolerant creeping plants like lippia (*Phyla nodiflora*); or go for a winter-green lawn using cool-season annual or perennial grasses sown each autumn, and accept that the turf will die back with the summer heat.

SOIL DRAINAGE
Provided you have dealt with any hard-pan, drainage should not be a problem in sand or gravel soils. Clay soils, on the other hand, are often poorly drained, and in regions where the rainfall in winter is higher than is necessary to meet the needs of plants, clay and clay-loam soils may lie wet and cold around plant roots, putting the crowns or collars of sensitive plants at risk of damage from surface moisture. This may be true even of plants that, in the wild, grow in wet soils, such as red hot pokers (*Kniphofia* species – see pp. 3 and 242).

Standing water also deprives plant roots of oxygen, a problem at any season. To open and aerate the soil, it can help to add generous quantities of sharp grit to the surface layer of clay or clay-loam soils at the same time as you are adding your chosen organic matter. If it is not enough to add organic material and grit, and to continue year after year to add more, it may be necessary to instal drainage pipes leading to a soakaway or into a storm drain.

Sometimes a localized drainage problem can be solved by planting shrubs or trees tolerant of wet soils; even a shrubby willow, let alone a full-sized weeping willow or a tall alder, can suck up astonishing amounts of water, so that what was a boggy patch or even an area of standing water turns into something quite manageable. Beware, however, of planting thirsty trees with moisture-searching roots near a building; they may well follow and penetrate the drains, or take so much moisture from the soil that cracks develop in foundations and walls.

While wet soils where the water lies stagnant are a problem in temperate climates there are many plants to choose from which enjoy a soil that is moist because of moving water: candelabra primulas, rodgersias and astilbes, globe flowers (*Trollius europaeus*), *Gunnera manicata*, the sensitive fern (*Onoclea sensibilis*). The yellow European flag, *Iris pseudacorus*, grows in wet soil or even with its feet in water; the Japanese *I. laevigata* also does well in shallow water. Soggy streamsides suit both the yellow *Lysichiton americanum* and its white Far Eastern counterpart *L. camschatcensis*. Some British gardeners, experimenting with plants that resent the alternating frost and thaw of stop-go winters, have found a few that will survive if grown with their crowns actually under water, where they do not freeze: among them are the kaffir lily, *Schizostylis coccinea*, and the arum lily, *Zantedeschia aethiopica*.

Part Two

WEATHER

4

Understanding
weather and climate

I have looked briefly, in Chapter 1, at some of the difficulties and challenges of gardening in different broadly recognized types of climates; in Chapter 2, at how plants adapt to different types of climate and weather; and in Chapter 3, at what we can do to modify the conditions under which we garden, to enable us to grow as wide a range of plants as possible. I now want to consider the various factors which produce the different types of climate and the weather which typefies them. Although beyond a certain point we cannot modify its effects or adapt to them, it is helpful to know as much as possible about the particular climate in which we garden.

The key to the atmospheric processes that make up our climates and our weather is the energy received from the sun in the form of light and heat. The atmosphere consists of gases – chiefly nitrogen, oxygen and carbon dioxide, with traces of others – in more or less constant proportion, with varying amounts of other constituents. The main variable is water vapour, transferred to the atmosphere by evaporation from surface water and by transpiration from plants. The amount of water vapour in the atmosphere – the humidity – varies with the season and with altitude; it is related to air temperature, and is highest in summer in low latitudes, near the equator – except, of course, in tropical desert areas. It is the humidity in the air that makes even quite modest summer temperatures in temperate maritime climates so uncomfortable by comparison with, for example, the hotter but drier

Mediterranean. The sun is constantly emitting energy, and the amount which the earth receives is chiefly affected by the distance between the earth and the sun, the altitude of the sun (its height above the horizon), and the day length.

The distance between the sun and the earth varies with the seasons because the earth's orbit is an ellipse, rather than a circle; and the angle at which the sun's rays strike the earth alters due to the tilting of the earth's axis relative to its plane of rotation around the sun. The further north or south of the equator (the higher the latitude), the greater the difference between the sun high in the sky on a summer's day at noon and the slanting rays of the low sun of winter. The higher the sun, the greater the heat received by a given area of the earth's surface, and the higher (other things being equal) the air temperature as a result. Day length, too, varies with seasonal changes, and it is evident that the longer the sun is shining, the more heat the earth will receive at a given point on its surface each day.

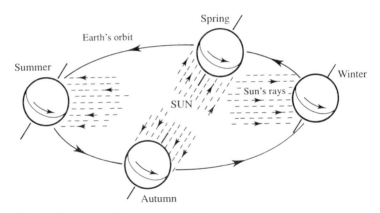

The earth's tilted axis and the astronomical seasons

At the earth's surface, land and sea are differently affected by heat received from the sun. Land warms up more quickly than water, which, being a poor conductor of heat, must absorb five times as much heat as a comparable mass of dry soil to achieve the same increase in temperature. Land also cools and returns heat to the atmosphere rapidly, while water cools and releases its stored heat slowly; the planet's oceans thus act as massive reservoirs of warmth. In both heating and cooling much more slowly than land masses, oceans induce a much narrower annual variation between maximum and minimum temperatures in coastal areas than is experienced in continental areas. This is why the

Mean sea-level temperatures (°C) in January. The position of the thermal equator is shown approximately by the dashed line.

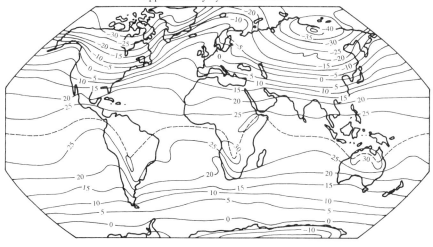

Mean sea-level temperatures (°C) in July. The position of the thermal equator is shown approximately by the dashed line.

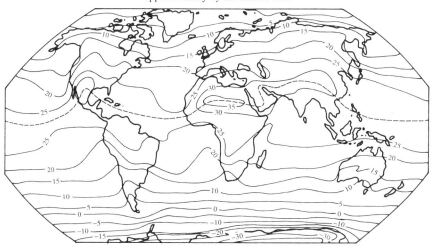

Source: Atmosphere, Weather & Climate (Barry & Chorley)

World mean sea-level temperatures, January and July

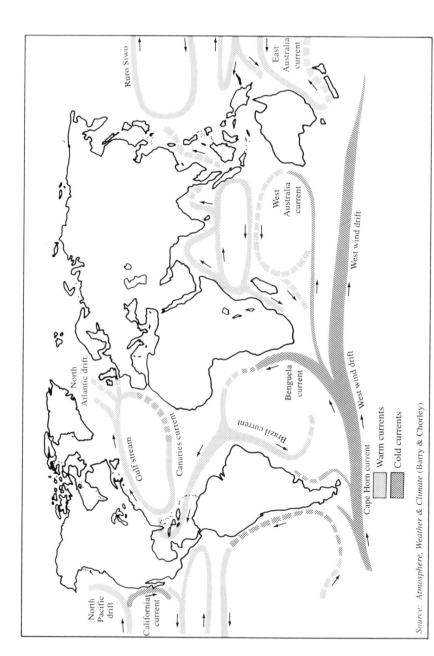

Source: *Atmosphere, Weather & Climate* (Barry & Chorley)

Main ocean currents

Labels visible in figure:

Ruro Siwo

East Australia current

West Australia current

West wind drift

North Atlantic drift

Benguela current

Brazil current

Gulf stream

Canaries current

North Pacific drift

California current

Cape Horn current

West wind drift

Warm currents

Cold currents

southern hemisphere with its huge oceans has, on average, cooler summers but milder winters than the northern hemisphere, dominated by large land masses.

Added to the heat reservoir effect is the effect of ocean currents. The Florida and Gulf Streams on the one hand, and the Kuro Siwo current on the other, bring warm tropical waters to the north Atlantic and the north Pacific oceans, raising the temperature of these regions. It is above all the Gulf Stream which makes the British climate suitable for such a wide variety of plants.

Maritime or oceanic climates occur in cool temperate regions on islands, and on the edges of large land masses; they are probably the gardener's dream, characterized as they are by comparatively small seasonal variations in temperature, and by adequate, evenly distributed rainfall. The moderating influence of the ocean diminishes further inland, resulting in wider variations in temperature, more frequent frosts in winter, and a shorter growing season. Towards the interior of large land masses the seasons are much more clear-cut, with consistently cold winters and warm or hot summers, and usually a fleeting spring and autumn – a continental climate.

Land is not only unevenly distributed about the globe; its relief varies greatly as well. For every rise of 100 m above mean sea level there is a fall in temperature of 0.6 °C (1 °F per 330 ft), and a mountain on the equator which has year-round snow on its peaks reproduces on its slopes the temperature gradient of an entire hemisphere. The alpine plants that gardeners grow come mainly from mountains in higher latitudes – such as the Alps, the Rockies, the high Himalayas – and the conditions they experience are not so very different from those of subpolar regions, where the growing season is short and the winters are long and severe.

The meteorological tropics extend roughly from 30 °N to 30 °S, from Cairo to Johannesburg, from New Orleans almost to Buenos Aires. As conditions under them are almost constant and temperatures are consistently high (in contrast to the changeability of weather driven by the buffeting westerlies of the temperate zone), tropical seasons are defined by variations in rainfall, and particularly the monsoons. The easterly trade winds converge from the NE and SE in a belt of light winds and calms (formerly known to sailors as the Doldrums); this belt occurs at the latitude where the sun's heat has recently been most intense, and so it migrates, following the sun, from north to south

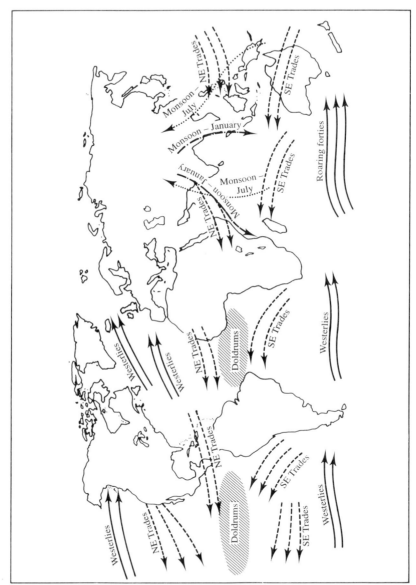

Prevailing winds

and back again during the course of the year. The monsoons are caused when mild, moist air, blowing over the oceans from the SE, meets hot, dry air blown down from the deserts of North India and Africa, and both are forced to rise. Clouds build up, advancing a little further each day and receding at night until at length, all being well, the two airflows converge in violent thunderstorms, the rains fall, and the year's harvest is assured.

Permanently drier regions of the tropics are often semi-desert, with plants adapted to long dry spells, while true deserts, the driest regions of all, are virtually devoid of vegetation except for short periods after the occasional rains.

Warm-temperate and subtropical climates, which may both experience frost, are broadly speaking of two types: Mediterranean, occurring on the western coasts of continents and characterized by cool, wet winters and summer drought; and the humid subtropical climates of eastern coastal regions which are hot in summer, warm in winter and humid all year.

In various combinations the components of weather – temperature, moisture, wind – produce these different climates and, in conjunction with soil, affect plant distribution.

Temperature and plant distribution

The effect of climate on plant distribution shows up clearly in the case of temperature, with the frost-line the most important of all climatic demarcations. Very few genera are found the world over, and few large genera have a balanced distribution either side of the frost-line, a distinction which is even more marked, at the species level, as between tropical and temperate plants. Whether or not they will tolerate frost, all plants appear to have a specific minimum temperature below which they cannot survive in the wild. This is not to say that the range of temperatures within which they can *exist* is narrow – most plants seem able to endure over a fairly wide temperature range – but rather that the temperature necessary for the production of viable seed is a limiting factor for plants in the wild: plants which survive happily in cold gardens may nevertheless be unable to reproduce themselves by seed.

Temperature is mainly affected by latitude and altitude; lesser factors are the slope and aspect of the land, and the extent and density of cloud cover and rainfall. Temperatures in the tropics may have a diurnal variation of as little as 2 °C/3–4 °F on cloudy days, but as much as 9 °C/

16 °F on sunny days; and even though it lies in equatorial and tropical regions, where the level of sunshine is generally high, the Amazon Basin experiences comparatively less because of frequent heavy rainfall and cloud cover. By contrast, where high pressure systems prevail, there is commonly very little cloud and the sun's rays are hot. Deserts, lacking the moderating influence of cloud cover, experience extreme temperature variations between day and night. Dust, pollutants or fog all reduce the intensity of sunlight. Away from the equator, slopes that face the midday sun receive direct sunlight for longer, and at angles nearer to the perpendicular, than do level plains.

Plant cover itself can reduce temperature, often quite markedly. Clearly, shaded ground is cooler than that which is open to the sun; but vegetation also interrupts air movement, thus reducing the amount of heat returned into the atmosphere. In a forest, the cooler, shaded soil beneath the canopy absorbs heat from the forest air and cools it. Furthermore, because trees and other vegetation transpire, the forest will be more humid than adjacent clearings, and will therefore warm more slowly. By night, the canopy acts as insulation, keeping both air and soil beneath it warmer; diurnal variations in temperature (that is, those over a 24-hour period) are therefore smaller in forested areas than in open places or areas of widely dispersed plants. There is also an exchange of heat between plants and their environment: leaves are warmed by absorbing radiation from sunlight, scattered light, reflected sunlight, and infrared wavelengths. If the air is warmer than a leaf, the leaf will heat up; but if it is cooler, the leaf will give off heat. In cold weather, therefore, the temperature is fractionally warmer in a close planting, even of small plants, than where they are dispersed.

SEASONAL TEMPERATURE RANGES

The astronomical seasons of spring, summer, autumn and winter are caused by the movement of the sun relative to the earth. The sun is at its furthest south in December. During the following months it tracks northwards to cross the equator on March 21 and reach its northernmost position, the Tropic of Cancer, on June 21; the process is reversed over the following six months, the sun re-crossing the equator in September and reaching the southern Tropic of Capricorn once again in December.

The meteorological seasons, which are the ones that concern gardeners, do not, however, correspond fully with the astronomical seasons, because the sun chiefly heats the atmosphere indirectly, by heating the land masses and oceans and other bodies of water, which then release

	21 Dec	21 Feb	21 Apr	21 June	21 Aug	21 Oct	21 Dec
SUN POSITION							
LAND TEMP.	Cold	Cool, warming rapidly	Warm, warming	Warm	Warm, cooling rapidly	Cool, cooling	
TEMP. OF BODIES OF WATER	Cold, cooling	Cold	Cold, warming	Warm, warming	Warm	Warm, cooling	
SEASON	Mid-winter	Early Spring	Late Spring	Mid-Summer	Early Autumn	Late Autumn	

Source: The Weather-wise Gardener (Calvin Simonds)

The six seasons of temperate climates (northern hemisphere)

their heat to warm the air. The weather of the various meteorological seasons is determined largely by the relative temperatures of the globe's land and water surfaces. For gardeners in higher latitudes, north and south of the tropics, the seasons are effectively six: winter, early spring, late spring (or early summer), midsummer, high summer (or early autumn), and autumn (late autumn/early winter). Go to the tropics, to the monsoon areas, and you will discover a completely different pattern of seasonal variations.

In the northern hemisphere, December 21 is the start of midwinter, for it is then that the sun is vertical over the southern Tropic of Capricorn, and furthest from the northern hemisphere. At the Arctic Circle, the sun no longer rises – the weeks of unbroken night have already begun. By late January, the land masses are at their coldest, for the days are short, the sunlight weak, and the land continues to cool.

Large bodies of water exercise their moderating influence: the Gulf of Mexico remains warm enough to give a virtually unbroken growing season in Florida and the coastal region, though further inland there may be thirty or more days of temperatures below freezing. The warm Gulf Stream ensures that the western coasts of mainland Britain experience growing temperatures for between 200 and 250 days, while in parts of New Hampshire (the same latitude as the south of France) the growing season averages a mere 90 days a year.

In early spring, which can be taken as starting on February 21 in the temperate northern hemisphere, the sun moves northwards at its fastest rate; day lengths and sun angles increase, and with them, most dramatically in the higher latitudes, the amount of solar radiation. The land is slow to respond, however, while water surfaces, which lag even more in their reaction time, are still cooling; not until the equinox of March 21 do they begin to warm again. In regions closest to the tropics the growing season has begun, but in the northern parts of the great land masses, and at high altitudes further south, it is still bitterly cold. By March 1 maximum daytime temperatures in the extreme south-west of Britain and over much of Ireland already exceed 10 °C/50 °F, but the rest of southern England will not enjoy such warmth until March 11, on average; inland, in central England, the critical date is March 21, in the north-east April 1, but not until late April will such temperatures be reached in north-east Scotland.

In late spring, there is progressively less and less difference between subtropical regions and the higher latitudes in the amount of heat received from the sun. Air and land temperatures rise, followed more slowly by those of large lakes and oceans. Not until about 30 May, however, can growers throughout the more northerly regions of the United States or in northern Britain be reasonably confident that there will be no more killing frosts until autumn.

The midsummer season begins on 21 June, when the sun stands directly over the northern Tropic of Cancer. The concern now of most gardeners in the temperate regions is whether it will rain or not; the growing season is in full swing, and the need for water at its height.

Early autumn mirrors early spring; the days shorten rapidly, and the sun descends in the sky. The result is a sharp decline in the amount of heat received from the sun, especially in the higher latitudes. By the end of September, or even earlier in some regions, gardeners in the northern United States and in much of Britain will have had at least one sharp frost, but the onset of the still colder weather of late autumn and winter will be delayed in maritime regions by the effect of the slowly-cooling oceans. The days continue to shorten until on 21 December the shortest day is reached, the start of midwinter once again.

Although these dates apply only to the northern hemisphere, the principle of the cycle of seasons is the same for the southern hemisphere. Gardeners in the cool-temperate regions of New Zealand, Tasmania or southern Chile will find many similarities with the maritime climate of Britain, and those in western and parts of southern

Australia with the Mediterranean or much of California. What is missing from the southern hemisphere is the equivalent of the continental climate, because of the absence of large land masses at higher latitudes (except, of course, for the wholly ice-bound continent of Antarctica).

FROST

Warmth from the sun heats the atmosphere, and is absorbed by the earth; after the sun sets, everything on the earth's surface gives off heat; without the sun to make good these losses, the temperature falls, and if it falls below freezing there will be what is called a radiation frost. The heat loss is greatest where there is no overhead shelter – be it clouds, tree canopy, horticultural fleece or other protection – to provide insulation. Following a frost-free day, quite a flimsy overhead shelter can keep frost at bay during the night. The nineteenth-century gardener John Loudon experimented with a cambric handkerchief supported on four stakes 15 cm/6 in above a patch of grass, and found that the temperature beneath the handkerchief was between 4 and 6 °C (7–11 °F) higher, even though the thin fabric gave virtually no protection against the wind. Even such partial cover as bare branches or wire mesh can suffice.

Under a clear sky this radiation cooling is very rapid, which is why in hot desert regions the nights are often surprisingly cold. Clouds, even very high clouds, provide the best natural protection against frost by reflecting back some of the heat given off by the earth during the night. Gardeners soon learn to observe the sky at dusk, to assess the amount of cloud cover, and even to notice the trend – if the clouds are thinning at dusk, the sky may well be clear by dawn, but if the clouds become more dense as afternoon yields to dusk, there is less likelihood of frost.

Generally speaking, it will be slightly warmer at ground level on a windy night than on a still one, when the heavier cold air sinks to hug the ground and there is no air movement to mix it with the warmer layers. The air at ground level cools more rapidly if the soil is already cold and dry; warm, moist soil releases more heat and moisture into the atmosphere, raising the air temperature. And of course, there is more time during the long nights of winter for the earth to lose heat and for the coldest air to settle at ground level. The greatest risk of frost comes with the combination of clear skies, little or no wind, long nights, and a cold air stream giving temperatures that are already low at dusk.

Although a windy night might avert a frost, frost can also be caused by winds, if their temperature is below freezing. Unlike radiation frost, this advection frost is not the result of on-the-spot cooling, but arrives from elsewhere. Advection frosts can be killers, especially as they are often longer-lasting than radiation frosts, and are frequently accompanied by cloud – the insulating qualities of which, helpful at night in retaining warmth, are equally effective in keeping out the sun's warmth during short winter days. Hoar frost, which transforms the garden into a sparkling landscape of ice crystals, occurs when the water vapour in moist air is frozen rather than being deposited as dew.

Local topography can have a marked effect on the incidence of frost. Cold air, being denser and heavier than warm air, tends to flow down slopes and hillsides; as we have already seen, at the lowest point, or sooner if there is an obstacle – which may be a mere hollow in the slope, or even something as slight as a hedge or fence – this cold dense air will collect: where this happens, there are the makings of a frost hollow.

The interaction of frost and other climatic factors

Gardeners in the United States, and increasingly elsewhere too, are familiar with the USDA hardiness zones based upon average minimum winter temperatures across the continent. Minimum temperatures, however, reflect only one of the factors that determine whether a plant is winter-hardy. The range of temperatures between summer and winter, and the duration of the seasons, also affect a plant's cycle of growth and dormancy. The growing season is defined, in temperate zones, by the period from last frost to first frost; more accurately, from the time when the temperature reaches 5.5 °C/42 °F, at which point grass and many other plants of temperate climates start to grow. Stop–go winters, in which frosts alternate with thaws that tempt plants into growth, can be more damaging than steady frost, even if the minimum temperatures reached in each frosty period are not so low.

Wind-borne frosts rapidly cause plant tissues to become not only cold, but dehydrated; plants suffer even more acutely when frozen soil prevents their roots from making good the moisture lost, and their cells become unable to function. Plants adapted to growing in frosty regions have various antifreeze mechanisms based on chemical changes in their tissue fluids; if those fluids are reduced, the ability of the tissues to withstand freezing is impaired. Most dangerous of all

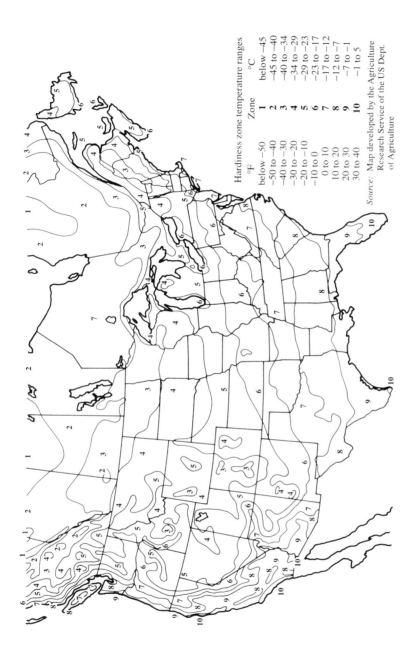

Hardiness zone temperature ranges

°F	Zone	°C
below −50	**1**	below −45
−50 to −40	**2**	−45 to −40
−40 to −30	**3**	−40 to −34
−30 to −20	**4**	−34 to −29
−20 to −10	**5**	−29 to −23
−10 to 0	**6**	−23 to −17
0 to 10	**7**	−17 to −12
10 to 20	**8**	−12 to −7
20 to 30	**9**	−7 to −1
30 to 40	**10**	−1 to 5

Source: Map developed by the Agriculture Research Service of the US Dept. of Agriculture

Plant hardiness zones in the United States

is the combination of a wind-borne frost, frozen soil and a bright sunny day, which imposes severe cold and dehydration stress. On still, sunless days plants can survive lower temperatures than when frost, sun and wind combine.

Very severe frost can rupture the cell membranes within the plant, but even lesser frosts can cause damage if they are followed by exposure to bright sunlight, which stimulates metabolic action before the ice that has formed in the plant tissues can melt to rehydrate the cells.

Plants native to regions where winters are severe but without thaw until the spring may be especially vulnerable when grown in milder regions with a less constant climate; they are easily lured into growth by a spell of mild weather, only to be damaged, perhaps even killed, as their prematurely moisture-filled tissues are frozen by the return of winter temperatures, or their tender new shoots are frosted. Other plants, more circumspect about unfurling their leaves, may however be prompted to flower too early, and fruit tree buds can be damaged or killed if they have begun to swell in an early mild spell.

Newly-planted or shallow-rooted plants are easily uprooted by successive thaws and frosts; the ground, wet from the thaw, heaves and cracks as the frost returns, exposing roots and leaving them vulnerable to cold and desiccation.

Unseasonable frosts – unseasonable, that is, in relation to the normal cycle of a particular species – may mean more than the loss of a spring display or a fruit crop, or a premature end to autumn's flowers: early frost in autumn may damage or kill plants which have not yet fully ripened, since soft and sappy growths, containing more cell moisture, are particularly vulnerable. Premature frosts following a damp or dull summer or a wet autumn spell can cause untold damage.

Frost can nevertheless be a labour-saver as well as a killer. A ground frost in autumn, which clears the next morning, makes hand weeding much easier, as the shallow roots of annual weeds are lifted half out of the soil; and soil that is dug in autumn and left as large clods will be broken down by hard frosts, as the water they contain expands on freezing to force the soil particles apart.

DIURNAL TEMPERATURE RANGE
The ability to withstand frost is only part of the story; the diurnal temperature range also affects the way plants grow. Some plants may be checked or damaged by cool nights following high daytime temperatures, even though the night may not have been frosty.

In equatorial regions there is little difference, at sea level, between

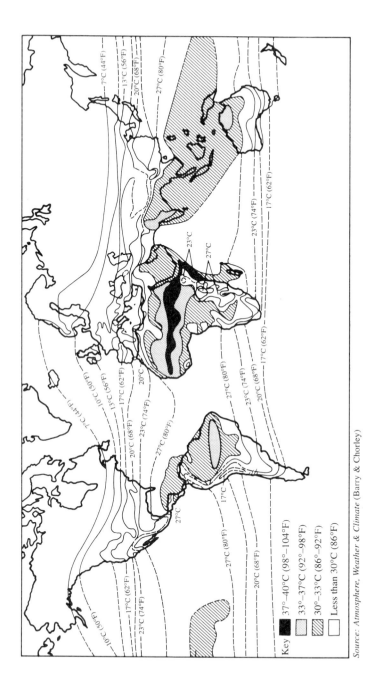

Source: Atmosphere, Weather & Climate (Barry & Chorley)

Mean daily maximum shade air temperatures (°C)

day and night temperatures, and the seasons too are very similar. At higher altitudes the nights may be much cooler than the days, with heavy dews forming as the moisture-saturated air cools; there may even be frosts, at very high altitudes. Plants from such regions are very specialized, able to endure the difference between extreme midday heat and several degrees of frost at night, but ill-adapted to cope with major *seasonal* fluctuations in temperature.

As one moves from the equator to the tropics there is a greater variation in day length and the diurnal temperature range widens, with summer daytime temperatures often much higher than those of equatorial regions. Maximum temperatures at the earth's surface occur at the tropics, in part because the sun remains directly overhead for longer during spring and autumn – for 86 consecutive days as against only 30 days at the equator – and in part because these days are themselves longer. A typical tropical plant is the date palm which, while in the cold months withstanding frosts that would kill equatorial plants, yet needs very high temperatures to ripen its fruits: it is not therefore a success in equatorial regions.

In high latitudes the normal pattern of diurnal temperature variation is one of warm to cool daylight hours, with colder nights. The range is greater under clear skies than cloudy, and in winter the usual pattern may be reversed, a clear frosty day being followed, when clouds gather in the evening, by a warmer night; but the general rule is that, as the sun goes down, so does the thermometer.

Rain, snow and other forms of precipitation

Moisture is as important as temperature for plant life, and a finite amount, present in the atmosphere as water vapour, is constantly recycled. Condensation is the direct cause of precipitation in all its forms – rain, snow, sleet, soft hail, hailstones, dew, hoar-frost, and fog. Moisture percolates into natural underground water reservoirs (aquifers), and is carried by rivers down to lakes or oceans; evaporating from open water, or from plants and the earth's surface, it re-enters the atmosphere. Rainfall, the single most important form of precipitation, is the easiest to measure, but measurements of total rainfall over a given period may be misleading: seasonal deficits may occur even in regions that seem to have plenty of rainfall, while a very heavy downpour, though it adds to the total, may do as much damage as good, through run-off, soil erosion, and physical damage to crops. Gardeners

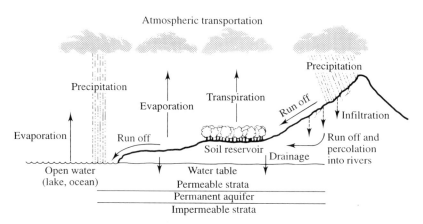

Atmospheric transportation

Precipitation

Precipitation

Evaporation

Transpiration

Run off

Infiltration

Evaporation

Run off

Soil reservoir

Drainage

Run off and percolation into rivers

Open water (lake, ocean)

Water table

Permeable strata

Permanent aquifer

Impermeable strata

The hydrologic cycle

are well aware of the value of intermittent spells of fine drizzle, as opposed to a prolonged dry period followed by heavy rain, much of which is wasted as it runs off parched soil; bald statistics do not reveal the difference.

The incidence of rainfall is not related to latitude, but mainly to the distribution of land and sea, and to the height of the land above sea level. Oceanic climates occur where the prevailing winds, coming off a warm sea, are consequently moist and cloudy. The warmer the air, the more moisture it can carry; air masses warmed as they pass over warm ocean currents draw up water vapour, and when this warm, moist air meets cooler land, as in the Pacific northwest or western Britain, very high levels of coastal precipitation result. However, proximity to the ocean does not always mean a damp climate: coastal deserts are formed in some regions, such as Baja California, Peru, and south-western Africa, where air cooled by passing over cold ocean currents then blows over a warm land mass; the air, warming, draws up what water vapour is available, causing very high evaporation. Continental climates, far from the influence of the ocean, tend to experience drier air and less precipitation.

Polar and high altitude climates, as well as being very cold, tend to have little precipitation (mostly falling as snow) even though the air may be comparatively moist. At the other extreme, tropical climates range from warm and humid to hot and dry, and experience little seasonal variation; rainfall may be more or less constant – or constantly deficient – throughout the year, or seasonally variable. Two climatic types show a marked seasonal variation in rainfall: monsoon climates,

World distribution of precipitation

Legend:

- Snow
- Seldom rains or snows
- Light seasonal rain or snow
- Heavy seasonal rain
- Rainfall every month

Pacific Ocean

Indian Ocean

Atlantic Ocean

Pacific Ocean

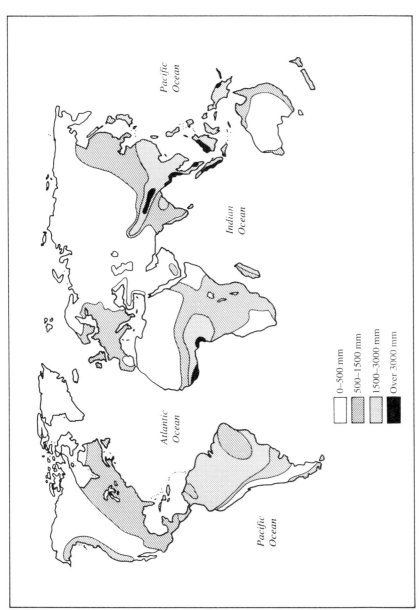

World distribution of total annual precipitation

0–500 mm

500–1500 mm

1500–3000 mm

Over 3000 mm

Pacific Ocean

Indian Ocean

Atlantic Ocean

Pacific Ocean

most of which fall within the tropical zones, experience hot, wet seasons alternating with dry ones, while subtropical Mediterranean climates have summers that are warm to hot and dry, with winters mild to cool and wet. In the tropics, the seasonal pattern of rainfall varies broadly with latitude; at the equator rain falls at all seasons; in the zone from about 3° to 10° north and south there are two wet and two dry seasons; and further away from the equator there is one wet and one dry season each year.

PRECIPITATION AND VEGETATION

If the species of plant which will grow in a given region are largely determined by temperature, the type of plant community in a given region – the vegetation – is determined by the pattern of precipitation, and reflects the major climatic types. Similar climates, as Carl Ludwig Willdenow noted two hundred years ago, produce similar vegetation, even in regions that are thousands of miles apart. Wet regions are characterized by tropical or rain forests; humid regions with more seasonal rainfall, by savannah or grassland. Forests cover more than half the cold temperate and tropical zones, but less than half the warm temperate zone; they will grow wherever there is sufficient precipitation at all seasons, and are limited in those regions not by winter cold but by the duration of summer. In the short summers of the tundra regions the frozen soil does not melt except at the very surface; with soil moisture largely locked up in the permafrost (the permanently frozen subsoil), only a sparse and highly adapted vegetation of stunted shrubs and dwarf herbaceous plants can survive the cold-induced drought.

More than half of the warm temperate zone consists of grasslands or desert; grasslands form where a shortage of winter rainfall gives them an opportunity to compete with trees. Deserts, of course, suffer from almost continual moisture deficits. The other possible pattern, of adequate winter but inadequate summer rainfall, characteristic of Mediterranean climates, gives rise to vegetation known as hard-leaved or sclerophyllous forest, where the plants are adapted to minimize moisture loss during the summer; a great many of the woody plants of the Mediterranean, of California, and of other regions with a Mediterranean type of climate, are indeed characterized by hard leaves, or by some other form of protection against the heat of the sun and excessive transpiration.

As common sense and observation suggest, the greater the precipitation and the more even its distribution, the more luxuriant the

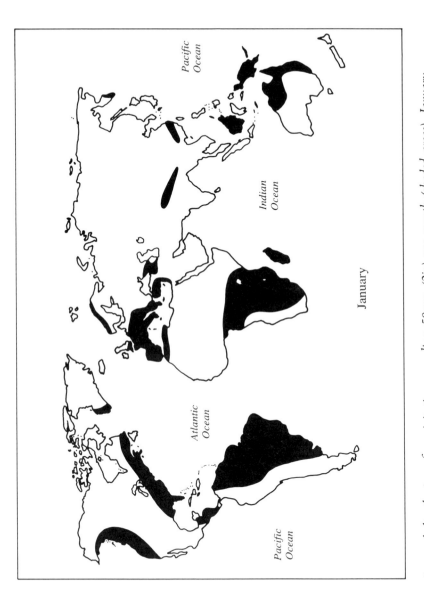

Seasonal distribution of precipitation exceeding 50mm (2in) per month (shaded areas), January

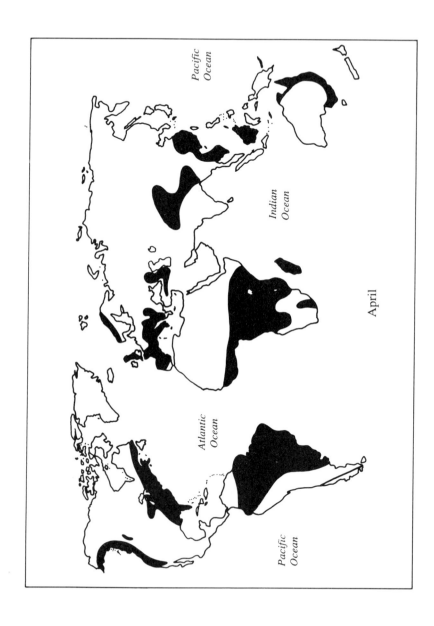

Seasonal distribution of precipitation exceeding 50mm (2in) per month, April

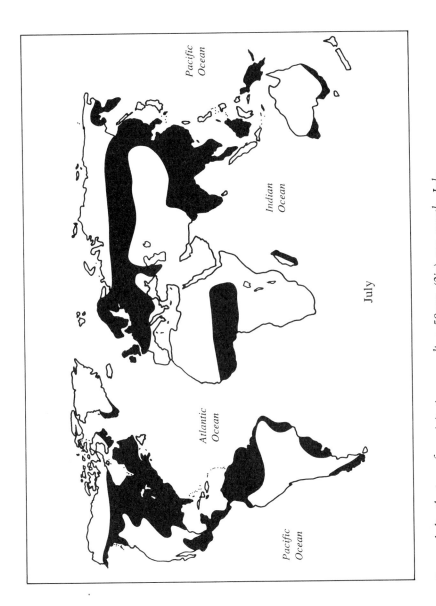

Seasonal distribution of precipitation exceeding 50mm (2in) per month, July

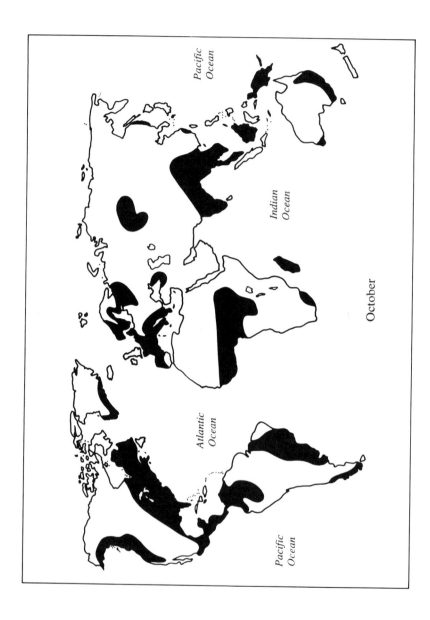

Pacific
Ocean

Indian
Ocean

Atlantic
Ocean

Pacific
Ocean

October

Seasonal distribution of precipitation exceeding 50mm (2in) per month, October

vegetation, though its precise components will vary according to temperature. The tropical rain forests contain mainly broad-leaved evergreen trees; in monsoon areas the trees and shrubs range from broad-leaved evergreen to deciduous, which lose their leaves to conserve water during the dry season. In the moist and equable oceanic climates of the temperate regions, broad-leaf forests or lush pasture are common.

In extreme continental climates, the vegetation is more limited – conifer forests, dry grasslands, or desert – a pattern well demonstrated in temperate North America, where the climate becomes progressively drier as one moves westwards across the continent; the mixed forest of the east, influenced by the Atlantic ocean, yields to open woodland with a grassy understorey, then to savannah with scattered trees, and finally to grassland; sometimes the transition is quite abrupt. The grasses of the prairies in their turn alter as precipitation decreases from east to west, from the tall grass prairie of the east to the short grass prairie of the west. There is also a small region of desert grassland, in Texas, New Mexico, Arizona and northern Mexico.

In South Africa as a whole the rainfall is rather low, and here too decreases westwards from a maximum on the east coast; almost all the western half of the country (except for a narrow coastal strip in the south and the mountains of the south-west) has less than 23 cm/10 in each year. This distribution results from winds which blow in warm, wet air from the Indian Ocean during the summer, producing rainfall that decreases in quantity from the coast inland; during the winter the winds, originating over the colder, drier air of the Southern Ocean, bring rain only to the coastal belt. High rainfall is confined in South Africa to the summits of the higher mountains, such as the Drakensberg and on the Transvaal–Natal border, small areas on the escarpment in north-eastern Transvaal, and the coastal mountains of the south-west. The result of this pattern is a great variety of vegetation types, from forest in the regions with continuous moisture and no dry season, through grassland and savannah (dry winters, rainfall in summer) and sclerophyllous forest (dry summer, wet winter), to desert and semi-desert. It is not only the absolute amount of precipitation which is significant, but also its predictability. Desert regions may have on average as much rainfall as regions that support a more luxuriant vegetation, but it is commonly very unpredictable, and there may be several years between effective amounts.

In the wetter regions of the Himalayas to the south of the snowy crests, where the monsoon is felt, the vegetation type is temperate rain forest. The rainy season is interrupted by a short winter, so that mois-

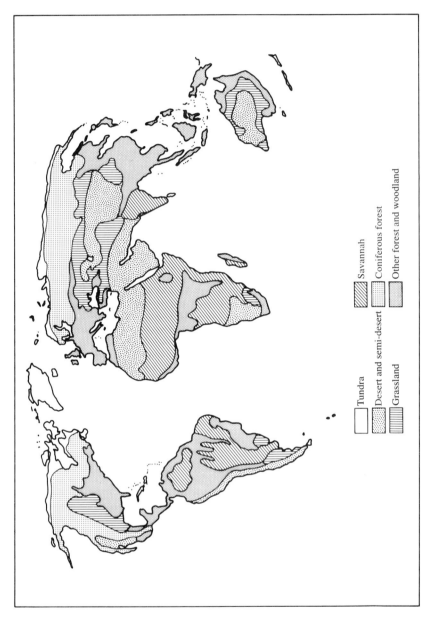

Tundra

Desert and semi-desert

Grassland

Savannah

Coniferous forest

Other forest and woodland

World distribution of vegetation

ture is always available. Frank Kingdon Ward writes of the forests of Upper Burma that

> . . . moisture and darkness have filled the forest with lurking death. The very ground from out of which the tree Rhododendrons grow is permanently mulched, the air is rank with the breath of decay, and between the stems of trees and Bamboos, silently, caressingly, steals the cool wet mist. Nothing is ever dry. Everything is choked and stifled with moss . . . And embedded in these cushions are the perching plants . . . From this spongy bed the epiphytes draw their water . . . up here in the swaying branches are light, air, and space, never drought.

As for the winter, 'In the rain forest the snow is soft and yielding, ready to melt at a glance from the sun, and to disappear altogether when a warm breath from the valley blows upon it.'

The regions of maximum rainfall are nearly all equatorial: the whole of Malaysia and the Pacific, the lowlands of Brazil, and parts of west Africa. Other, more localized wet regions occur on the east coast of Brazil, parts of the west coast of South America, the east coast of Madagascar, the Himalayas and Burma, parts of south India, New Zealand, and a small area in Alaska. By contrast, the regions of very low rainfall are in the Arctic, parts of western North America and of temperate South America, North Africa and Arabia, Central Asia, South Africa, and the Australian interior. A glance at an atlas will show that these patterns of precipitation resolve themselves into two distinct belts, one of high rainfall from the Himalayas through Malaysia and across the Pacific, and the other of low rainfall which has resulted in the chain of deserts stretching from the west coast of North Africa almost to China.

RAINFALL AND TOPOGRAPHY

As well as these great patterns, local topographical factors affect precipitation. When warm, moist air is forced upwards to cross a mountain range it cools, eventually reaching the point where moisture begins to condense and to fall as precipitation. As a general rule, more falls on the heights than in the plains, more on the windward side than on the leeward. When an air mass has crossed the summit of a mountain range or hills, it begins to warm again as it descends, which increases its water-holding capacity and decreases precipitation on the lee side, creating a dry belt known as a rain-shadow. In middle

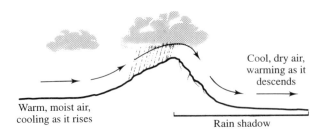

Cool, dry air,
warming as it
descends

Warm, moist air,
cooling as it rises

Rain shadow

Formation of a rain shadow

latitudes, for example in the Alps, precipitation increases up the mountain slopes, to about 3–4,000 m/10,000 ft, and even quite low hills can
affect local rainfall. In western Britain, where the hills are at most only
about 1,000 m/3,000 ft, the maximum falls are actually recorded to
leeward of the summits, probably because the air tends to go on rising
for a while after passing the crest, and there is a time-lag between condensation and precipitation; it is also possible that eddies in the airflow
may distort the picture, causing less rain to be collected in gauges on
the windward side and more on the leeward than has actually fallen.

The middle elevations of very high mountain ranges, such as the
Sierra Nevada in California, often receive more precipitation than the
peaks. Air masses will continue to move upwards after jettisoning their
moisture, or will frequently move through gaps in the mountain chain,
leaving the peaks comparatively dry. In the tropics and subtropics too,
the maximum precipitation generally occurs below the highest mountain crests, decreasing upwards towards the summit. The great snowy
range of the Himalayas presents a massive barrier to the monsoon
winds, so that to the south there is heavy rainfall in summer, while
the Tibetan plateau belongs for the most part with the arid zone of
Central Asia.

ATMOSPHERIC HUMIDITY
Like rainfall, atmospheric humidity can be quite startlingly affected by
local conditions. When I was a child, the air in our mountain valley
in Switzerland was extremely dry; even in winter, our thick, raw-wool
mountain socks, washed in the evening and hung outside, would be
dry by morning. But about thirty years ago the great Dixence dam
was built, at the time the tallest in Europe, creating a large lake to
satisfy the increasing demand for electricity. Although the lake is two
valleys away, the climate perceptibly changed, and now our socks are
still wet the morning after washing.

Another striking illustration of the effect of atmospheric moisture is the fog belt along the Pacific coast of North America, north and south of San Francisco. The general climate of the region is dry, with about 500 mm/20 in of rain each year, almost all falling in the winter months; the summers are hot and dry. But in the fog belt summers are cool and cloudy, and the rainfall in favoured places is twice as high as in the rest of the region. The fogs are caused by mild, moist air which, blowing onto the California coastline from far out in the Pacific Ocean, crosses just offshore a belt of cold water that wells up from the depths. The giant coast redwood forests of northern California exist only because fog drip provides them with summer moisture; the high atmospheric humidity reduces transpiration and keeps the soil moist. On the warm and sunny heights above the fog level the red-woods give way to the typical chaparral vegetation of drought-resistant shrubs. In the coastal desert of Chile, although there is virtually no rain, areas of persistent winter fog create wet zones which support a seasonal flora, the 'loma'.

Local variables also affect the formation of dew – the condensation which occurs when moist, warm air encounters a colder surface. Condensation is greatest: under clear skies, when the ground cools faster than it does under clouds; at low wind speeds; when the air pressure is high (which reduces the amount of cooling necessary for condensation to occur); beneath vegetation with open branching and leaf canopy; on cool surfaces such as poleward-facing slopes; and in valleys into which cold air has already drained. The theoretical maximum dewfall in a single night is minute, compared with rainfall – less than 1 mm/1/30 in. None the less, like fog, dew appears to benefit plants that are subject to drought.

HAIL, SLEET, AND SNOW

Showers of soft hail, small opaque grains of ice, are quite common in winter and spring in the high latitudes. True hailstones can, as their name implies, cause considerable damage, large ones on occasion reaching the size of cricket balls, smashing through glasshouses and flattening crops. In the wine-growing areas of Europe, where summer hailstorms can jeopardize the grape harvest, special rockets have been developed which are fired into the air; the heat of their explosions melts the threatened hail, which falls instead as rain. The summer months are punctuated by the thuds of rockets exploding in their several stages. I recall one summer in Switzerland when the rockets failed to do their job, and we had a storm of hailstones the size of ping-pong balls; as they hit the waters of the lake, its surface was transformed into a million tiny waterspurts.

Precipitation of all kinds starts as tiny particles of condensed water in clouds. If the temperature is well below freezing, the particles grow in the form of microscopic ice crystals into the intricate and beautiful structures we call snowflakes. If the air is below freezing all the way to the ground, these flakes will fall as snow. In high latitudes where rapidly cooling land is accompanied by very low air temperatures, snow, or its variants such as sleet and ice pellets, is more usual than rain. The cold of Siberia or of the northern parts of North America is far more severe than the coldest western European winter; in Britain's mild maritime climate, however, the lowest temperature is seldom very far from the melting level of snow, so it is difficult to forecast whether rain or slushy snow will occur.

For a heavy fall of snow, there must be ample moisture in the clouds where the precipitation forms, and the air must be very cold. Air cold enough to make snow cannot hold much moisture, however, and the extra moisture essential for heavy snow is usually derived from warmer, wetter air blowing into the freezing air at cloud level.

Snow storms may also arise from local conditions; freezing air blowing over open water will become moister and warmer near the water than in the upper layers; being lighter, this warmed air will tend to rise, forming clouds which, cooling again, may give snow. This is known as lake-effect snow, though the water could as well be a sea or an ocean as a lake.

Orographic snow, from the Greek for mountain, occurs on the windward side if the temperature is below freezing when a relatively warm, moist air mass is forced upwards by a mountain range. In North America, the regions that get more than 1.5 m/5 ft of snow in an average winter are found on the crests of the mountain ranges, and along the shores of the Great Lakes and the Gulf of Maine, where the snow may be orographic, lake-effect, or a combination of both.

The vegetation of subalpine regions the world over is modified by snow. Within subalpine forests, accumulations of deep snow, being slow to melt, shorten the growing season and thus give rise to areas of meadow instead of forest. Avalanches can clear sizeable areas of forest. In alpine tundra habitats where summer rainfall is typically very low, melting snow is the major source of soil moisture. Snow cover and soil moisture are the most important limiting factors for plants in alpine zones: downhill from the snow beds there is a constant supply of summer water, giving rise to meadow in drained areas, and to sedge–sphagnum communities in boggy hollows; on the higher slopes, above the zones of snow accumulation and melt, the combination of maximum winter exposure and summer desiccation usually results in almost bare boulder field.

Snow is an excellent insulator; if it falls on cold or frozen soil it keeps the cold in, but if it falls thickly early in the season on unfrozen soil, even quite severe subsequent frosts will not penetrate the blanket. A thin layer, however, will clear fast from bare, warmer soil but more slowly from grass or low-growing plants where – air being a poor conductor of heat – the air trapped between the plants will insulate the snow from the heat of the soil. The temperature beneath a thick snow blanket is surprisingly moderate and fairly constant, giving alpine plants a long, uninterrupted dormancy. The value of snow as protection was clearly seen in the freak winter of 1978–9 in Britain, when the temperature remained below freezing for days on end. The parts of plants below the snow were in many cases undamaged while above, exposed to frost and wind, they were blackened and split.

Snow drifting against the glass can help to reduce draughts inside glasshouses, but wet snow or, worse still, a combination of wet snow and freezing rain, can cause physical damage. It is best only to leave snow on glasshouses and plastic tunnels if it is not too thick – plastic tunnels can collapse under the weight of a layer of sodden snow – and to shake heavy snow off bushes and tree branches that are at risk of breaking under its weight.

Snow varies in moisture content (as skiers know well), but 8–12 cm is equivalent to 1 cm of rain. In many areas of the world, it is a source both of soil moisture and of water to replenish underground supplies; but its effectiveness depends on the melt rate. During rapid melting, caused by sudden rises in temperature, much of the moisture will be lost through run-off, which may also cause flooding and erosion, especially if the soil is frozen or already saturated. The slow melt of a gradual thaw, on the other hand, allows moisture to penetrate gradually into the soil.

DROUGHT

Drought, almost as much feared by gardeners as severe frost, does not necessarily imply a Saharan deficit; it is a relative condition. A lack of moisture in the soil which is enough to disrupt normal biological activity constitutes drought – which, by that definition, occurs in temperate regions after about three weeks without rain; little wonder that, almost every summer, water companies in Europe ban the use

Source: *Atmosphere, Weather & Climate* (Barry & Chorley)

The average number of years in ten when irrigation is theoretically necessary for crops in England and Wales

of hosepipes after barely a week of fine weather. In parts of the tropics, on the other hand, because the different patterns of biological activity are less readily disrupted by a lack of rain, several rainless months may pass without a drought resulting.

There is, then, no absolute level at which drought occurs. For example, the annual precipitation in a region of arid grassland may be scarcely more than in a desert where only true xerophytes (drought-adapted species) survive; the difference is that, falling at a time when it can accumulate in the soil instead of being lost through evaporation and run-off, it can support the growth of grasses, even if in the most marginal regions only annual species survive. In Mediterranean climates where droughts are a regular feature in summer, the vegetation is adapted in a variety of ways to withstand them, while the plants of

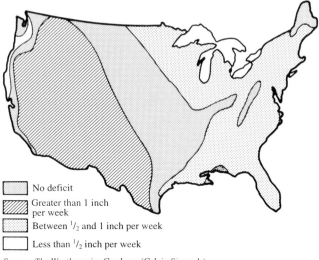

No deficit

Greater than 1 inch
per week

Between $\frac{1}{2}$ and 1 inch per week

Less than $\frac{1}{2}$ inch per week

Source: The Weather-wise Gardener (Calvin Simonds)

Weekly water deficits to be expected by gardeners in the United States; most places have a deficit of ½ inch or more through the growing season

climates where precipitation is more regular will show distress after only a week or two without rain, being ill-adapted to cope with a shortfall, especially during the growing season.

Certainly, the traditional garden plants of temperate regions – eastern North America, Europe, Japan, to name three where gardening is extensively practised – are not adapted to spells of drought. Without a regular supply of water (roughly 2.5 cm/1 in every week to ten days) plants begin to wilt, and the supply of nutrients is interrupted.

In many parts of the world there is not enough rainfall during the growing season, and this is a problem for gardeners where winter rains are inadequate to compensate. In all but the driest parts of the United States and of Britain there is a water surplus in the winter which restores soil moisture levels to provide a reserve for plants to draw upon during the growing season, but in the face of a rising demand from cities and towns, industry and agriculture for the finite resource of water, gardeners are having to learn how to cope with drought without turning to the hosepipe.

Prevailing winds and local effects

Wind may be less important than temperature and moisture as an evolutionary force affecting plants, but it can have a major effect on

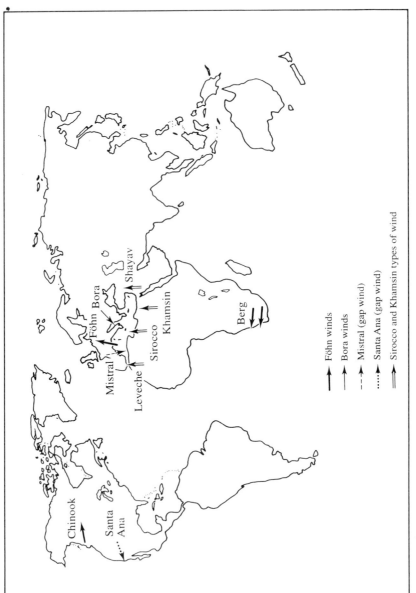

Chinook

Santa
Ana

Föhn Bora

Shayav

Mistral

Leveche

Sirocco

Khamsin

Berg

→ Föhn winds

↑ Bora winds

⇢ Mistral (gap wind)

⋯⋯ Santa Ana (gap wind)

⇉ Sirocco and Khamsin types of wind

'Local' winds

the way we garden. Air masses have an important part to play in climate; they may be polar, arctic or tropical, maritime or continental, according to their origin and temperature. Cold air masses originate in winter over areas such as Canada or Siberia, when there is extensive snow-cover, or over polar sea-ice at any time of the year; warm air masses arise over tropical continental areas in summer, or as deep, moist layers over tropical oceans.

The patterns of movement of these air masses are the source of the prevailing winds – those that are the most frequent in a given area. In the higher latitudes, westerly winds prevail, while in the tropics the easterly trade winds dominate, with seasonal variations in the monsoon areas. Everywhere, topographical features determine more localized effects.

Oceans, lakes and large expanses of level ground offer little resistance to winds, which sweep across them almost without slowing or turbulence. The 'bracing' climate of the coastal resorts of north-eastern Britain, for example, results from such winds sweeping eastward from the Urals without let or hindrance.

Mountain ranges which present a barrier to the movement of air masses are a major influence on the way winds and weather develop. In the middle and higher latitudes, air forced upwards over such a barrier gives rise to strong winds at the summits, and this may be noticeable, even over quite low hills, by comparison with the surrounding lowland.

The föhn is a strong and blustery, warm, dry wind which develops on the lee of a mountain range in certain circumstances. Temperatures can rise quite dramatically when the föhn blows, and on the northern slopes of the Alps, for example, this temperature rise frequently triggers spring avalanches. In the New Zealand alps and the Rocky Mountains this type of wind is known as the chinook, and in the Andes as the zonda. The berg wind of coastal South Africa and Namibia, blowing down from the escarpment, is also a föhn wind. Even such minor hill ranges as the Pennines, Grampians and Welsh mountains in Britain have their föhn, which is mainly of significance to gardeners and growers because it disperses cloud and contributes to the 'rain shadow' of the hills.

Another kind of lee wind is the cold, dry, gusty bora of the northern Adriatic, northern Scandinavia and elsewhere. Bora winds occur chiefly in winter and early spring. On the eastern slope of the Rocky Mountains both bora and chinook type winds can occur, and may reach hurricane force.

Wind may also be channelled through gaps and along valleys that lie in the direction of the wind, increasing its speed; in valleys that lie across the wind direction, eddies form. Since mountains often act as barriers between contrasting climates, mountain gap winds are often unusually warm or cold, as well as strong. The mistral, a cold, violent north-easterly wind that blows down the Rhône valley to the Mediterranean coast of France, mainly in winter and spring, is an example of a cold gap wind. When the mistral blows in summer it adds greatly to the risk of forest fires. The Santa Ana wind, which blows from the Mojave desert through the gaps around the Los Angeles basin, is a hot, dry gap wind.

Another hot, dry wind, of another kind, is the sirocco, a blisteringly hot, dry south wind blowing from the north coast of Africa across the Mediterranean to Italy and the south of France, where, having picked up moisture on its passage across the water, it is warm and humid. Associated in the southern and eastern Mediterranean with high temperatures and dust storms or a hazy atmosphere, it is locally known as the ghibli (in Libya), the khamsin (in Egypt, Palestine, Syria and Lebanon), leveche (in southern Spain) and sharav (in Israel).

Mountains, hills and valleys also create their own local conditions, such as the anabatic or valley winds which blow gently up the slopes on warm sunny days. After sunset the upper air cools, and a cold wind develops down the slope: the katabatic or mountain wind, draining into the valley. At the lowest point, or sooner if there is an obstacle, this cold dense air will be arrested and a frost hollow may be formed.

LAND AND SEA BREEZES

Land and sea breezes are further local phenomena caused by the differences in temperature which occur as the land heats more rapidly by day than the sea, and cools faster at night. Warm air over the land rises (creating the thermals that birds, and gliders, use to ascend), drawing cooler air from the sea in underneath itself and creating an onshore or sea breeze; this weakens in late afternoon and then swings round as the land cools, until at night a land or offshore breeze blows from the cooler land to the warmer sea. These breezes occur during fine, calm weather around the Mediterranean in the summer months, bringing welcome relief at the hottest time of day; they are also common on coasts in the tropics, and on most tropical islands. Once the land

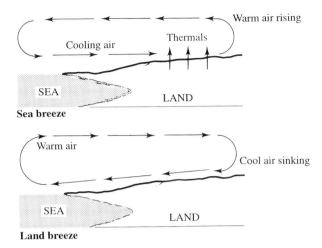

Sea and land breezes

temperature has risen to match that of the ocean, it is slow to rise further because each additional degree of warmth on land draws in cooling sea breezes.

The 'equinoctial' gales of spring and autumn, familiar to gardeners in coastal regions, are an example of the same effect on a much larger scale. In spring in the northern hemisphere the land gains heat much faster than the sea, and colder air from the great oceans of the southern

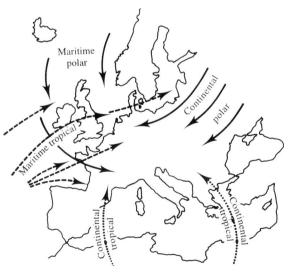

Air masses affecting Europe

hemisphere is drawn northwards over the warmer continental land masses; in autumn the process is reversed, with cold air from the rapidly-cooling land masses being drawn southward over the warmer oceans. The general westerly motion of the winds in the temperate zones constantly brings warm, moist maritime air from the west over the continents, and cold, continental air masses over the warmer oceans.

AIR MOVEMENTS AND TOPOGRAPHY IN EASTERN NORTH AMERICA

The interaction between air movement and topography is clearly illustrated by the winter weather of the east coast of North America. As arctic winds blowing from the north-west pass over the Atlantic, the lower layers are moisturized and warmed, and clouds form a few miles offshore, fair weather clouds nearest the shore and thicker, greyer clouds out to sea; further out still, over the open ocean, snow squalls form. By the time it reaches Bermuda, however, 500 miles offshore, air that was near-freezing is barely cool, thanks to heat gained from the ocean. Conversely, when maritime tropical air is carried over the freezing land by easterly winds, its moisture condenses instantly into fog. In early summer, the south-west winds bringing maritime tropical air across the still-cold waters of the Gulf of Maine cause fog to form along this coast.

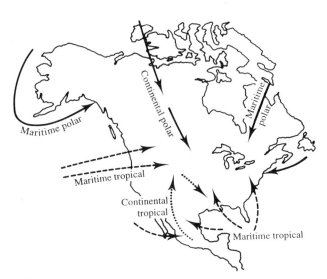

Air masses affecting the United States and Canada

The mountains of the eastern United States also have their effect: the Appalachians lying along the western boundary of the region form a low but effective barrier to continental polar air from the west which, being cold and dense, tends to hug the ground. The mountains both slow its passage and lift it, and if it is also moist from its passage over the Great Lakes, snow will fall over the Appalachians. The mountains affect air moving in the opposite direction, too; even the low foothills of the Appalachians are enough to lift the maritime air brought ashore by easterly winds to the point where it loses its moisture as precipitation.

Thanks to the Appalachians, the winters of the eastern seaboard are a little slower to set in and a little less harsh than those in corresponding states west of the mountains. But the mountains also act as a barrier to warm air from the Midwest, delaying the onset of spring in a New England under the influence of the still-cold Atlantic.

Soil, climate and vegetation

The type of soil can affect climate locally. Dark soils absorb more heat and tend to have a higher range of surface temperatures than light-coloured soils; moist clay soils tend to warm and cool more slowly than dry sands, in which there is a large quantity of trapped air – surface-layers of sandy soil tend therefore to be warmer than the upper layers of clay during the day and in spring and summer, but colder by night and in winter. Linked with this, moist clay soils, being more efficient at conducting heat into their depths than dry sand soils (since water is a better conductor of heat than air), experience there a greater range of temperature; saturated sands will tend to behave more like clay than like dry sands.

Interference by human activity in the delicate balance between climate and soil can have a major impact on plants. The dust bowl of the Great Plains region of western North America, an area of often violent and very dry winds, was caused when overgrazing and ploughing for cereals in the late nineteenth and early twentieth centuries resulted in cycles of erosion and deposition of wind-blown material (loess) which have changed the pattern of vegetation.

The type of vegetation, or lack of it, covering the surface of the earth affects the local climate. Above rain forests, whether equatorial or coniferous, the air will be warmer than above grassland, which is lighter in colour. The forest canopy has the effect of reducing daytime

Part Three

PLANTS

It is now time to consider some of the plants that have contributed to our gardens, not merely by referring them to this or that country of origin, as do so many reference books, but by giving more detail about the climates of their native regions, and even the specific habitats where they are to be found.

The chapters that follow are based, on the whole, on the same climatic types as those of the different sections of Chapter 1, beginning with the two major climates of high latitudes, the maritime and the continental. Next come two chapters that deal with plants from climates characterized by drought: the warm-temperate world with a Mediterranean pattern of dry summers and wet winters; and the arid lands where rainfall is unpredictable and sparse, but still sufficient to support a surprising variety of plants. By contrast, the next two chapters deal with plants that have evolved in regions where moisture is almost always abundant all year round: the warm, humid subtropics, and the cool rhododendron heartlands of the Himalayas and western China. On the higher slopes of these and other mountain ranges grow the plants gardeners generally call 'alpines'; as we have seen, the ways in which they adapt to the extreme conditions of high altitudes are similar to the protective devices adopted by plants from subpolar regions, and plants from both areas are considered in the penultimate chapter. The final chapter deals with some of the plants that grow in the tropics, where wet seasons alternate with dry, and in the equatorial regions, where the weather is hot and wet all year round.

In a book of this length it is clearly impossible to refer to every plant that is in cultivation, but I have tried to include at least a reasonable proportion of our well-known garden plants or their forebears, together with some less familiar but not less attractive or useful, and even a few that are mentioned only because they are typical of the climate or habitat under consideration.

5

Plants from cool-temperate maritime and island climates

In the cool-temperate regions of the world, cool summers and relatively mild winters, with rain falling in every month, are the norm in regions where the influence of oceans moderates the climate. The weather is often changeable, but rarely extreme; spells of prolonged deep cold or long droughts are the exception, and though it may often be windy, hurricane-force winds are rare. As gardeners in the British Isles have long known, all this adds up to a climate which is kind to an exceptionally wide range of plants. British gardens are the envy of the world; and it is widely recognized that the climate has had much to do with making the British a nation of gardeners.

The chief source of this benign British climate is the Gulf Stream, that vast wind-driven, sea-borne river of warm waters from the Gulf of Mexico that rolls across the Atlantic to wash the west coasts of England and Scotland, even reaching part-way down the east coast after its journey through the northern isles. Any great mass of water acts to some extent as a moderating influence, slow to lose heat in winter and to gain it in summer; the Gulf Stream is so effective as a heat source that Britain is markedly warmer in winter than areas at the same latitude on the east coast of North America, chiefly due to the south-westerly winds that draw heat from the Gulf Stream waters and warm the northern lands over which they blow.

Much of western Europe is also cooler in summer and warmer in winter than the interior of the continent. However, because Britain

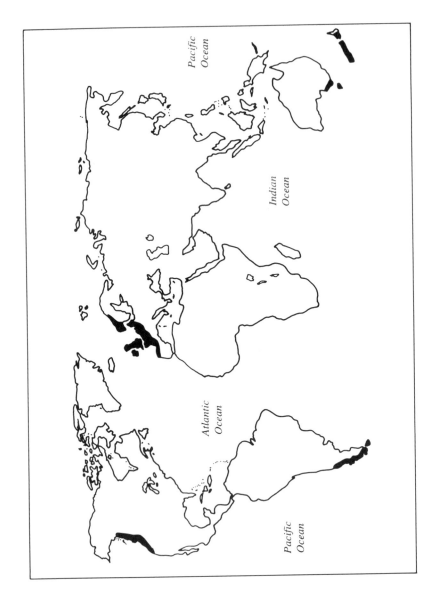

Cool-temperate maritime and island climates

and mainland western Europe were covered by icecaps during successive ice ages, the flora of the region is comparatively poor. Few gardeners in Europe are therefore content to grow only native plants; at the very least, they want to draw on the greater floral riches of other regions of the world blessed with a maritime climate: the Pacific coast of North America, south-west coastal South America, New Zealand, Tasmania and parts of coastal south-eastern Australia.

The Pacific north-west

Much of California has a typically Mediterranean climate, and the plants of this region will be described in a later chapter. But further north, and along the coast, the climate is cooler and moister, though still characterized by mild, wet winters and relatively dry summers. In the coastal regions the temperatures are mild, cloudy weather is frequent, and diurnal temperature fluctuations are small. Unusually for such a temperate climate, the coastal forest extending south from the Gulf of Alaska to the Mendocino coast of California is overwhelmingly dominated by conifers, renowned for their size and longevity. The most famous are the coast redwoods, *Sequoia sempervirens*, but others are scarcely less familiar: Douglas fir (*Pseudotsuga menziesii*), incense cedar (*Calocedrus decurrens*), western red cedar (*Thuja plicata*), grand fir (*Abies grandis*), Lawson's and Nootka cypress (*Chamaecyparis lawsoniana, C. nootkatensis*), Sitka spruce (*Picea sitchensis*), western hemlock (*Tsuga heterophylla*). The largest of all pines, *Pinus lambertiana* or sugar pine, is one of several species native to the region. Among the few hardwoods of the Pacific north-west forests are Oregon white oak (*Quercus garryana*), black cottonwood (*Populus trichocarpa*), red alder (*Alnus rubra*) and the evergreen tan oak (*Lithocarpus densiflorus*); these are often confined to specialized habitats.

In the narrow coastal strip where maritime influences are most marked, the dominant tree species are *Picea sitchensis* and *Tsuga heterophylla*; the spruce is very tolerant of salt spray and may form nearly pure stands, or associate with lodgepole pine (*Pinus contorta*) in exposed coastal sites. There is a rich shrub and herb understorey and the forest floor is mossy. Typical of the shrubs are *Vaccinium alaskaense* and *V. parvifolium, Menziesia ferruginea, Rubus spectabilis* and *Acer circinatum*, with herbaceous plants such as *Tiarella trifoliata, Claytonia sibirica* and *Maianthemum dilatatum*, and ferns – *Polystichum munitum* and *Blechnum spicatum*.

The main components of the Pacific north-west forests are *Pseudo-tsuga menziesii*, *Tsuga heterophylla* and *Thuja plicata*; *Abies grandis*, *Picea sitchensis* and western white pine (*Pinus monticola*) are less abundant. In central Oregon they are joined by *Calocedrus decurrens*, *Pinus lambertiana* and *P. ponderosa*. The Pacific silver fir, *Abies amabilis*, is commonly found near the northern limits of Douglas fir forests. Lawson's cypress (*Chamaecyparis lawsoniana*), so successful as a garden plant, is a localized endemic in south-western Oregon. *Acer macrophyllum*, *Prunus emarginata* and *Fraxinus latifolia*, *Alnus rubra* and *Populus trichocarpa* grow along waterways, and madrona (*Arbutus menziesii*), golden chinquapin (*Chrysolepis* [*Castanopsis*] *chrysophylla*) and *Quercus garryana* belong on warmer, drier sites, as does salal (*Gaultheria shallon*).

Understorey trees to Douglas fir, *Tsuga heterophylla* and *Thuya plicata* include *Cornus nuttallii* and *Taxus brevifolia*, which is found everywhere though it is never dominant. Beneath these smaller trees is a layer of evergreen shrubs, subshrubs, flowering plants and ferns, including *Mahonia nervosa*, *Rhododendron macrophyllum*, *Trillium ovatum*, *Vancouveria hexandra*, *Synthyris reniformis*, *Iris tenax*, *Coptis laciniata*, *Disporum hookeri*, *Asarum caudatum* and, in the wetter regions, *Polystichum munitum* and *Oxalis oregana*. *Ceanothus velutinus* appears after the herbaceous species that colonize burned sites have begun to give way to shrubs. On very wet sites *Thuja plicata* may be dominant, with an understorey of *Oplopanax horridum*, lady fern (*Athyrium filix-femina*) and *Lysichiton americanum*. *Lilium pardalinum*, the panther lily, forms large colonies on stream banks in the coastal forest of northern California and Oregon, and *Veratrum californicum* grows in wet meadows; the quamash, *Camassia quamash*, is also a plant of damp meadows, but at lower elevations.

In the coastal forests of northern California and southern Oregon grow the world's tallest trees, the coast redwood, *Sequoia sempervirens*. They are associated with various other trees, typically Douglas fir and *Lithocarpus densiflorus*, with *Umbellularia californica* in moist places and *Arbutus menziesii* on dry sites. Many of the understorey herbs and ferns just listed grow with the sequoias, together with *Disporum smithii*, *Lilium columbianum*, *Viola glabella*, *Vancouveria planipetala*, *Clintonia andrewsiana*, *Heuchera micrantha*, *Dicentra formosa* and others; on the upper slopes there are evergreen shrubs such as salal, *Rhododendron macrophyllum* and *Vaccinium ovatum*.

Between the coastal forests and the subalpine *Abies* forests of high elevations is mixed evergreen forest, with Douglas fir and *Lithocarpus densiflorus*, *Quercus chrysolepis*, madrona and *Chrysolepis chrysophylla*. The evergreen ericaceous and other shrubs, among them the Oregon grape (*Mahonia aquifolium*), form a dense layer beneath the trees, with *Polystichum munitum* and a range of herbaceous plants – *Chimaphila umbellata*, *Disporum hookeri*, *Smilacina stellata*, *Linnaea borealis*, *Trientalis latifolia*, *Achlys triphylla*, *Aquilegia formosa*, and *Clintonia uniflora* or bride's bonnet.

Several of the trout lilies, so called because of their marbled leaves, belong to the woods and forests of north-western America: *Erythronium hendersonii* and *E. oregonum*, *E. revolutum* from damp places in the redwood and mixed evergreen forests and along wooded streams, *E. californicum*, and *E. tuolumnense*, growing in open foothill woodlands. As in the eastern states, there are several species of trillium: *T. chloropetalum*, a plant of the redwood and mixed evergreen forests along the coastal range of the mountains, in moist places; *T. ovatum*, which grows at higher altitudes, in shadier places; and the brook trillium, *T. rivale*, from moist places in the humid transition zone, and also in rocky places in the Siskiyou Mountains, on magnesium-rich serpentine soils.

The shooting stars, also called American cowslip, are primula relatives with reflexed, cyclamen-like petals; one of the most robust is *Dodecatheon jeffreyi*, which resembles the eastern *D. meadia*, and usually grows on wet ground, as do *D. pulchellum* and *D. dentatum*. Others, such as *D. clevelandii* and *D. hendersonii*, grow in drier places on the mountain slopes. A curious little plant resembling the European *Saxifraga granulata*, *Romanzoffia californica* grows in moist rocks and on alpine fellfields. *Luetkea pectinata* inhabits damp rocky slopes in the red fir and subalpine forests.

The plants of temperate South America

Where the cool temperate regions of the northern hemisphere are dominated by deciduous forests, in the southern continents areas with similar climates are chiefly dominated by evergreens. The southern coastal regions of Chile have a wet, windy, mild climate, progressively cooler towards the Straits of Magellan in the south. Much of the country is mountainous, the southernmost reaches of the Andes forming the border between Chile and the Argentine.

The mixed evergreen forest of lowland and central Valdivia and Chiloé provinces contains many of the trees most typical of Chile, largely evergreen: *Eucryphia cordifolia*, *Persea lingue*, *Drimys winteri*, *Laurelia aromatica*, and *L. sempervirens* (*serrata*), which is more common to the south and in the cordilleras, *Cryptocarya peumus*, *Crinodendron hookerianum* (*Tricuspidaria lanceolata*), *Citronella gongonha* (*Villaresia mucronata*), the Chilean hazel (*Gevuina avellana*), *Weinmannia trichosperma*, *Caldcluvia paniculata*, and *Nothofagus* species, *N. obliqua* and *N. dombeyi*. Unusually, *Eucryphia glutinosa* is deciduous. The siete camises, *Escallonia rubra*, grows along stream-sides and in damp ravines, and *E. revoluta* is found in moist thickets or *matorral*. *Luzuriaga radicans* and *L. marginata* (which is also found in New Zealand) may form dominant undergrowth with *Blechnum magellanicum* and *B. arquatum* in forests of eucryphia, *Nothofagus dombeyi* and *Laurelia*, with climbing *Cissus striata*, *Elytropus chilensis*, *Lardizabala biternata* and *Hydrangea serratifolia*, and the climbing bamboo, *Chusquea quila*. In the damper, more sheltered regions of the temperate rain forest filmy ferns (*Hymenophyllum* species) grow on tree trunks and *Nertera depressa* and *Calicera colitricia* on the forest floor; in the high atmospheric humidity, ferns and mosses flourish. *Sarmienta repens* grows in leafy, cool, shady conditions at forest margins, creeping over and up mossy rocks and tree-trunks. The Chilean bell flower, *Lapageria rosea*, also needs conditions of high atmospheric humidity. Another climber of the forest margins is the coral plant, *Berberidopsis corallina*, with a narrow range in the coastal cordillera between Concepción and Valdivia, where the climate changes from Mediterranean to maritime. Bamboos such as *Chusquea quila* and clump-forming *C. culeou* associate with bromeliads – *Greigea sphacelata* and the chupalla, *Fascicularia bicolor*, sometimes growing as an epiphyte on tall forest trees or on low shrubby trees in open sites, as well as in rocky clefts. In drier places their associates are *Quillaea saponaria*, *Lithraea caustica*, *Cryptocarya peumus*, *Peumus boldus*, *Cereus chilensis* and *Acacia cavenia*, with *Eccremocarpus scaber* from the more open parts of the forest; in wetter sites among palms grow *Aristotelia chilensis* (*macqui*), *Persea lingue*, *Luma apiculata* and *Rhaphithamnus cyanocarpus*.

In infertile but humid soils in the forests grows *Lomatia ferruginea*, with *Luma apiculata* and *L. chequen*. The related *Tepualia stipularis* also favours damp sites, from the River Maule southwards. *Sophora macrocarpa* grows near streams and rivers. The culen, *Psoralea glandulosa*, also prefers damp sites, especially to the north of its range in central Chile. A common habitat of the flame flower, *Tropaeolum speciosum*, is dusty roadside bramble thickets, though it also grows in *Nothofagus* forests. The maiten, *Maytenus boaria*, and *M. magellanica* also grow in open places, not in the rain forest. *Berberis valdiviana* grows, as its name suggests, in Valdivia province, where another common shrub is *Abutilon ochsenii*. *Azara microphylla* is most common in Valdivia too, and in

Chiloé province, where *A. serrata* also grows, in the lower reaches of the coastal cordilleras, while *A. lanceolata* is common as far south as the Straits of Magellan. The murtillas, *Ugni molinae*, is widely cultivated in the region for its aromatic fruits.

The habitat of the monkey puzzle, *Araucaria araucana* (*imbricata*), is at about 1,000 m/3,300 ft in the high cordilleras towards the north of the maritime-climate region, where it grows with *Nothofagus dombeyi* and *Maytenus boaria*, and at higher altitudes with *N. pumilio* and *N. antarctica*. *Berberis linearifolia* was introduced from moist woodlands at mid altitudes on the Argentine slope of the Andes.

The cordillera of the Valdivia coast and the marshy plateau at 1,000 m is rich in conifers, with *Podocarpus nubigenus* and *P. salignus*, *Libocedrus tetragona* and *Dacrydium fonckii*. *Saxegotha conspicua* is common from the River Maule southwards, growing in dense forests both in Chile and in neighbouring Patagonia. *Austrocedrus chilensis* is most often found in the interior. *Fitzroya cupressoïdes* (*patagonica*) ranges from approximately the latitude of Valdivia southwards, in Chile and south-western Argentina, with two distinct types, one growing in poorly drained lowlands and the other at altitude in the Andean Cordillera, almost to the treeline. The coastal type grows with *Nothofagus dombeyi*, *N. betuloïdes and Drimys winteri*, with a shrub layer of *Chusquea*, *Berberis*, *Ugni candollei* and *Desfontainea spinosa*. Where the drainage is most seriously impeded another South American conifer, *Pilgero-dendron uviferum*, occurs, with *Tepualia stipularis*. The Andean fitzroyas grow with *Podocarpus nubigenus*, *Nothofagus nitida* and *Laurelia philip-piana* at the lower altitudes and *Nothofagus antarctica*, *N. pumilio* and *Weinmannia trichosperma* at higher elevations, with a shrub layer of *Philesia magellanica*, *Drimys winteri* var. *andina*, *Gaultheria myrsinoïdes* (*Pernettya prostrata*), *Maytenus magellanica* and *Berberis* species.

Some species occur throughout the range and at varying altitudes. One such is *Drimys winteri*, which varies from shrubby, in the Andean var. *andina*, to tree-like in var. *chilensis* (var. *latifolia*), with the tallest from the southernmost ranges of its distribution, among other forest vegetation; it is usually found in moist places and along stream-banks. The fire bush, *Embothrium coccineum*, and its botanical variants with longer or shorter, more or less persistently evergreen leaves, is a low shrub at high altitudes and along the exposed coastline of the Magellan Straits, but is of tree stature further north, especially at low altitudes. *Mitraria coccinea* also grows as far south as the Straits of Magellan. *Berberis darwinii* extends into western Patagonia. The most southerly conifer native to South America is *Libocedrus tetragona*, which grows on the islands of Tierra del Fuego; it also occurs in Patagonia, with *Podocarpus nubigenus*. *Discaria serratifolia* ranges from Coquimbo in central Chile south to Magallanes province and, as such a wide distribution might suggest, is a variable shrub. The most widely distributed of Chile's species of *Solanum* is *S. crispum*, a lax scrambling shrub; *S. valdiviense* grows in scrub and moist sunny meadows in Valdivia and Chiloé provinces. One of the most familiar of Chilean shrubs is *Fuchsia magellanica*, often found by waterfalls and other perpetually damp places. The wettest places also suit *Gunnera tinctoria* and the monkey flower, *Mimulus luteus*.

In open scrub, the climbing mutisias, *M. decurrens*, *M. oligodolon* and *M. ilicifolia*, drape themselves over *Fabiana imbricata* or *Colletia spinosa* hosts where calafate (*Berberis buxifolia*) also grows. The Andean broom-mimic *Diostea juncea* and *Rhaphithamnus spinosus* (*R. cyanocarpus*) are also mainly from the drier interior regions and Andean foothills, as are *Colletia hystrix* (*C. armata*) and *C. infausta*, shrubs with sharp green spines doing the duty of leaves, and *Trevoa trinervis*. The shrubby slipper flower, *Calceolaria integrifolia*, is common as far south as Chiloé, and the related *Jovellana violacea* grows in the north of the maritime-climate region.

ANTARCTIC FLORA OF SOUTHERN CHILE
Beyond Chiloé, the flora becomes more antarctic in character, with *Nothofagus betuloïdes*, *Podocarpus nubigenus* and *Libocedrus tetragona*. At the forest margins grow *Philesia magellanica* (*buxifolia*) and the creeping gesneriad *Asteranthera ovata*, which attaches itself to mossy rocks or tree trunks. *Desfontainea spinosa* forms low thickets, often with *Philesia magellanica*, and with the creeping *Myrteola nummularia* covering the ground.

Further south still, into the windswept regions of Tierra del Fuego, the vegetation ranges from Patagonian steppe in the north-east, *Empetrum rubrum* heath on acid soils and coastal scrub – dominated by *Lepidophyllum cupressiforme*, with *Berberis buxifolia* (widespread throughout the region from Santiago southwards) and *B. empetrifolia*; or by *Chiliotrichum diffusum*, which also grows in open deciduous and evergreen forest and, further north, at altitude in the Andes of Chile and Argentina – to deciduous forests and, in the regions of highest rainfall, evergreen forest. Among the shrubs of the deciduous *Nothofagus pumilio* forest are *Berberis ilicifolia* and *Maytenus disticha*, with undergrowth of *Blechnum penna-marina*, while the associates of *Nothofagus antarctica* are *Berberis buxifolia*, *Chiliotrichum*, *Embothrium coccineum* and *Empetrum rubrum*, with perennials including *Anemone multifida*. In the wetter sites this forest grades into scrub of *Gaultheria* (*Pernettya*) *mucronata*; *G. insana* (*furiens*) is found between the River Maule and the River Palena. *Nothofagus pumilio* (which extends to the snow line as a low shrubby tree in the north and interior) grades into evergreen *N. betuloïdes* forest, with *Empetrum*, *Berberis ilicifolia*, *Blechnum magellanicum* and *B. penna-marina*, *Gunnera magellanica* and *Luzuriaga marginata*.

In coastal regions *Drimys winteri* often dominates together with *Nothofagus betuloïdes*, and in better-drained sites they are joined by *Embothrium coccineum* and *Maytenus magellanica*, with *Desfontainea spinosa*. Filmy ferns grow on partly decomposed tree trunks; in these cool, damp regions decomposition is very slow. At the limits of altitude and exposure *Nothofagus betuloïdes* is often shrubby. Other species forming shrubby communities are *Fuchsia magellanica*, common in exposed coastal sites, with *Ribes magellanica*, *Gaultheria mucronata* and *Chiliotrichum*. In the most exposed coastal places *Hebe elliptica* is dominant, with *Berberis ilicifolia*, *Empetrum rubrum*, *Escallonia serrata* and *Gaultheria mucronata*.

The iris family is represented in the southern hemisphere not by *Iris* itself but by various other genera, including the South American and antipodean *Libertia*, of which *L. formosa* and *L. caerulescens* are Chilean species, growing in moist sites. A Chilean irid often seen in European gardens is *Sisyrinchium striatum*, and from the Falkland Islands, where the weather is continually wet and windy and the winters chilly and changeable, comes *S. filifolium*. Another Falkland Islander is *Oxalis enneaphylla* or scurvy grass; *O. adenophylla* is a Chilean native, and so are the tiny *O. lobata* and *O. magellanica*.

Ourisia is a genus confined to the southern hemisphere; *O. coccinea* is from the Chilean Andes, favouring clay soils on shaded stream-sides and moist banks, and *O. magellanica* (*ruelloïdes*) is found in wet places. *Nierembergia repens* (*N. rivularis*) grows along river banks, ranging from Chile to Argentina and Uruguay. There are some choice slipper flowers (*Calceolaria* species) too, the smallest perhaps *C. tenella*; others are *C. biflora*, and *C. darwinii*, from the Straits of Magellan. From the Falkland Islands and the Straits of Magellan comes *Azorella trifurcata* (*Bolax glebaria*).

The antipodean contribution

Only a small region of Australia can be considered to have a maritime climate: Tasmania, and perhaps part of coastal Victoria, where the rainfall is evenly distributed throughout the year. Because many of the plants native to eastern Tasmania in particular also occur in Victoria, often at higher elevations (and some are more widespread still), this southerly portion of the mainland will be considered here as well as Tasmania. As a whole, Tasmania is mountainous, with a climate markedly drier in the east (annual rainfall of 500–800 mm/20–31 in) than in the south-west, where the annual precipitation can be as much as 1750 mm/69 in.

Lomatia tinctoria is a Tasmanian endemic growing on open, sunny hillsides and in light, dry sclerophyll forest; a far more spectacular proteaceous genus is *Telopea*, the waratah; the Tasmanian *T. truncata*, which grows both at lower elevations in open eucalypt forest, and at altitude as part of the heathland community, is less striking than the mainland species. *Telopea speciosissima* grows in the sandstone regions near the coast of New South Wales, and *T. oreades* in moist upland eucalyptus forests in New South Wales and Victoria, reaching its maximum stature in the valley bottoms in wetter sclerophyll forest. On drier ridge-tops it grows in the heathy shrub layer beneath the open canopy of *Eucalyptus obliqua* forest.

The majority of eucalypts come in fact from Australia, but among Tasmanian species are some of the most suitable for cooler climates, at least if grown from seed collected at high altitude: *Eucalyptus gunnii*, which every florist sells for its almost circular, blue-glaucous juvenile foliage; the mountain gum, *E. dalrympleana*; *E. urnigera*, the urn gum, which seems to become windfast more readily than many species; and the Tasmania snow gum, *E. coccifera*. The juvenile form of the heart-leaf silver gum, *E. cordata*, and *E. globulus*, are both used in bedding schemes in northern hemisphere gardens, being quick to raise from seed; in mild climates such as that of California *E. globulus* grows into a tall tree within a very few years. *Eucalyptus viminalis*, the manna gum – said to be the favourite food of koala bears – forms the canopy above a forest of blackwood (*Acacia melanoxylon*), *Nothofagus cunninghamii*, myrtle, native sassafras (*Atherosperma moschatum*) and an understorey of tree fern (*Dicksonia antarctica*).

Some of the richeas grow in the Tasmanian eucalyptus forest, where *R. scoparia* becomes fairly tall, while in the open it forms a hummock. *Richea dracophylla* is a large shrub from moist, low-altitude mountain slopes. The giant grass tree, *R. pandanifolia*, grows in the rain forest of King Billy pines, *Athrotaxis selaginoïdes*, in a dense gloom of moss and fern.

The vegetation of Mount Wellington in southern Tasmania passes through four distinct zones, starting with dry, open woodland, which yields to tall forest, subalpine woodland and finally the alpine zone. The forest and scrub zones are composed of a variety of eucalypts, including *E. regnans*, *E. coccifera*, *E. delegatensis* and *E. obliqua*, with shrubs such as waratah, richeas, *Anopterus glandulosus*, *Olearia*, the climber *Prionotes cerinthoïdes* (which often behaves as an epiphyte, growing for example on *Nothofagus cunninghamii*). Eucalypts can also be found in the rain forest, with *Pomaderris*, *Bedfordia*, *Phyllocladus*, *Aristotelia peduncularis*, *Orites diversifolia*, *Eucryphia milliganii*, and plants also native to Victoria's wet forests: *Atherosperma moschatum*, lancewood (*Phebalium squameum*) and stinkwood (*Zieria arborescens*). *Nothofagus cunninghamii* forms large stands, and there are various wattles – *Acacia mucronata*, *A. dealbata*, *A. riceana* and *A. verticillata*. On the wind-swept summit, which is snow-covered in winter, grow shrubs in the protea family such as waratah, *Bellendena montana*, *Orites revoluta* and *O. acicularis*, with *Bedfordia linearis*, *Leptospermum rupestre* (*humifusum*), *Richea sprengelioïdes* and *R. scoparia*, *Exocarpos strictus*, *Melicytus* (*Hymenanthera*), epacrids such as *Cyathodes* species, *Trochocarpa thymifolia*, *Epacris serpyllifolia* and *Pentachondra pumila*, *Microcachrys tetragona*, *Tasmannia* (*Drimys*) *aromatica* and *Hakea lissosperma*, with dwarf eucalypts immediately below the summit – *E. coccifera*, *E. urnigera* and *E. johnstonii*. *Ozothamnus ledifolius* grows in exposed places at mid to high altitudes.

From the high-rainfall south and west of the island comes *Eucryphia lucida*, a tall, columnar tree growing with *Nothofagus cunninghamii* and *Atherosperma moschatum*, often rising from an undergrowth of ferns as it does in the moist fern gullies of the mountains of Victoria. The Huon pine, *Lagarostrobos franklinii* (*Dacrydium franklinii*), is a long-lived member of the Tasmanian temperate rain forest flora, and *Athrotaxis selaginoïdes* grows in light forest with *Nothofagus cunninghamii* and the giant grass tree, *Xanthorrhoea australis*; the pencil pine, *Athrotaxis cupressoïdes*, grows at higher altitudes. *Diselma archeri* is also found in the damper subalpine regions of Tasmania, while *Acradenia frankliniae* grows on stream margins in the forest of the west coast.

Tasmania is home to some of the antipodean Ericaceae: *Gaultheria depressa* from boggy places on the mountain plateau of Tasmania, and also from New Zealand, *G. hispida* from the wet forests at middle

133

elevations, and G. (*Pernettya*) *tasmanica*. The non-woody plants of the south and west include the Christmas bells (*Blandfordia punicea*), which grows in moist acid soil, *Isophysis tasmanica*, *Milligania densiflora* and *M. longifolia*, and the widespread irid *Diplarrena moraea*.

SOUTHERN AUSTRALIA

Many of the plants of the drier east coast of Tasmania also occur in south-eastern Australia: among them are eucalypts (there are 29 species native to Tasmania), *Acacia dealbata* (but *A. pataczekii* from the north-eastern uplands is a Tasmanian endemic), *Epacris impressa* of coastal heaths and the wetter foothills of Victoria, *Leucopogon ericoïdes*, *Correa alba*, which also grows on the rocky sea cliffs and dunes of Victoria, *Hibbertia fascicularia*, *Leptospermum grandiflorum* (*rodwayanum*) from granite formations at middle elevations, *L. lanigerum* (*pubescens*) from damp places across a wide altitudinal range, and *L. scoparium* from montane and coastal regions, *Prostanthera lasianthos* from cool woodlands, *Ozothamnus rosmarinifolius*, and the daisy bush *Olearia phlogopappa*, which in Victoria grows in the wet sclerophyll forests of the mountains. *Bauera rubioïdes* is a low, spreading shrub with wiry stems, forming the undergrowth in open parts of the forest.

The heath-like *Olearia floribunda* and *O. ramulosa* inhabit dry, sunny heaths in their native Tasmania, and the Tasmanian and southern Australian *Melalenca squarrosa* grows in wet heaths. Also from damper heaths or foothill forests on the mainland and Tasmania are *Pimelea flava*, *Pultenaea gunnii*, the scrub sheoke (*Casuarina paludosa*) and the velvet bush (*Lasiopetalum dasyphyllum*). *Correa backhouseana* grows in open or shady places in Tasmania and Victoria, and *Callistemon salignus* also grows in a variety of habitats, from swamps and stream banks to dry, rocky heights. The rosemary-like *Westringia angustifolia* and *W. brevifolia* are Tasmanian coastal and montane plants, and *Cyathodes juniperina* has a wide altitudinal range from the coast to 1,000 m/ 3,300 ft or more. The irids *Patersonia longiscapa* and *Libertia pulchella* grow in damp places, by mountain streams and in wet peaty soils.

In parts of coastal, lowland and upland Victoria the vegetation is also cool-temperate, with *Eucalyptus oreades* and *E. delegatensis*, *Eucryphia moorei* from damp gullies in the coastal forest, *Correa reflexa* and, at higher elevations, the manna or ribbon gum, *Eucalyptus viminalis*, and the scribbly gums such as *E. mannifera* var. *maculosa*; *E. delegatensis* and other species grow at altitude with *Bedfordia* and *Acacia obliquinervia*. Also from Victoria and New South Wales are the spinning gum, *Eucalyptus perriniana*, the willow peppermint, *E. nicholii*, the Argyle apple, *E. cinerea*, *E. polyanthemos* and *E. pulverulenta*. On sandy coastal heaths or dunes grow *Banksia serrata*, *Billardiera scandens*, and the paroo lily (*Dianella caerulea*).

Several of Tasmania's plants also grow in the wet sclerophyll forests of the Main Dividing Range in eastern Victoria, where the rainfall is in excess of 1,000 mm/40 in a year; these forests occur at elevations above 330 m/1,000 ft. Here *Eucalyptus globulus*, *E. regnans*, *E. delegatensis*, *E. nitens*, *Acacia melanoxylon* and *Nothofagus cunninghamii* grow above understorey trees such as *Acacia mucronata* and *Persoonia arborea*, with *Acacia verticillata* and *A. howittii*, *Banksia spinulosa*, *Tasmannia aromatica* (*Drimys lanceolata*), *Olearia phlogopappa*, *Coprosma nitida* and *C. hirtella*, *Epacris paludosa*, *Boronia muelleri*, *Pultenaea cunninghamii*, *Gaultheria appressa*, *Hovea rosmarinifolia*, *Pomaderris apetala*, the satinwood, *Phebalium squameum*, and the tree fern *Cyathea australis*. Climbers include *Billardiera longiflora* and *Clematis aristata*, which grows in moist, sheltered gullies and along forested stream-banks. Similar habitats suit *Prostanthera melissifolia* and *P. rotundifolia*, *Lomatia fraseri* and, in mountain valleys in the regions of highest rainfall, *Correa lawrenceana*. *Eriostemon myoporoïdes*, growing in the wetter highland areas, also occurs in the dryish north escarpment of Mt Galore with cypress pines (*Callitris*). *Banksia marginata* grows in the eucalypt forests of the eastern states and in the wetter regions of South Australia and Tasmania. Among the the herbs of the wet forest are *Scaevola aemula*, the fairy fanflower, *Viola hederacea*, *Pratia pedunculata* and *Drymophila cyanocarpa*.

Olearia argophylla is a native of Tasmania and south-eastern Australia, where it occupies humid, shady fern gullies in *Eucalyptus regnans* forest, with *Bedfordia salicina*, *Pittosporum bicolor*, *Olearia stellulata* (*lirata*), the liana *Parsonsia brownii*, *Dicksonia antarctica* and other ferns, and *Dianella tasmanica*. The kangaroo fern, *Microsorium diversifolium*, grows as an epiphyte on the trunk of tree ferns and the branches of *Olearia argophylla*.

The characteristic eucalypt of the higher Alps of Victoria is the snow gum, *E. pauciflora niphophila*, with *Olearia frostii*, *Acacia alpina*, *Westringia semifolia*, *Prostanthera cuneata* (also from northern Tasmania) and *P. walteri*, *Grevillea victoriae*, *Orites lancifolia*, *Exocarpos nanus*, *Leucopogon hookeri*, and species of *Celmisia* and of *Pratia* and *Wahlenbergia*, *Herpolirion novae-zelandiae*, *Aciphylla glacialis*, *Astelia alpina*, *Scleranthus biflorus* and the brown edelweiss, *Ewartia nubigena*.

135

NEW ZEALAND'S FORESTS

New Zealand's forests are of two main types: conifer–hardwood forests dominated by gymnosperms, mainly podocarps but also kauri and libocedrus; and beech forest in which one or more of the four native species of *Nothofagus* are dominant. The conifer–hardwood forests fall into three main types: the kauri–podocarp–hardwood forests of the northern parts of North Island; the podocarp–hardwood lowland rain forests of North Island and the west coast of South Island; and the podocarp–hardwood–beech forests that grow along mountain ranges in both islands, especially South Island. The kauri pine, *Agathis australis*, grows in the lowland and coastal forests of North Island. Also grown for timber are *Dacrydium intermedium* and *D. colensoi*. *Dacrydium cupressinum*, the rimu, is a rain forest species forming the canopy, with *Dacrycarpus* (*Podocarpus*) *dacrydioïdes*, *Podocarpus totara* and *Prumnopitys ferruginea*, black maere (*Nestegis cunninghamii*) and *Nothofagus solandri*, above celery pine (*Phyllocladus* species), *Carpodetus serratus* and tree ferns *Dicksonia squarrosa* and *D. fibrosa*, *Alsophylla tricolor* and *A. smithii*, and *Cyathea medullaris*, with white rata (*Metrosideros albiflora*) scaling the trunks, and filmy ferns and fragrant orchid (*Earina autumnalis*) growing as epiphytes.

Dacrydium cupressinum also grows with podocarps, *Nothofagus fusca* and *N. menziesii* in the forests, and with mountain totara (*Podocarpus hallii*) and *Weinmannia racemosa* forms the canopy for *Aristotelia serrata*, *Cordyline indivisa*, *Rubus cissoïdes*, *Dracophyllum filifolium* and a ground covering of *Gaultheria antipoda*, with rata (*Metrosideros robusta*) as an epiphyte. The pahautea, *Libocedrus bidwillii*, is a tree of wet montane forest, fringing mountain totara; this and the kawaka, *L. plumosa*, are allied to the Chilean *Austrocedrus*. The bog pine, *Dacrydium bidwillii*, grows both in boggy and in dry, sandy soil. On mountain slopes the alpine totara, *Podocarpus nivalis*, makes spreading mounds; it is matched in Tasmania and southern Australia by *P. alpinus*.

The celery-topped pines are most unlike the conventional image of a conifer. *Phyllocladus glaucus*, the toatoa of New Zealand, grows in lowland and montane forests of North Island, and the tanekaha, *P. trichomanoïdes*, in lowland forests. The most frost-resistant is the alpine celery-topped pine, *P. aspleniifolius* var. *alpinus*, which grows with *Dacrycarpus dacrydioïdes* and *Dacrydium cupressinum* on the lower slopes of the mountains and also at higher altitudes.

Apart from the forests of the northern and coastal parts of North Island, New Zealand's forests are of the cool-temperate type, predominantly evergreen, with a dense undergrowth of shrubs, lianas, epiphytes and ferns. The forest floor is a soft, thick litter layer; the atmosphere is still and damp, and mosses, lichens and epiphytic orchids such as *Earina autumnalis* are abundant, with filmy ferns along moist seepages and creeks.

Among the trees of the forest that form the canopy, sometimes with podocarps, are the beeches, *Nothofagus menziesii*, the black beech *N. solandri* and its mountain form *cliffortioïdes*, and the red beech, *N. fusca*; the hinau, *Elaeocarpus dentatus*; and the karaka, *Corynocarpus laevigatus*, a coastal species. The southern rata, *Metrosideros umbellata*, grows in the higher-rainfall areas of South Island, and is rare on North Island; it is terrestrial, whereas the rata, *M. robusta*, starts as a high epiphyte, gradually working its way down the host trunk to become itself, in time, established in the soil; in its turn it becomes the host for many epiphytes and lianas, such as *Freycinetia* and *Astelia*. Astelias are not all epiphytes: *A. nervosa* grows in subalpine forests and grasslands, in moist or even swampy soil, and wet peaty soil also suits *A. chathamica*.

Shrubs and understorey trees of the lowland forest include *Macropiper excelsum*, which grows in gullies and on shaded rocky outcrops, *Pseudowintera colorata*, *Fuchsia excorticata*, *Pittosporum umbellatum*, *Lophomyrtus bullata* and *L. obcordata*, *Hoheria populnea*, the lacebark, and *H. sexstylosa*, *Weinmannia racemosa*, *Ixerba brexioïdes*, *Quintinia acutifolia*, the turepo, *Paratrophis microphylla*, *Schefflera digitata*, *Pseudopanax laetus* and the lancewood, *P. crassifolius*, *Olearia albida*, *Griselinia littoralis* and *G. lucida*, which often starts life as an epiphyte in rimu or hinau. *Griselinia littoralis* is commonly associated in the understorey with *Aristotelia serrata*, *Elaeocarpus hookeriana* and *Fuchsia excorticata* beneath a canopy of *Podocarpus totara*, matai (*Prumnopitys taxifolia*) and kahikatea (*Dacrycarpus dacrydioïdes*). Striking components of the understorey are the tree ferns such as *Cyathea dealbata* and *C. medullaris*, *Dicksonia squarrosa* and *D. fibrosa*.

At the margins of the forests, and in forest clearings and open scrub, many of New Zealand's wind-resistant shrubs and trees are found. The tutu, *Coriaria arborea*, is a poisonous shrub or small tree of the forest margins from sea level to 1000 m/3,300 ft, a range matched by *Aristotelia serrata*, the wine berry, *Olearia arborescens* and *Carpodetus serratus*. Other forest-margin trees and shrubs include *Olearia paniculata*, *O. furfuracea* and *O. rani* and, mainly at higher altitudes, *O. ilicifolia* and *O. macrodonta*, *Plagianthus betulinus*, *Sophora tetraptera* and *S. microphylla*, *Myrsine australis*, the mapou, *Coprosma lucida*, the karamu, and *Solanum aviculare* and *S. laciniatum*, the poroporo. At the forest margins of both islands grows the climbing *Parsonsia heterophylla*, a relative of the humble periwinkle. One of New Zealand's rarest plants is its native trumpet vine, *Tecomanthe speciosa*, reduced to one surviving specimen in the wild. Another scandent shrub growing in open places is the lobster claw or parrot's bill, *Clianthus puniceus*.

Some New Zealand plants are widespread, occurring both in forest habitats, where they often grow tall and slender, and in the open, where they tend to be more bushy and spreading – an outline better adapted to deflect wind and spare the shrub a battering. Such are the wharangi, *Melicope ternata*; *Pomaderris kumeraho*, a scrubland plant from North Island, and several species of *Brachyglottis*, such as *B. compacta*, *B. laxifolia* and *B. greyii*. *Melicytus ramiflorus* is wind-hardy, but becomes gnarled and stunted in exposed places. *Pittosporum eugenoïdes*, the tarata, *P. colensoi*, *P. crassifolium*, the karo, and *P. ralphii* grow in clearings and on stream banks; *P. eugenioïdes* can also be found in the wild growing in forests with *Podocarpus hallii*, *Olearia ilicifolia*, *Carpodetus serratus* and *Pseudopanax* species. The rare *Pittosporum dallii* grows in the mountains of South Island, while *P. tenuifolium* is found in the drier, eastern regions only. In grass and low scrubland on the eastern side of North Island and southwards grows *Leucopogon suaveolens* (*Cyathodes colensoi*).

The Nelson mountains are rich in shrubs, especially on the mountain tops and in the valley bottoms; where the valley bottoms are too wet and frosty for *Nothofagus* forest, it is replaced by tall shrubs – olearias, hebes, pittosporums, dracophyllums and *Melicytus*.

Wet places at the forest's edge are where coprosmas such as *C. propinqua*, the mingimingi, *Cordyline australis* and *C. indivisa*, the mountain cabbage tree, occur. The cabbage tree can be found in the wild in a variety of habitats, sometimes on the lower mountain slopes with *Phormium cookianum* or mountain flax, *Rubus* species, and the wild Irishman (*Discaria toumatou*). Elsewhere it gives way to *Cordyline banksii*, still with mountain flax, *Metrosideros robusta*, and nikau palm, *Rhopalostylis sapida*; the broader-leaved *Cordyline indivisa* grows at higher altitudes. Another montane plant is the mountain neinei, *Dracophyllum traversii*. *Gaultheria oppositifolia* is a North Island montane species from rocky places, while *G. antipoda* has a wide altitudinal range, growing in scrub or open, rocky sites. *Phormium tenax*, the common New Zealand flax, grows in swamps and damp areas, normally in the lowlands, in contrast to the drier, often shadier habitats favoured by the mountain flax; *Olearia virgata* also favours boggy sites. The mountain ribbonwoods grow on upland slopes on South Island, *Hoheria lyallii* on the drier, eastern slopes and *H. glabrata* on the wet, west-facing slopes.

The lancewood, *Pseudopanax crassifolius*, grows in drier regions, in scrubland with *Kunzea ericoïdes* and *Nothofagus menziesii* and *N. solandri*, at low elevations, as well as in forest. *Leptospermum scoparium*, the manuka or tea tree, often forms scrub that protects regenerating forest and native orchids. New Zealand's brooms often grow in open scrub; among them are *Notospartium glabrescens*, the coastal *Carmichaelia williamsii*, *C. odorata* which grows on shady banks beside streams, and *Chordospartium stevensonii*, native of the silty flats of river basins at mid-altitude in a small area of North Island only. The bizarre *Pseudopanax ferox* with its variable leaf forms is a rare tree in both North and South Islands; *P. lessonii* grows in coastal scrub on North Island and the Three Kings group, and *P. arboreus* in forests and open scrub on both North and South islands. The wild Irishman, *Discaria toumatou*, grows in open tussock or dune country and rocky places, chiefly on the east of South Island.

Dodonaea viscosa grows in exposed, windy places on the coast as well as in lowland forests and scrub. It stands salty winds well, as does the coastal *Coprosma repens*. *Olearia angustifolia* grows on the coasts of South Island and Stewart Island, *O. solandri* on the coasts of North Island and the northerly parts of South Island. *Olearia nummulariifolia*, tall in sheltered places, can stand the full force of the wind but then becomes a squat hummock, alongside *Cassinia vauvilliersii* and hebes. *Cassinia leptophylla*, another of the shrubby composites in which New Zealand is rich, is a variable species; ssp. *fulvida* rather resembles *Olearia solandri*, and ssp. *vauvilliersii*, especially in its form *albida*, recalls *O. algida*. More wind-resisters are found in the genus *Corokia*, to which belongs the wire netting bush, *C. cotoneaster*. It has given rise to a natural hybrid, × *virgata*, with *C. buddleioïdes* from New Zealand's North Island.

Brachyglottis reinoldii is a South Island coastal native, whereas the visually similar *B. elaeagnifolia* grows at middle altitudes on North Island, and large-leaved *B. repanda* in scrub and forest from the coast to middle altitudes on North Island. The ngaio, *Myoporum laetum*, is found in exposed coastal sites and on coastal and lowland forest margins. Another coastal plant is *Pomaderris apetala*, which is also found in Australia. Chatham Island trees and shrubs are often very wind-resistant; among them are *Olearia traversii*, an extremely wind-proof but very frost-tender tree, *Corokia macrocarpa*, and *Brachyglottis huntii*, which is adapted to withstand drought. *Olearia semidentata* and the similar *O. chathamica* both need the high atmospheric humidity of an island climate to thrive.

Most hebes are very wind-tolerant; they range from *H. salicifolia* and *H. elliptica*, which are also native to Chile, to tiny shrubs found on mountain slopes. A typical association in the wild would include *Hebe odora*, *Corokia cotoneaster* and *Coprosma parviflora*, with *Dracophyllum* and *Clematis* species. New Zealand's clematis mainly grow among scrub: they include *C. australis*, *C. forsteri* and *C. petriei*, the almost leafless *C. afoliata*, and *C. paniculata* (*C. indivisa*), the largest New Zealand species. The Chatham Islands have their own species of hebe, *H. dieffenbachii*, a wind-resistant but not very frost-tolerant species, and of myrsine, *M. chathamica*, which grows in the wild with *Olearia semidentata*.

New Zealand is rich in woody plants of divaricate habit – that is, with branches, often thin, wiry and interlacing, spreading almost at right angles from the stem. The phenomenon is seen in *Pittosporum anomalum*, *P. lineare* and *P. divaricatum*, which is not unlike *Corokia cotoneaster* in aspect. The coprosmas run greatly to the divaricate habit, with *C. rugosa*, *C. rotundifolia* and *C. propinqua* reaching tall shrub or small tree size. Others are low and spreading: *C. acerosa*, *C. petriei* and *C. brunnea*. The smaller species of *Melicytus*, shrubby members of the violet family, have thick, angular branches and small leaves; *M. crassifolius* is one of these (formerly classed as *Hymenanthera*); *M. angustifolius* has a native range that extends to Tasmania and southern Australia. The malvaceous *Plagianthus divaricatus*, a typical member of the coastal vegetation of New Zealand, also has divaricate branches.

Some species superficially resemble divaricators, forming low, tangled mounds when growing in exposed places: *Leptospermum scoparium*, some *Clematis*, *Muehlenbeckia* and *Rubus*. Some of these brambles may form a tangle of leafless, prickly stems, but change their looks with their habitat; so that *R. squarrosus*, for example, is a tall climber with foliage in the forests, but a low skeletonized mound in open sites. Others, such as *R. cissoïdes*, appear to indulge in the common New Zealand habit of looking different in the juvenile and adult stages. The muehlenbeckias are not thorny, but form tangled mounds of slender, sparsely-leaved stems; they are very resistant to salt winds, and the larger *Muehlenbeckia complexa* can be used to clothe a fence or bank with dense growth; *M. axillaris* is one of several small species from mountain slopes, compact and slow-growing.

Various theories are put forward for the phenomenon of divarication. Some say it may have evolved as a protection from the cold of higher altitudes or latitudes: in cold weather the temperature within the network of branches is higher than that outside. Many species display differing juvenile and adult forms, with juvenile plants divaricate in habit; these are known in New Zealand as mikimikis. The most striking forms of juvenility are found in tropical and subtropical plants, and despite the temperate, maritime climate New Zealand's flora has a strong tropical element. This characteristic is seen in a wide variety of families from the podocarps (in *Podocarpus spicatus*, the matai or black pine, only) and beeches (only in *Nothofagus solandri*, and that not always) to Compositae; a common feature is that the plants displaying it grow in open, windy habitats, especially on exposed coastlines. It is seen in *Carpodetus serratus* and *Plagianthus betulinus*, which grow at the margins of coastal and lowland forests and along river banks. The sophoras, members of the pea family, also display juvenile and adult forms. *Sophora tetraptera* and *S. microphylla* both grow into small trees, but the shrubby *S. prostrata* makes a low mound; it may be a fixed juvenile form of *S. microphylla*. The divaricate juvenile form of *Hoheria angustifolia* yields to an elegant adult tree, while in *H. sexstylosa*, which is also evergreen, the difference between juvenile and adult forms is in the leaf, not the habit. Differing juvenile and adult foliage is common in eucalypts and acacias too; in the acacias the first true leaves are pinnate or bipinnate, but in the adult form the function of the leaves is performed by flattened leaf-stalks or phyllodes; in some species the adult form takes over completely. The most striking example of differing leaf forms in juvenile and adult is found in *Pseudopanax*, especially the lancewood or horoeka, *P. crassifolius*, and *P. ferox*, which have three or four distinct stages of varying leaf form and habit.

Like the sophoras, *Libertia* is a genus also native to both Chile and New Zealand, with the antipodean *L. ixioïdes* and *L. peregrinans*, the first inhabiting forest clearings and scrub and the second damp hollows; damp places among shrubs also suit the tiny *L. pulchella*. *Arthropodium cirrhatum* is a lily-relative inhabiting, in the wild, dry, rocky places. Moisture-loving *Bulbinella hookeri* is rather like a small asphodel, while *B. rossii* grows in drier places.

New Zealand has some spectacular buttercups, such as *Ranunculus buchananii*, *R. insignis* and *R. lyallii*, which thrives in deep moist or even wet soils, in regions of high atmospheric humidity. The Chatham Island forget-me-not, *Myosotideum hortensia* (*M. nobile*), is a plant of the seashore, growing in pockets of decayed seaweed at the base of cliffs or even in sand along the high-tide line.

141

The aciphyllas are an umbelliferous genus of New Zealand and Australian plants with divided, stiletto-sharp leaves, which earn them such common names as wild Spaniard (*Aciphylla colensoi*) or bayonet plant (*A. squarrosa*).

New Zealand has some fine native sedges and grasses, much appreciated by gardeners today, which include elegant cousins of the South American pampas grass, *Cortaderia fulvida* and *C. richardii*, and *Chionochloa rigida* and *C. conspicua*, the hunangamoho grass, and the bronze-haired sedges such as *Carex buchananii*. *Stipa arundinacea* is a beautiful grass with airy, shining flower-heads. New Zealand is also well endowed with ferns, ranging from tree ferns which are barely frost-resistant to filmy ferns which revel in the high rainfall, *Blechnum capense*, red-tipped *B. procera*, the crown fern (*B. discolor*), tiny *B. pennamarina* and other blechnum species, *Paesia scaberula*, the kidney fern (*Trichomanes reniforme*) and others.

Western Europe's flora

Compared with all these riches, the western European flora is modest indeed. Small wonder that, as they were introduced, British gardeners seized upon the aromatic shrubs of the Mediterranean and the bright bulbs of Asia Minor, the flowering trees, shrubs and herbs of North America and later the Far East and, before long, the huge range of lovely things from temperate South America and Australasia, of which we have just had a glimpse.

For all that, western Europe is not wholly devoid of garden-worthy plants. As soon as gardens began to be more than just places to grow plants for medicinal and household use, variant forms of native species were sought out and treasured: coloured primroses and those with double or hose-in-hose flowers, or blooms set in a frilly calyx earning them the name Jack-in-the-green, sweet violets in not only blue and white, but also pink and carmine, lavender and sulphur and skimmed-milk, double daisies (*Bellis perennis*) and the viviparous hen and chickens daisy, *B. perennis* 'Prolifera', double buttercups and lesser celandines and wood anemones, the double cuckoo flower or lady's smock of water meadows (*Cardamine pratensis*) and the double kingcup or marsh marigold (*Caltha palustris*) of wet ditches, double soapwort (*Saponaria officinalis*) and meadow cranesbill (*Geranium pratense*), double catchfly (*Lychnis viscaria*) ... the list is long.

Native shrubs, too, have their garden forms: the double gorse, *Ulex europaeus* 'Flore Pleno', the snowball tree (*Viburnum opulus* 'Roseum'), coloured variants of broom (*Cytisus scoparius*) and hawthorn (*Crataegus monogyna* and *C. laevigata*), rowans (*Sorbus aucuparia*) with coloured bark or unusually-coloured fruits and whitebeams (*S. aria*) with exceptionally fine foliage, the double gean or white cherry (*Prunus avium*), and fastigiate or Irish yew (*Taxus baccata*) and miniature box (*Buxus sempervirens* 'Suffruticosa') as evergreen accent and edging shrubs. The crab apple was developed into the sweet fruit we know today, and the hop (*Humulus lupulus*) began to be used to flavour ale, giving the bitter beers so popular in England today.

Other natives were valued for their intrinsic beauty or for their medicinal properties, such as Solomon's seal (*Polygonatum multiflorum* and *P. odoratum*), lily of the valley, monkshood (*Aconitum napellus*), columbine (*Aquilegia vulgaris*), the pasque flower of chalk downs (*Pulsatilla vulgaris*), the Cheddar pink (*Dianthus gratianopolitanus*) and the maiden pink (*D. deltoïdes*), the white *Anemone narcissiflora* and the snowdrop anemone, *A. sylvestris*, the snake's head fritillary (*Fritillaria meleagris*), the summer snowflake (*Leucojum aestivale*), the stinking hellebore (*Helleborus foetidus*), the foxglove (*Digitalis purpurea*), the woodbine or honeysuckle (*Lonicera periclymenum*). The sweet flag, *Acorus calamus*, was used as a fragrant strewing herb, and is now grown in its variegated-leaved form in gardens. Sweet Cicely, *Myrrhis odorata*, can be used to take the acidity from cooked fruit, lemon balm (*Melissa officinalis*) to make wine, and blanched shoots of seakale (*Crambe maritima*) are a delicacy being rediscovered today.

The globe flower (*Trollius europaeus*), the yellow gentian (*Gentiana lutea*) and the willow gentian (*G. asclepiadea*), the martagon lily (*Lilium martagon*) and *L. pyrenaicum*, *Ornithogalum pyrenaicum*, bistort (*Persicaria bistorta*), the white buttercup *Ranunculus aconitifolius*, water avens (*Geum rivale*), lungwort (*Pulmonaria longifolia*), *Iris spuria*, and the Welsh poppy (*Meconopsis cambrica*): all these are beautiful plants, worth a place in gardens wherever the climate allows. In woodland conditions they can be joined by *Paris quadrifolia*, which is wide-ranging from Europe to temperate east Asia, associated in the wild in Europe with dog's mercury, Solomon's seal (*Polygonatum multiflorum*) and the orchid tway-blade (*Listera ovata*).

Many western European natives are valued in gardens today in selected forms, variegated leaves being especially popular. Among plants with variegated or coloured leaves are meadowsweet or queen

6

Plants from
continental climates

In contrast to the cool-temperate oceanic or maritime climate with rain in every month and no great variations in temperature between summer and winter, the continental climate of eastern and central Europe, and of central and eastern Canada and the USA, is characterized by cold winters and warm to hot summers. Here too precipitation is normally year-round, frequently falling as snow or freezing rain in winter; there is often a summer maximum, but there may also be spells of drought and heatwave in summer. In northern North America the climate of the east coast is somewhat modified by the proximity of the Atlantic, so that it is less extreme than that of the interior; in the higher latitudes of the interior, winters are very severe.

Northern China and Korea, except for the south and coastal regions, also have a continental-type climate with very cold winters, merging in the interior to the cold desert climate of Central Asia. The climate of northern Japan is modified by the influence of the sea, so that precipitation is heavier on average than in mainland China, while both eastern China and Japan feel the influence of the monsoon, with high humidity in summer. Central China has a climate not unlike that of the mid-Atlantic states of the US, with cold, wet but not too severe winters.

These regions have given the gardens of today some of their most familiar plants. Some of these made their way westwards along the trade routes from the east: oriental poppies, bearded irises and tulips were early arrivals from the Mediterranean-influenced Near East and

145

Continental climates

the dry regions of Central Asia. The wild rhubarb, *Rheum rhaponticum*, originates from the cold-winter, drier regions of Central Asia, as does the statice, *Limonium suworowii*, and *Astragalus tragacantha*. The opium poppy (*Papaver somniferum*) provides poppy seed for confectionery and flavouring bread, as well as the drug which has both medicinal and other less desirable uses. Woody plants from the interior of Asia Minor include *Platanus orientalis*, the summer jasmine (*Jasminum officinale*), and the old mock orange, *Philadelphus coronarius*. Plants from the Russian interior include *Iris sibirica* (an early introduction), *Nepeta racemosa* (*N. mussinii*), bergenias, and gypsophila.

Early settlers in and travellers to North America found a whole new range of plants which soon began to make their way back to the Old World: Michaelmas daisies, bergamot or bee balm (*Monarda didyma*) and horsemint (*M. fistulosa*), the false spikenard (*Smilacina racemosa*), scarlet *Lobelia cardinalis*, the butterfly silkweed (*Asclepias tuberosa*) and the spiderwort, *Tradescantia virginiana*, named for the Tradescants – Tradescant *fils* travelled and collected extensively in the eastern coastal regions. Other collectors of the seventeenth and eighteenth centuries introduced to Europe *Magnolia virginiana*, the great laurel or rose bay (*Rhododendron maximum*), the hop tree, *Ptelea trifoliata*, *Rosa virginiana*, *Hydrangea quercifolia*, and many phlox species. The first settlers made use of the seeds of *Gymnocladus dioica* as a substitute for coffee – by all accounts a pretty nasty one, but it gave the tree its nickname of Kentucky coffee tree.

North America

Grasslands cover a huge area of the interior of the North American continent, the precise type of vegetation varying with decreasing precipitation from east to west. The easternmost, wettest portion is the tall grass prairie, which yields to the mixed or mid grass prairie and, in the area of lowest rainfall in the west, to the short grass prairie or plains. From the prairies come the precursors of many herbaceous border plants, especially among the composites: sunflower (*Helianthus* species), *Aster ericoïdes*, *Gaillardia* or blanket flower, the tickseeds (*Coreopsis*), *Helenium autumnale*, the prairie coneflower *Echinacea purpurea*, and *Rudbeckia hirta*, as well as the Kansas gayfeather (*Liatris pycnostachya*). In their prairie habitat flights of butterflies – monarchs and swallowtails and fritillaries – feed on the nectar of these plants, which in cultivation do best in sun with a deep, well-drained soil.

147

Sagebrushes such as *Artemisia ludoviciana* also grow among the prairie grasses. The leguminous baptisias or false indigos, and the eupatoriums, ranging from the big Joe Pye weed (*Eupatorium purpureum*) and *E. fraseri* to the mistflower, *E. coelestinum*, add a different, cooler note of colour to border plantings of these grassland flowers, while in moist soils grows the queen of the prairies, *Filipendula rubra*.

The other great vegetation type of the cold-temperate North American regions is deciduous forest. Unlike the conifer forests of the more northerly regions, it is more open, and enough light reaches the forest floor for a rich diversity of woodland plants to flourish; both its woody plants and the perennials of its forest floor and margins have gone to enrich European gardens. The dominant trees of the canopy vary from region to region. In northern Ontario in Canada, jack pine (*Pinus banksiana*) grows as part of the boreal forest, with a well developed understorey of shrubs and herbs such as dwarf huckleberry (*Vaccinium angustifolium*), bush honeysuckle (*Diervilla lonicera*) and big-leaf aster (*Aster macrophyllus*), with a moss floor. The northern taiga yields gradually, southwards, to deciduous forest; balsam fir (*Abies balsamea*) and white spruce (*Picea glauca*), and the tamarack (*Larix laricina*) of boggy places, become less abundant, and a mix of hard-woods and other conifers takes over. In the Appalachians red spruce (*Picea rubens*) dominates, with *Abies fraseri* south of Pennsylvania, and broadleaves such as mountain ash (*Sorbus americana*) and maple (*Acer spicatum*). Virgin hemlock–hardwood forest, as in north-western Pennsylvania, is more than half hemlock (*Tsuga canadensis*), with beech (*Fagus americana*) the next most common tree, and smaller proportions of yellow birch, sugar maple, black birch (*Betula lenta*), red maple (*Acer rubrum*), black cherry (*Prunus serotina*), white ash (*Fraxinus americana*), basswood, yellow poplar or tulip tree (*Liriodendron tulipifera*) and *Magnolia virginiana*.

In the eastern lowland deciduous forest, sugar maple (*Acer saccharum*), yellow birch (*Betula alleghaniensis*, syn. *B. lutea*) and paper birch (*B. papyrifera*), beech (*Fagus grandifolia*) and basswood (*Tilia americana*) grow with pines (*Pinus banksiana*, *P. resinosa* and *P. strobus*) and hemlock. Associated with these are *Acer rubrum*, white ash, black cherry, *Quercus rubra* the red oak, and *Magnolia acuminata*, the cucumber tree. The shrub layer includes *Rhododendron maximum* and the calico bush, *Kalmia latifolia*, which favours dry, sandy soils. Further south this mixed forest merges into beech–maple or oak–hickory (*Quercus–Carya*) forest.

The mixed forest of the Cumberland Mountains and Alleghany Mountains is rich in its variety of species. Sugar maple, buckeye (*Aesculus octandra*), beech, tulip tree, white oak (*Quercus alba*) and northern red oak (*Q. borealis* var. *maxima*), and basswood are among those forming the overstorey; other trees of these regions well-known to gardeners throughout the cool-temperate regions include the sweet buckeye (*Aesculus flava*) and silver maple (*Acer saccharinum*). Understorey trees and shrubs in this complex community include some of our favourite flowering trees, such as redbud (*Cercis canadensis*), dogwood (*Cornus florida*), witch hazel (*Hamamelis virginiana*), *Amelanchier* and species of *Rhododendron* and *Magnolia*, with *Liquidambar styraciflua*, ironwood or blue beech (*Carpinus caroliniana*), hop hornbeam (*Ostrya virginiana*) and hackberry (*Celtis occidentalis*). There are species of *Viburnum* such as the hobble bush, *V. lantanoïdes* (*V. alnifolium*) and the sheepberry, *V. lentago*, and of sumac; there are climbers and creepers such as *Parthenocissus quinquefolia*, the Virginia creeper, and various *Vitis* species; and an abundance of berrying shrubs such as huckleberry and blueberry (species of *Vaccinium*) and blackberry (*Rubus*).

The false acacia or black locust, *Robinia pseudoacacia*, is a native of the eastern North American region, associated with the central forests of oak–pine and oak–hickory, where on the drier ridge tops *Quercus coccinea*, the scarlet oak, is one of several species associated with *Pinus rigida*, *P. pungens* and *P. virginiana*. The shrub layer includes species of euonymus and vaccinium. To the immediate east of the Appalachians, where the climate is slightly more temperate, grow the Indian bean tree, *Catalpa bignonioïdes*, the box elder, *Acer negundo*, the fringe tree, *Chionanthus virginicus*, the cockspur thorn, *Crataegus crus-galli*, the shrubby buckeye, *Aesculus parviflora*, and *Liquidambar styraciflua*. The herbaceous layer has some of the characteristics of grassland, with bugbane (*Cimicifuga* species), eupatorium, *Phlox stolonifera* and golden rod.

As well as *Kalmia latifolia*, its dwarfer relatives *K. polifolia* and *K. angustifolia*, and species of rhododendron and azalea, North America is home to many more fine ericaceous shrubs: *Zenobia pulverulenta*, *Leucothoë fontanesiana*, the Labrador tea (*Ledum groenlandicum*), *Andromeda glaucophylla*, *Leiophyllum buxifolium*, the sand myrtle of the New Jersey pine barrens, the stagger bush, *Lyonia mariana*, the tree-like sorrel bush, *Oxydendron arboreum*, the huckleberries, *Gaylussacia brachycera* and *G. baccata*, and species of *Vaccinium* including the lowbush blueberry, *V. angustifolium*, the highbush or swamp blueberry, *V. corymbosum*, cranberries, and the rabbit-eye blueberry, *V. virgatum*.

Clethra alnifolia, the sweet pepper bush, the witch hazel relatives *Fothergilla gardenii* and *F. major*, and the partridge berry, *Mitchella repens*, need similar conditions in the garden: an acid, leafy soil, and shade. Dry soil, so long as it is acid, suits the bayberry, *Myrica pensylvanica*, but the wax myrtle, *M. cerifera*, prefers it damp. Improbably related to the humble buttercup, the yellowroot, *Xanthorhiza simplicissima*, is at its best in cool, neutral to acid soil. North America boasts few rose species compared with Asia, but among them are not only *Rosa virginiana* and the smaller *R. nitida*, but also the lax or scrambling prairie rose, *R. setigera*, and *R. carolina*.

WILDINGS OF THE WOODLAND FLOOR
The complex plant communities of the deciduous or mixed forest, with their overstorey and secondary canopies, their shrub layers and light-seeking creepers, are completed by a forest-floor vegetation of shade-tolerant bulbs, perennials, ground-creeping shrubs, mosses and ferns. These seasonally-active plants commonly burst into leaf and flower early in the year, while the canopy is leafless and there is still light and moisture enough for them to grow; by high summer, many will have died back and become dormant once again, though a few, such as golden-rod (*Solidago*), grow throughout the summer to flower in early autumn.

The Virginian cowslip, *Mertensia pulmonarioïdes* (*M. virginica*), is typical of these spring-flowering woodland plants. The false spikenard (*Smilacina racemosa*), the merrybells (*Uvularia grandiflora*), *Clintonia umbellata*, the bloodroot (*Sanguinaria canadensis*), *Streptopus roseus* and the trout lily, *Erythronium americanum*, all flower in the leafy litter of the forest floor in spring, with the wake robin, *Trillium grandiflorum*, which grows in rich, moist woodlands, at increasing altitudes towards the south of its range. In New Hampshire the wake robin associates with the Indian poke, *Veratrum viride*, and *Osmunda cinnamomea* in open, mixed woodland. The squawroot, *Trillium erectum*, is most abundant further north than the wake robin, into the Canadian Shield (the vast lake- and river-pitted U-shaped area centred on Hudson Bay, between northern Ontario and Quebec and the Arctic Ocean); the trillium that extends furthest north is *T. cernuum*, a native of damp woodlands on acid soils on the coast, but found on calcareous soils further inland. The snow trillium, *T. nivale*, is the first to flower, on rocky ledges in moist woodland clearings near streams, even before the snows have disappeared. The painted trillium, *T. undulatum*, grows in moist woods and bogs in coniferous and mixed woodland in very acid soils, at altitude, while *T. sessile*, by contrast, has a more southerly distribution on calcareous and alluvial soils in woodlands.

Jack-in-the-pulpit, *Arisaema triphyllum*, is an aroid of the woodlands, and other familiar woodland plants from North America include *Galax urceolata* (*G. aphylla*); the foam flower, *Tiarella cordifolia*; and the May apple, *Podophyllum peltatum*. Violets such as *Viola pensylvanica* and *V. labradorica* spread carpets among shrubs and beneath trees, as do the wild gingers, *Asarum canadense*, *A. virginicum* and others. In late summer the baneberries come into their own: *Actaea alba*, the white baneberry, and *A. rubra*. A less familiar berrying plant is the blue cohosh, *Caulophyllum thalictroïdes*.

Further north, in the white spruce–balsam fir woodlands where paper birch, trembling aspen (*Populus tremuloïdes*) and balsam aspen (*P. balsamifera*) also form part of the overstorey and alder (*Alnus crispa*) and chokeberry (*Aronia* species) grow with wild gooseberry and blackberry and *Rosa acicularis*, the herb layer includes creeping *Cornus canadensis*, twin flower (*Linnaea borealis*) and false lily of the valley (*Maianthemum canadense*), *Pyrola* species, *Streptopus roseus*, woodland star (*Trientalis borealis*), willowherb (*Epilobium angustifolium*), and the orchid *Goodyera repens*, with club moss and ferns. The lake iris, *I. lacustris*, grows in the Great Lakes region, in moist areas in sandy woods and bogs; its larger cousin *I. cristata* grows in moist habitats in the mid southern states east of the Mississippi river, and in the Appalachian and Ozark mountains.

Parallels in Asia and North America

As in North America, the forest communities of eastern Asia are composed of many species – far more than in Europe, where comparatively few woody species survived the severe ice ages. Apart from hickory (*Carya*), many of the same genera occur in Asia as in North America; only the species are different. Instead of the paper birch and the yellow birch we find *Betula ermanii* and *B. costata*, and the Japanese white birch, *B. platyphylla* var. *japonica*; in place of *Fraxinus americana*, the Manchurian ash, *F. mandschurica*; and replacing the American beech, *Fagus grandifolia*, there is the Japanese *F. crenata*. These genera, of course, also have their European species: *Betula pendula*, the silver birch; *Fagus sylvatica*; and *Fraxinus excelsior*, the common ash, with its black winter buds.

Among conifers, the eastern North American *Thuja occidentalis* is matched by *T. orientalis*, the Chinese arbor vitae, while Asia, like North America, has many species of pine; those from cold-winter regions include the Japanese white pine, *Pinus parviflora*, the Japanese red pine, *P. densiflora*, the black pine, *P. thunbergii*, and the Korean pine, *P. koraiensis*. Silver firs from north-eastern Asia include the Manchurian fir, *Abies holophylla*, the Nikko fir, *A. homolepis*, A. *veitchii* from Japan, and the adorable *A. koreana* with its symmetrically conical outline and navy blue cones. *Juniperus rigida*, the Manchurian weeping juniper, is very cold-hardy, thriving in conditions similar to those that suit *J. virginiana*, the pencil cedar.

Asia is also home to several maples, among them some of our finest garden trees: the Chinese paperbark maple, *Acer griseum*, and its lesser-known relatives *A. nikoense* from mountain forests in Japan and China and *A. triflorum* from Manchuria and Korea; the trident maple, *A. buergerianum*; snakebarks such as *A. capillipes* and *A. rufinerve* from Japan and Korea's *A. tegmentosum*, which grows in deep mountain sites (these three echoed by *A. pensylvanicum* from eastern North America), *A. grosseri* and *A. davidii* from China; and shrubby *A. tataricum* ssp. *ginnala*. Japan's endemic *A. pycnanthum* has a counterpart in *A. rubrum*, the red maple, from eastern North America. This is an example of what plant geographers call the Magnolian Distribution, in which similar Asian and American species have no close relatives in other regions.

Whereas in North America several species of maple are common as part of the mature forest canopy, Japanese and Korean maples are more often understorey trees and shrubs, frequently growing near streams. One above all, *A. palmatum*, is very much part of the garden heritage of Japan and Korea. *Acer japonicum*, a native of cool-temperate to sub-alpine zones of Japan, is less adaptable to cultivation in North America than *A. palmatum*.

Europe can boast a single rowan, *Sorbus aucuparia*, while North America has its *S. americana*, but more fine species have been introduced to western gardens from northern China and Japan: *S. discolor* and *S. commixta*, and *S. pohuashanensis*. The Korean rowan, *S. alnifolia*, is not of the mountain ash type; it is native not only to Korea but also to northern China and Manchuria and northern Japan. Among crabs in cultivation are the Chinese *Malus transitoria*, Japanese *M. tschnonoskii*, and *M. floribunda*, known simply as the Japanese crab, and shrubby *M. toringo* ssp. *sargentii*. A North American crab valued in gardens is *M. coronaria*.

In both north-eastern Asia and eastern North America grow species of deciduous azalea. The sweet azalea, *Rhododendron arborescens*, *R. viscosum* the swamp azalea, and the pinkshell azalea, *R. vaseyi*, are echoed by *R. japonicum*, the Korean *R. schlippenbachii*, and *R. albrechtii* from

Japan. The yellow or honeysuckle azalea, *R. luteum*, is a native of eastern Europe and the Caucasus. Several other ericaceous genera occur in both Asia and North America, but as they are mostly from milder regions they will receive attention in a later chapter.

The snowbell trees of Asia, *Styrax japonica* and *S. obassia* among them, have more quality than the North American snowdrop trees, *Halesia tetraptera* (*H. carolina*), *H. diptera*, and *H. monticola*, while the Asiatic *Pterostyrax* are again less showy. Like these the stewartias – camellia relatives, mainly deciduous – do best in cool woodland soils; not all are from the cold-winter regions, but the Japanese *Stewartia pseudocamellia* and Korean *S. koreana* are both suited to continental climates. North America's hardy stewartia, *S. ovata*, is more of a shrub.

Diospyros is a mainly tropical genus, but the North American persimmon, *D. virginiana*, is echoed by the Chinese persimmon, *D. kaki*, and by the date plum, *D. lotus*. North America has its grape vines, *Vitis labrusca* the fox grape and *V. riparia* the riverbank grape, while Asia runs to ornamental vines such as *V. coignetiae*, *V. amurensis*, and *V. flexuosa*.

America's dogwoods have their Asian counterparts: from Japan and Korea comes *Cornus kousa*, with a Chinese variant *C. kousa* var. *chinensis*, which is more lime-tolerant. Their tabular habit of growth shows up more markedly in *C. controversa*; its American counterpart is shrubby *C. alternifolia*. The shrubby *C. alba*, with a native range from Siberia to Manchuria in north-east Asia, has its American 'twin' in *C. stolonifera*.

Viburnum is another widespread genus; some of its finest representatives come from cold-winter regions of Asia, such as *V. farreri* and *V. carlesii*. There are species, such as *V. dilatatum* and *V. wrightii*, whose chief glory is their fruits; the tree-like *V. sieboldii*; and *V. sargentii*, which resembles the guelder rose (*V. opulus*, a European species with a North American lookalike in *V. trilobum*).

Far less familiar in gardens are the members of the genus *Zanthoxylum*, improbably related to oranges and lemons. They are represented in North America by the toothache tree or prickly ash, *Z. americanum*, and in north-eastern Asia by the Japan pepper, *Z. piperitum*, and *Z. schinifolium*. The yellowwoods are a small genus both North American and Asian: *Cladrastis lutea* has its counterpart in *C. sinensis*. The white fringe tree of North America, *Chionanthus virginicus*, is matched in Asia by the Chinese fringe tree, *C. retusus*.

One of the most brilliant flowering climbers of the cold-winter regions of eastern Asia is the trumpet vine, *Campsis grandiflora*. The North American species is *C. radicans*, with its yellow variant, f. *flava*.

153

These illustrate plainly the need of plants from continental climates for a good summer ripening if they are to flower well; they are less successful in cloudy Britain, for example, than on mainland Europe. The Boston ivy, *Parthenocissus tricuspidata*, was originally introduced from Japan; like the Virginia creeper, *P. quinquefolia*, it colours just as brightly without the help of a continental summer.

For floral beauty, the North American witch hazels cannot compare with the Asiatics. *Hamamelis mollis*, the Chinese witch hazel, and *H. japonica*, the Japanese, flower on bare branches in winter. Similarly, the flowers of *Prunus* species from Asia are on the whole superior to those from North America. The apricot, *P. armenaica*, and the peach, *P. persica*, were both first introduced to Europe from western Asia and have been so long cultivated that their countries of origin are uncertain, but they may well have come originally from further east. The Japanese apricot, *P. mume*, is a native of China and Korea – like many Asiatic plants, it has been cultivated for centuries in Japan and was first introduced to European gardens from that country, hence the mis-leading common name. The Manchurian apricot, *P. mandschurica*, is accurately so called, however.

One of the most beautiful of cherries is *Prunus sargentii*, a native of northern China and Japan. *Prunus maackii*, the Manchurian cherry, is occasionally grown for its polished bark. The first of the 'Japanese cherries' to be planted in European gardens was *P. serrulata*, a form of the Chinese hill cherry, but the prototype of most of our flowering cherries was *P. jamasakura* (*P. serrulata spontanea*), which varies from pink to white in flower and from coppery to rich mahogany in young leaf.

The tough and cold-hardy *Hydrangea paniculata* is another Asiatic shrub cultivated, in the sterile form 'Grandiflora', by the Japanese and introduced to the west from Japan. The North American *H. arborescens* also comes in fertile and sterile or lacecap and mophead forms, while *H. radiata* is a species from Carolina. The hardy climbing hydrangeas, *H. anomala* ssp. *petiolaris* and the related *Schizophragma hydrangeoïdes* and *S. integrifolium*, are Asiatic. The climbing relatives of the spindleberries are found in both continents, *Celastrus orbiculatus* in north-east Asia and *C. scandens* in North America.

Asia is very rich in clematis, compared with North America: the spring-flowering *C. macropetala*, lantern-flowered *C. tangutica* and *C. serratifolia*, *C. terniflora* (*C. maximowicziana*) and the parents of the large-flowered garden hybrids, are all from the cold-winter regions.

The plants of north-eastern Asia

The golden rain tree, *Koelreuteria paniculata*, is a native of northern China and Korea, and needs summers hot enough to ripen the wood if it is to flower freely; maritime-region summers are apt to be too grey. The same seems to be true of *Sophora japonica*, the pagoda tree. The tree of heaven, *Ailanthus altissima*, another native of northern China, is very adaptable, however, tolerant even of atmospheric pollution.

The katsura, *Cercidiphyllum japonicum*, grows in Japanese mountain valleys where cold air is trapped, so it is very frost-resistant, unless lured into untimely spring growth by a premature mild spell, when the young leaves are easily scorched – a common problem with woody species from continental climates grown in more temperate regions. Plants valued for their ornamental fruits, such as species of *Euonymus* from northern China or Japan – *E. planipes* (*E. sachalinensis*), *E. hamilton-ianus* ssp. *sieboldianus*, *E. bungeanus*, *E. oxyphyllus*, and *E. phellomanus* – callicarpas, or *Symplocos paniculata*, may fail to ripen their wood enough to fruit freely in regions with cooler summers. Fruiting barberries such as *Berberis koreana* are less demanding, while the Japanese *B. thunbergii* is most familiar in gardens in its coloured-leaf forms.

The weigelas are more familiar in gardens than these fruiting shrubs. *Weigela florida* and *W. praecox*, parents of many garden hybrids, both originate in Japan, Korea and Manchuria, together with *W. middendorf-fiana*; the beauty bush, *Kolkwitzia amabilis*, is related to these. Several forsythias are Asiatic too: *Forsythia suspensa*, *F. giraldiana*, and the dwarf Korean *F. ovata*. *Kerria japonica*, a Chinese native first introduced to the west in its double-flowered Japanese garden form, and the winter jasmine, *Jasminum nudiflorum*, are known to almost every gardener in cool temperate regions, but *Rhodotypos scandens*, the jetbead, is seldom grown. The herbaceous *Clematis heracleifolia* grows in ravines in the hills north of the Great Wall in China.

Though the parent of many hybrid lilacs is the eastern European *Syringa vulgaris*, Asia has given us *S. reticulata* from the woodlands of the Amur region of north-east Asia, *S. pubescens* from the arid regions of northern China, *S. villosa* and *S. oblata* from northern and western China, and the Korean lilac, *S. patula*, which is also found in northern China as well as Korea. The rhododendron heartland is farther west, in the wet foothills and slopes of the Himalayas, but outliers are found in the north-east of the Asian continent, such as winter-flowering *R. dauricum*.

Most magnolias are natives of the northern and temperate regions, usually growing in mixed deciduous and coniferous forest. The most northerly species are *M. hypoleuca* from the forests of the Kuriles and Hokkaido, and *M. kobus*, another forest species growing throughout Japan and on the island of Quelpaert. *Magnolia sieboldii* is also adapted to very cold winters, with a range from southern Manchuria and Korea, where it grows in river valleys, to the forests of Japan.

One of the hardiest of rose species is *Rosa rugosa*, a native of north-eastern Asia which can be found growing on the shores of northern Japan. With a distribution from northern China to Turkestan, *R. primula* is also very much a rose of warm summers and cold winters. Another single yellow rose is *R. xanthina*, long cultivated in northern China and Korea.

Without doubt the most opulent of north-eastern Asia's flowering shrubs is the tree peony or moutan, *Paeonia suffruticosa*, developed by the skill of Japanese growers to a range of huge-flowered, full-petalled beauties. They are winter-hardy but easily tricked into early growth in spring by an untimely mild spell, so the steady continental winter suits them better than milder maritime climates.

Hostas are among the most popular of perennials in the United States and in Britain, with new varieties introduced yearly and many nurseries and societies specializing in the genus. Japanese gardeners appreciated their qualities generations before we in the west did so, and many of the original introductions from Japan were of garden forms, so long cultivated that their original parentage can scarcely be determined. Familiar kinds like *H. fortunei*, *H. ventricosa* and *H. crispula* have been grown in western as well as Japanese gardens for a long time. The wild species from which these garden forms were developed grow on the hillsides and mountains of Japan, often in rocky or grassy places. Among them are *H. elata* and *H. sieboldiana*, which is also found on forest margins; *H. nakaiana* and *H. capitata* are to be found in Korea, too, and both favour limestone.

The first of the day lilies to be introduced to the west from Japan, as long ago as the sixteenth century, was *Hemerocallis fulva*, the tawny day lily; three hundred years later came its double form, and other species native to Japan or China, such as *H. citrina*, and the branch-headed *H. multiflora*. Like hostas, day lilies are now the subject of inten-sive breeding programmes. Yet another group of highly-bred perennials is the herbaceous Chinese peonies, of which the forerunner is *Paeonia lactiflora*, long treasured by the Chinese. More fleeting but no less beau-tiful are *P. obovata* and *P. mlokosewitchii*.

The perennials of China and Japan often have an air of quality lacking in the colourful but formless composites of North America. Among such garden plants are *Astilbe chinensis taquetii*; the toad lilies, *Tricyrtis* species, with their intricate structure; aroids like *Arisaema sikokianum*; the poppy *Hylomecon japonicum*; the bleeding heart, *Dicentra spectabilis*, and its yellow Chinese counterpart *D. macrantha*; *Kirengeshoma palmata*; the Asiatic globe flowers (*Trollius ledebourii* and others), which have flowers shaped like saucers rather than globes; *Deinanthe caerulea* and *D. bifida*; the dawn poppy, *Eomecon chionanthum*, and the poppy-like, but unrelated, *Glaucidium palmatum*. *Aquilegia flabellata* is a Japanese native, as are the water irises, *I. ensata* and *I. laevigata*, and the moisture-loving *Primula japonica* with its candelabra flowers. From Kamchatka come the black *Fritillaria camtschatcensis*, *Delphinium brachycentron*, and one of the finest monkshoods, *Aconitum carmichaelii*.

The bugbanes are both Asiatic and North American, *Cimicifuga racemosa* typifying the American species and *C. simplex* the Asiatic. The skunk cabbage, *Symplocarpus foetidus*, also occurs wild in both north-east Asia and north-east North America. Despite its name, *Persicaria virginiana* (*Tovara virginiana*) is also both North American and Japanese, while one of the toughest of irises, *I. setosa*, extends in the wild from North America to Japan to Siberia.

Eastern Europe to western and central Asia

The climate of western Europe is modified by the proximity of the Atlantic ocean, but eastern Europe has a truly continental climate with cold winters, warm to hot summers and a fleeting spring, as does much of European Russia. Parts of western and central Asia also have a continental-type climate, though the summers are also generally dry to very dry, giving rise to arid or semi-desert regions in much of central Asia.

The naturally occurring grassland or steppe of Eurasia extends from the north coast of the Black Sea eastwards to central Asia, across to the Altai Mountains of southern Siberia. To the north is boreal forest; to the south, mountains or desert. There is a westerly extension of modified steppe vegetation on free-draining soils in Europe, its last traces as far west as the dry, sandy fields of the Breckland in East Anglia in eastern England, where one of the steppe species that survives is *Veronica spicata*. Accordingly, although the typical climate of the steppe is continental, with long, hard winters and hot, dry summers, some steppe species are also found in regions where the climate is more properly described as maritime.

As in much of eastern Asia and North America, the climax vegetation of areas where there is sufficient rainfall is winter-deciduous forest. A wedge of such forest extends eastwards from western Europe to the Urals, separating the northern coniferous forests and the southern steppes and reappearing in the Caucasus region. In the oak woods of Europe, pedunculate oak (*Quercus robur*) or sessile oak (*Q. petraea*) are dominant, with ash (*Fraxinus excelsior*), poplars, birches, alder (*Alnus glutinosa*) and wild cherry (*Prunus avium*). Oak forests are fairly open, so that small trees and shrubs like hazel (*Corylus avellana*), hawthorn (*Crataegus monogyna*), field maple (*Acer campestre*), crab apple (*Malus sylvestris*), rowan (*Sorbus aucuparia*) and the evergreen holly (*Ilex aquifolium*) and yew (*Taxus baccata*) are able to thrive in the light shade. The ground layer is herbaceous, grassy and shrubby. Ivy (*Hedera helix*) and honeysuckle or woodbine (*Lonicera periclymenum*) are common climbers.

By comparison beechwoods, dominated by *Fagus sylvatica*, are densely canopied and dark, with almost no undergrowth except early-flowering perennials and bulbs – *Anemone nemorosa* or wood anemone, bluebells (*Hyacinthoïdes non-scripta*) – and perhaps some brambles. In clearings there may be ash, wild cherry, whitebeam (*Sorbus aria*), holly, yew, elder (*Sambucus nigra*), the spindle tree (*Euonymus europaeus*), dogwood (*Cornus sanguinea*) and the wayfaring tree (*Viburnum lantana*).

In wet places, in cold-temperate Eurasia as in North America, alders, willows, poplars and birches form thickets, with sedges, and ferns such as the magnificent royal fern (*Osmunda regalis*). Some of the willows have qualities that endear them to gardeners: foliage in the case of *Salix alba*, especially its variety *sericea*, and *S. elaeagnos*; coloured stems in *S. acutifolia* and the violet willow, *S. daphnoïdes*, the North American *S. irrorata*, *S. alba* var. *vitellina* and *S. alba* 'Britzensis', and the purple osier, *S. purpurea*; catkins in *S. triandra*, the almond willow. The sweet gale or bog myrtle, *Myrica gale*, grows in acid, boggy soils in Europe and across to north-eastern Asia, as well as in North America.

The colder northern regions are dominated by conifers – Scots pine (*Pinus sylvestris*) in the west, Norway spruce (*Picea abies*) to the south and east. The common juniper, *Juniperus communis*, and the savin, *J. sabina*, grow in open places, including chalk downs. A common tree of the cold-winter regions of the Balkans, the Serbian spruce, *Picea omorika*, is valued in gardens for its graceful outline, more open than the finely-textured *P. orientalis*.

If the peach and apricot originate, to the best of our knowledge, in eastern Asia, western Asia is the native region of the myrobalan or cherry plum, *Prunus cerasifera*, and of the sour cherry, *P. cerasus*. Unlike these, the bird cherry, *P. padus*, does not produce edible fruits, nor does the evergreen cherry laurel, *P. laurocerasus*; the dwarf Russian almond, *P. tenella*, is also purely ornamental.

Another shrub from cold-winter areas is the Siberian crab, *Malus baccata*, and *M. niedzwetskyana* is also from central Asia. This, the parent of many of today's hybrid crabs, has imparted to some its reddish leaf colouring, and also its tendency to suffer from scab; however, it also enters into the parentage of the Rosybloom group, bred to cope with Canadian winters.

Some crabs bear fruits that make good jelly, but nothing beats quince jelly, made from the fruits of *Cydonia oblonga*, a native of northern Persia and Turkestan. A single fruit is so powerfully aromatic as to perfume a room; half a fruit will transform an apple pie. Some of the flowering quinces or 'japonicas' of farther east, Chinese *Chaenomeles speciosa* and Japanese *C. japonica*, though grown mainly for their flowers, also bear fruits which make a passable jelly. The black mulberry, long valued for its juicy fruits, is a native of western Asia.

Flowering shrubs and trees from these regions may fail to flower freely if they do not receive the summer ripening they are accustomed to in nature; and even if they bear flowers, they may fail to ripen their fruits. The shrubby honeysuckles are typical; *Lonicera tatarica* and *L. korolkowii*, which put on a good show given a hot and sunny summer, are barely worth growing in the maritime climates of north-western Europe. The red-berried elder, *Sambucus racemosa*, will be laden with fruits on well-ripened wood.

A continental climate is important too for the mimosa-like *Albizia julibrissin*, which grows in hot-summer, cold-winter regions from Persia to China; and the chaste tree, *Vitex agnus-castus*, is never so spectacular as when well baked in summer. Other flowering shrubs are less dependent on ripening heat: the common lilac, *Syringa vulgaris*, is a native of eastern Europe, yet its cultivars are as generous in grey, cloudy Britain as in sunnier climes. One of the most cold-hardy lilacs is *S. josikaea*, which crossed with the Chinese *S. reflexa* gave rise to 'Bellicent' and other tough hybrids raised in Ottawa, Canada. One of the best of the tamarisks, even under grey skies, is the central Asian *Tamarix ramosissima*.

Some of central Asia's roses are easygoing, such as *Rosa fedtschenkoana* from Turkestan and the Afghan *R. ecae*. The double Persian Yellow,

R. foetida 'Persiana', and the two-tone Austrian Copper, *R. foetida* 'Bicolor', are derived from the vivid single wild form, and are less demanding than the sulphur rose, *R. hemisphaerica*, whose very double blooms need a hot, dry spring in order to open before mouldering in the bud. The European dog rose, *R. canina*, and the cinnamon rose, *R. cinnamomea*, hardly merit a place in the garden, but other wild roses of Europe are worthy of space: the sweet brier or eglantine, *R. rubiginosa*, with scented foliage, the apple rose, *R. villosa*, and *R. glauca* (*R. rubrifolia*). The suckering *R. pimpinellifolia* or burnet rose has a wide native range, from western Europe to northern Asia.

North America's evergreen rhododendrons, valued more for their toughness than for their grace, have counterparts in western Asia, with *R. ponticum* – so adaptable that it has naturalized widely in Britain to colour hillsides with its mauve flowers – *R. smirnowii*, and *R. caucasicum*, and the honeysuckle azalea, *R. luteum* (*Azalea pontica*). Several lesser members of the family Ericaceae are common to both Eurasia and North America, either as a single widespread species – such as the cowberry, *Vaccinium vitis-idaea*, and the cranberry, *V. oxycoccus*, the bearberry, *Arctostaphylos uva-ursi*, the bog rosemary, *Andromeda polifolia*, or the blue heath, *Phyllodoce caerulea* – or as separate species in each continent. Thus the mayflower or trailing arbutus of eastern North America, *Epigaea repens*, has a Japanese counterpart in *E. asiatica*, both with tubular pink bells, while the western Asian *E. gaultherioïdes* (*Orphanidesia gaultherioïdes*) has open saucer flowers.

PERENNIALS FROM EURASIA
One of the most cold-hardy of perennials, the yarrow or milfoil (*Achillea millefolium*), is a European grassland native. Also from the grasslands of Europe or Asia (some of them natives also of Britain and other maritime-climate regions of Europe) are the dropwort (*Filipendula hexapetala*), the clustered bellflower (*Campanula glomerata*), the meadow geranium (*Geranium pratense*) and *G. sylvaticum*, *Veratrum album*, and *Veronica spicata* ssp. *incana*, a plant of the Russian steppes. *Dictamnus albus*, the burning bush, favours gravelly slopes and fields on dry, calcareous soils, *Lychnis viscaria* is usually found on dry, poor soils, and the globe thistles such as *Echinops ritro* grow on grassy or gravelly slopes and sunny wastelands. The bloody cranesbill, *Geranium sanguineum*, grows in dry scrub, but in Britain it favours limestones and coastal rocks and sands. *Aster amellus* grows on lime soils in open brush with other calcicole plants such as *Carlina acaulis* and *Aster linosyris*. The peach-leaved bellflower, *Campanula persicifolia*, grows in

open woodlands and meadows. *Veronica austriacum* ssp. *teucrium* grows at woodland margins, in open beech and oak forests and in dryish grasslands.

Damper places are inhabited by *Iris sibirica*, the marsh spurge (*Euphorbia palustris*), the meadowsweet (*Filipendula ulmaria*; *F. palmata* and *F. purpurea* are natives of north-eastern Asia), the purple loosestrife (*Lythrum virgatum*) and the yellow loosestrife (*Lysimachia punctata*), goat's rue (*Galega officinalis*), *Geranium wlassovianum* and the bistort (*Persicaria* [*Polygonum*] *bistorta*). The lemon lily, *Hemerocallis lilioasphodelus*, is found in moist meadows and woodland clearings. Similar sites in the Caucasus mountains are the habitat of *Inula magnifica*, while in damp meadows and at woodland margins from the mountains of Europe eastwards into Russia grows the mourning widow, *Geranium phaeum*. *Campanula latifolia* grows in woodlands and lush meadows throughout most of Europe and into Central Asia.

Plants of woodland margins and clearings include the foxglove (*Digitalis purpurea*), the wood spurge (*Euphorbia amygdaloïdes*), *Eupatorium cannabinum*, the Christmas and Lenten roses and their kin (*Helleborus niger*, *H. orientalis*, *H. purpurascens*, *H. viridis* and others) and the stinking hellebore (*H. foetidus*), the Solomon's seals (*Polygonatum multiflorum* and *P. odoratum*, the former in deciduous woodlands and the latter generally at the sunny margins of oak woodlands or in open coniferous forests). *Geranium platypetalum* grows in spruce woods and hazel scrub in the Caucasus and northern Turkey and Iran. *Aconitum lycoctonum* ssp. *vulparia* grows with other herbaceous plants among deciduous forests, and *A. napellus* is found in a variety of habitats from forests and stream-sides to meadows. The fireweed, *Epilobium angustifolium* (sometimes grown in its white form *album*), is adaptable to almost any site from barren wasteland to forest margins, streams and thickets; the choicer *E. dodonaei* is a plant of sandy soils in the hills and subalpine regions, growing along streams and rivers and in rocky places.

161

7

Plants from Mediterranean climates

The Mediterranean climate is warm-temperate, with mild, wet winters and warm or hot summers during which little or no rain falls. As well as the lands to the north, south and east of the Mediterranean itself, this type of climate is found in central Chile, California, the south-western Cape district of South Africa and parts of western and southern Australia. The vegetation of regions with this type of climate, typically a mix of evergreen shrubs and some trees, is known as maquis and garrigue in southern France, macchia in Italy, chaparral in California, matorral in Chile, and fynbos in the Cape region. Bulbs and perennials adapted to the winter-growing, summer-dormant life cycle also grow in these regions.

The Mediterranean maquis and garrigue

Before the natural vegetation was disrupted by felling and grazing, the Mediterranean was a region of thin sclerophyllous woodlands, dominated by oaks – cork oak (*Quercus suber*) and holm oak (*Q. ilex*) – and pines: umbrella stone pine (*Pinus pinea*) and, extending into the southern Black Sea region, Aleppo or Jerusalem pine (*P. halepensis*). Apart from a few isolated patches of original pine forest, what now remains is only scattered, gnarled trees, with a thin scrub on limestone known as garrigue, and elsewhere a taller, denser cover called maquis, in which

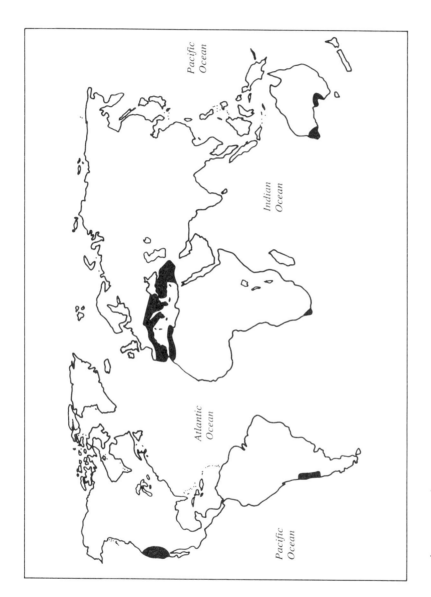

Mediterranean climates

some trees remain – not only pines and oaks, but also the Judas tree (*Cercis siliquastrum*) and carob (*Ceratonia siliqua*).

The larger shrubs include wild olive (*Olea europaea* ssp. *africana*, *O. verrucosa*), Phoenician juniper (*Juniperus phoenicia*), lentisk or mastic tree (*Pistacia lentiscus*) and terebinth tree (*P. terebinthus*), the evergreen buckthorn (*Rhamnus alaternus*), and species of strawberry tree: *Arbutus unedo*, which occurs as far west as south-west Ireland, and *A. andrachne*, more common in Greece, together with the natural hybrid *A.* × *andrachnoïdes*. The tree heath (*Erica arborea*) occurs in the northern and southern Mediterranean, extending as far as the Caucasus and East Africa in the east; in the west its place is taken by the Portugal heath, *E. lusitanica*. *Erica erigena* (*E. mediterranea*) is also a westerly species, ranging as far as south-west Ireland. Myrtle (*Myrtus communis*) and bay laurel (*Laurus nobilis*) are widespread, and the common fig (*Ficus carica*) is abundant, both cultivated and wild. Gum storax (*Styrax officinalis*) grows in the warmer, more sheltered places.

The smaller shrubs that compose the maquis and garrigue are the subdominants of the original woodland. Many are both evergreen and aromatic: the labiates rosemary (*Rosmarinus officinalis*) and sage (*Salvia officinalis*), lavender – including *Lavandula stoechas*, the French lavender, *L. lanata*, *L. dentata* and *L. pinnata* – and *Phlomis fruticosa* or Jerusalem sage, rue (*Ruta graveolens*), the 'curry plants' such as *Helichrysum italicum*, and *Cistus*. Several plants used in cooking for their aromatic qualities are Mediterranean natives: savory (*Micromeria*), oregano or marjoram (*Origanum*), hyssop, and many thymes.

Spiny shrubs are also common in the maquis: kermes oak (*Quercus coccifera*), pomegranate (*Punica granatum*), butcher's broom (*Ruscus aculeatus* and *R. hypoglossum*), species of *Asparagus*, and the prickly broom (*Calycotome villosa*). There are several other species of broom and broom-relatives in the Mediterranean region: *Genista monosperma*, *G. aetnensis*, the Mount Etna broom, and *G. cinerea*, from the south-western regions, the Spanish broom (*Spartium junceum*), *Coronilla valentina* and the larger ssp. *glauca*, *Anthyllis barba-jovis*, the moon trefoil (*Medicago arborea*) and *Adenocarpus*.

Shrubs with a felted or hairy coating to the leaves, as protection against the heat of the sun and excessive transpiration, include *Quercus alnifolia*, *Convolvulus cneorum*, *Artemisia arborescens*, the cotton lavenders (*Santolina*), *Lithodora rosmarinifolia*, *Teucrium fruticans*, *Vella pseudocytisus*, and the shrubby mallow, *Lavatera maritima* (*L. bicolor*). Others, such as rue and *Linum arboreum*, have a waxy glaucous coating.

A genus typical of the Mediterranean, with outliers in the Canaries, is *Cistus*, the sun roses, ranging from the tall gum cistus, *C. ladanifer*, to spreaders such as *C. parviflorus* and *C. salviifolius*. The halimiums are related, among them *H. ocymoïdes* and *H. lasianthum*; some species, including *H. lasianthum*, grow in light shade at woodland edges. In the wild cistuses are often confined to certain soil types: *Cistus palhinhae* grows on the limestone promontory of Cape St Vincent in the Algarve, but the closely related *C. ladanifer* is more widely distributed, on neutral or acid soils.

The familiar oleander, *Nerium oleander*, a native of the Mediterranean region, is grown in many countries of the world. This and the chaste tree, *Vitex agnus-castus*, are the only native shrubs that flower in late summer. The olive, so characteristic of the Mediterranean countries, probably originates from further east, though cultivated in southern Europe for centuries, perhaps millennia. No less typical of the region is the vine, also thought to be an age-old import from further east. The fig, *Ficus carica*, and the caper bush, *Capparis spinosa*, are true natives, and another important economic plant of the region is the cork oak, *Quercus suber*. *Chamaerops humilis*, the Mediterranean fan palm, is a pygmy compared with the Canary Island *Phoenix canariensis*, a relative of the date palm. As well as umbrella and Aleppo pines, the conifers typical of the region are the Italian cypress, *Cupressus sempervirens* 'Stricta', and the maritime pine, *Pinus pinaster*. The Phoenician juniper, *Juniperus phoenicia*, and the Syrian juniper, *J. drupacea*, are among several species native to this region.

BULBS, PERENNIALS AND EPHEMERALS OF SOUTHERN EUROPE

As we have seen, going to ground is one of the ways in which plants cope with a dry season, and the Mediterranean is rich in plants with corms, bulbs or tubers, many of which flower in the spring and spend the summer in a state of dormancy, to be revived by the autumn rains. The hillsides and olive groves of the northern Mediterranean are bright in spring with *Anemone pavonina* or poppy anemone and its kindred *A. coronaria*. Wide expanses of colour also come from annual poppies (*Papaver* and *Roemeria* species) and the corn marigolds (*Chrysanthemum segetum* and *C. coronarium*).

Unlike the anemones, which range eastwards from south-west France, the tuberous-rooted *Ranunculus asiaticus* grows in the eastern Mediterranean, the Near East and North Africa. Many tulips are natives of Central Asia, but the Mediterranean has its *Tulipa saxatilis* and *T. cretica*, Cretan natives, *T. sylvestris*, the tulip of Italian meadows, *T. orphanidea* which grows wild in the eastern regions, and the latest of all to flower, *T. sprengeri* from north-western Turkey. One of the earliest bulbs to be introduced to the west was the musk hyacinth, *Muscari ambrosiacum*, to be followed by the more familiar blue-flowered species. Some of the ornamental onions, too, are Mediterranean natives, among them *Allium zebdanense* and *A. neapolitanum* (which grows not just in the region of Naples, as the name might imply, but throughout the northern Mediterranean), *A. roseum*, *A. sphaerocephalum*, *A. flavum* and *A. carinatum*.

Some of the crocuses most familiar in European gardens are natives of the Mediterranean region: *Crocus chrysanthus*, *C. biflorus*, *C. imperati* flowering in late winter and spring, and *C. longiflorus*, *C. nudiflorus*, and *C. medius* flowering in autumn. Colchicums are sometimes, inaccurately, referred to as autumn crocuses; several species are native to Mediterranean regions, as is the colchicum-like *Sternbergia lutea*. *Leucojum autumnale* occurs in the Iberian peninsula and in North Africa, and *Cyclamen* species are found in both the northern and southern Mediterranean lands. Many narcissi grow in moist meadows, in regions influenced by the wetter Atlantic climate, but *Narcissus papyraceus* and *N. tazetta*, together with its subspecies *aureus*, and the jonquil, *N. jonquilla*, are true Mediterraneans.

Many species of iris grow wild in Asia Minor, but some are native to the Mediterranean region, including *Iris histrio*, as well as the related *Gynandriris sisyrinchium* and the snake's head or widow iris, *Hermodactylus tuberosus*. The bearded *Iris* 'Florentina', probably an age-old hybrid, grows in the fields and orchards of Italy. Southern Europe has its own *Gladiolus* species too, typified by the corn flag, *G. communis* ssp. *byzantinus*. The wild Roman hyacinth, *Hyacinthus orientalis*, comes from the eastern regions of the Mediterranean and Asia Minor, where grow also the Madonna lily, *Lilium candidum*, and *L. chalcedonicum*. The asphodels, *Asphodelus microcarpus* and others and *Asphodeline lutea*, are common.

There are several species of spurge: shrubby *Euphorbia characias* and its subspecies *wulfenii* and variety *sibthorpii*, and the smaller *E. rigida* and *E. myrsinites*, and spiny *E. acanthothamnos*, which grow in rocky places. Rocks are the usual habitat of *Convolvulus althaeoïdes* and its subspecies *tenuissimus*. Spain, North Africa and the Near East have given to gardens a trio of poppies, *Papaver atlanticum*, *P. pilosum* and *P. rupifragum*. Also from North Africa is the thistle, *Cynara hystrix*. Other Mediterranean thistles are *Onopordum acanthium*, *Silybum marianum* and *Galactites tomentosa*. Mulleins include *Verbascum olympicum*, *V. undulatum* and *V. phoenicium*. The Corsican hellebore, *Helleborus argutifolius*, and the closely related *H. lividus*, grow in rocky places on the island of Corsica. The foxgloves of the Mediterranean region include *Digitalis ferruginea* and *D. lanata*, and the shrubby *D. obscura* from Spain. There are several species of peony: *P. clusii* from Crete, *P. rhodia* from Rhodes, *P. russii* from Corsica and *P. cambessedesii* from the Balearic Islands.

PLANTS OF THE SEASHORE

Sandy beaches and dunes are the home of the southern European horned poppies, *Glaucium flavum* and *G. corniculatum* (*G. phoenicium*), of the sand lily, *Pancratium maritimum*, of sea lavender such as the florists' statice, *Limonium sinuatum*, and of stocks, *Matthiola sinuata* and *Malcolmia maritima*. The sea squill, *Urginia maritima*, is another Mediterranean and Near Eastern native, not confined to seashores despite its common name. The sea holly, *Eryngium maritimum*, is found even on British coasts, in dry, sandy places. The shrubby *Euphorbia dendroïdes* grows on cliffs and rocky places, usually within sight of the Mediterranean sea.

PLANTS OF NORTH AFRICA

Many of the plants of the northern and eastern Mediterranean also grow in North Africa. The north coast of Morocco is characterized by cork oak (*Quercus suber*) forests, and a maquis of *Cistus salviifolius*, *Erica arborea* and *E. umbellata*, and *Lavandula stoechas*. *Tamarix africana* and *Genista monosperma* grow on sandy soil, and in damp meadows on both sides of the Straits of Gibraltar grows *Narcissus viridiflorus*.

The High Atlas is the home of *Adenocarpus anagyroïdes*, *Colutea arborescens*, *Teucrium fruticans* and juniper, with *Iris tingitana*, a parent of the big Dutch irises, *Convolvulus sabatius* (*mauretanicus*) and *Rhodanthemum gayanum* (*Chrysanthemum mawii*). The Anti Atlas forests are composed of *Quercus lusitanica*, with thickets of *Cistus albidus*, while the forests of the Middle Atlas plateau are of *Cedrus libani* var. *atlantica*, now treated as a variety of the cedar of Lebanon rather than as a species in its own right. Here too grow holly, ilex and *Viburnum tinus*, and the Moroccan broom, *Cytisus battandieri*. In glades in the forest grow *Paeonia coriacea*, *Geranium atlanticum* and *Ranunculus calandrinioïdes*. In the Rif mountains of northern Morocco grow cistuses, *Salvia interrupta* and *Lithodora diffusa*. The winter-flowering *I. unguicularis* (*I. stylosa*) is a native of Algeria.

Plants of Macaronesia

The region known as Macaronesia – the Atlantic islands of Madeira, the Azores, the Canary Islands and the Cape Verdes – is not strictly part of the Mediterranean, but the flora is related to that of the Mediterranean region and North Africa, and some species, such as the evergreen climber *Smilax aspera*, have a range that includes all these regions. One of the best known plants of the region is the Paris daisy (*Argyranthemum frutescens*), together with *A. foeniculaceum* and *A. maderense*, while the dragon tree of the Canaries, *Dracaena draco*, is almost legendary.

On most of the islands the forest has been largely destroyed, but on Madeira laurel forest survives on the central mountain spine of the island, gaining moisture from the clouds that form on the heights, in contrast to the drier coastal regions. The Lauraceae that chiefly compose the forest are *Laurus azorica*, *Ocotea foetens* (*Laurus maderensis*), *Persea indica*, and *Aponomias barbujana* (*Laurus canariensis*). Among them grow *Clethra arborea* and *Euphorbia mellifera*, the pride of Madeira (*Echium candicans*), and the shrubby foxglove *Isoplexis sceptrum*, with *Geranium palmatum* in clearings in the forest. *Geranium maderense* is less common, growing at higher altitudes. The montane zones above the forest are also the home of the tree heath, *Erica arborea*, and the besom heath, *E. scoparia*, and of *Vaccinium padifolium* (*maderense*).

The forests of the Canary Islands were composed of the same four laurel species, but are now very degraded. From sea level to about 700 m/2,300 ft the vegetation is a semi-desert succulent scrub, typical of arid regions, with *Phoenix canariensis*, species of *Euphorbia*, *Aeonium* and *Aichryson*, and *Senecio kleinia*, and Compositae. On the cliffs of the coastal mountains grow *Marcetella moquiniana*, *Genista monosperma* and *Argyranthemum foeniculaceum*, the palomera (*Pericallis lanata* [*Senecio heritieri*]), the pico paloma (*Lotus berthelotii*) and *L. maculatus*. *Jasminum odoratissimum* grows in rocky places in the lower zone. At the upper limits the succulent scrub merges into juniper scrub, with *Juniperus phoenicia* and *Erica arborea*, on the southern slopes and, in the wetter regions, into tree heath and the evergreen laurel forest.

Other trees of the forest zone are *Arbutus canariensis*, *Prunus lusitanica*, *Picconia excelsa* and *Ilex perado* ssp. *platyphylla*. The shrub and herb layer has *Viburnum rigidum*, *Euphorbia mellifera*, *Chamaecytisus proliferus*, *Hypericum grandifolium*, *Hedera canariensis*, *Semele androgyne*, *Echium pininiana*, *Geranium canariense*, *Woodwardia radicans*, *Isoplexis canariensis*, *Canarina canariensis* and *Senecio cruentus*, the ancestor of the florists' cineraria. Above the laurel forest, from about 1,200 m/4,000 ft, there is a savannah-like vegetation of *Pinus canariensis* with *Adenocarpus foliolosus*, *Cistus symphytifolius*, *Daphne gnidium*, *Lotus* species, *Sideritis candicans* and the asphodel, *Asphodelus microcarpus*. Higher again, in the montane zone, grow *Echium wildprettii* and *Cytisus supranubius*.

There are instances of species closely resembling each other on different islands. The Madeiran whortleberry is matched by *V. cylindraceum* from the Azores, where *Erica azorica* is endemic; *Pericallis aurita* (*Senecio maderense*) by *P. lanata* (*S. heritieri*) from Tenerife. Not all Macaronesian plants are allied to European genera: isolated species include *Clethra arborea*, *Pittosporum coriaceum* and *Sideroxylon marmulano*, of Madeira.

California chaparral and upland forests

Chaparral as generally understood is the evergreen sclerophyllous shrub vegetation of California; chaparral is also found in Arizona and northern Mexico, however, with a winter-deciduous variant, petran chaparral, in the Rocky Mountains. The summer-deciduous variant, soft chaparral, is also known as coastal sage scrub. The California chaparral, which like the maquis has its characteristic fragrance from the aromatic plants which comprise it, forms an almost continuous cover of shrubs, especially on the steeper slopes. The inland mountain slopes are in the rainshadow of the prevailing winds, and consequently hotter and drier than coastal slopes at the same elevation.

Some California species are closely related to Mediterraneans. The Judas tree of the Mediterranean, *Cercis siliquastrum*, has its counterparts in *C. occidentalis*, the western redbud of North America, and *C. reniformis*, a Texan–Mexican species; the Greek *Arbutus andrachne* is matched in California by the madrona, *A. menziesii*, and in Mexico by species such as *A. xalapensis*. Only slightly more distant is the relationship between the bay laurel of the Mediterranean, *Laurus nobilis*, and the California bay or headache tree, *Umbellularia californica*.

There are many evergreen shrub species in the chaparral. A typical, and dominant, genus is *Ceanothus* or California lilac, which is very diverse in habit, ranging from prostrate shrubs such as the squaw carpet, *C. prostratus*, to the tree-like *C. arboreus*, *C. thyrsiflorus*, the blueblossom or blue brush, which grows with the azalea *Rhododendron occidentale*, and *C. cyaneus*, which grows in association with the California tree poppy, *Romneya coulteri*. Some grow on coastal bluffs – *C. gloriosus*, *C. griseus horizontalis* – and others in stony soil on the slopes amid other shrubs of the chaparral, such as the manzanitas (*Arctostaphylos* species, themselves widespread and often dominant), sumac (*Rhus* species), and native oaks, and *Yucca whipplei*. Yet other California lilacs, for example *Ceanothus incanus*, *C. leucodermis* and *C. papillosus*, grow in broken woodland, and a few, among them the squaw carpet, come from altitudes where there is snow in winter.

The most widely distributed chaparral shrub is chamise (*Adenostoma fasciculatum*), either as pure stands or mixed, co-dominant with *Arctostaphylos* or *Ceanothus* species; at its lowest elevations, it yields to coastal sage subshrubs, *Salvia* and *Eriogonum fasciculatum*. Other local dominants are *Dendromecon rigida*, chaparral pea (*Pickeringia montana*) and *Fremontodendron*. Among other well-known California shrubs are *Mahonia fremontii*, which grows on hot slopes facing the desert, and the western redbud, *Cercis occidentalis*, from dry slopes and canyons in the foothill woodlands and chaparral.

In slightly wetter regions other shrubs, often taller, join chamise, manzanita and California lilac: oaks (scrub oak, *Quercus dumosa*, often in pure stands, and others), *Garrya*, mountain mahogany (*Cercocarpus betuloïdes*) and *C. ledifolius*, chaparral holly (*Heteromeles arbutifolia*), chaparral cherry (*Prunus ilicifolia*), *Rhamnus* and *Rhus* species, and *Malosma laurina*. At higher elevations dominants include *Castanopsis sempervirens*, *Quercus vaccinifolia*, prostrate species of *Arctostaphylos* and *Ceanothus*, and some winter-deciduous shrubs. On the interior side of the Sierra Nevada, this montane chaparral forms a mosaic with coniferous forest, pinyon–juniper woodlands, or scrub vegetation of the type associated with the Great Basin, between the Sierra Nevada and the southern Rocky Mountains.

Conifers are sometimes associated with the chaparral, forming stands within the shrubby growth – *Pinus attenuata*, *P. muricata* and species of *Cupressus* – or more dispersed – bigcone pine, *Pinus coulteri*, digger pine, *P. sabiniana* and *P. torreyana*. Occasionally hardwood trees more characteristic of the upland forests, such as *Quercus agrifolia*, *Q. wislizenii*, *Q. chrysolepis*, the madrona (*Arbutus menziesii*) and the California laurel (*Umbellularia californica*), grow in the chaparral, often in the moister places such as ravines and north-facing slopes.

SUBSHRUBS, PERENNIALS AND BULBS
Although evergreen sclerophyllous shrubs are the typical chaparral vegetation, there are shrubs and subshrubs, climbers and some herbaceous plants to be found too. The monkey flowers, *Mimulus aurantiacus*, *M. longiflorus* and *M. puniceus*, the matilija poppy (*Romneya*), penste-

mons such as *P. heterophyllus*, *Dicentra chrysantha*, *Eriogonum fasciculatum*, *Zauschneria* and species of salvia and *Ribes* such as *R. menziesii* from the chaparral and lower forests and *R. roezlii* from dry open slopes and the forests of the inner coastal ranges, are sub-shrubby or semi-deciduous. Climbers may be woody (*Clematis* species, *Keckiella* [*Penstemon*) cordifolia*] or herbaceous (species of *Convolvulus* and *Lathyrus*). *Keckiella cordifolia* grows through *Ceanothus* or *Arctostaphylos*, *Cercocarpus* or sumac.

Among bulbous plants of the chaparral are *Brodiaea* species, *Dichelostemma ida-maia*, *Triteleia laxa*, *Zigadenus fremontii*, several fritillary species, such as scarlet *Fritillaria recurva*, and *Calochortus* or mariposa lilies, among the best-loved of California's bulbs; they grow in open, dry places among sagebrush or other dwarf shrubs and extend into the desert regions (another section, Eucalochortus, are woodland plants from the mountainous regions). Familiar annuals include *Phacelia*, *Gilia*, *Collinsia*, *Eschscholtzia*, *Clarkia*, *Nemophila menziesii* from the chaparral and coastal sage scrub, *Limnanthes douglasii* from grasslands and foothill woodlands, and lupins. Several species of perennial lupin are California natives, among them the widespread *Lupinus polyphyllus*, the tree lupin, *L. arboreus*, and *L. chamissonis*, which grow in sandy places on the coast, and *L. albifrons*, which grows in sandy or rocky places in a wide range of lower-altitude habitats. Other perennials include *Sisyrinchium*, *Delphinium* and *Sidalcea malviflora*, from grassy slopes and coastal prairies.

COASTAL SAGE SCRUB AND INTERIOR CHAPARRAL

The soft chaparral, also known as coastal sage scrub, grows on the Coastal Range, on both coastal and interior slopes. It is a low-altitude, summer-deciduous vegetation tolerating drier conditions than evergreen chaparral. The subshrubs that are associated with chaparral, among them *Artemisia californica*, *Salvia mellifera* and *S. leucophylla*, are often dominant in coastal sage scrub, together with *Encelia californica*, *Baccharis pilularis* and others. The fuchsia-flowered gooseberry, *Ribes speciosum*, grows both in the coastal sage scrub and the chaparral. *Mentzelia lindleyi* (*Bartonia aurea*) is an annual of the soft chaparral. To the south and near the coast there are many succulents. Two widely-cultivated coastal conifers are the Monterey cypress, *Cupressus macrocarpa*, and the Monterey pine, *Pinus radiata*, both able to resist salt-laden gales, though twisted into a gnarled caricature of a tree on the most exposed bluffs.

The interior chaparral is very similar to the California chaparral,

171

although it is separated from it by desert and experiences a different climatic pattern, most of the sparse rainfall taking the form of intense summer storms, when much of it is lost through evaporation. However, chamise is absent, and *Quercus turbinella* fills the role that chamise holds in California, dominating most of the interior chaparral. It intergrades with desert scrub or grassland at low elevations and with yellow pine forest or pinyon–juniper forest at higher altitudes. Mexican chaparral is markedly evergreen, with *Quercus*, *Garrya*, *Cercocarpus*, *Rhus*, *Ceanothus* and *Arctostaphylos* species; the rain falls only in summer. Chamise often forms pure stands, *Arbutus texana* is a small tree, and *Yucca whipplei* is sometimes named chaparral yucca in these regions. Petran chaparral, at high elevation in the central Rocky Mountains, is winter-deciduous, with *Quercus gambelii* dominant.

CALIFORNIA UPLAND FORESTS

The upland woodlands and forests are dominated by trees rather than shrubs; rainfall increases with altitude, and it is this rather than differences in temperature patterns that allows for the development of forests. Around the Central Valley of California is a ring of pine–oak woodland dominated by blue oak, *Quercus douglasii*, with digger pine (*Pinus sabiniana*), coast and interior live oaks (*Q. agrifolia* and *Q. wislizenii*), and two deciduous oaks, valley oak (*Q. lobata*) and, at higher elevations, black oak (*Q. kelloggii*) and canyon live oak (*Q. chrysolepis*). There are scattered specimens of *Aesculus californica*, and a few shrubs, including some of the evergreen genera of the chaparral, and *Cercis*, which is deciduous. At higher elevations in the Coast Range, blue oak woodland is replaced by mixed evergreen forest dominated by *Pinus coulteri* and oaks, especially *Q. chrysolepis*, with *Acer macrophyllum* and *Umbellularia californica*. Another type of mixed forest is dominated by *Pseudotsuga menziesii* and *Umbellularia californica*; oaks (*Q. chrysolepis*, *Q. kelloggii*) are also present, with *Lithocarpus densiflorus* and madrona. Shrubs of the mixed forest include *Oemleria* (*Osmaronia*) *cerasiformis*, *Rhododendron macrophyllum* and *R. occidentale*, *Gaultheria shallon*, and *Vaccinium ovatum*. Irises such as *I. innominata* and *I. douglasii* are found in the forest, the latter also in coastal prairie and open grassy slopes.

In the central Coast Range and the Transverse Ranges the major dominant is *Quercus agrifolia* on the steeper, moister slopes, associated to the south with California walnut (*Juglans californica*) and *Quercus engelmanii*, which predominates on more arid slopes. In the Transverse and Peninsular ranges, bigcone pine (*Pinus coulteri*) is associated with *P. ponderosa*, canyon live oak, *Quercus chrysolepis*, and *Q. kelloggii*, and a shrubby layer of *Arctostaphylos*, *Ceanothus* and *Cercocarpus*. On steep north-facing slopes and in ravines, bigcone spruce (*Pseudotsuga macrocarpa*) is common, at low altitudes as scattered individuals above a canopy of *Quercus chrysolepis* and higher up in greater numbers. Throughout this region of the Coastal Range, bigcone pine and canyon live oak grow together in the drier sites adjacent to chaparral, and bigcone spruce and canyon live oak share the moister, fire-free sites, joined by *Acer macrophyllum*, *Populus trichocarpa* and California laurel in moist, cool ravines. In some parts, either following removal of conifers by logging or fire, or on steep slopes and in steep canyons, the forest is dominated by broad-leaved trees.

The most extensive forest in California is the conifer forest or yellow pine forest of middle elevations, in which *Pinus ponderosa* is almost always present, though in drier or colder parts its place may be taken by *P. jeffreyi*. Another four species share dominance with these: sugar pine (*P. lambertiana*), Douglas fir (*Pseudotsuga menziesii*), California white fir (*Abies concolor* var. *lowiana*) and incense cedar (*Calocedrus decurrens*). Conifers form the canopy, with *Pinus lambertiana* and *Sequoiadendron giganteum* the largest trees; this, the giant sequoia of the Sierra Nevada, grows in moist sites. Smaller trees are both deciduous (*Quercus kelloggii*, *Acer macrophyllum*, *Cornus nuttallii*) and evergreen (*Quercus chrysolepis*, *Cercocarpus ledifolius*), and both evergreens and deciduous species also make up the shrub layer, with *Quercus*, *Arctostaphylos* and *Ceanothus*, *Lithocarpus*, *Castanopsis*, *Prunus*, *Carpenteria californica*, *Ribes*, *Symphoricarpus* and *Vaccinium*. There is also a herbaceous, mainly perennial layer, with *Clintonia*, *Disporum* and *Smilacina*, *Iris*, *Pyrola*, *Lupinus* and *Viola*. Trout lilies, *Erythronium califoricum* and *E. hendersonii*, are also found in the conifer forest.

At higher elevations lodgepole pine (*Pinus contorta* var. *murrayana*) is typical, sometimes supplanted by red fir (*Abies magnifica*). Lodgepole pine grows both on arid, windswept sites on shallow soils and in cold, damp sites by lakes or at the edge of meadows. With it grow shrubs of familiar California genera: *Arctostaphylos*, *Ceanothus*, *Castanopsis* and *Ribes*. Where red fir is dominant it is accompanied by several other conifer species. In moist and shady places *Spiraea douglasii* and the flowering currant, *Ribes sanguineum*, grow, while boggy places are the habitat of *Leucothoë davisiae*.

173

The fynbos of the south-western Cape

The fynbos of the Cape, South Africa's version of the maquis vegetation that has evolved to withstand hot, dry summers and wet winters, extends from the western Cape to Humansdorp, to the west of Port Elizabeth in the southern Cape; most of this area has a Mediterranean, winter-wet climate, through in the easternmost parts there is some summer rain as well. The fynbos gives way abruptly to other types of vegetation, especially to semi-desert scrub in the low rainfall areas. The rainfall in the south-western Cape increases with altitude, and there are pronounced rain-shadow effects in the lee of the mountains. The western Karoo and Namaqualand have a similar climate but a different flora.

The fynbos is rich in Proteaceae, Ericaceae, Rutaceae, shrubby Compositae and Restionaceae, but there are few grasses. There are about twenty-five species of *Protea* including *P. neriifolia, P. magnifica* and, growing on dry rocky ridges, on hill and mountain slopes and in mountain grassland, and in moist, sheltered places, *P. caffra*. The moister places at altitude in the fynbos vegetation are also the habitat of *Mimetes argenteus*. The silver tree, *Leucadendron argenteum*, and *Leucospermum reflexum* and *L. cordifolium*, are also in the protea family. *Heeria argentea*, the rockwood, grows on dry, rocky mountain slopes.

The Cape region is known for its many species of *Erica*; the fynbos includes more than fifty species, offering a range of colours and forms vastly greater than those native to Europe: scarlet, green, yellow, coral and crimson join the muted purples, mauve-pinks and whites of the northern hemisphere heaths. Among tree-like heaths are *E. caterviflora* and the high-altitude *E. triflora; E. canaliculata* grows in the dry mesophytic forest of the southern Cape.

Many of the Cape members of the Rutaceae are also needle-leaved or heath-like shrubs of the fynbos: among them are *Adenandra* (*Diosma*) *uniflora, Coleonema* (*Diosma*) *album* and *C. pulchrum*, from the mountain slopes. Other shrubs of the region include the mountain saffronwood, *Cassine parvifolia*, which grows in the dry forest and fynbos of the south-western Cape, and the needle hardleaf, *Phylica villosa*, which ranges from the coastal to the mountain fynbos. The honeybell bush, *Freylinia lanceolata*, grows over a wide altitudinal range in moist areas by streams or fringing vleis, in the western and southern Cape.

The lion's ear, *Leonotis leonurus*, is widespread from the south-western Cape to Natal, growing on flats and hillsides. Even wider-ranging is the ironwood olive, *Olea capensis*, a plant of the bush and

174

littoral scrub. On arid slopes grows *Anisodontea capensis*; this extends into the Karoo, where also grow *Gazania krebsiana* and others. *Arctotis acaulis* is one of many daisies from the south-western Cape and Namaqualand. *Chrysanthemoïdes monilifera* is found in a wide variety of habitats from coastal dunes and rocky hillsides to forest margins, in the western, southern and eastern Cape and northwards to Natal and southern Transvaal. *Melianthus major* ranges from Clanwilliam to the Peninsula and eastward to the southern Cape and Karoo.

The Clanwilliam cedar, *Widdringtonia juniperoïdes*, is endemic to a narrow altitudinal range on the Cedarberg Mountains, forming open vegetation on rocky soils with other plants of the mixed shrub community; *W. cupressoïdes* grows in similar communities but is more widespread.

NAMAQUALAND VELD
Extending up the western coast of South Africa to the Orange river is the semi-arid region of the Namaqualand veld, where in wetter years the land is vividly coloured in spring with many composites – *Arctotis*, *Gazania*, *Venidium*, *Osteospermum*, *Dimorphotheca*, *Ursinia*, *Senecio* and *Felicia* – while in drier years semi-succulents of the mesembryanthemum family such as the giant sour fig, *Carpobrotus quadrifidus*, and *Lampranthus* species, provide the colour. Often just one or two species will colour a wide area: *Venidium fastuosum*; *Senecio elegans*, a plant of grassy slopes, which also grows on dunes and coastal rocks just above the high-tide level; the Namaqualand daisy or star of the veld, *Dimorphotheca sinuata*, with *Heliophila longifolia*; the rain daisy, *Dimorphotheca pluvialis*; *Grielum grandiflorum* with the kingfisher daisy, *Felicia bergeriana*. *Gazania krebsiana* is a plant of dry grasslands, *Osteospermum caulescens* grows on grassy slopes, and *O. barberiae* among rocks and on grassy plains. The blue-flowered *Felicia amelloïdes* is found on exposed, stony hillsides, and *F. filifolia* (*Diplopappus filifolius*) grows on dry hillsides and in poor soils in semi-arid areas.

MONOCOTS OF THE SOUTH-WESTERN CAPE
One of South Africa's great contributions to the world's gardens is the range of monocotyledonous plants that grow there, extending not only throughout the Mediterranean-climate western Cape region but also northwards and eastwards into regions where the rains occur mainly in summer. Those from the western Cape region where the rain falls mainly in winter almost all have a winter-growing habit and are dormant in summer.

Some genera are endemic to the region. The Cape cowslips, species of *Lachenalia*, are confined to the south-western part of southern Africa, most of them in the western Cape – among them are *L. aloïdes* from the Cape peninsula and its var. *vanzyliae*, and *L. elegans* from the north-western Cape region. The species of *Polyxena* include *P. corymbosa* and the wider-ranging *P. ensifolia*, which extends to the Karoo and eastern Cape. Bulbous species of Namaqualand include *Lapeirousia speciosa*, and from the drier east, *Homeria collina* (*breyniana*). Most species of *Homeria* are natives of the western and south-western Cape, with one (*H. pallida*) extending from central Namibia to eastern Transvaal. *Geissorhiza* is almost wholly confined to the winter-rainfall area, with a large number of species – such as *G. radians*, the wine cup – in the south-western Cape. Of South Africa's many orchids, the pride of Table Mountain, *Disa uniflora*, grows in permanently damp places by waterfalls and vleis in high mountain localities in the winter-rainfall area.

Ixia and *Sparaxis* are endemic to Cape Province, mainly in the south-west and extending into the Karoo; all are winter-growing and summer dormant, among them the red ixia, *I. campanulata*, the green ixia, *I. viridiflora*, and the harlequin flower, *Sparaxis tricolor*. Many of the species of *Babiana* and of *Lapeirousia* are also from the south-western Cape. *Hesperantha*, a genus endemic to sub-Saharan Africa, has many species in southern Africa, especially in the north-western Cape region. The southern African endemic *Freesia* are all winter-growing, from the Cape, mainly in the south-west with *F. refracta* extending into the Karoo and southern Cape and *F. corymbosa* reaching the eastern Cape. The montbretia-like *Antholyza* is endemic to the winter-rainfall areas of the Cape, mainly in coastal areas; and the related *Tritonia*, wider-ranging in the continent, is represented by, among others, *T. crocata* from the south-western Cape. *Chasmanthe aethiopica*, despite its specific name, is a winter-growing species from the Cape, as are *C. bicolor* and *C. floribunda*. Of the two species of forest lily, *Veltheimia capensis* from the western Cape and Little Karoo has a long summer dormancy. The peacock flower, *Moraea neopavonia*, and *M. villosa*, are from the western Cape and winter-growing, like *M. polystachya*, which extends into Orange Free State and the Karoo. *Aristea major*, from the south-western Cape, is evergreen. *Wachendorfia paniculata*, though it extends into the eastern Cape, is also summer-deciduous and winter-growing. Even fresh-water aquatics, such as the Cape hawthorn (*Aponogeton distachyos*), or marsh plants such as the arum lily (*Zantedeschia aethiopica*) are adapted to a winter-growing regime.

Two species of African lily, *Agapanthus africanus* and the rare *A. walshii*, are from the south-western Cape, as are some red hot pokers or torch lilies, among them *Kniphofia sarmentosa*, which grows alongside mountain streams, and *K. uvaria*, which also favours stream-sides and marshy areas in the fynbos of the south-western Cape, flowering profusely after veld fires. The belladonna lily (*Amaryllis bella-donna*), which grows wild on the coastal hillsides of the south-western Cape, is known to be shy-flowering in cooler, maritime climates; but it is equally so in its native haunts when the leaves are hidden by scrub growth. Only after a bush fire does it flower freely. The related species of *Brunsvigia* are from the winter-rainfall areas: *B. josephinae*, *B. marginata* and the candelabra flower, *B. orientalis*. The Guernsey lily, *Nerine sarniensis*, is also from the western and south-western Cape.

Other genera, though extending to other regions of the world, are well represented in south-western Africa. The chincherinchees such as *Ornithogalum thyrsoïdes* are mainly from the western Cape and the Cape peninsula. The majority of African *Romulea* species are from the Cape, winter-growing with a long summer dormancy. *Gladiolus* extends throughout Africa except in desert regions and also occurs in the Middle East and Mediterranean regions; several species are found in the winter-rainfall areas of Cape Province, among them a handful known as painted lady (*G. angustus*, *G. brevifolius*, *G. carneus* and *G. undulatus*), the blue afrikaner (*G. carinatus*), brown afrikaner (*G. liliaceus*) and marsh afrikaner (*G. tristis*), the cliff gladiolus (*G. carmineus*), *G. citrinus*, *G. aureus* and the waterfall gladiolus, *G. cardinalis*, which grows on moist, rocky ledges near streams in the mountains of the south-western Cape. The closely related *Homoglossum merianellum* and *H. watsonianum*, the red afrikaner, are also winter-growing Cape species. Several species of *Watsonia* have the same growth pattern and are native to the south-western Cape, among them *W. borbonica* (*W. pyramidata*), *W. marginata*, *W. aletrioïdes*, *W. meriana*, *W. stenosiphon* and *W. versfeldii*.

The flora of south-western and southern Australia

Two regions of Australia have a Mediterranean climate: the south-western part of Western Australia, and the area around Spencer Gulf in South Australia with part of western Victoria. The two regions are separated by the arid coast along the Great Australian Bight. The summers are marked by virtually total drought, and the winters are wet and frost-free; the south-west has much wetter winters than the south

177

and the transition to desert is more gradual as a result. In the southwest, soil type is more significant than rainfall or altitude in determining the plants that grow in a given community.

The area around Perth is known as the Swan Coastal Plain, and is characterized by poor, sandy soils, with a limestone ridge inland from the coastal dunes; it is bounded on the east by the rocky Darling Scarp. The windswept coast has a low heath of prickly Moses (*Acacia pulchella*) and *Hibbertia hypericoïdes*, and on the coastal limestone ridges is a dense heath of *Hakea*, *Dryandra*, *Melaleuca* and *Templetonia retusa*. This is the home of the Swan River daisy, *Brachyscome iberidifolia*. On sheltered limestone slopes and valleys grow *Melaleuca lanceolata* and *Callitris preissii*, with tuart (*Eucalyptus gomphocephala*), a large tree on deeper soils, forming forest at the southern end of its range. Understorey trees and shrubs include *Agonis flexuosa*, wattles and *Grevillea* species.

The mangrove, *Avicennia marina*, grows in salt water lagoons and estuaries, with the berry saltbush, *Rhagodia radiata*, and the salt-water paperbark, *Melaleuca cuticularis*, around the shores. Seasonal freshwater swamps, wet only in winter, are the habitat of *Melaleuca rhaphiophylla* and *M. preissiana*, *Leptospermum ellipticum*, some species of *Banksia*, and the white myrtle, *Hypocalymma angustifolium*, with basket flower (*Adenanthos obovatus*) at the margins. On slightly drier ground grow the kangaroo paws including *Anigozanthos viridis*, and the red swamp cranberry, *Astroloma stomarrhena*.

On sandy soils a few trees are widespread, above all jarrah, *Eucalyptus marginata*, which forms extensive forest on gravelly soils at the edge of the Darling Scarp, and mixes with other trees in more open woodland on the sands. Marri, *E. calophylla*, prefers the clays of the eastern regions. The southern hemisphere family Proteaceae is well represented in Australia's Mediterranean-climate regions, with several tree species of *Banksia* on the coastal plain, among them *B. menziesii* and the bull banksia, *B. grandis*, which often grows with she-oak, *Allocasuarina fraseriana*. The other widespread tree is the semi-parasitic tree mistletoe, *Nuytsia floribunda*. *Acacia saligna* is a common and widespread wattle.

The shrub flora is very rich, with many members of the Myrtaceae – tea trees, bottlebrushes, featherflowers, and honeymyrtles. On the coastal limestone the chenille honeymyrtle (*Melaleuca heugelii*) grows, and further inland the Swan River myrtle (*Hypocalymma robustum*) and *Calytrix flavescens*. *Acacia meisneri* grows near York, on ridges and plains and along the roadsides. The sand bottlebrush, *Beaufortia squarrosa*, grows on the coastal plain, and several shrubby melaleucas are found on the winter-wet soils at the foothills of the scarp. Other myrtle relatives of the Perth region are *Darwinia*, *Calothamnus* – the common net bush, *C. quadrifidus*, and the silky net bush, *C. villosus* – and *Chamelaucium*. Other families are represented too: winter bell, *Blancoa canescens*, grows in sandy heaths and banksia woodland, and the blueboy, *Stirlingia latifolia*, is a common shrubby protea relative growing on sandy soils. *Hakea prostrata*, though low-growing on the windswept south coast, is a shrub or small tree in the Perth region. Thickets of *Dryandra sessilis*, the parrot bush, form on limestone soils. *Grevillea thelemanniana* occurs on gravelly clay soils.

The pea-flowered *Hovea trisperma* is common on sandy soils; another familiar legume is the Swan River pea, *Brachysema lanceolatum*, which grows in a wide variety of habitats. *Acacia pulchella* and others grow on the coastal hills, with *A. rostellifera* forming thickets on coastal dunes. On the granite soils of the Darling Scarp grow a variety of shrubs such as *Cryptandra arbutiflora*, *Borya nitida*, *Verticordia acerosa*, *Petrophile biloba*, *Thomasia glutinosa*, and *Grevillea endlicheriana* and *G. bipinnatifida*. In the deeper soils grow wandoo (*Eucalyptus wandoo*) and marri (*E. calophylla*), and on the laterite the dominant tree is jarrah (*E. marginata*). The jarrah forest covers over a million hectares (2½ m acres), chiefly on laterite soils where the annual rainfall is over 1,100 mm/44 in. It occurs as an almost pure stand, with marri in loam soils on the lower valley slopes, wandoo on clay valley soils and where the rainfall is too low for jarrah, and *E. patens* in alluvial soils along creeks.

As on the coastal plain, she-oak is a common understorey tree. Other common trees in the forest are *Banksia grandis* on laterite soils, and *B. menziesii* and *B. attenuata* on sands, with *B. littoralis* on river flats, and *Acacia extensa* in jarrah forest, especially along creek banks. The southern jarrah forest is wetter than the north, so the water bush, *Bossiaea aquifolia*, and native willow, *Oxylobium linearifolium*, are common, with *Xylomelum occidentale* or woody pear, and the snotty-gobbles, *Persoonia longifolia* and *P. elliptica*. There are many lianas in the jarrah forest: wild sarsaparilla (*Hardenbergia comptoniana*), coral vine (*Kennedia coccinea*), *Clematis pubescens* and *Billardiera floribunda* among them. The arborescent monocots blackboys (*Xanthorrhoea preissii* and *X. gracilis*), black gin (*Kingia australis*) and pineapple bush (*Dasypogon hookeri*) grow in the forest. The shrub layer is composed of species of banjine, *Pimelea rosea*, *P. suaveolens* and *P. spectabilis*, *Hibbertia miniata* and *H. stellaris*, *Leschenaultia biloba* and fanflower, *Scaevola platyphylla*.

Acacia strigosa also grows in the understorey, and blueboy grows on deep sands. There are shrubby protea relatives including *Hakea lissocarpha*, *Isopogon* and *Dryandra* species. *Gastrolobium villosum* is one of several toxic pea-flowered shrubs. *Boronia fastigiata* occurs in jarrah forest and on swampy flats. The yellow-eyed flame pea, *Chorizema dicksonii*, grows in open, gravelly forests. Among the herbs of the jarrah forest are *Dampiera linearis* and *Scaevola striata*, *Tetratheca viminea*, *Orthrosanthus laxus*, yellow flags (*Patersonia xanthina*), and the widespread purple flags, *P. occidentalis*. The blue lady orchid, *Thelymitra crinita*, grows in the woodlands, as does the silky blue orchid, *Caladenia sericea*.

EUCALYPT FORESTS AND MALLEE

Karri (*Eucalyptus diversicolor*) forms forests in the south-western part of Western Australia, on sandy loams in regions with scarcely less rainfall than jarrah forest and a less well-marked dry season. Pure karri forest is composed of two or three layers, with karri forming the entire upper layer. In the main karri forest there is a second layer of smaller trees, including *Casuarina decussata*, *Agonis flexuosa*, and *Banksia grandis*. Other trees which may mix with karri are *Eucalyptus jacksonii* and *E. guilfoylei*, and *Agonis juniperina*. There is always a dense shrub layer in karri forest, with *Trymalium spathulatum*, *Chorilaena querciflora*, *Crowea angustifolia*, *Boronia gracilipes*, the tree *Hovea elliptica* and shrubby *H. trisperma*, the holly flame pea (*Chorizema ilicifolium*) and *C. cordatum*, *Hakea oleifolia*, *Hibbertia cuneiformis*, water bushes (*Bossiaea* species) and species of *Acacia*, especially *A. pentadenia*, *A. urophylla* and *A. myrtifolia*, with *Paraserianthes distachya* (*Albizia lophantha*). Many of the lianas of the jarrah also grow in karri forest, and there are ferns and herbs such as *Dampiera hederacea* in the leafy forest floor.

From the southern coastal strip comes one of the most widely cultivated eucalypts, *E. ficifolia*, rare in the wild; other species are dominant in the region, including bullich, *E. megacarpa*, near the coast and along creeks, *E. occidentalis* on low-lying flats, and mallees in the eastern heath areas – *E. preissiana* among them. *Banksia coccinea* grows in deep sands and heathlands, favoured also by scallops, *Hakea cucullata*, and other species, *Isopogon formosus* and *I. cuneatus*. These also grow in woodland, as do smokebushes (*Conospermum*), *Crowea angustifolia* and *Acacia myrtifolia*. On the granite outcrops grow *Banksia verticillata* and *Hakea suaveolens*, which is such a pernicious weed in the fynbos of the Cape region of South Africa; gravels are the preference of *Dryandra formosa*, one of several species from the region. On the coast grow *Boronia alata*, *Anthocercis viscosa* and *Banksia praemorsa*. *Andersonia sprengelioïdes* is an epacrid which grows on coastal granite slopes; other epacrids from the region are *A. caerulea*, *Lysenema ciliatum* and *L. fimbriatum*, and *Sphenotoma* species.

The area has many swamplands with their own range of plants. Swamp or gravel bottlebrush, *Beaufortia sparsa*, grows in areas that are wet in winter, dry in summer; it also grows in nearby jarrah forests, as does the flame pea, *Chorizema reticulatum*. *Callistemon speciosus* favours the margins of swamps. There are many species of *Melaleuca*, with *M. cuticularis* near salt water and *M. rhaphiophylla* along rivers and freshwater lakes; other swamp dwellers are *Leptospermum firmum*, *Agonis linearifolia* and *A. juniperina*, *Hypocalymma cordifolium*, *Actinodium cunninghamii*, *Banksia quercifolia* and *B. occidentalis*, *Cosmelia rubra*, *Boronia megastigma* and *B. heterophylla*. At the margins of swamps grow herbs such as *Goodenia*, *Dampiera* and *Scaevola* species.

The Stirling Range, near the southern coast, has the highest peaks in southern Western Australia; they are clad in dense scrub, extending down over the plains, where it is broken by woodlands. Many of the plants that grow there are endemic to this range; among them are many eucalypts, in addition to jarrah, marri, wandoo, and in sheltered valleys yate (*E. occidentalis*) and bullich. Some are mallees – tallerack (*E. tetragona*), *E. preissiana* and *E. tetraptera*. There are several species of *Darwinia*, including *D. macrostegia*, and of bottlebrushes, *Beaufortia decussata* and others and the one-sided bottlebrushes, *Calothamnus*. Wattles that grow here include *Acacia costata* and *A. drummondii*. The mountain kunzea, *K. recurva* var. *montana*, and two endemic myrtles, *Hypocalymma myrtifolium* and *H. speciosum*, grow here, with some featherflowers (*Verticordia habrantha* and others), and waxflower (*Chamelaucium confertiflorum*). Several of the banksias already mentioned grow here, and *B. solandri* is common; smokebushes (*Conospermum*), coneflowers (*Isopogon* and *Petrophile* species, including *I. latifolius* which grows on the peaks) and dryandras too are found here: *D. formosa* and others. There are many species of *Hakea* and of wild honeysuckle (*Lambertia*). Mountain pea (*Oxylobium atropurpureum*) grows on the upper slopes and several bitter peas (*Daviesia*) including *D. oppositifolia* in the woodlands. There are several small epacrids, including *Andersonia axilliflora* on the higher slopes and the paper heath, *Sphenotoma drummondii*, in rock crevices near the summits. Trigger plants include the climbing *Stylidium scandens*. *Velleia foliosa* is prominent on the upper slopes. As in other regions of south-western Australia there are several species of orchid, including the butterfly orchid, *Caladenia lobata*, which grows in sheltered gullies at lower elevations.

Along the south coast east of the Stirling Range, and extending to the western edge of the Great Australian Bight, is a region of sand plains, relatively flat and unwatered – the rivers are mainly seasonal and saline. The vegetation is low or tall heath, often with emergent mallee eucalypts, and here and there taller eucalypt woodlands including the salmon gum, *Eucalyptus salmonophloia*, in loamy pockets. The heath vegetation is very diverse, with many species of *Banksia*, including *B. speciosa*, *B. caleyi* and the tree-like *B. media*; several *Dryandra* species, many grevilleas and hakeas, among them *H. laurina*, the widely cultivated pincushion hakea, chittick (*Lambertia inermis*), nodding coneflower (*Isopogon teretifolius*) and several other coneflower and *Petrophile* species, smokebushes (*Conospermum amoenum* and others) and *Franklandia fucifolia* or lanoline bush.

Tallerack, *Eucalyptus tetragona*, is one of several mallees from the region. In clay soils, wet in winter, *E. platypus* is dominant. There are many melaleucas; one that grows in clay heaths or mallee communities is *M. uncinata*, the broom honeymyrtle. Bottlebrushes, species of *Beaufortia* and *Calothamnus*, are common. Silver tea tree, *Leptospermum sericeum*, grows on only granitic slopes. On the sand heaths grow many species of featherflower (*Verticordia*) and waxflowers (*Chamelaucium*, including *C. megalopetalum* on sands); *Boronia scabra* grows on clay or gravel soils. *Kennedia nigricans* is common on deep coastal sands, and *Leschenaultia tubiflora* grows on sandheaths.

PLANTS OF THE HEATHLANDS
The Barrens are a small area of isolated low peaks on the south coast near the western end of the southern sand plains. The vegetation is a tapestry of heath, mallee and swamp. The climate is typically Mediterranean, with low precipitation falling in winter. The dominant plants of the heaths, which cover the hills among rocky outcrops, are members of the protea and myrtle families, such as *Regelia velutina*, banksias, grevilleas and dryandras. The royal hakea (*Hakea victoriae*) grows on the sandy plains around the hills. The weeping gum, *Eucalyptus sepulcralis*, grows on the lower slopes, as well as other mallee species, melaleucas, *Baeckea* species, clawflowers (*Calothamnus*) and many other myrtle relatives. *Leschenaultia superba* grows in thick scrub and on some peaks the endemic *Goodenia stenophylla* is found.

On the west coast, north of Perth and extending northwards to beyond the Murchison River, is another region of sand plain or sand heath, mostly consisting of poor sands and gravels and supporting many endemics. The vegetation is mainly low scrub and includes mallee eucalypts, but north of the Murchison River there is tall, dense scrub. The same families dominate these northern sand plains, with several species of banksia, dryandra, hakea, smokebushes, and grevillea –

including the white plume, *G. leucopteris*, and *G. thyrsoïdes*. River gums, *Eucalyptus camaldulensis*, grow along river courses and there are pockets of marri (*E. calophylla*). Near the coast north of the Murchison grows the illyarrie, *E. erythrocorys*. There are many species of *Verticordia*, *Calothamnus*, *Melaleuca* and *Calytrix*, three of coppercups, *Pileanthus*, and a few of the mountain bells type of *Darwinia*, with many other myrtaceous genera. *Eremaea*, a genus close to *Melaleuca*, is centred in this region. The Geraldton wax, *Chamelaucium uncinatum*, grows along this part of the coast in sandy hollows. Wattles are prominent in the tall scrub north of Murchison River, among them bowgada, *Acacia linophylla*, and curara, *A. tetragonophylla*. The pea family is also represented, by *Brachysema*, *Jacksonia*, *Sphaerolobium*, *Hovea*, *Daviesia* and *Mirbelia*. The native foxglove, *Pityrodia oldfieldii*, appears soon after bush fires. The kangaroo paws are represented here, as elsewhere, including the state flower, *Anigozanthos manglesii*, and the black kangaroo paw, *Macropidia fuliginosa*. There are several species of native conifers on the heaths, among them the sand plain cypress, *Actinostrobus arenarius*, and the dwarf cypress, *A. acuminatus*. The orange banksia, *B. prionotes*, and the white plume grevillea grow in the sands.

East of the jarrah forest lies the agricultural wheat belt, a tapestry of habitats and vegetation types, with only a few uncleared areas remaining of hilltop thickets, savannah woodland and sand plain, as well as extensive salt lakes. The dominant woodland trees are wandoo, York gum (*Eucalyptus loxophleba*) and salmon gum. York gum usually grows with the jam tree, *Acacia acuminata*. The wandoo woodlands of *Eucalyptus wandoo* and, on gravelly hills, the powderbark wandoo (*E. accedens*) are interspersed with York gum woodlands. Among the understorey plants is *Lechenaultia biloba*. There are several species of mallet (*Eucalyptus astringens* or brown mallet, *E. gardneri*, *E. falcata*, and the swamp mallet, *E. spathulata*) with only scattered shrubs below. The yates such as flat-topped yate, *E. occidentalis*, are common in the south of the wheat belt. The most widespread tree here is the salmon gum, *E. salmonophloia*. There are many mallees throughout the region, such as the rose mallee, *E. rhodantha*.

The tall thicket known as wodjil is dominated by acacias, with other shrubs including *Casuarina*, hakeas and grevilleas. Tamma is a lower-growing shrubby thicket dominated by *Casuarina campestris*. The broom honeymyrtle, *Melaleuca uncinata*, also forms dense thickets. A few specimens of sandalwood, *Santalum spicatum*, remain; quandong, *S. acuminatum*, is more common. Laterite hilltops are covered with shrubs, sometimes dense thickets of dryandra such as *D. nobilis* or golden dryandra and *D. proteoïdes* or king dryandra. The open heath and mallee heath that develop on deep sands or on shallow sand over laterite are rich in wild flowers. The shrubs are mainly low-growing, with the usual families, the epacrids, myrtles and Proteaceae, with bottlebrush grevillea (*G. paradoxa*) and flame grevillea (*G. eriostachya*), and featherflowers.

The highly weathered granite outcrops of the south-west, scattered throughout the region and rising from the surrounding scrub to form flat expanses or large domes, support their own flora. Where the soil is deep, dense thickets of she-oak or wattle are common; in crevices and soil pockets many shrubs are to be found. The granite outcrops are wet in winter due to run-off, and very dry in summer; there are rock pools, around which the microclimate is very extreme. The most common plant in shallow soil pockets is pincushions, *Borya nitida*, which dries out and becomes dormant in summer, plumping up again after the first rains of winter. Under overhangs, where it is protected against desiccation, grows rock fern (*Cheilanthes tenuifolia*). The shrubs of the granite outcrops all have various adaptations to protect them from the intense summer heat; most have deep-ranging roots. *Kunzea pulchella* has silky leaves, while others such as *Calothamnus rupestris*, *Kunzea baxteri*, *Verticordia huegelii* and *Melaleuca radula* have needle leaves. *Hakea petiolaris* has tough, leathery foliage, and *Dodonaea attenuata* is covered with a sticky resin which also helps to reduce moisture loss. There are few trees; among them are the she-oak, *Casuarina huegeliana*, and the gungurru, *Eucalyptus caesia*.

SOUTHERN AUSTRALIA

The Mediterranean-climate region of eastern South Australia and western Victoria is very roughly bisected by the Spencer Gulf; to the west the vegetation is chiefly shrubby open scrub and low shrubland, while to the east is a more grassy open scrub and heath. The heathlands develop on low-fertility sands near the coast and around the Grampians.

A few plants of Western Australia are also found in southern regions; among them are *Alyogyne huegelii* and *A. hakeifolia*, *Acacia cyclops*, the climbing *Sollya heterophylla*, the irid *Orthrosanthus multiflorus*, and the Swan River daisy (*Brachyscome iberidifolia*). More commonly, montane plants and those that grow in damp sites in the heathlands also range quite widely in southern Australia into the regions where rain falls in summer as well as winter, some even into Tasmania. Among the plants of damp heathy places are *Melaleuca squarrosa* and *M. gibbosa*, *Hakea nodosa*, *Casuarina paludosa*, *Leucopogon ericoïdes, Bauera rubioïdes, Pimelea flava, Pultenaea gunnii, Correa reflexa, Olearia ramulosa, Apalochlamys spectabilis, Stypandra caespitosa, Patersonia longiscapa*. Other plants typical of the heathlands are the horny cone bush (*Isopogon ceratophyllus*), the coral heath (*Epacris microphylla*), the dwarf wedge pea (*Gompholobium ecostatum*), the cranberry heath (*Styphelia humifusa*), the running postman (*Kennedia prostrata*), *Bossaia cinerea, Lomatia ilicifolia*, and *Kunzea ambigua*. The umbrella fern, *Gleichenia microphylla*, grows in damp shade, as in thickets of paperbark by streams. One of the paperbarks, *Melaleuca ericifolia*, originally formed vast thickets in lowland Victoria, but is now represented by mere vestiges along creeks and river flats. Orchids of the genus *Thelymitra* are widespread.

The Grampians themselves, an isolated range of mountains in western Victoria, have a varied vegetation from mountain forest with fern gullies in the cooler ravines to open woodland, heathy scrubs and swamps. In damp places grow *Melaleuca squamea* and *M. decussata, Prostanthera rotundifolia*, and *Epacris impressa*. Drier heaths and sandhills are the habitat of *Xanthorrhoea australis* and *X. quadrangulata, Dillwynia sericea, Westringia glabra, Baeckea crassifolia, Conospermum mitchellii, Stephelia behrii (Astroloma conostephioïdes)* and *Cryptandra tomentosa*. Plants of the rocky hills include *Leptospermum nitidum, Calytrix alpestris*, and *Thryptomene calycina*. *Correa aemula* grows in the mountain forests, and *C. lawrenceana* is also found in eastern Tasmania. *Ozothamnus (Helichrysum) thyrsoïdeum* grows in montane regions of Victoria from the Grampians to the eastern heights. The Oyster Bay pine, *Callitris rhomboidea*, grows on the slopes and ridges of the Grampians as well as in coastal regions.

Banksia serrata grows in sandy coastal tracts, while right by the sea, on coastal dunes and cliffs, *B. integrifolia* is found. Other coastal plants are *Leptospermum laevigatum, Bursaria spinosa, Correa alba* and *C. pulchella, Calocephalus brownii*, the boobialla, *Myoporum insulare*, and *M. parvifolium* and *M. viscosum*. *Acacia sophorae* is valued for its ability to bind sandy dunes with its extensive root system. As in the west, another type of specialized habitat in southern Australia is granite outcrops, which support their own vegetation, with *Allocasuarina stricta, Dodonaea cuneata, Isotoma axillaris, Stypandra glauca, Callistemon pallidus*, and *Kunzea parvifolia*.

Central Chile

Extending from southern Coquimbo province to Concepción, roughly centred around Valparaiso in central Chile, is a region which is climatically equivalent to much of California, with winter rain (falling as snow at higher elevations). At low altitudes it is often foggy, but higher up it is sunny, and midsummer can be quite arid on the upper slopes and on plateaux and in broad valleys. In deep valleys that remain moist all year, wet forest develops, but this is replaced on north-facing slopes and on steep mountainsides by a vegetation very like chaparral.

The trees of the wet forest are boldo (*Peumus boldus*), peumo (*Cryptocarya peumus*), *Crinodendron patagua*, and *Escallonia rubra*, with ferns as a dense understorey. At the forest margins grow bamboos and species of *Mutisia* – *M. ilicifolia*, *M. retusa*. At higher altitudes the soap tree, *Quillaea saponaria*, grows with an understorey of *Berberis*, *Escallonia* and *Cestrum*. *Aristotelia maqui* is found in damp places, gullies and streamsides, and *Abutilon vitifolium* grows along watercourses. The solanaceous *Vestia foetida* and *Cestrum parqui* grow in shady, damp places; the cestrum is often found near *Loasa acanthifolia*, the ortiga brava, and can be used to relieve the pain of its stinging leaves.

Central Chile has its own species of palm, the kankan or honey palm, *Jubaea chilensis*, from which a sugary sap is extracted to make palm honey or wine. It grows on dry slopes of the narrow belt of the coastal cordillera at low altitudes, with *Quillaea saponaria*, *Lithraea caustica*, quisco (*Cereus chilensis*), espino (*Acacia cavenia*), and even peumo and boldo in damper places, with macqui, *Persea lingue*, *Luma apiculata* and *Rhaphithamnus cyanocarpus*. On arid hills the chagual (*Puya coerulea*) grows, often with columnar cacti, over which *Tropaeolum tricolorum* trails, and in the most arid zones of the central valleys there are spiny shrubs such as *Acacia*, *Adesmia*, and *Proustia*, with the poison-ivy relative *Lithraea caustica*, a small tree. Another plant of the drier regions, extending as far south as Patagonia, is *Fabiana imbricata*. The deep tubers of *Tropaeolum azureum*, which grows in the drier regions of the Andean foothills, protect it against the long seasonal droughts. *Tropaeolum polyphyllum* comes from further south, in the high screes near the snow line. The nasturtium, *Tropaeolum majus*, is also a Chilean plant. The Chilean glory flower, *Eccremocarpus scaber*, grows in the coastal ranges, in dry scrub and rocky ravines.

Lobelia tupa grows more commonly in coastal regions, on light, sandy soils and even in dune country, than in the interior. Also mainly coastal are *Luma chequen* and *Aextoxicum punctatum*, the olivillo. The ortega, *Schinus polygamus* (*dependens*), and the maiten, *Maytenus boaria*, occur as scattered individuals southwards into the southerly regions with a more maritime climate; the range of *Buddleja globosa* is similar.

Chile's evening primrose, *Oenothera berteriana*, is known as Don Diego de la noche because it opens only at night; it is widespread in sunny places in the central and southern regions, preferring sandy soils with access to ground water. The Peruvian lily, *Alstroemeria haemantha*, grows in river valleys in the Valparaiso district. The poor man's orchid or butterfly flower (*Schizanthus*) is represented in central Chile by *S. pinnatus*, the pajarito. *Calceolaria corymbosa* grows in the shade of shrubs, and *C. arachnoidea* is a plant of humid places in the cordillera at middle elevations.

In the summer-dry regions of central Chile the fire lily, *Pyrolirion tubiflorum* var. *flammeum*, grows in fields and cornfields; var. *aureum* is found further north, in Peru, and *P. boliviense* grows on dry, clay slopes in Bolivia. *Habranthus andersonii* is also from central Chile, as well as southern Brazil, Uruguay and eastern Argentina. *Hippeastrum bicolor* and *H. chilense* are endemic amaryllids from the central regions. Also from central Chile is *Leucocoryne ixioïdes*. The sought-after blue crocus, *Tecophilaea cyanocrocus*, grows high in the Cordillera of Santiago, ranging from Valparaiso to Coquimbo, on stony slopes where it is snow-covered in winter.

8

The plants
of arid lands

Near-absolute deserts such as the Sahara, where there is little rain at any season and no really cold weather (though night-time temperatures are much lower than during the day) are beyond the scope of this book, though one extremely important economic plant, the date palm, has its origin in the oases of the North African desert. Though they are often described as the most absolute deserts in the world, I shall briefly touch on the plants of the coastal deserts of Peru and northern Chile. At the margins of true desert regions in which virtually no vegetation can survive, where desert merges into less extreme climatic zones, a wide variety of species and of plant forms has developed. In other arid lands, though there may be little more rain than in these parched regions, it normally falls at a season when enough accumulates in the soil to sustain plant growth instead of being lost through evaporation and run-off. In some such regions the soil is moist enough for part or all of the year to sustain the growth of grass, whereas elsewhere the vegetation known as desert scrub, which is mainly woody, is typical. In western North America there are extensive desert regions supporting desert scrub; the arid parts of western Argentina are similar.

In Africa and Asia there is a great series of more or less dry regions covering parts of both continents, stretching from the west coast of North Africa to north-eastern Mongolia. The Saharan, Arabian, Persian and Thar (Great India) deserts, and their easternmost extension in Rajasthan, are warm deserts, while the Turkestan, Tibetan and Gobi

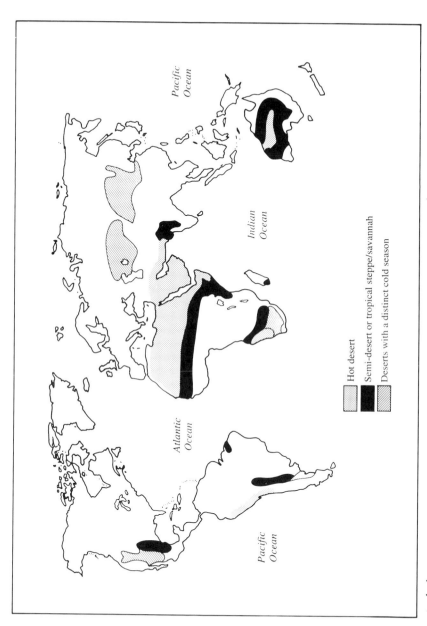

Pacific
Ocean

Indian
Ocean

Atlantic
Ocean

Pacific
Ocean

Hot desert

Semi-desert or tropical steppe/savannah

Deserts with a distinct cold season

Arid climates

are mainly cold deserts, the first with a fairly well-developed vegetation and the other two very cold due to their great elevation. Even in the warm deserts frosts are not unknown, and the diurnal temperature range is very wide. Much of the western part of southern Africa is also desert; like the American deserts, but unlike those of the African–Indian desert region and the desert that covers much of the interior of Australia, its flora is rich in drought-adapted species. Parts of eastern South Africa are also very arid.

Semi-arid climates capable of supporting the type of vegetation known as dry grassland are found in both tropical and temperate regions. The term savannah is often used for tropical grasslands, ranging from pure grassland to grassland with scattered shrubs and trees such as species of *Acacia* or even savannah woodland, while steppes or prairies are the mid latitude equivalent, with grasses, bulbous plants, herbaceous annuals and perennials, and some woody shrubs. The constant feature of these regions, with their variety of climatic regimes, is a dry season resulting in regular and pronounced moisture deficits.

The desert scrub of North America

The four desert regions of North America – based on climatic, vegetational and floristic distinctions – are the Great Basin desert or cold desert, between the Sierra Nevada and the Southern Rocky Mountains, which experiences both snow and hard frost in winter, and is dominated by big sagebrush (*Artemisia tridentata*), or locally by shadscale (*Atriplex confertifolia*), winterfat (*Eurotia lanata*) or salt sage (*Atriplex nuttallii*); and the warm deserts, the Mojave, Sonoran and Chihuahuan (the first and last warm-temperate, the Sonoran subtropical, climatically speaking), all three dominated by the creosote bush, *Larrea tridentata*. The Chihuahuan, a high-altitude desert, receives about the same average annual precipitation as the others (less than 300 mm/12 in) but about two-thirds of it falls in summer, against one-third to less than half in the case of the other three.

The lower slopes of the bajadas are dissected with channels, known as arroyos or washes, in which streams flow only after heavy rain. The bajadas support a typical desert vegetation in which species diversity correlates more closely with soil texture than with rainfall. The truly xerophytic evergreens such as creosote bush and jojoba (*Simmondsia chinensis*) give the desert its characteristic appearance, dominating the bajadas. The plant communities often show cyclic succession, as exemplified by open areas in the desert scrub of Texas, which are first invaded by creosote bush and then by Christmas tree cholla (*Opuntia leptocaulis*), followed by reversion to bare ground, which is then again invaded by creosote bush growing from wind-dispersed seed.

In the warm deserts, succulents are also important on the bajadas. The largest plants in the desert are cacti. The cardón cactus of Baja California and Sonora, Mexico (*Pachycereus pringlei*) can reach 18 m/ 60 ft; the saguaro cactus of Arizona and Sonora (*Carnegiea gigantea*) can reach 10 m/33 ft. Drought-deciduous species such as ocotillo or desert coachwhip (*Fouquieria splendens*) are also important on bajadas, with summer annuals dominant only in playas. Annual species, both winter and summer types, often form communities based on micro-environments. Some grow on bajadas, some at the edge of playas, some in playas; some grow beneath certain canopies but avoid others, while yet others grow only in the open.

The larger arroyos may have scattered trees, able to survive because their root systems can reach water supplies greater than those available on the surrounding bajadas. Only in the Arizona Sonoran desert, where there is significant summer rainfall, do trees occur on the bajadas as well. Common species are smoke tree (*Dalea spinosa*), desert ironwood (*Olneya tesota*), feather bush (*Lysiloma thornberi*), mesquite (*Prosopis* species) and palo verde (*Cercidium* species), all legumes with large seeds. *Acacia greggii* or catclaw also grows along washes, as does Apache plume (*Fallugia paradoxa*). The desert willow, *Chilopsis linearis* (*Bignonia linearis*), is another riparian plant, tolerant of heat, cold, drought and wind. The California fan palm, *Washingtonia filifera*, grows in permanent water soak. Many desert riparian species in North America are winter-deciduous, and growth, leaf expansion and flowering are controlled by day length rather than moisture-dependent.

THE GREAT BASIN

The cold desert of the Great Basin is overwhelmingly dominated by sagebrush, *Artemisia tridentata*, just below the pinyon–juniper woodland of the lower montane regions. Formerly, this shrub steppe contained sagebrush, bitterbrush (*Purshia tridentata*), desert peach (*Prunus andersonii*) and horsebrush (*Tetradymia glabrata*), with perennial, mainly bunch grasses. Intensive grazing has reduced the grasses and palatable shrubs, and introduced weedy annuals have gained as a result; sagebrush, which is unpalatable, has been reduced by fire – it is not a sprouter. Although few succulents are frost-resistant, two species of beavertail cactus (*Opuntia* species) extend throughout the Great Basin

191

desert. At lower elevations, associates of sagebrush are shadscale (*Atriplex confertifolia*), spiny hopsage (*Grayia spinosa*), winterfat (*Eurotia lanata*) and Mormon tea (*Ephedra* species). Some species of *Calochortus* grow in dry conditions: the Mariposa lilies are often found among sagebrush. The species of section Cyclobothra have a more southerly distribution still, in even hotter and drier conditions.

In parts of southern Nevada and eastern Utah, shadscale becomes the dominant, with budsage (*Artemisia spinescens*), greasewood (*Sarcobatus baileyi*) and *Ephedra nevadensis*. The shadscale zone of the Great Basin is significantly warmer and drier than the sagebrush zone, and the ground cover is much less – only 10 per cent. At the Great Basin–Mojave transition zone, big sagebrush and shadscale give way to creosote bush, and here too grow blackbrush (*Coleogyne ramosissima*), wolfberries (*Lycium* species) and hopsage.

THE MOJAVE DESERT

The warm Mojave desert is dominated by an overstorey shrub layer mostly of creosote bush, and an understorey of burro bush or white bur sage, *Ambrosia dumosa*. In fine soils with high percentages of carbonate at the base of bajadas desert holly (*Atriplex hymenelytra*) is dominant, while where there is less carbonate cattle spinach (*A. polycarpa*) dominates. Other shrubs locally abundant on the bajadas with creosote bush are spiny menodora (*Menodora spinescens*), wolfberries, Mormon tea (*Ephedra*), ratany (*Krameria parvifolia*), goldenhead (*Acamptopappus schockleyi*), *Dalea fremontii*, and yellow paper daisy (*Psilostrophe cooperi*). On the middle zones of the bajadas, creosote bush is displaced by blackbrush, Joshua tree (*Yucca brevifolia*), spiny hopsage, matchweed (*Gutierrezia* species) and winterfat. Other species of yucca also occur at the middle elevations of bajadas – *Y. baccata* or banana yucca, and *Y. schidigera*, with desert Spanish bayonet (*Y. whipplei*) along the western edge of the Mojave desert. Many cacti grow on the bajadas, some endemic to the Mojave; among the most conspicuous are the beavertail (*Opuntia basilaris*), *O. echinocarpa* and *O. acanthocarpa* (chollas), *Echinocactus polycephalus* and the barrel cactus *Ferocactus acanthodes*. Along rills, cheesebush (*Hymenoclea salsola*) may dominate, with *Cassia armata*, *Ambrosia eriocentra*, *Brickellia incana*, and catclaw (*Acacia greggii*).

On very calcareous soils with a caliche layer, creosote bush often grows with *Atriplex confertifolia*, with *Krameria*, *Ephedra*, *Lycium*, yuccas, and *Opuntia ramosissima*. The trailing or climbing *Asarina antirrhiniflora* grows on limestone cliffs and rocky slopes. At higher elevations and in the northern zone, where there is no caliche layer, creosote bush grows with *Lycium andersonii* and *Grayia spinosa*, and Joshua tree, in a transition zone to the higher elevations or slightly cooler, moister sites where Joshua tree is dominant. At the lower levels Joshua tree grows with creosote bush and *Ambrosia dumosa*, at higher elevations with *Ephedra nevadensis*, *Ceratoïdes lanata*, *Lycium*, *Salazaria mexicana*, *Thamnosma montana* or *Coleogyne ramosissima*. Opuntias and barrel cacti also grow in these zones. At the upper levels of the Joshua tree zone it yields to pinyon–juniper woodland. Where the Sonoran and Mojave deserts meet, saguaros, junipers, Joshua trees, paloverdes and crucifix-ion thorn (*Canotia holocantha*) grow together.

THE SONORAN DESERT

The Sonoran desert is much more complex, ranging from the very arid Colorado desert in the north with vegetation similar to the Mojave (creosote bush and burro bush dominating) to, at the other extreme, in central Baja California, the Arizona uplands and parts of Sonora, a four-layered community with an overstorey of arborescent cacti such as saguaro, and trees – *Cercidium microphyllum*, *Olneya tesota*, *Celtis pallida* and, in the northern Arizona uplands, *Canotia holocantha*; in southern sites *Bursera microphylla* and large cacti are prominent. The tall shrub–cactus layer below this has creosote bush, *Acacia* species such as *A. greggii*, ocotillo and chollas. A third layer has two species of burro bush (*Ambrosia dumosa* and *A. deltoidea*), brittle bush (*Encelia farinosa*) and a variety of cacti, including barrel, fish hook, cholla, and beaver-tail – there are about five times as many species of cacti in the Sonoran desert as in the Mojave. Further up the bajadas grow *Calliandra erio-phylla*, *Zinnia grandiflora*, *Psilostrophe cooperi*, *Jatropha cardiophylla*, jojoba, *Encelia farinosa* and *Krameria parvifolia*. A fourth layer is com-posed of perennial grasses and winter and summer annuals – approx-imately the same number of each type of annual in the Sonoran, with its two nearly equal peaks of rainfall in winter and summer, whereas in the winter-wet Mojave there are about six times as many winter as summer annuals.

Encelia farinosa frequently inhabits dark volcanic soils, and here too grows *Agave deserti*. On sandy soils perennial grasses grow with shrubs such as *Ephedra trifurca*, *Dalea schottii*, *D. emoryi* and *Eriogonum deserti-cola*. In saline soils *Atriplex polycarpa* often forms nearly pure stands; other plants growing in saline soils include *Isocoma* species, *Lycium fremontii*, and *Atriplex canescens* or *A. lentiformis*. Screw bean mesquite (*Prosopis pubescens*) grows on moderately saline, sandy soils.

In the regions of the Sonoran desert bordering the Gulf of California are some plants with very limited distribution, such as boojum (*Fouquieria columnaris*), and dominants such as *Bursera microphylla* and *B. hindsiana*, *Jatropha cuneata* and *J. cinerea*, growing with the widely distributed tesota, blue paloverde (*Cercidium floridum*), ocotillo, and teddy bear cholla (*Opuntia bigelovii*). Close to the shores low-growing plants form a community, with *Frankenia palmeri*, *Atriplex*, *Lycium*, *Suaeda*, *Encelia* and *Ambrosia*. On bajadas and inland, the *Bursera–Jatropha* community includes a different range of species, among them *Opuntia cholla*, *Lysiloma candida*, boojum, *Ficus palmeri*, *Ambrosia* species, *Viscainoa geniculata*, *Solanum hindsianum*, and the chuparosa or hummingbird bush, *Justicia (Beloperone) californica*.

In the plains of Sonora, ironwood (*Olneya tesota*) is prominent, with paloverdes, *Parkinsonia aculeata*, ocotillo and mesquite (*Prosopis*). Along washes grow *Jatropha cordata*, *Bursera laxiflora*, *Ipomoea arborescens*, *Ceiba acuminata* and other subtrees. Brittlebush is widespread and there are several species of cholla. Among shrubs, *Caesalpinia pumila*, *Calliandra*, and *Mimosa laxiflora* are common, with others more localized, such as *Cordia parvifolia*, *Croton sonorae*, *Jacobinia ovata*, *Tecoma stans* and *Zizyphus obtusifolia*. In the southernmost parts of the Sonoran desert creosote bush is dominant on many sites, and there are several conspicuous cacti. Paloverdes grow with *Jatropha cuneata* and *J. cinerea*, *Bursera microphylla*, *Lycium*, *Encelia farinosa*, *Lysiloma candida* and *Krameria parvifolia*. There are virtually no agaves or yuccas except for *Y. valida*. *Opuntia cholla* is common.

Agaves, however, dominate regions of the Sonora open to the Pacific ocean and thus to the cooling effect of westerly breezes and to moist air and fog. With agaves, including *A. shawii* and *A. deserti*, the other dominant genus is *Ambrosia*. Here too grow jojoba, *Opuntia prolifera*, *Yucca valida* and *Eriogonum fasciculatum*. In the south of this region the valleys contain creosote bush and *Atriplex polycarpa*, and the slopes *Lycium californicum*, ocotillo, *Yucca whipplei*, and *Ephedra*; barrel cacti are prominent but chollas and columnar cacti are uncommon. Southwards boojum and *Pachycormus* become more numerous, associated with ocotillo and elephant trees (*Bursera*). In Baja California the blue hesper palm or grey goddess, *Brahea armata*, grows on rocky outcrops, often of limestone, and in low woodland and steep gullies (the Guadalupe hesper palm, *B. edulis*, grows in similar sites in Guadalupe).

THE CHIHUAHUAN DESERT
The Chihuahuan desert lacks trees, but has a great diversity of species in two shrub layers. Beneath creosote bush, ocotillo, mesquite and

Acacia are tarbush (*Flourensia cernua*), guayule (*Parthenium incanum* – which produces rubber almost as good as that of the rubber tree, *Hevea brasiliensis*), leather plant (*Jatropha* species), *Koeberlinia spinosa*, many cacti, and several distinctive agave-relatives with spinescent basal leaves: century plant (*Agave lechuguilla* and others), sotol (*Dasylirion wheeleri*), Spanish bayonet (*Yucca elata*, the soaptree, most common in desert grasslands, and *Y. baccata*) and *Nolina*. In the Saladin region *Yucca filifera* woodland may develop. *Agave lechuguilla* and *Fouquieria* are common on limestone, with *Leucophyllum frutescens* and others. In Mexico, some areas just above the desert are dominated by large yuccas and sotols, forming yucca woodland. The Chihuahua desert is also rich in cacti, such as *Opuntia phaeacantha* and *Echinocactus horizonthalonius*.

MEXICO'S MESQUITE GRASSLANDS

The mesquite grasslands of Mexico are almost as dry as the Sonoran and Chihuahuan deserts of the northern plateau. The groundcover is typically grama or mosquito grass, *Bouteloua gracilis*. In the transition from desert to grassland, creosote bush, *Yucca elata* and other desert plants are present. At the upper range of precipitation, grassland merges into pine–oak woodland via junipers, oakbrush and agaves. With the grasses grow many very similar compound-leaf shrubs and trees: honey mesquite (*Prosopis juliflora*), screwbean mesquite (*P. pubescens*), ironwood (*Olneya tesota*), paloverde (*Cercidium* species), Jerusalem thorn (*Parkinsonia aculeata*), the frijolito (*Sophora secundiflora*) and others. The succulent sangre de drago, *Jatropha cuneata*, and the related Mexican jumping beans, *Sapium biloculare* and *Sebastiana pavoniana*, grow in the grasslands, as does the trompillo, *Cordia boissieri*. The prickly poppies, *Argemone mexicana*, *A. platyceras* and others, are common throughout the grasslands. Hillsides in the upper desert are the habitat of *Buddleja sessiliflora*. Desert hackberry, *Celtis pallida*, grows in both the desert and the grasslands, and western soapberry, *Sapindus drummondii*, ranges from the valleys of the upper desert to the woodland zone. The related Mexican buckeye, *Ungnadia speciosa*, grows in mountain canyons on limestone hillsides on both sides of the Rio Grande, and *Rhus sempervirens* is found on dry, rocky slopes in northern Mexico. The Texas algerita (*Mahonia trifoliolata*) extends into the dry grasslands from the Texas desert.

As its name implies the seep willow, *Baccharis glutinosa*, grows along watercourses, where it forms dense thickets. Moist soils along streams or in the desert mountains are the natural habitat of the fan palm, *Washingtonia robusta*. *Sabal* and *Erythea* also extend into the mesquite grasslands, though more properly associated with the thorn forest of further south. The curious drooping agave, *A. attenuata*, is a native of the mesquite grasslands.

The thorn forest of Central America and the Caribbean

In tropical Mexico, the Caribbean region and northern Colombia and Venezuela, a type of vegetation known as thorn forest develops in the drier tropical regions. It is in effect a transitional vegetation between the tropical deciduous forest and the arid lands where mesquite and creosote bush are dominant. As the name implies, many species that make up the thorn forest are spiny – in Mexico's thorn forest are acacias such as *A. macracantha*, *A. hindsii* and the less ferocious *A. farnesiana*, *Jacquinia pungens*, *Caesalpinia cacalaco*, *Randia echinocarpa*, and species of *Condalia*. Not all are thorny, however; unarmed trees and shrubs include *Lysiloma thornberi* (*microphylla*), *Guaiacum coulteri*, *Pithecellobium dulce*, *Enterolobium cyclocarpum*, *Cassia oxyphylla*, the cycad *Dioön edule*, and others. The tree morning glory, *Ipomoea arborescens*, is common in the thorn forest.

Between Mexico City and Acapulco in the Rio Balsa valley is a zone of arid tropical scrub akin to the thorn forest of the north. *Beaucarnea inermis*, the zoyate, grows in the mesquite grasslands but is more common in the arid southern regions of Mexico, and here too and in Guatemala grow species of *Furcraea*. One of the organ cacti, *Cephalocereus mezcalaensis*, is prominent in the arid scrub of the south, together with bullhorn acacias (*A. spadicigera* [*cornigera*]) and prickly pears (flat-pad *Opuntia* spp). *Randia echinocarpa* grows both in the thorn forest of the north and in southern Mexico. Similar thorn forest extends to Costa Rica, south-western Ecuador and Peru.

The thorn forest of the drier regions of the Caribbean islands and of northern Colombia and Venezuela is composed of similar trees and shrubs: algorrobo (*Prosopis juliflora*), species of *Acacia* and *Caesalpinia*, and the smaller *Cercidium praecox*, *Guaiacum officinale*, *Randia* species, and *Bursera simaruba*, with species of *Erythrina* and *Tabebuia* in the most favourable sites, and many cacti in the most arid.

The arid zones of South America

In the dry regions of north-eastern Brazil, a type of dry forest known as *caatinga* (from the local Indian word) is the climatic climax. Deciduous in the dry season, it is composed of woody and some thorny species of tree; there are virtually no epiphytes (except for some *Tillandsia* species), few climbers, and only an ephemeral herbaceous layer. There are many cacti, together with species of *Acacia*, *Cassia*, *Erythroxylon*, *Jatropha*, *Mimosa* and *Zizyphus*. *Prosopis* is absent. The high caatinga includes bottle trees or barrigudas and arborescent cacti. The vegetation known as *agreste* is transitional between the caatinga and coastal forest: typical species include *Cassia excelsa*, *Parkinsonia aculeata*, *Erythrina velutina*, *Schinopsis brasiliensis*, *Tabebuia caraiba*, *Copaifera langsdorfii*, the palm *Syagrus coronata* and Spanish moss, *Tillandsia usneoïdes*.

Much of the Chaco of Paraguay and northern Argentina is also semi-arid, with rainfall in summer in the north and in winter in the south; the xerophytic vegetation, known as *monte*, is of two types. Algorrobo forest is formed of species of *Prosopis*: algorrobo (*P. juliflora*) and tamarugo (*P. tamarugo*), palo santo (*Bursera graveolens*) and the pea-flowered *Gourliea decorticans*, with columnar cacti. A typical plant of the margins of cultivated land is the pepper tree, *Schinus molle*. In open places there is an abundance of terrestrial bromeliads such as *Dyckia* species. Quebracho forest is dominated by two species: *Aspidosperma quebracho-blanco* and *Schinopsis quebracho-colorado*, with a shrub layer of cacti, *Capparis*, *Schinus*, *Maytenus*, *Brunfelsia uniflora* and *Cercidium*. The large *Bromelia hieronymi* is widespread. In many ways the most arid regions of the Argentina monte vegetation resemble the desert scrub of northern Mexico, and they share a characteristic species, *Larrea tridentata*. In the east the climate is less dry and may indeed become seasonally flooded: here savannah or *palmares* develop. A variant of quebracho forest occurs on the rising ground near the Andes, characterized by *Schinopsis haenkeana* and *Chorisia insignis*. In Argentina the vegetation known as *espinal* is effectively the same as that of the Chaco, except that *Schinopsis quebracho-colorado* is absent.

The high plateaus of the Andes are semi-arid; because of the dryness of the climate, the snow-line is very high. On the high arid plains of southern Bolivia grow species of stinging *Loasa* and *Caiophora*, with *Verbena peruviana*; in the fields the native *Tropaeolum tuberosum* is cultivated in rows, with potatoes and oxalis, for food. In northern Peru there are small groves of *Bombax* and scattered *Acacia* and *Capparis*. In the north-eastern ridges of Chile *Polylepis incana* is abundant up to

4,000 m/13,200 ft, and *Baccharis tola* grows at similar altitudes; the solanaceous *Iochroma grandiflora* often grows among *Baccharis*. At lower altitudes columnar and barrel cacti are common, and in the lowlands the algorrobillo, *Caesalpinia brevifolia*, grows. Species of bromeliad such as *Puya chilensis* and *P. coerulea* grow in the uplands of northern Chile; others grow further south, such as *P. berteroniana* in central Chile, and *P. alpestris*, high in the southern Andes but always in dry places.

The extreme desert climates of coastal Peru and northern Chile support little more than a fog-watered winter flora, known as the loma. The climate is so hostile that there are wide stretches with no vegetation at all, or at most small communities of shrubs, many of which are summer-deciduous, leafing only with sufficient precipitation, and very deep-rooted. *Proboscidea altheifolia* has a very large storage root enabling it to remain dormant for several years, if necessary. Shrubs of the region include the composites *Tessaria absinthioïdes*, *Baccharis petiolata* and *Pluchea chingoyo*, with *Atriplex chilense*. South of Antofagasta the characteristic plant is *Euphorbia lactifolia*, with *Nicotiana solanifolia*, *Alstroemeria violacea*, *Hippeastrum* species, *Calandrinia* species and various cacti and composites. The lily of the Incas, *Alstroemeria pelegrina*, grows in coastal sand dunes in Peru and Chile.

The lomas or fog deserts of southern Peru and northern Chile are the home of species of *Nolana, Solanum* and *Tigridia, Tropaeolum tricolorum, Loasa bertrandii*, with cacti, *Oxalis gigantea*, and ephemerals recalling the annual flora of the coastal hills of California. Where the coastal desert yields, towards the south, to the Mediterranean climate of central Chile, spiny shrubs such as *Acacia, Adesmia* and *Proustia* grow, together with *Lithraea caustica*.

The Pampas region of South America which has given its name to the pampas grass so familiar in gardens, *Cortaderia selloana*, is a flat, treeless region, bordered on the south and west by *monte*, on the north by the Chaco, and to the north-east by the savannah grasslands of the *parque mesopotámica* of northern Argentina and Uruguay. It is not only the home of pampas grass: here too grow tobacco flowers (*Nicotiana affinis*), petunias, and *Tropaeolum majus* or nasturtium.

In the south of the continent, east of the Andes, lies the region known as Patagonia, where the vegetation is mainly steppe. Grasses are dominant, with species of *Acaena, Calceolaria, Draba, Erigeron, Silene, Sisyrinchium* and, in moist places, *Anagallis, Azorella*, and the tiny fern *Blechnum penna-marina*. In the far south of the region another type of Patagonian steppe vegetation is composed of scrub dominated by *Lepidophyllum cupressiforme*, with shrubby berberis and *Oxalis enneaphylla*.

The dry lands and deserts of southern Africa

About one third of South Africa, mainly in the Cape Province, is very arid, with rainfall of less than 300 mm/12 in. This region is made up of a large inland area, part of the plateau of southern Africa, and a small, low-lying coastal strip extending along the west coast. The inland portion, known as the Karoo, is bounded on the south and west by the coastal mountain ranges, on the east by the foothills of the highlands of eastern Cape Province, and on the north by the Orange River valley. In the upland portions or Upper Karoo, temperature changes are extreme and night frosts occur regularly in winter, while in the low-lying or Great Karoo, frosts are less severe. In the region as a whole the rainfall decreases from east to west, and inland from the coastal mountains. Such rain as there is falls in the eastern parts in summer but in the western portions and the coastal strip in winter. In the Upper Karoo the vegetation is of the type known as arid bush, while in the Great and Little Karoo (the belt of dry country between the Swartberg and the coastal mountains) succulent bush predominates.

THE UPPER KAROO
In the arid bush, small-leaved, low-growing shrubs predominate, such as *Pentzia* species and *Chrysocoma tenuifolia*. There are many annuals, especially annual grasses, which appear after the rains and quickly seed and flower. In areas with saline soils the common Karoo bushes are replaced by small succulents and *Lycium*, with *Atriplex* species. In the very dry north-west of the region *Rhigozum trichotomum* dominates, and the koppies or rocky outcrops have a vegetation of small bushes or succulents, among them the quiver tree, *Aloe dichotoma*. In some of the less elevated country *Gnidia polycephala*, an almost leafless plant, is also found. At the margins of sandy areas grows *Parkinsonia africana*.

In the river valleys, apart from those that are permanently watered, the dwarf *Acacia detinens* is common, with *Euryops multifidus*, *Aloe* and *Pentzia* species, *Zizyphus mucronatus*, *Acacia karroo* and *A. giraffae*. Another type of valley community is characterized by *Boscia* trees. Though still drought-adapted, the river valley communities need more moisture than the arid bush; the dwarf acacia community is transitional between arid bush and bush savannah. Acacia grassland is composed of a ground layer of close-growing grasses, with scattered small trees, especially species of acacia. The commonest, and in the driest part the only, acacia is *A. karroo*, with *A. caffra* common in the south-east Cape. Growing with the acacias are *Zizyphus mucronatus*, *Gymnosporia buxifolia*, species of *Euclea*, *Royena*, *Cussonia* and others, with aloes. Where the acacias cease to be dominant, these are joined by *Commiphora*, *Harpephyllum caffrum*, *Ekebergia* and other plants of the drier forests, with *Aloe marlothii* and tree euphorbias in rocky places, and *Encephalartos* on the steep slopes. Where the grasses are sparse *Haemanthus* and *Sansevieria* become abundant.

The bush savannah is found in open, dry parts of the plateau where winter temperatures are low; it is a grassland with scattered shrubs and miniature trees: *Acacia caffra* and *Protea caffra* in the south, *Acacia rehmanniana* and *Combretum* species, *Euclea lanceolata*, and *Peltophorum africanum* in the north. Another type of bush savannah is found in Cape Province, north of the Orange River. A characteristic shrub here is the wild camphor bush, *Tarchonanthus camphoratus*, sometimes with *Acacia stolonifera* and *A. detinens*, *Rhus ciliata*, *Royena pallens* and *Zizyphus mucronatus*, the buffalo thorn. On very shallow soils *Royena pallens* is found with *Pentzia*, and in the south *Lebeckia macrantha* with aloes. On limestone soils the wild olive, *Olea europaea*, is associated with *Tarchonanthus*, *Acacia stolonifera* and others. The most luxuriant of the bush savannah types is dominated by *Acacia giraffae*, *A. robusta* and *A. karroo*.

THE FROST-FREE ARID LANDS
Succulent scrub is found on the southern coastal belt in frost-free regions of rather low rainfall. It is characterized by an abundance of large succulents, especially species of *Aloe*, *Euphorbia* and *Portulacaria*. Shrubby plants accompanying these arborescent succulents are generally spiny, and small climbers such as *Asparagus* are abundant. In the driest parts *Aloe ferox* and euphorbias such as *E. grandidens* or *E. tetragona* – the first reaching to 20 m/65 ft, the second to 10 m – form an open upper layer; elsewhere the upper layer is dominated by the aloe and *Acacia karroo*.

The African savannah of dry grassland with scattered trees extends in a great arc to the north, east and south of the wet tropical regions of the continent. The seasonal rainfall is sufficient to support perennial grasses such as the deep-rooted elephant grass, which comes into leaf and flower with the rains. On the dry semi-desert grasslands of northern Africa the doum palm, *Hyphaene thebaica*, sends its roots deep into ground water to survive the long dry spells. The Sudanese grass-lands are also the home of another palm, *Phoenix reclinata*; species of palm, grasses and *Acacia* are the most conspicuous plants of the region. Among the trees or tree-like plants of the savannah, the dracaenas are related to and resemble the arborescent yuccas of the North American deserts. The baobab, *Adansonia digitata*, is widely distributed in the arid regions of Africa, growing at low altitude in hot, dry woodland. The impala lily, *Adenium obesum*, grows in hot, dry areas among rocks or in sandy woodlands in the low veld.

Among the plants of the desert regions of the Karoo are highly specialized succulents, such as *Lithops* or stone plants, which mimic pebbles. There are also species of *Crassula*, such as *C. falcata* and *C. coccinea* (*Rochea coccinea*), *Senecio articulatus*, and the 'mesems', species which used to belong to the genus *Mesembryanthemum* and are now separated into *Carpobrotus* and *Lampranthus*, *Delosperma* and *Ruschia*. They vary from small ground-covering plants to succulent shrublets. Species of *Gasteria* and *Haworthia* are also natives of the African contin-ent, specifically of the Karoo desert in the south. There are also many cactus-like succulents belonging to the family Stapeliaceae, chiefly an African group but with a few species in the Indian subcontinent.

The arid lands of Australia

Much of Australia is extremely arid, and part of the interior is true desert. Between the Mediterranean-climate region south-west of Western Australia and the desert lies an area of transitional woodland giving way to arid shrubland, while to the south the Nullarbor Plain lies between the dry woodland along the Great Australian Bight coast and the Great Victoria Desert. The inland regions of the Northern Territories and the northern parts of South Australia are also arid or desert.

Several arid-land plants are widespread throughout the continent. The desert oak, *Allocasuarina decaisneana*, grows on sand dunes through-out central Australia, and the desert poplar, *Codonocarpus cotinifolius*, *Atalaya hemiglauca*, the inland tea tree (*Melaleuca glomerata*) and the black tea tree (*M. bracteata*), the native fuchsia (*Eremophila latrobei*) and the weeping emu bush (*E. longifolia*), the silvery senna (*Cassia arte-misioïdes*) and *C. sturtii*, and the butterfly bush, *Petalostylis cassioïdes*, are all more or less widespread in dry inland regions. The wild orange, *Capparis mitchellii*, extends into the dry parts of Queensland and

Northern Territories and down to South Australia. Acacias such as *A. tetragonophylla*, the gidgee (*A. cambagei*), the red mulga (*A. aneura*), and *A. dictyophleba*, the waxy wattle, grow throughout the dry zones.

THE ARID LANDS OF WESTERN AUSTRALIA

The vegetation of the transitional woodlands of Western Australia results from low and unpredictable rainfall without a definite seasonal pattern, in some years so low that the vegetation remains dormant. Several of the plant groups of the wetter south-west are found here, but not in such numbers: Proteaceae and pea flowers, epacrids, trigger plants (*Stylidium*) and native buttercups (*Hibbertia*). They are joined by grasses, mulla mullas (*Ptilotus*), species of *Solanum*, poverty bushes (*Eremophila*) and composites. The woodlands are dominated by eucalypts, usually in mixture; the most widespread is salmon gum, *E. salmonophloia*, often seen with gimlets (*E. salubris* and *E. campaspe*). There are also varieties of blackbutt (*E. corrugata*, *E. lesouefii*, *E. clelandii* and others), and coloured-flowered species such as the coral gum (*E. torquata*), *E. stricklandii* and *E. woodwardii*. In the northern regions tall thickets of wattles and she-oaks are common, and much of the southern part is covered by mallees.

The understorey in eucalypt woodland is a mixture of shrubs and herbs, especially the poverty bushes, *Eremophila* species, among them *E. oppositifolia* and *E. clarkei* or turpentine bush, both widespread in the arid regions of the south, as is burrobunga, *Olearia pimelioïdes*. The south-eastern woodland understorey is often dominated by *Cratystylis conocephala* or greybush; also common is bluebush, *Kochia sedifolia*, both in the woodlands and on the Nullarbor Plain. Shrubby wattles are numerous, and there is a great variety of herbs – everlastings, vetches (*Swainsona colutoïdes* among them) and Sturt's desert pea, *Clianthus formosus* (*C. dampieri*), which grows on dry sands, its deep roots seeking out the moisture retained deep in the soil after the rare rainstorms.

The native cypresses, *Callitris huegelii* and *C. preissii*, grow in sandy soil, especially near salt lakes, and the desert kurrajong, *Brachychiton gregorii*, appears as scattered individuals. There are inland extensions of many species of the wetter south-western region, both in the sand heath and with the mallee or small tree eucalypts. East of the Goldfields the soil changes from red loam to limestone and, quite abruptly, the vegetation changes to that typical of the Nullarbor Plain. There are no more eucalypts; black oak or belar (*Casuarina cristata*) is common, and at the margins of the plain is a bluebush–myall association (*Kochia sedifolia* and *Acacia sowdenii*). In the depressions or dongas on the

Nullarbor Plain ephemerals – *Clianthus formosus*, white everlasting (*Helipterum floribundum*) and others – grow with shrubs such as *Pittosporum phillyraeoïdes* and miljee (*Acacia oswaldii*), and extend into the arid regions of central Australia.

Inland, between the transitional woodland and the desert, wide plains are covered with mulga and wattle scrub, with here and there spinifex, low hills and salt lakes. Mulga (*Acacia aneura*) is the dominant small tree, replaced in the north-west by other, similar wattles. Curara, *A. tetragonophylla*, and bowgada or wanyu (*A. linophylla*) are also widespread, the former favouring heavy soils along water-courses and creeklines, the latter often growing with mulga, eucalypts and grevilleas. Gidgee, *A. anostema*, grows on sand dunes, with wanyu, rattle bush (*Grevillea stenobotrya*) and limestone wattle (*Acacia sclerosperma*). Another gidgee, *A. pruinocarpa*, is a prominent large tree in inland summer-rainfall areas, growing in a variety of habitats; along water-courses it is found with cottonbush (*Ptilotus obovatus*) and tall saltbush (*Rhagodia eremaea*).

Mulga scrub is open, low woodland with undershrubs, among which the poverty bushes such as *Eremophila maculata* or native fuchsia are the most prominent; cassias are also common, among them silver cassia, *C. artemisioïdes*. Both sandalwood, *Santalum spicatum*, and quandong, *S. acuminatum*, are widespread, the first found in a variety of habitats but generally favouring the moister woodlands. Hakeas are of the corkwood type, *H. lorea* in the north and *H. recurva* in the south. *Hakea preissii*, needlebush, grows in sandhills and around salt lakes, with Gascoyne bluebush (*Maireana polypterigia*), salt bushes, sago bush (*M. pyramidata*), curara and prickly acacia (*A. victoriae*). There are few tall trees, but the ubiquitous river red gum, *Eucalyptus camaldulensis*, grows along rivers, as do the coolabah, *E. microtheca*, *Callistemon phoeniceus*, and the yulbah or bat's-wing coral tree, *Erythrina vespertilio*.

The mulga scrub is brilliantly coloured after rain with the flowers of ephemerals: *Helichrysum* and *Helipterum* with their everlasting daisies, the mulla mullas (*Ptilotus*), Sturt pea, and *Swainsona* species. Unlike the North American and southern African deserts, with their cacti and euphorbias respectively, there are few succulents in the Australian arid lands; an exception is parakeelya, *Calandrinia* species. Where the soil is sandy, the dominant plant is usually no longer mulga but coarse spinifex grasses of the genera *Triodia* and *Plectrachne* with the occasional bara gum (*Eucalyptus gongylocarpa*) or bloodwood (*E. dichromophloia*). Around salt lakes many species of saltbush (*Atriplex*) grow,

203

with bluebushes (*Kochia*), kopi poverty bush (*Eremophila miniata*), bindieye (*Bassia*) and samphires.

THE DRY NORTH-WEST

The north-west Cape Range peninsula of Western Australia is also an arid region, with such rain as there is falling mainly in summer as heavy cyclonic showers, but with light though regular rain in winter, enabling some of the plants of the wetter south-west to survive – *Banksia*, *Thryptomene* and *Hibbertia* among them. The vegetation is mostly shrub steppe, dominated by wattles (ranji bush, *Acacia pyrifolia*, and curara, *A. tetragonophylla*) and eucalypts, among them bloodwood (*E. dichromophloia*), weeping box (*E. patellaris*) and occasional coolabah (*E. microtheca*). The understorey is of spinifex and small shrubs – *Cassia*, *Abutilon*, *Hibiscus*, *Sida* and *Gossypium*, including Sturt's desert rose, *G. sturtianum*. There are species of shrubby morning glories (*Ipomoea*) and of grevilleas.

The north-west coast, with its wide beaches and mangrove mudflats, borders sandy plains and salt marshes. The plains carry scrub, usually dominated by wattles such as bowgada, ranji and curara, as well as *Acacia farnesiana* which also occurs in North America. There are species of *Cassia*, *Solanum*, *Sida*, *Abutilon*, *Corchorus*, and *Scaevola*, of which the most common is currant bush, *S. spinescens*. In the northern region there are areas of low open savannah with cork tree (*Hakea lorea*), whitewood (*Atalaya hemiglauca*) and native walnut (*Owenia reticulata*). Coolabah (*Eucalyptus microtheca*) grows in non-saline depressions and river red gum (*E. camaldulensis*) along water-courses. Another riverbank tree is the white dragon tree, *Sesbania formosa*. There are many grasses and colourful herbs of the genera already described. Saline depressions support the expected saltbushes, bluebush, bindieye and *Rhagodia*. Here on open flats grows one of the ten species of *Crinum* native to Australia, *C. flaccidum*.

The inland range of northern Western Australia experiences a similar rainfall pattern to the Cape Range, and is covered with spinifex steppe and mulga woodland, similar to the mulga scrub already described. Bloodwood and several mallees are widespread, and cork tree is common. There are many species of cassia and other pea-flowered shrubs, a variety of wattles besides mulga, and a number of shrubby mallows. *Corchorus walcottii* is common and there are a number of spiny, woolly *Solanum* species. The iron plant, *Astrotricha hamptonii*, is endemic, and *Livistona alfredi*, the millstream fanpalm, is a tropical relic, echoed by the Australian cabbage palm, *L. marias*, in the arid regions of central

204

Australia. In the gorges grows the cajeput, *Melaleuca leucadendron*, with ferns beside pools and in moist places deep in sheltered rock crevices.

CENTRAL AUSTRALIA

The plants of central Australia can be divided into groups according to their habitat. In sandy soils and dunes grow *Exocarpos sparteus*, *Acacia maitlandii* and *A. ligulata*, with *A. pruinocarpa*, the black gidgee, desert oak (*Allocasuarina decaisneana*), *Atalaya hemiglauca*, and *Acacia coriacea* in deep sands. The redbud mallee, *Eucalyptus pachyphylla*, also favours the deeper sands. *Crotalaria cunninghamii* is a dune plant, and others are the desert fringe myrtle (*Calytrix longiflora*) and desert heath myrtle (*Thryptomene maissonneurii*), *Maiomyrtus flaviflorus*, and the sand-hill native fuchsia (*Eremophila willsii*). The desert broom bush, *Daviesia eremaea*, grows on sand plains with spinifex and desert oak.

Other plants of the dry interior grow in rocky places, hillsides and gorges: the ghost gum (*Eucalyptus papuana*), *Macrozamia macdonnellii*, the curry wattle (*Acacia spondylophylla*) which grows among spinifex, and *A. strongylophylla*, *Grevillea* species such as *G. wickhamii*, species of *Indigofera*, Sturt's desert rose, which also grows on the sand plains, the wild passionfruit (*Capparis spinosa* ssp. *nummularia*), the flannel flower (*Actinotus schwarzii*), *Hibbertia glaberrima*, the rock fuchsia bush (*Eremophila freelingii*) and *Prostanthera striatiflora*. *Pandorea doratoxylon* is a climber inhabiting rocky gorges. The gum coolibah, *Eucalyptus intertexta*, grows as a mallee up on the rocky ranges, but becomes tree-like in salty swamp areas, and the river red gum grows along river courses.

Lastly, there are plants adapted to growing in saline environments: *Halosarcia*, the ruby salt bush (*Enchylaena tomentosa*), old man saltbush (*Atriplex nummularia*) and other saltbushes, needlewood (*Hakea leucoptera*) and tea tree (*Melaleuca glomerata*).

Other plants characteristic of central Australia are beefwood, *Grevillea striata*, which grows along water-courses, and other grevillea species, the white cypress pine (*Callitris glaucophylla*), *Acacia victoriae*, the red mallee (*Eucalyptus socialis*) and others.

INLAND SOUTH-EASTERN AUSTRALIA

Rather less extreme are the dry regions of inland southern and eastern Australia, between the mountains and the deserts. Several types of vegetation develop in these regions: mallee, dry heath, tussock grassland, open shrubland, open eucalypt forest of various types. Mallee takes its name from the multi-stemmed, fire-resistant eucalypts collectively known as mallee; they are often accompanied by shrubby growth of

Acacia, Cassia, Olearia, Eremophila and *Prostanthera*, and may be interspersed with heath or grassland and salt bush; succulent halophytes grow on the salt pans and gypsum flats. In the dry regions of north-western Victoria and South Australia the shrubs of the mallee (*Eucalyptus incrassata, E. gracilis* and others) include *Acacia rigens* and *A. glandulicarpa*, the grey mulga (*A. brachybotrya*), *Olearia pimelioïdes* and *O. magnifica*, *Eremophila oppositifolia*, the silvery emu bush (*E. scoparia*) and *E. longifolia*, the fringe myrtle (*Calytrix tetragona*), *Prostanthera aspalathoïdes*, *Eriostemon pungens*, the desert heath myrtle (*Baeckea crassifolia*), the shrub violet (*Hybanthus floribundus*), *Boronia caerulescens, Melaleuca wilsonii*, and *Pittosporum phillyraeoïdes*.

Callitris verrucosa, a cypress pine, is sometimes dominant on mallee sand ridges. *Acacia ligulata*, the small cooba, the sugarwood (*Myoporum platycarpum*) and *Hakea vittata* grow on sandhills or in cypress pine–belar (*Casuarina cristata*) forests, or with eucalypts. Sugarwood also grows with bullock bush (*Heterodendron oleaefolium*) and emu bush (*Eremophila longifolia*), along creek banks and gullies. The paper sunray, *Helipterum corymbiflorum*, is one of several species making sheets of seasonal colour in the dry lands. Among the halophytes of the south-east are the rosy bluebush (*Kochia eriocladon*) and the bladder saltbush (*Atriplex vesicaria*); *A. semibaccata* and the ruby saltbush, *Enchylaena tomentosa*, are widespread throughout the drier regions of Australia.

In the south-east, eucalyptus forests may be classified according to the type of species that are dominant. In western Victoria and southern New South Wales, north of the Dividing Range, the open, dryish forest is of eucalypts of the box and ironbark types. Red box (*E. polyanthemos*) and long leaved box grow on rocky ridges with thin soils, while grey box (*E. punctata*) and yellow box (*E. melliodora*) grow with yellow gum (*E. leucoxylon*) on loamy flats; red gum (*E. camaldulensis*) follows water-courses, and red ironbark (*E. sideroxylon*) occurs on grassy, gravelly slopes. The understorey is composed of *Acacia* (*A. pycnantha* in Victoria and across into South Australia, *A. hakeoïdes* var. *angustifolia* in the Murray mallee, *A. verniciflua* and *A. armata* throughout), *Grevillea rosmarinifolia, G. alpina* and others, *Hibbertia linearis*, with *Eriostemon verrucosus, Cryptandra tomentosa, Boronia anemonifolia*, and *Baeckea ramosissima*. *Brachyloma daphnoïdes* is often dominant in box woodland on drier rocky hills. There are many species of terrestrial orchids, species of *Thelymitra, Caladenia* and others.

On the drier foothills box–ironbark forests grade into stringybark and peppermint forests, while on wetter sites with good soil stringybark–peppermint grades into taller mountain forest. The sclerophyllus undergrowth is of *Acacia* and other legumes, and heaths. *Eucalyptus radiata*, the common peppermint, forms pure stands or grows with stringybarks and gums (*E. rubida*, *E. mannifera*, *E. ovata*, *E. bicostata*); on poor, stony ridges it is replaced by *E. dives*. Understorey shrubs include *Acacia ulicifolia* (*juniperina*) and *A. stricta*, *Hovea heterophylla*, and the climbers *Hardenbergia violacea* and *Billardiera scandens*. The dry inland regions are the habitat of *Melaleuca wilsonii*.

The tropical *Eucalyptus papuana* or ghost gum extends into the river flats of the drier subtropical regions of the east, usually as solitary specimens, while in the savannah grasslands it often accompanies other eucalypts of the bloodwood, lancewood, messmate or coolabah type. The black box or river box (*E. largiflorens* [*bicolor*]) grows in the dry plains of western New South Wales and adjacent regions, either as pure stands or, in wetter depressions, with the weeping myall (*Acacia pendula*) and *A. salicina*, the coobah. The dry western plains are also the habitat of the poplar-leaved kurrajong, *Brachychiton populneus*, and the white kurrajong or lacebark tree, *B. discolor*. The Queensland bottle tree, *B. rupestris*, stores water in its swollen trunk as a reserve in times of drought. Australia has its own species of baobab, *Adansonia gregorii*, from the arid north-east and the western regions of the Northern Territory.

In the dry inland plains of New South Wales and Queensland, as in Western Australia, the wilga (*Geijera parviflora*) occurs; in the east it grows with leopardwood, *Flindersia maculosa*, or bordering stands of the burrum, *Acacia shirleyi*, with emu bush and other acacias. The plains and slopes of New South Wales are the home of the boonery or river oak, *Heterodendron oleifolium*, where the sweet quandong, *Santalum acuminatum*, also grows.

Cold deserts

Much of Central Asia has an extreme climate, very hot in summer, very cold in winter, and extremely dry, with a short and windy spring. Summer temperatures in China's far western province of Xinjiang, which is fairly typical of the Central Asian interior, can reach 40 °C/ 104 °F, and in winter they commonly fall to − 40 °C/ − 40 °F. Despite this, plants do grow; and in cultivated areas, where man's ingenuity brings water from the mountains that surround Xinjiang, or from the snow-melt rivers, they grow remarkably well and vigorously in the yellow clay which needs only breaking up and irrigating to release its nutrients.

In between the oases, the desert seems barren; but it has its plants, including tamarisks with their vestigial leaves and spectacular pink or white plumes of flower. There are even forests here and there in the desert, with trees such as *Populus diversifolia* and willows.

The steppes of Central Asia are a region of grassland, with some shrubs and expanses of bare soil. Here, where the continental climate merges into that of the cold desert, the climate is fairly extreme, very dry with long, cold winters and hot summers. South-west Asia, between the Himalayas and the Mediterranean, the Black and Caspian seas, is also a semi-arid region with cold winters and hot, dry summers. Some highly specialized salt-tolerant plants, known as halophytes, grow in the salty deserts around the Caspian and Aral seas: tamarisks, species of *Artemisia*, and the salt tree, *Halimodendron halodendron* (*argenteum*). The salt tree is also found in the Elburz Mountains to the north of !ran's Dasht-e-Kavir or salt desert, with *Elaeagnus orientalis*, *Rosa persica* (*Hulthemia persica*, *Rosa berberifolia*), *Pistacia vera*, poppies, the globe thistle (*Echinops sphaerocephalus*), *Eryngium* species and *Geranium tuberosum*.

Many of the bulbs that have become indispensable components of today's temperate gardens originate in these dry regions: tulips and irises such as *I. caucasica* and *Gynandriris sisyrinchium*, alliums and crocuses, together with the foxtail lilies (*Eremurus* species) and fritillaries. As we have seen, several of these genera also occur in the Mediterranean regions into which the dry, cold-winter interior of Asia Minor merges.

9

Plants from humid warm-temperate and subtropical climates

The Mediterranean climate, with its dry, hot summers and cool, wet winters, is one type of warm-temperate or subtropical climate. Another, found in much of eastern central China, southern Japan, eastern coastal Australia and South Africa, and the south-eastern states of the USA, is characterized by rain at all seasons, most falling during the summer, when temperatures are warm to hot. The winters, in such regions, are mild with occasional cold spells. Before the great ice ages, this was the climate of much of today's temperate regions. Forests of primitive temperate genera – *Magnolia*, *Liriodendron*, *Liquidambar*, *Ginkgo* among them – probably then encircled the globe to much higher latitudes in the north than now. The ice age virtually destroyed them in Europe, but in both North America and China/Japan they survived in the southerly regions, and to this day the floras of these two regions have much in common.

The south-eastern Atlantic states of the USA are progressively warmer the further south; the coastal lowlands of Georgia and the Carolinas experience mild winters, during which frost and snow seldom occur, and Florida has an almost tropical climate, modified by the oceanic and Gulf waters, with only rare frosts. The Gulf states are cool and moist in winter, warm and moist in summer; in coastal regions frosts are uncommon, but inland the moderating influence of the warm Gulf waters diminishes fast and occasional very cold spells may occur when polar air penetrates southwards.

Humid warm-temperate and subtropical climates

The climate of southern Brazil, Uruguay and northern Argentina is also warm-temperate, with a moderate annual rainfall, well distributed throughout the year but with a summer or autumn peak; Antarctic polar air brings occasional cold spells in winter when frosts may occur, and the summers are not so hot as those of the south-eastern United States or of south-eastern Australia.

In the eastern interior or high veld of South Africa, which includes much of Transvaal, Orange Free State, and parts of Lesotho, both altitude and exposure to the moist winds coming off the Indian Ocean produce ample and reliable rainfall, as compared with the dry western regions, mainly in the summer. During the dry, sunny winter there is a wide daily variation in temperature and night frosts are frequent, with snow at altitudes over 1,500 m/5,000 ft. The climate of the eastern Cape is intermediate between the Mediterranean climate of the western Cape and the subtropical eastern coastlands; the rainfall is relatively plentiful, at least near the coast, and occurs in both summer and winter. In coastlands further north and in the low veld of Natal and Swaziland the climate comes nearer to being tropical, with warm, humid summers and frost-free winters.

South-eastern Australia comprises the states of Victoria and much of New South Wales. There is no real cold season in the coastal regions: cold spells are brief and not severe. Inland and at altitude, winter temperatures can be lower and moderate frosts may occur. The summers are warm to hot; long hot spells are common, and although rainfall is on average well distributed throughout the year, summer droughts can be severe on occasion. Parts of Queensland also experience a warm-temperate to subtropical climate; the north is tropical, and the interior arid. The climate of coastal North Island, New Zealand is warm-temperate or subtropical, unlike the mainly cool-temperate maritime climate of the greater part of the country.

As we have seen, the climate of north-eastern China is continental, with severe winters; that of south-eastern China is tropical. Between, and to the east of the mountainous region of the south-west, lies eastern central China, a region of variable winters, alternating wet and chilly, with frosts during the colder spells, and of warm, wet summers. Further inland, in the middle to upper Yangtze valley, the Sichuan basin has a climate which is less humid in summer, with milder winters. In south-western and southern China the climate is subtropical. The vegetation of the Himalayan foothills, in northern India, Assam and Burma, is also subtropical to warm-temperate in character. In southern Japan, and especially around the coasts of the Inland Sea, the winters are mild, almost subtropical, and the summers warm and very humid. Similarly, though much of Korea has a continental climate, in the extreme south and on the island of Quelpaert the climate is warm-temperate; oranges thrive there.

At higher altitudes, subtropical and even tropical climates may be characterized by warm wet summers and cool, drier winters, as in the *tierra templada* or intermediate slopes of mountains in Central and South America, where the temperature is rarely excessively hot and never gets very cold, and the rain falls mainly in the summer months. Much of Mexico, south of the north-western desert regions and away from the tropical east coast (where the climate is known locally as *tierra caliente*), has such a climate; at higher altitudes – from about 1,800 m/6,000 ft – frost and snow can occur, giving rise to the term *tierra fria*. In Central America the seasons are marked by rainfall variations rather than temperature differences. The trade winds are the source of the cloud forest of the windward mountain slopes; as they are forced upwards over the mountain ranges their moisture condenses and falls, so there is a pronounced rain shadow on the leeward side of the mountains. Most of the Pacific slopes and many of the valleys in the mountains have a monsoon type of climate with up to six rainless months a year.

The same descriptions of climatic zones, based on temperature rather than precipitation, are used in the other mountainous countries of Central and South America where Spanish is spoken. In the *tierra fria* zones of Columbia and Ecuador the days are warm, the nights cool but frost-free, and rain often falls in the afternoon; the weather is perpetually very like that of spring in the temperate regions.

Warm-temperate and subtropical Asia

The Himalayas can be divided geographically into three zones, of which the lower or foothills, rising from the plains to altitudes of 1,800–3,000 m/6,000–10,000 ft, are covered on the outer slopes with dense subtropical evergreen rain forest below and semi-evergreen temperate rain forest at higher altitudes. The floristic zones grade into each other more or less abruptly and are delineated more or less clearly by altitude. At the lowest levels, from the plains and lower river valleys to the foothills, is the cultivated zone, with a subtropical or warm temperate flora; this is succeeded by the rain forest belt, composed mainly of broad-leaved evergreens. Typically, the lower foothills abound in epiphytic orchids – species of *Dendrobium*, *Vanda*, *Coelogyne*, *Cymbidium* and others.

Nepal, and the much smaller Bhutan and Sikkim to the east, are chiefly mountainous. Above 1,000 m/3,300 ft the chir pine or long-leaved Indian pine, *Pinus roxburghii*, is dominant, especially in the drier west and Kumaon. The chir pine is a subtropical species from the monsoon belt of the outer Himalayas from Bhutan to north-east Pakistan, often as extensive pure forests, always at lower altitudes than *P. wallichiana*. Other trees of the lower temperate forest that grow in the same zone as the chir pine include *Michelia kisopa*, *Lithocarpus spicata*, *Castanopsis tribuloïdes* and *Machilus duthei*.

In the outer foothills of eastern Nepal, subtropical deciduous species have to compete with *Schima wallichii* and *Castanopsis*. Subtropical evergreen trees such as *Eugenia tetragona* and *Ostodes paniculata* grow between 900–1,600 m/3,000–5,500 ft in the areas of highest rainfall. At higher elevations in the lower temperate forest grow *Michelia doltsopa*, Lauraceae, *Bucklandia populnea*, *Castanopsis tribuloïdes* and *C. hystrix*.

In the big river valleys, valley winds blow daily upstream, significantly reducing rainfall on the lower slopes, though the higher elevations are still very wet. Most of the rivers run approximately north–south, so west-facing banks get little sun and are damp and shady at lower altitudes, allowing subtropical evergreen forest to develop, with *Pandanus furcatus*, *Toona ciliata*, the magnolia relative *Talauma hodgsonii*, *Drimycarpus racemosus*, Lauraceae, epiphytic ferns and orchids, and species of *Aeschynanthus*, *Hoya* and *Rhaphidophora*. The subtropical deciduous hill forest is composed of species (some of them evergreen) such as *Anogeissus latifolia*, *Ehretia laevis*, *Terminalia tomentosa*, *Flacourtia indica*, *Lannea grandis*, *Mallotus philippinensis*, *Bauhinia variegata*, *Ougerina dalbergoïdes*, and *Alangium salviifolium*. In the wetter zones deep in the mountains, semi-evergreen hill forest develops, with *Pandanus furcatus* and *Cyathea spinulosa*, *Dalbergia hircina*, *Albizia mollis*, *Toona ciliata* and *Erythrina suberosa*. Other species occurring in the hill forest are *Beilschmiedia roxburghiana*, *Cinnamomum* species, *Clerodendron* species, and climbers *Dregea volubilis* and *Trachelospermum lanceolatum*. Eastern Himalayan species such as *Podocarpus neriifolius*, *Talauma hodgsonii* and *Dysoxylum procerum* are near their western limits here.

Some of the subtropical species are still found in the *Schima–Castanopsis* zone: *Mallotus philippinensis*, simul (*Bombax malabaricum*), *Terminalia chebula* and *Syzygium cumini* (*Eugenia jambolana*). They are joined by the champa (*Michelia champaca*), *Anthocephalus cadamba*, *Dysoxylum procerum* and *Heteropanax fragrans*, with at higher levels

213

Macaranga pustulata, Rhus succedanea, Ilex doniana, Engelhardtia spicata and, in wet gullies, tree ferns and *Pandanus furcatus*. Shrubs that appear where the forest has been lopped and opened are *Camellia kissi, Viburnum erubescens* and *V. coriaceum, Eurya acuminata, Myrsine semiserrata, Osbeckia stellata, Pyrus pashia, Phyllanthes* species and the widespread *Rhododendron arboreum*. Other plants of the warm-temperate to subtropical zone are *Mahonia napaulensis* and *M. acanthifolia, Jasminum dispermum*, and the yellow flax, *Reinwardtia indica*.

In Assam and Burma, that wedge between India and China, two mountain systems meet: the east–west oriented Himalayas, and the mountain ranges that run south from Yunnan through Burma to the ocean. Assam is the valley of the Brahmaputra river: to its north, the Himalayan foothills; to its south, the Naga, Khasi and Garo hills and Manipur. Burma is dominated above all by the Irrawaddy. The lower jungle has three seasons: the rains, in summer and autumn; the hot season, spring; and the cold season, which is hardly winter as we understand it in temperate regions, characterized by clammy mists, not frost. On the jungle floor flowers are few, for little light penetrates; mosses and ferns dominate, with species of *Arisaema*, and the flowers belong mainly to epiphytic orchids high in the trees where the light reaches them.

In the Irrawaddy hill jungle of Burma's foothills, the woody flora includes *Acer niveum, Gmelina arborea, Magnolia pterocarpa, Quercus thomsonii* and *Q. semiserrata*, the ironwood (*Mesua ferrea*), *Dipterocarpus alatus, Eriobotrya wardii, Schefflera wardii, Schima khasiana*, and species of *Sterculia, Ficus, Elaeocarpus, Nephelium, Engelhardtia, Bauhinia* and *Michelia*, growing at altitudes of 600–900 m/2,000–3,000 ft with epiphytic *Fagraea*, the gingers *Hedychium coccineum* and *Costus speciosus, Impatiens, Begonia, Lysionotus* and *Aeschynanthus*. Several species of *Hedychium* are native to the warm temperate or subtropical regions of the Himalaya: *H. coccineum* occurs not only in the central and eastern Himalayas but also north-east India and Bangladesh, while *H. gardnerianum* is found in Nepal, Sikkim and east to the Khasia Hills of Assam, *H. greenei* in Bhutan, Assam, Khasia and the Lushai Hills, in marshy ground at the forest margins, and the subtropical *H. coronarium* in north India and Burma and *H. ellipticum* from Garhwal eastwards to Thailand.

The commonest genus of trees of the warm temperate belt is *Wightia; W. gigantea* starts life as an epiphyte, but ends by strangling the life out of its host. At around 1,200–1,500 m/4,000–5000 ft other woody plants make an appearance: *Altingia excelsa, Terminalia myriocarpa,*

Bucklandia populnea, Litsea, Cinnamomum species, *Actinodaphne*, and *Rhododendron dendricola*. This is one of the first species of rhododendron, many of them epiphytic, to be found in the forest of evergreen oaks, *Cinnamomum* and *Michelia*.

SOUTH-WESTERN CHINA

Although the Chinese and Himalayan floras each have their own character, and there are climatic differences between the eastern Himalayas and western China, the vegetation of western China is essentially cool-temperate except in the extreme south-west. At low altitudes in some of these regions, however, the flora is more characteristic of warm-temperate or subtropical climates. The zone of cultivation, up to about 600 m/2,000 ft, is typically warm-temperate, with bamboos, *Melia azedarach, Lagerstroemia indica, Ficus infectoria* and a variety of other trailing, climbing and arboreal *Ficus, Ardisia crispa, Gardenia florida, Rosa laevigata, Machilus hanmu, Ligustrum lucidum, Paulownia duclouxii, Sloanea chinensis* and an undergrowth of begonias, gesneriads, arisaemas, and ferns such as *Gleichenia linearis*.

The low, hot valleys of the Salween which lead up to the Yunnan plateau are characterized by a subtropical, Indo-Malayan forest flora, with trees such as *Bombax* species, *Engelhardtia, Clerodendron, Tripterigium, Ficus cunia* and *Caesalpinia nepalensis*, with on the lower slopes *Osbeckia, Luculia, Buddleja, Schima* and large-leaved woody araliads. Here too grows *Primula malacoïdes*, familiar to gardeners in colder climes as a glasshouse plant. *Magnolia delavayi* grows in southern Yunnan, on sandstone and limestone formations among *Lithocarpus* scrub. The related *Manglietia forrestii* is a native of western and southern Yunnan, *M. hookeri* extends into Upper Burma, and *M. insignis* has a wide range from the eastern Himalayas to central China and north Vietnam. Also from subtropical Yunnan are *Gordonia chrysandra*, which grows in moist, open sites among thickets and scrub or on rocky slopes, and *G. axillaris*, a tree of groves and open forests.

From Yichang (Ichang) on the Yangtze eastwards, the high mountains give way to plains and low hills, and the flora is essentially warm-temperate or even subtropical, with a sprinkling of cool-temperate plants. Plants of of the Yichang region include the tung oil tree (*Aleurites fordii*), *Toddalia asiatica*, the bead tree of northern India and central China (*Melia azedarach*), the Chinese tallow tree (*Sapium sebiferum*), *Platycarya strobilacea, Firmiana simplex (Sterculia platanifolia), Dalbergia hupeana, Sapindus mukorosii, Xylosma racemosum*. These last two are native not only to central China, but also to Taiwan (Formosa)

215

and Japan, as is *Neolitsea sericea*. The related *Persea ichangensis*, by contrast, is found only in western Hubei.

SOUTHERN CHINA, HAINAN AND HONG KONG

Oranges, lemons and other citrus have been cultivated for so long that their native habitat is often unknown, though it is accepted that they originate in the subtropical regions of south-east Asia. Neither *Citrus sinensis*, the orange, nor *C. limon*, the lemon, is known except in cultivation; the mandarin or tangerine, *C. reticulata*, and the pomelo, *C. grandis*, are also widely cultivated, as Robert Fortune noted when travelling in Guangdong (Canton). The most generally cultivated fruits, he observed, in addition to oranges and pomeloes, were mango, guava, wangpee (*Cookia punctata*), litchi, jujube (*Zizyphus jujuba*) and longan (*Dimocarpus [Euphoria] longana*); further north, in the Ningbo region, where the tea plantations flourished, kumquat (*Fortunella margarita*) grew in groves. Several species are grown for their fragrant flowers, which are dried and added to tea; not just the familiar jasmine, but also *Osmanthus fragrans*, *Michelia figo (fuscata)*, *Chloranthus inconspicuus*, the orange jessamine (*Murraya paniculata [exotica]*) and the mock lime, *Aglaia odorata*. Tea itself is made from the leaves of *Camellia sinensis*, in its two main variants, *C. sinensis* var. *sinensis* and *C. sinensis* var. *assamica*, the first originating in the forests, open scrub and dry hillsides of Yunnan and the second so long cultivated that its original habitat is uncertain.

Bamboos are used for a great variety of purposes. Some species are edible, others are used for household utensils, for making musical instruments, furniture or paper; sections of the larger canes are used as waterwheel buckets; entire canes are used for scaffolding and construction (the frame, walls, floor and roof of buildings can all be made of bamboo); some species are used for hedging or barriers. In the more southerly regions of China, from the south face of the Nan Ling mountains to Hainan, bamboos mainly have a clumped habit, as in *Sinocalamus* and *Bambusa*, though at altitude in the mountains bamboos with the stoloniferous habit typical of more northerly species are encountered.

The centre of distribution of the genus *Camellia*, to which the tea plant belongs, is southern and south-western China, in the regions straddling the Tropic of Cancer. In the province of Guangxi (Kwangsi) which borders Vietnam, there are a score or so of species with yellow flowers after the style of *C. chrysantha*. They are one of the main understorey elements in the evergreen broad-leaf forests at the northern edge of the tropical zone, where tropical forest yields to sub-tropical. Rainfall in this region is abundant, the rains falling from May to September, and the atmospheric humidity is high all year; the annual average temperature is 21.5°C/71°F, and frost is almost unknown. *Camellia oleifera* grows in woods and thickets in the southern provinces of China and the island of Hainan, while the white-flowered *C. grantham-iana* is native to the cooler wooded ravines of a mountain in Hong Kong's New Territories.

Hong Kong is mountainous, with rugged, well-watered ravines; like the adjacent mainland, it has a markedly seasonal rainfall, with hot, humid summers, and sunny winters that can be surprisingly cold (frost is rare, but not unknown). Many of the species that grow there also occur in the southern mainland provinces and some also on Hainan. Among the trees of the region which have some economic use are the wood oil tree, *Aleurites montana*, the incense tree (*Aquilaria sinense*) from which joss sticks are made, and the cassia bark (*Cinnamomum cassia*). Hong Kong has its own magnolia, *M. championii*, and mang-lietia, *M. fordiana*, growing in sheltered valleys, where the rare *Rhodoleia championii* was also discovered. On damp rocks in the ravines *Chirita sinensis* grows.

JAPAN AND TAIWAN

The coastal regions of southern Honshu, Shikoku and the Pacific side of Kyushu, together with the Ryukyus and lowland Formosa, have a warm-temperate or subtropical climate, influenced by the warm Japan current that flows along the Pacific side of the archipelago. However, much of the flora is temperate rather than subtropical, albeit with a considerable broad-leaved evergreen element. The closest cor-respondence in mainland eastern Asia to Japan's warm-temperate south is found in the lowlands and hills of South Korea to the Yangtze valley and the mountains of western China, and the highlands of Burma and the Himalaya – the rhododendron heartland, rather than the subtropics, and therefore belonging in another chapter. A number of the plants of southern Japan also extend into warm-temperate China and For-mosa, *Cinnamomum camphora*, *Illicium religiosum*, *Viburnum odoratis-simum*, *Loropetalum chinense*, *Ficus pumila* and the shell ginger, *Alpinia zerumbet*, among them. Subtropical elements, occurring not only in southern China but also in the Malay Peninsula or India, include *Caesal-pinia nuga*, the soap tree (*Sapindus mukorossii*), *Eurya japonica*, the Chinese banyan (*Ficus microcarpa*), *Schefflera octophylla*, and *Hoya carnosa*. The widely cultivated *Gardenia jasminoïdes* is a native of the forest's edge in Kyushu. The Chinese fan palm, *Livistona chinensis*, grows in sub-tropical woodland not only in southern China but also in Japan, the Ryukyus, and the islands to the south of Taiwan.

Undisturbed rain forest in southern Japan is dominated by tall ever-green oaks, with members of the laurel and magnolia families, and a dense shrubby undergrowth, with lianas, epiphytic ferns, and some orchids. In the predominance of oaks and the presence of Magnoliaceae, Japanese warm-temperate rain forest resembles that of the south-eastern United States.

The south-eastern United States

The coastal plain of the Atlantic and Gulf states has a much more diverse vegetation than the rest of the eastern United States, where the climax vegetation is broad-leaved deciduous forest. In the coastal plain are grasslands and savannahs, sandhills and dunes, dry pinelands, shrublands, sclerophyllous woodlands and rich mesophytic forest, pocosins, bogs, swamps and oxbows, often jostling one another within very small distances and differences in altitude. Much of this variation derives from the dramatic diversity of physical and chemical character-istics of soils in the region. Fast-draining sands with very low water retention and fertility are common, while alluvial soils, also generally infertile, vary greatly in texture and drainage. Soils with a shallow water table are common, while clay subsoils border the alluvial plain of the Mississippi River. Highly weathered soils occur widely, varying in fertility according to the parent material. Fire has also had a signifi-cant influence on the vegetation of the region.

The climate is humid warm-temperate to subtropical, with rainfall distributed evenly throughout the year. Rainfall tends to decrease away from the coast; it is highest in the south-eastern section where the pat-tern is more tropical than subtropical, with dry winters and wet sum-mers. The length of the frost-free season increases toward the coast and to the south. Hurricanes and severe convectional storms bring high winds to the region, causing physical damage to vegetation and a very high incidence of lightning, giving rise to frequent fires.

The longleaf pine, *P. palustris*, grows in the coastal plain from south-east Virginia to central Florida and across to Texas, mainly at sea level in sandy or gravelly soils. In the poorest sands longleaf pine grows with *Quercus laevis* dominating the understorey tree layer, and occasional specimens of black gum or tupelo (*Nyssa sylvatica*) and persimmon

(*Diospyros virginiana*). Staggerbush (*Lyonia mariana*) and dwarf huckle-berry (*Gaylussacia dumosa*) form scattered clumps. Where there is clay subsoil, blackjack oak (*Quercus marilandica*), sandhill post oak (*Q. margaretta*) and bluejack (*Q. incana*) are co-dominants, with other sub-canopy trees such as black gum, persimmon, and sweet gum (*Liquid-ambar styraciflua*). Where the clay comes to the surface boggy habitats result, with sweet pepperbush, *Clethra alnifolia*, *Cyrilla racemiflora*, and *Lyonia lucida*.

The slash pine, *Pinus elliottii*, is another important constituent of the lower coastal plain pine forests, from South Carolina to south Florida and north Louisiana, sharing dominance with longleaf pine on sandy soils. On finer-textured soils bluejack oak is characteristic, with live oak (*Quercus virginiana*) common in the overstorey. In south-central Florida the southern Florida slash pine, *P. elliottii* var. *densa*, is the dominant canopy tree. Further west, in eastern Texas, longleaf pine shares dominance with shortleaf pine, *P. echinata* (the most widespread of all the southern pines, which also occupies large areas of the coastal plain as well as the Piedmont plateau of the Carolinas, and the moun-tains) and loblolly pine, *P. taeda*, which takes its name from the moist hollows or loblollies where it often grows; here the dominant oaks are *Quercus incana* and post oak (*Q. stellata*). Common understorey trees are yaupon (*Ilex vomitoria*) and *Cornus florida*.

The sand pine scrub of Florida is dominated by sand pine, *Pinus clausa*, as the overstorey, with a lower shrub layer of saw palmetto (*Serenoa repens*) and scrub palmetto (*Sabal etonia*) and an upper shrub layer dominated by scrub live oaks (*Quercus geminata*, *Q. myrtifolia* and *Q. virginiana*), *Carya floridana*, and *Lyonia ferruginea*. Another type of sand pine scrub has a more broken canopy, and the understorey is com-posed of sandhill rosemary (*Ceratiola ericoïdes*) and *Quercus inopina*. These are sclerophyllous communities, possibly as an adaptation to the very low level of nutrients in the sandy soil. The shrubs and palms reproduce from underground rhizomes and burls rather than from seeds, following fire.

Where there is more moisture available, dry sandhill communities grade into pine-dominated flatwoods and savannahs. Savannahs have an open canopy and grass-dominated understorey; in the flatwoods the canopy is denser and the understorey is composed of shrubs and sub-canopy trees. They are very varied in composition, with *Pinus elliottii* often co-dominant in the canopy, and scrub oaks replaced by *Ilex glabra* and *Myrica cerifera*. In Texas, pine–oak forest roughly corresponds to the Florida flatwoods: longleaf or shortleaf pines dominate the canopy, with some loblolly pines, various oaks, and sweet gum. Among the understorey species are *Callicarpa americana*, *Ilex vomitoria* and *Cornus florida*. The Carolina allspice, *Calycanthus floridus*, grows in mixed pine/hardwood forest.

The savannah of the coastal plain is transitional between the dry pine communities and the wetlands. In the drier parts, the tree canopy is composed only of longleaf pine; the herb layer includes many legumes, such as *Cassia fasciculata*, *Lespedeza capitata*, *Clitoria mariana*, and *Amorpha herbacea*, with woody species such as *Myrica cerifera* and *Smilax glauca*. In the moister savannahs there is a great diversity of non-woody plants, including insectivorous plants such as *Pinguicula*, *Sarracenia* and *Drosera* species and the Venus flytrap, *Dionaea muscipula*. Wet savannahs are found in depressions, and here grow bog species such as *Cyrilla racemiflora*, *Illicium floridanum* and highbush blueberry, *Vaccinium corymbosum*. In place of longleaf pine there are scattered specimens of pond pine (*Pinus serotina*), *Taxodium ascendens*, and tupelo, as well as *Magnolia virginiana*.

The climax vegetation for most of northern Florida, southern Georgia, the Carolinas and Virginia is mixed deciduous and evergreen forest, where the relative importance of evergreens varies according to the availability of nutrients and water; on the driest and most sterile soils more than 80 per cent of the trees are evergreen, falling to only 10 to 30 per cent on the most fertile soils. Among the evergreens are *Magnolia grandiflora* and occasional red bay (*Persea borbonia*), and the semi-evergreen laurel oak (*Quercus laurifolia*); deciduous species include beech (*Fagus grandifolia*), sweet gum, tulip tree, limes (*Tilia* species), and hickories (*Carya* species). This is sometimes called beech–magnolia forest, although beech is absent from parts of Georgia and Florida and *Magnolia grandiflora* is not common in the Carolinas and Virginia. Along the lower Mississippi and by river swamps and ponds the magnolia grows with other moisture-lovers such as the water oak (*Quercus nigra*), sweet gum and *Nyssa sylvatica*. *Magnolia fraseri* grows in mixed woodlands from the southern Appalachians to north-western Florida and Texas. A deciduous tree not seen in the wild since the eighteenth century is *Franklinia alatamaha*, originally discovered along the Alatamaha river near the Georgia coast, where it was growing with the fever tree, *Pinckneya bracteata* (*P. pubens*).

In wet sites, river swamp forest is dominated by bald cypress (*Taxodium distichum*) on silty soils, with *T. ascendens* growing over sand; they often grow with species of tupelo. On soils that are not regularly inundated, laurel oak, red maple, American elm (*Ulmus americana*) and sweet gum may become established on drier hummocks. The under-storey is composed of small trees such as water elm (*Planera aquatica*), pop ash (*Fraxinus caroliniana*) and pumpkin ash (*F. profunda*), with sweet bay (*Magnolia virginiana*), red bay, and *Cyrilla racemiflora* on peaty soils. Around bases of trees grow swamp leucothoë (*L. racemosa*), fetterbush (*Lyonia lucida*), sweet pepperbush and several *Ilex* species. Another type of swamp forest is distinguished by a spell in late summer when the soil becomes quite dry, although for about half the year it is saturated. The most typical trees here are overcup oak (*Quercus lyrata*) and water hickory (*Carya aquatica*), with an understorey of winterberry (*Ilex verticillata*), water locust (*Gleditsia aquatica*), *Itea virginica*, *Styrax americana* and stiff dogwood (*Cornus foemina*).

Where the soils are saturated only during winter and spring, *Quercus laurifolia* is a common dominant, with willow oak (*Q. phellos*), *Fraxinus pennsylvanica*, American elm and sweet gum. Typical of the smaller trees and shrubs of this zone are possum haw (*Ilex decidua*), *Crataegus* species, *Viburnum obovatum*, ironwood (*Carpinus caroliniana*) and several species of rhododendron, with dwarf palm (*Sabal minor*) forming dense thickets, and a variety of climbers such as poison ivy (*Rhus radicans*), *Smilax* species, supplejack (*Berchemia scandens*), *Decumaria barbara* (often growing into sweet gum or tulip tree), *Lonicera sempervirens* and cross vine (*Bignonia capreolata*). The least damp locations in the wetlands, at the highest points of the flood-plain, are inundated for only a short time each year, and not at all during the growing season. Here grow basket oak (*Quercus michauxii*) and cherry bark oak (*Q. falcata* var. *pagodaefolia*), with occasional water oak (*Q. nigra*) and *Q. virginiana* on local high ground, and several hickory species. Spruce pine (*Pinus glabra*) grows in the wetter areas, and loblolly pine in the drier places. The understorey includes American holly (*Ilex opaca*), pawpaw (*Asimina triloba*) and spicebush (*Lindera benzoin*). In Florida and the Gulf states these higher locations also feature *Sabal palmetto* and *Serenoa repens*.

In the lakes, submerged aquatics include *Potamogeton*, with floating-leaved aquatics including *Nelumbo* and *Nymphaea*, and floating aquatics such as *Eichornia crassipes* forming a mat on the water surface. Along the shore, cattail (*Typha latifolia*) grows with button bush (*Cephalanthus occidentalis*) and emergent *Taxodium ascendens*, water elm, and *Persea* species.

Non-alluvial wetlands may take the form of shallow marshes, dominated by grass, sedge and rush species; the Florida Everglades are the best-known and most extensive example of this type of vegetation, which is common across the lower coastal plain. Another type of

221

non-alluvial wetland is the pocosin, shrub-dominated peatlands with a dense cover of evergreen and deciduous shrubs and scattered emergent trees. One type is characterized by *Pinus serotina*, *Cyrilla racemiflora* and *Zenobia pulverulenta*; these grow on the poorest and deepest peats. On slightly elevated sites the pine grows with loblolly bay (*Gordonia lasianthus*) and *Lyonia lucida*. Other species growing in the pocosins are *Ilex glabra*, *Chamaedaphne calyculata*, *Kalmia angustifolia* and *Woodwardia virginica*. Up to half the ground cover is provided by *Sphagnum* species which over time decompose into peat.

Atlantic white cedar (*Chamaecyparis thyoïdes*) ranges from New England south to northern Florida and Alabama. It grows in a variety of wetland habitats, with sphagnum and *Woodwardia virginica*, *Lyonia lucida*, *Ilex coriacea*, *I. glabra* and *Clethra alnifolia*. Older stands of Atlantic white cedar become invaded by bay forest species such as *Ilex cassine*, red bay (*Persea borbonia*), loblolly bay, and the wide-ranging and adaptable sweet bay (*Magnolia virginiana*); of these species with 'bay' as their common name, only red bay is in the bay laurel family. Many of the shrubby species already mentioned as growing in various wetland communities are associated with bay forest, together with cinnamon fern (*Osmunda cinnamomea*), *Vaccinium atrococcum*, and climbers including *Smilax* species, *Parthenocissus quinquefolia*, the Virginia creeper, and Confederate jasmine or evening trumpet flower (*Gelsemium sempervirens*), which is also native from Mexico to Guatemala. The red morning glory, *Quamoclit* (*Ipomoea*) *coccinea*, grows in thickets and waste places, often along the roadside.

Compared with bay forest, cypress domes or wet hammocks form in poorly drained depressions that are inundated for longer periods each year. *Taxodium ascendens* is the dominant canopy, and the understorey is composed of many of the same evergreen shrubs as in the pocosins. Epiphytes are common, among them Spanish moss (*Tillandsia usneoïdes*), the resurrection fern (*Polypodium polypodioïdes*) and – in central and southern Florida – other *Tillandsia* species.

Some of the species of Asia which echo those of North America are described with the plants of the rhododendron heartland (Chapter 10). Thus *Magnolia rostrata* of the lower slopes in Burma and Assam has its counterpart in *M. tripetala*, which grows in wetter sites in the rich forests of the Allegheny region and the Appalachian and Ozark mountains southwards to Florida, Arkansas and Missouri, where it is accompanied by *Liquidambar styraciflua*, red maple, *Liriodendron tulipifera* and *Betula lenta*. *Magnolia macrophylla*, another of the umbrella-leaved types, grows in sheltered woodland in ravines and river valleys, again with sweet gum and tulip tree, and the southern red oak (*Quercus texana*); its ssp. *ashei* has a southerly distribution in the north-western Florida lowlands, growing with hop hornbeam (*Ostrya virginiana*) and red buckeye (*Aesculus pavia*). The sassafras of the eastern United States, *S. albidum*, has a frost-tender counterpart in the Chinese *S. tzumu*. The North American tulip tree is matched by the widely distributed *Liriodendron chinense* of western, central and eastern China's moist, dense woodlands.

Mexico and the Central American *tierra templada*

Central America is partly subtropical, partly tropical, with uplands in which, at the higher elevations, a temperate flora also grows. Subtropical and upland Mexico and Central America, which are our concern in this section, are often struck by tropical storms and hurricanes, whereas the tropical parts lie south of the normal hurricane paths. Because of the variation in altitude, with mountains and volcanoes, there is great diversity and species-richness in the vegetation of the region. Unlike that of North America, however, it has not been comprehensively surveyed.

The lower mountain slopes of northern Central America support subtropical moist forest, with a mix of temperate trees such as *Alnus*, *Carpinus*, *Cornus*, *Nyssa*, *Ostrya*, *Platanus* and *Ulmus*, and tropical trees such as *Brunellia*, *Beilschmiedia* and *Phoebe*, and *Alchornea*. The low-mountain pine forests of Belize, Guatemala, Honduras and Nicaragua are usually composed of fairly pure stands of *Pinus oocarpa*, sometimes with *P. caribaea*.

Leaving the coastal plain of Mexico and climbing, the vegetation changes from desert-type plants. Oaks appear, with *Arbutus xalapensis* in the drier oak forest and *Oreopanax peltatus* in the wetter parts. At higher elevations still, pines appear, first in the form of pinyon–juniper woodland on the more arid foothills, and at higher elevations above pure oak woodland and mixed pine–oak forest, dense pine forest of different species sometimes forming pure stands. The pine–oak forest zone alone occupies over a quarter of Mexico's total land surface. On the higher slopes of south central Mexico, western Guatemala, Costa Rica and Panama, subtropical montane vegetation develops, with subtropical subalpine vegetation only on the high peaks of Mexico, western Guatemala, and Costa Rica. The low-latitude centre of diversity for conifers is Guatemala's highlands, with *Abies*, *Cupressus*,

223

Juniperus, several species of *Pinus*, *Podocarpus*, *Taxodium* and *Taxus*. The high-mountain humid forests of northern Central America are fairly open, generally dominated by *Juniperus standleyi*, *Pinus ayacahuite* or *P. rudis*.

The typical trees of upland central and southern Mexico are evergreen oaks and long-needled pines. There are many species of both – over a hundred oaks, and many pines, more being discovered almost yearly; it seems that the genus *Pinus* is still evolving quite fast in Mexico. *Pinus cembroïdes*, the Mexican pinyon, is widespread at low altitudes in the mountains bordering the arid plateau of northern Mexico, often associated with junipers such as *J. deppeana* and sometimes with scrub oak. Among the best known pines are *Pinus montezumae* (a major constituent of the pine forests of central Mexico and south to Guatemala, sometimes growing with *Cupressus lindleyi*), and its more frost-tender subspecies *lindleyi* and *rudis* and hardier *hartwegii*. *Pinus ayacahuite* grows at high elevations in central and south Mexico to Guatemala, El Salvador and west Honduras (it is replaced by *P. strobiformis* in the north) and *P. patula*, the Mexican weeping pine, is restricted to eastern Mexico, in the subtropical parts of the country, where it grows at altitude in relatively cool, humid regions. The oaks include *Quercus laurina*, *Q. rugosa* and *Q. mexicana*, *Q. acatenangensis* and *Q. brachystachys*, *Q. polymorpha* and *Q. rysophylla*. The most abundant oak in the pine–oak forest of northern Mexico is *Q. emoryi*, the black oak. *Fuchsia microphylla* grows with oaks and *Pinus montezumae* as an undershrub. *Bouvardia terniflora* or trompetilla grows on rocky slopes in the oak and pine forest, while *B. multiflora* grows at lower altitudes in forested canyons. The sacred fir, *Abies religiosa*, which is the most southerly of firs, is almost more characteristic of the higher-altitude forest; it also occurs in the high mountains of northern Guatemala with *Cupressus lusitanica*, *Pinus pseudostrobus* and *Podocarpus oleifolius*. *Abies vejari* forms dense forest on the steep, rocky slopes of mountain summits, on poor but moist soils; also *Juniperus ashei* and *Taxus globosa*.

Buddleja cordata has an extensive range in the pine–oak forests of the uplands, while *B. crotonoïdes* extends from south Baja California to Costa Rica, occurring in rocky areas and pine forest, as in the Chiapas highlands of central Mexico, where it grows with the Mexican madrona, *Arbutus xalapensis*, pines and *Crataegus pubescens*, the tejocote, a plant of clearings in the forest. *Abelia floribunda* is a native of dry ledges in the Cordilleras of Mexico, at between 2,500–3,000 m/8,000–10,000 ft.

Several garden flowers originate from the pine–oak forest zone of Mexico, among them *Zinnia elegans*, *Tagetes*, *Cosmos* and dahlias, derived from *D. rosea* and *D. coccinea* of the lower pine forest in Chihuahua. *Lobelia laxiflora* ranges widely throughout Mexico and Guatemala, usually in rocky places, the favoured habitats too of *Achimenes longiflora*. The salvias of Mexico are many and varied; some grow in the *Abies* forest, with species of *Ribes* and the shrubby *Dahlia tenuicaulis*, which also grows in Colombia just below the *paramo* zone (see Chapter 12, Plants of the Tropics). The Mexican species range from *Salvia blepharophylla*, *S. buchananii*, *S. cacaliifolia* and *S. coccinea*, which grows among oaks and pines in the eastern coastal states, *S. elegans*, a western species from similar habitats, and tuberous-rooted *S. patens*, to the shrubby *S. involucrata*, *S. gesneriiflora* of the west-central pine–oak forest and *S. fulgens*, *S. greggii* from rocky hillsides at the desert margins, and *S. microphylla*. The bedding salvia, *S. splendens*, is also a pine–oak forest species. The Mexican star, *Milla biflora*, is a bulbous plant from open woods and grassy slopes in the pine–oak zone, and from the lower pine forest zone comes the flor de tigre, *Tigridia pavonia*, flowering during the rainy season. Another familiar bulbous plant, the very widespread *Zephyranthes grandiflora*, is also a native of Mexico.

The agave-like *Beschorneria* species – with the exception of *B. calcicola*, which grows in dry, stony places in the sclerophyllous scrub – are plants of the montane woodlands or scrub of central and southern Mexico, where they grow in deep, organic soils. *Beschorneria tubiflora* grows in oak, pine and *Liquidambar* woodland, and *B. rigida* grows in mountain scrub with oak and pine, *Garrya*, *Ceanothus*, *Ternstroemia* and agaves. The most widely cultivated in subtropical and Mediterranean climates is *B. yuccoïdes*, which grows in woodlands under a canopy of *Liquidambar* and *Alnus*.

In the cloud forest of conifers and evergreen oaks at middle altitudes in tropical Mexico, frost is unknown, and annual rainfall is heavy; the constant humidity is ideal for the many epiphytes. The overstorey is a combination of northern temperate and subtropical trees, the former including *Liquidambar styraciflua*, *Nyssa* and others. Mexico's tallest tree, the ramrod tree (*Chaetoptelea mexicana*), is common in the cloud forest and the cooler parts of the tropical evergreen forest. Other plants of the cloud forest are *Magnolia schiediana*, *Trema micrantha*, the tree ferns *Nephelia mexicana* and *Sphaeropteris horrida*, *Platanus mexicana*, the hand-flower tree (*Chiranthodendron pentadactylon*), *Cnidoscolus* (*Jatropha*) *liebmannii* and *Styrax glabra*. There is a variety of ericaceous shrubs in the understorey, and begonias, bromeliads and orchids thrive in the shade. *Sprekelia formosissima* also grows in this transitional zone, in rocky places, cliffs and on lightly wooded slopes. At higher altitudes *Abies guatemalensis*, *Cupressus lusitanica* and *Pinus ayacahuite* are accompanied by *Fuchsia splendens*, *Calceolaria mexicana* and *Malvaviscus arboreus*, which also favours the shady places that suit fuchsias and ferns. *Fuchsia fulgens* and *Maurandya erubescens* grow in rocky places in woodlands and open hillsides, the former occasionally as an epiphyte, the latter twining through shrubs and trees. The most widely distributed of New World buddlejas, the tree-like *B. americana*, occurs from central Mexico southwards towards Bolivia and Peru, at varying altitudes and in different habitats from Guatemalan cloud forest to sea level.

The climbing *Cobaea scandens* is a native of southern Mexico; other species are found in central America growing with *Mutisia* or *Bomarea* species. The climbing *Rhodochiton atrosanguineum* grows deep in the rain forests of southern Mexico, with the orchid *Epidendrum vitellinum*.

There are several native Mexican cycads, such as the variable and widespread *Ceratozamia mexicana*, which grows in a range of habitats from forest to semi-desert; *Dioön spinulosum*, a tall species forming very localized forests; or *Zamia fischeri*, which grows in high-altitude forests. High-altitude and coastal cycads (such as *Z. furfuracea*, which grows on sandy hummocks in exposed sites on the east coast of Mexico), like many *Encephalartos* from South Africa, are sclerophyllous in character, while the forest-dwellers have soft, lax foliage; unlike the former, these have no resting period but grow all year round. The demarcation between the two types is far from rigid, and several species are adapted to both bush and forest habitats.

Warm-temperate South America and the *tierra templada*

The Andean chain extends the length of South America and, as elsewhere in mountain country, climate is much modified by altitude. Southwards from Central America, the pines, firs and hemlocks of North America are replaced by *Podocarpus glomeratus* forest at the cooler, damper altitudes. Epiphytic and lithophytic orchids (*Epidendrum*, *Oncidium*, *Lycastes*, *Masdevallia* and other genera) and bromeliads, and epiphytic peperomias, are common; species of *Calceolaria* and *Fuchsia* such as *F. boliviana* and *F. denticulata* grow there, with ferns. Climbers include *Tropaeolum tuberosum*, *Cobaea scandens*, *Bomarea caldasii* and other species, and many species of *Passiflora*, such as *P. jamesonii* from the uplands of Ecuador.

Above the fog desert of coastal Peru and Chile there is enough precipitation to support trees such as *Lucuma obovata*, *Carica candicans* and *Acnistus* species, with epiphytic ferns and peperomias, and in rock crevices calceolarias, begonias, heliotrope, *Loasa* species, and *Solanum* species. The sacred flower of the Incas, *Cantua buxifolia*, grows at mid altitudes in the Andes of Peru, Bolivia and northern Chile. The angel's trumpet, *Brugmansia* (*Datura*) *arborea*, is one of several Andean species ranging from Ecuador to northern Chile, often growing along stream-sides or in scrub, where another solanaceous shrub, *Iochroma grandiflora*, grows among *Baccharis*. With these occur bulbous *Stenomessum* and *Zeyhyranthes*, and in the alpine meadows the irid *Orthrosanthus chimboracensis* is found. The *paramo* of the northern Andes is the habitat of fuchsias, scarlet passion flowers, bomareas, and puyas. In the lower valleys, the climate is drier and semi-tropical; *Bombax* is dominant, with *Schinus molle*, arborescent *Ipomoea* species, opuntias of the prickly pear type, *Jatropha* and the climber *Dalechampia*, *Argemone* species and *Asclepias curassavica*.

In southern Brazil, northern Argentina, Uruguay and Paraguay there are two not very clearly distinct seasons: six months of warm to hot, humid weather and six months of 'winter' when night frosts are possible. In the drier regions of the west the comparatively high atmospheric humidity and wide diurnal temperature variations lead to heavy dews which enable tillandsias and other epiphytes to survive the dry season; in the east there is no definite dry season.

The Atlantic forests of south-eastern Brazil, which extend into north-eastern Argentina, are humid, subtropical rain forests isolated from the Amazon basin and characterized by many endemic species. The paraná pine, *Araucaria angustifolia*, is dominant in places, with species of *Tabebuia* and the queen palm (*Syagrus romanzoffiana* [*Arecastrum romanzoffianum*]), and many tree ferns, lianas and epiphytes. One of the important timber trees of the region is *Cedrela tubiflora*; other trees include the floss silk tree (*Chorisia speciosa*), *Ficus* species, *Jacarctica dodecaphylla*, *Aspidosperma australe*, *Balfourodendrum riedelianum*, the very rare *Apuleia leiocarpa*, and *Holocalyx balansae* in which many epiphytes grow. The bamboo *Guadua trinii* grows with *Ocotea pulchella* and *Acacia tucumanensis*. The tree fern, *Phyla virens*, is a rare plant in damp places, and *Vanilla fragrans* is a terrestrial orchid climbing into trees. (The main source of commercial vanilla is the tropical *V. planifolia*.) Among woody climbers are *Passiflora caerulea*, *Cissus striata*, and the love charm (*Clytostoma callistegioïdes*).

Where the tree cover is thinner and the light levels consequently higher – along water-courses, in coastal scrub and on rocky outcrops – the arborescent *Philodendron bipinnatifidum* is to be found, in the sub-tropical regions of south-eastern Brazil, northern Argentina, Bolivia and Paraguay. Also from the shores of southern Brazil is the feijoa, *Acca sellowiana*, growing on exposed cliffs.

Solanum verbascifolium or fumo bravo, *Phytolacca dioica* or ambú, *Sapindus saponaria* or palo jabón (soap tree), and *Cecropia adenopus* grow along the roadsides, with cleomes and begonias. The edible palm, *Euterpe edulis*, grows in this region, and *Ilex paraguariensis*, the plant from the leaves of which maté tea is made, forms forests known as *yerbales*; it also grows in the araucaria forest. The coral tree, *Erythrina crista-galli*, grows on raised tussocks in marshy places and along water-courses; it is found in southern Brazil and Argentina, Bolivia, Paraguay and Uruguay, and is the national flower of Argentina. *Erythrina speciosa*, from south-eastern Brazil, also favours wet sites. *Abutilon megapota-micum* has its botanical name from the Rio Grande – the big river. Plants of the drier regions are *Schinus terebinthifolius*, the red powderpuff (*Calliandra haematocephala* [*inaequilatera*]), the copaiba balsam (*Copaifera langsdorfii*), and the widespread *Bougainvillea spectabilis* and *Passiflora coccinea*. Despite its common name, the Mexican flame bush, *Calliandra tweedii*, is a Brazilian native, naturalized in the West Indies and southern United States; so too is *Ipomoea* (*Pharbitis*) *learii*.

The climate of the Gran Chaco of Paraguay and Argentina is dry, and the vegetation of the mid western regions is described in Chapter 8; in the more humid east, the vegetation is largely savannah with wax palms (*Copernicia cerifera*) and the odd *Crataeva tapia*. The yatay palm or jelly palm, *Butia capitata*, grows in grasslands and lowland wood-lands. In the plains, where the soil is somewhat saline, the trees are *Prosopis juliflora* and *Schinopsis balansae*, the quebracho, with *Copaifera*, the queen palm, *Dolichandra* and *Passiflora*, and many epiphytic brome-liads, even growing on cacti. The bromeliad genus *Dyckia*, which occurs over a wide range of subtropical southern America, is always found in sunny places or rock crevices; some species, for example *D. brevifolia*, grow on hot, dry rocks in southern Brazil where they are flooded during the rainy season.

As the land rises towards the west and the *tierra templada* of Bolivia, the rainfall increases sharply, and the vegetation varies accordingly. On the wetter, south-facing slopes the bush yields to transitional and then to montane rain forest, where *Phoebe porphyria* is abundant, covered with epiphytes, chief of which are bromeliads, *Peperomia* and species of fern. Among the larger trees of the transitional zone are *Alnus acuminata* and *Tipuana tipu*; the canopy is formed of *Schinopsis quebracho-colorado*, *Aspidosperma quebracho-blanco*, *Ziziphus mistol*, *Caesalpinia para-guariensis*, and species of *Prosopis*. The Amazon lily, *Eucharis amazonica*, grows deep in the forests of the tributaries of the Amazon. In the montane rain forest *Phoebe porphyria* is still present, with *Rapanea laetevirens* and *R. ferruginea*, *Eugenia* species and *Ilex argentina*. There are many fuchsias including *F. boliviana*, and species of *Tibouchina* and *Heliotropium*. Here too grow climbers such as *Mandevilla laxa* (*suaveolens*) and *Caiophora lateritia*. The golden shower, *Pyrostegia venusta*, grows at the forest edges and *Macfadyena unguis-cati*, the cat's-claw vine, scales tall trees within the forest. Among the ground plants of forest glades is *Alonsoa warscewiczii*. The bamboo of the region is *Chusquea lorentziana*.

The roadside vegetation includes the tree tomato, *Syphomandra betacea*, *Bocconia pearcei*, petunias, and *Begonia micrantha*. *Salvia guaranitica* ranges across central South America from southern Brazil through Paraguay and Uruguay into northern Argentina. *Lantana camara*, which has become such a weed in some of the subtropical countries to which it has been introduced, also has a wide range in South America.

As well as the tree tomato, a great range of grains and fruits unknown as natives in Europe or the East grow in South America; some are now very familiar, such as the potato and tomato or, more recently commonplace, maize and passion fruit (*Passiflora edulis*) and granadilla (*P. quadrangularis*), while others remain exotic or unfamiliar, such as the Andean cherimoya, *Annona cherimola*, which is related to the pawpaw of the south-eastern United States, *Asimina triloba*, and *Carica stipulata*, the mountain papaya or chamburro, a relative of the true papaya of the tropics. Among Andean grains the quinoa (*Chenopodium quinoa*), a plant of the *tierra fria*, is now available in European shops.

Australia and New Zealand

In the warm-temperate regions of south-eastern Australia there are two main vegetation types: the two-layered dry sclerophyll or open forest, and the wet sclerophyll or tall open forest, composed of three or more storeys. Each is to be found in parts of Victoria and New South Wales near the coast. Much of eastern Queensland is also open forest.

Sclerophyll forest develops on soils with low water-holding capacity, such as those over sandstone.

In contrast to sclerophyll forest, the tropical rain forest of north-eastern Queensland yields, in northern New South Wales, to sub-tropical rain forest (also known as brush or jungle) composed increasingly of subtropical and temperate elements, with fewer species and a growing tendency to single-species dominance; for example, coach-wood (*Ceratopetalum apetalum*) in the Dorrigo highlands. The subtropical rain forest covers the floors and slopes of the upper part of valleys facing south-east, east and north-east, up to a varying altitudinal limit above which the winters are too cold. At its southern limit the subtropical rain forest yields to a cool-temperate rain forest dominated by *Nothofagus moorei* and, in Tasmania, *N. cunninghamii*.

In the warmer regions, the abundance of lianas and epiphytes, the predominance of evergreen trees, are typical of rain forest. Many of the species belong to the Indo-Malayan rain forest flora, whereas those of the sclerophyll forest are largely endemic to Australia, and on the whole the two types are to be found in separate communities. Here and there they mix, however, with *Eucalyptus saligna* and *Syncarpia laurifolia*, both abundant in eucalyptus forest proper, rising above the main rain forest canopy of *Dysoxylum*, *Ficus* and other, mainly evergreen, species; red cedar, *Toona australis*, and *Melia azedarach* are among the few deciduous species. Below this main canopy is a third storey of *Diospyros, Drimys, Eupomatia* and the tree fern *Alsophylla leichhardtiana*. A few of these trees are buttressed like the trees of true tropical rain forest, mainly those growing in the wettest hollows; the leaves of many have a characteristic, long-drawn-out drip-tip. There are many epiphytic ferns, orchids and mosses, such as *Asplenium bulbiferum*. *Eucalyptus grandis*, the rose gum, also grows in the rain forest valleys, and another species that sometimes forms an overstorey to the rain forest is the tallow wood, *E. microcorys*.

The hoop pine (*Araucaria cunninghamii*) extends from New South Wales to New Guinea, usually as individuals or small groups scattered through the rain forest, in rocky gorges or along stream banks. The silk oak (*Grevillea robusta*) grows along creeks and river-banks in the rain forest, in northern coastal New South Wales and southern Queensland, and several rain forest species have a wider range than this. The lilly pilly, *Acmena (Eugenia) smithii*, is found as far south as Victoria but extends right up to Cape York. This and other lilly pillies (*Acmena* and *Syzygium* species), such as *S. paniculatum*, the brush cherry or creek lilly pilly, often grow along streams. The Moreton Bay fig, *Ficus macrophylla*, is a rain forest species ranging from New South Wales to northern Queensland and inland to the Bunya mountains. The sweet shade, *Hymenosporum flavum*, is a coastal rain forest species from New South Wales and Queensland. The firewheel tree (*Stenocarpus sinuatus*) grows in a variety of rain forest types, in coastal New South Wales and Queensland and on the Atherton tableland. *Cordyline stricta* is both common and widespread in the rain forests and along stream-banks, and even in moist places in open forest; similar habitats suit *Ceratopetalum gummiferum*. *Macadamia tetraphylla* is a subtropical rain forest species from coastal northern New South Wales and southern Queensland.

As far south as East Gippsland, in eastern Victoria, there are outlying pockets of the rain forest of Queensland and New South Wales. As well as the lilly pilly and the climbing wombat berry (*Eustrephus latifolius*), plants of the East Gippsland jungles include *Pittosporum undulatum*, the kanooka (*Lophostemon* [*Tristania*] *laurina*), *Callistemon citrinus*, the Snowy River wattle (*Acacia boormannii*), the palm *Livistona australis* and the climbing *Kennedia rubicunda*. The incense plant, *Calomeria amaranthoïdes* (*Humea elegans*), ranges from the Blue Mountains southwards to the East Gippsland jungle.

Some species are commonly found at the rain forest margins, among them the rain tree (*Archidendron grandiflorum*), *Cassia floribunda*, the blueberry ash (*Elaeocarpus reticulatus* [*cyaneus*]), the bat's-wing coral tree (*Erythrina vespertilio*) in tropical and subtropical monsoonal regions of the north and east, but above all in the dry sclerophyll forests of the north, *Sideroxylon australe* (*Planchonella australis*), brush box (*Lophostemon confertus*, formerly *Tristania conferta*) and *L. suaveolens*, the swamp box, *Eugenia australis* along watercourses, *Acacia aulocarpa*, and the climbing *Hardenbergia violacea*.

Plants that are often found in the drier scrub include the widespread and common *Elaeocarpus reticulatus*, *Cupaniopsis anacardioïdes* growing in coastal scrubs and even in dune country, the black bean or Moreton Bay chestnut (*Castanospermum australe*) in rain forest and coastal scrubs on moist soil and along watercourses, the Illawarra flame tree (*Brachychiton acerifolius*) and the white kurrajong (*B. discolor*) in coastal scrubs and rain forest, the weeping bottlebrush (*Callistemon viminalis*) growing alongside or even in water, the Port Jackson fig (*Ficus rubiginosa*) on rocky hills and in open forest, the candlenut (*Aleurites moluccana*) along water-courses, and the wombat berry in shady, often moist places. *Hakea salicifolia* is generally found in wet gullies, in wet or dry sclerophyll forest or at the rain forest edge. The wonga vine, *Pandorea pandorana*, ranges from the most sheltered, humid fern gullies of the eucalyptus forests of Victoria to New Guinea and Indonesia, and the bower vine, *P. jasminoïdes*, has a narrower distribution in northern coastal New South Wales and Queensland.

THE SCLEROPHYLL FORESTS OF EASTERN AUSTRALIA

The sclerophyll forest is dominated by species of eucalypt, growing in varying associations according to local climatic and soil conditions. In the drier regions of the east coast and South Australia grow the sugar gum, *Eucalyptus cladocalyx*, and the spotted gum, *E. maculata*. The blackbutt, *E. pilularis*, grows in poorer soils in the coastal regions. The poorest country belongs to the scribbly gum (*E. haemastoma*) and the snappy gum (*E. racemosa*). The swamp mahogany, *E. robusta*, occurs in a narrow coastal strip in New South Wales and southern Queensland.

The Sydney red gum, *Angophora costata*, often forms almost pure stands on Hawkesbury sandstone; the river red gum, *Eucalyptus camaldulensis*, is found here, as it is in every other region, while the forest red gum, *E. tereticornis*, extends from the northern Queensland tablelands to north-eastern Victoria. Of the blue gums, there is the Sydney blue gum, *E. saligna*.

Banksia serrata is often found growing in deep sand on coastal dunes, or shallow sands among sandstone inland to the Blue Mountains, usually in dry sclerophyll forest. The sandy coastal lands are where *B. integrifolia*, *Melaleuca elliptica*, *M. armillaris* and *M. hypericifolia*, *Westringia rosmariniformis*, *Hibbertia scandens*, *Acacia suaveolens* and the Queensland silver wattle, *A. podalyriifolia*, are to be found. The black wattle, *A. mearnsii*, is often found near the coast, in a variety of soil types. The red silky oak, *Grevillea banksii*, is another near-coastal species, growing in open eucalyptus forest, on stony hillsides, and on secondary dunes, and *G. juniperina* grows in eucalyptus forest on sandy soils. *Hakea salicifolia* and *Rulingia pannosa* grow in dry, open forest. The heath banksia, *B. ericifolia*, inhabits heaths with a high water table and also grows on exposed seaside cliffs and in sandstone gullies inland to the Blue Mountains.

Allocasuarina verticillata (*Casuarina stricta*) grows above all near the coast, and withstands both salt winds and saline soils, while *Casuarina equisitifolia*, the coastal she-oak, has a more northerly distribution, sometimes forming pure stands in sand in the lee of large dunes. *Grevillea lanigera* ranges from coastal heaths and forest to subalpine woodland, usually in well-drained sites, and the pink spider flower, *G. sericea*, grows on Sydney sandstone, in dry sclerophyll forest and as far as the central western slopes. The red spider flower, *G. speciosa*, is another sandstone species, confined to near-coastal regions. The paroo lily, *Dianella caerulea*, grows in forests and coastal heaths. The cone flowers, *Isopogon anemonifolius* and *I. anethifolius*, grow in heaths and dry sclerophyll forests. *Lomatia silaefolia* is also from the coastal areas of New South Wales and Queensland. At the margins of near-coastal forests, and along streams, grows *Pittosporum rhombifolium*. *Acacia floribunda* is widespread in forests and woodlands in coastal New South Wales and along streams in East Gippsland, Victoria. Wet or swampy places near the coast are the habitat of *Leptospermum liversidgei*, *Melaleuca quinquenervia* (which has become a pest in southern Florida) and *M. linearifolia* or snow-in-summer, and *Blandfordia grandiflora*.

From the mountain ranges that run parallel to the east coast come *Hakea lissosperma*, *Melaleuca styphelioïdes*, and *Leptospermum petersonii*. *Lomatia myricoïdes* has a southerly distribution in eastern Victoria and southern New South Wales, growing in forests, on mountain slopes and along stream-sides; cool forests in these regions are also the habitat of *Pittosporum bicolor* and *P. undulatum*. The natural hybrid *Grevillea × gaudichaudi* (*G. laurifolia × G. acanthifolia*) occurs in rocky gullies in the Blue Mountains. The mountain banksia, *B. canei*, favours rocky slopes and gullies, in woodland and heath, in subalpine eastern Victoria and southern New South Wales. The green wattle, *Acacia decurrens*, grows in the cool hills and gullies of coastal New South Wales and the table-lands, and the swamp wattle, *A. elongata*, is usually found in damp areas of sandy heaths and woodlands in the central tablelands, slopes and coast of New South Wales and eastern Victoria. The downy wattle, *A. pubescens*, has a very limited range on gravelly clay ridges and shales in the Blue Mountains. Ovens' wattle, *A. pravissima*, grows on the banks of rivers and in the hills in the highlands of north-eastern Victoria and of New South Wales; the black wattle, *Callicome serrati-folia*, in damp places in the Blue Mountains, forming thickets along stream-banks. The alpine bottlebrush, *Callistemon sieberi*, is widespread in subalpine eastern Australia and also occurs in marshy places on the Darling Downs, Queensland. In the gorges and escarpments of the south-east grow *Crowea exalata*, *Myoporum viscosum*, the digger's speed-well (*Parahebe* [*Veronica*] *perfoliata*), *Pelargonium australe* and *Nicotiana suaveolens*. *Patersonia sericea* grows in rocky or sandy places, often near the coast, and *Blandfordia nobilis* is found in grassy, sandy sites.

The knife-leaf wattle, *Acacia cultriformis*, grows in forests and on ridges on the western slopes, tablelands and plains of New South Wales and southern Queensland, and the Wyalong wattle (*A. cardiophylla*) is found on sandy and gravel soils on the western slopes and plains. The dry inland areas, western slopes and tablelands, on sandy or gravel ridges, are the habitat of *A. triptera*, which sometimes forms dense impenetrable thickets. The mudgee, *A. spectabilis*, is widespread on the central western slopes and plains of New South Wales and Queensland.

Some of Australia's species are widespread in the east, occurring in regions with different climatic types and on different soils. Such are the silver banksia, *B. marginata*, *Grevillea rosmarinifolia*, *Acacia genistifolia* (*diffusa*), *A. longifolia*, *A. retinodes*, *A. rubida* and *A. flexifolia*, *Lhotskya* (*Calytrix*) *alpestris* and *Calytrix tetragona*, *Westringia rigida*, *Viminaria juncea*, *Callistemon citrinus*, *Crowea saligna* (*Eriostemon crowei*) from rocky, exposed places, the kurrajong (*Brachychiton populneus*) from rocky areas, river banks and flats, *Callistemon macropunctatus*, and *Solanum laciniatum*. Their very adaptability can make them a dangerous pest when they are introduced into other countries: thus, *Hakea sericea* has become a serious weed in the fynbos of South Africa.

The vegetation of Norfolk and Lord Howe islands, in the southern Pacific, belongs with that of Australia. One of Norfolk Island's best-known plants is the Norfolk Island pine, *Araucaria heterophylla* (*excelsa*). From Lord Howe Island comes the irid *Dietes robinsoniana*.

WARM-TEMPERATE TO SUBTROPICAL NEW ZEALAND
Much of New Zealand's climate is maritime cool-temperate, but in the northern coastal lowlands of North Island the climate is warm-temperate or even subtropical, and the Kermadecs, to the north of North Island, are distinctly subtropical. Of the country's three main forest types, kauri (*Agathis australis*) forest occupies (or occupied, for there is little virgin kauri forest left) the drier regions north of 38 °S, such as ridge-tops, with species of *Podocarpus* in the moister places. The kauri trees soar above the canopy of taraire (*Beilschmiedia tarairi*, formerly the most common medium-sized understorey tree of the warm rain forests), northern rata (*Metrosideros robusta*), towai (*Weinmannia silvicola*) and rewarewa (*Knightia excelsa*). These are associated with puriri (*Vitex lucens*), nikau and *Coprosma*.

The podocarps are rimu (*Dacrydium cupressinum*), miro (*Prumnopitys ferruginea*), totara (*Podocarpus totara*), matai (*Prumnopitys taxifolia*) and kahikatea (*Dacrycarpus* [*Podocarpus*] *dacrydioïdes*); in favourable sites all grow above the main canopy. The principal hardwoods are tawa (*Beilschmiedia tawa*) and kamahi (*Weinmannia racemosa*). Many smaller trees grow in the New Zealand forest too: *Litsea calicans*, the mangeao; *Hedycarya arborea*, the pigeonwood; the proteaceous *Persoonia toru*;

Paratrophis banksii or towai; *Pennantia corymbosa*; *Dysoxylum spectabile* or kohekohe; *Alectryon excelsus*; the puka, *Meryta sinclairii*; the tawapou, *Planchonella novi-zelandica*. Puriri grows with tree ferns and *Dacrycarpus dacrydioïdes* in the forests. One of the canopy trees of the lowland and coastal forest of North Island is karaka, *Corynocarpus laevigatus*. The pukatea, *Laurelia novae-zelandiae*, grows in the warm rain forests in damp gullies and creek beds. In sheltered gullies and at the base of cliffs the whau, *Entelea arborescens*, is found. *Pittosporum cornifolium* is usually epiphytic on large forest trees or rocks. One of New Zealand's many shrubby daisies, *Brachyglottis kirkii*, grows on wooded slopes at low altitudes on North Island. From north to south, in the lowland forests, grows the nikau palm, *Rhopalostylis sapida*, the most southerly palm in the world. There are many lianas in the northern forest, among them supplejack (*Rhipogonum scandens*), kiekie (*Freycinetia banksii*), rata vines (*Metrosideros*) and *Clematis*. Epiphytes are also common: kapuka (*Griselinia lucida*) and ferns and orchids.

The trees of the coastal districts include pohutukawa (*Metrosideros excelsa*), karaka, ngaio (*Myoporum laetum*) and kohekohe. The swamp maire (*Syzygium maire*) and *Laurelia novae-zelandiae* favour wet soils. In tidal waters grows the mangrove, *Avicennia resinifera*. Off the northern coast of North Island lies the group of islands called Three Kings; here grow *Pennantia baylisiana* and the rare *Elingamita johnsonii*. A familiar plant from the Kermadecs is *Metrosideros kermadecensis*.

South Africa

The southern part of Africa consists of an elevated continental plateau with raised margins, rather like a saucer with a raised rim, and a narrow coastal belt of much lower elevation. The eastern escarpment is made up of the long ridge of the Drakensberg, rising to over 2,100 m/ 7,000 ft in the Transvaal. In the southern Transvaal the altitudes are lower, but further south along the Natal border the plateau rim rises again, much of it to over 3,000 m/10,000 ft. Most of South Africa falls within the warm temperate zone, with only the northern portions in the tropics; but the climate in the interior is more temperate than its latitude might suggest, because of the elevation.

The vegetation of much of the eastern half of the country is savannah of various types. Savannah develops in regions of summer rainfall with a rather dry winter, as in most of the country between the escarpment and the coast in the south-east portion. In the low-lying country in the Transvaal and northern Natal a near-tropical type of savannah known as low veld occurs; frosts are rare and the summers are hot and wet (see Chapter 12). The bush veld occupies the northern part of the plateau; frosts occur, but they are seldom severe or prolonged. The bush savannah of the high plateau is characteristic of low rainfall areas; the annual temperature range is the largest in the country, and winter frosts occur regularly. The savannah is composed of varying proportions of trees and shrubs with grasses, unlike the grasslands of the inland plateau of southern Transvaal, Orange Free State and parts of Natal, where there are no trees. Here the average rainfall is higher than in the bush savannah, mainly falling in summer; the winters are dry, cold and sunny.

There are only small areas of forest vegetation in South Africa; they occur where the temperature is rather uniform, with no frosts in winter, and the rainfall is moderate and evenly distributed, as in the eastern part of the south coast where temperate or warm-temperate forest occurs from sea level to 750–900 m/2,500–3,000 ft; further east the higher temperatures, with a greater range, allow warm temperate forest to grow up to about 380 m/1,250 ft. Along the coastal strip in Natal, high rainfall and high temperatures produce almost tropical conditions and the forest is distinctly subtropical in character. Forest vegetation is also found in the better-watered ravines of the coastal slopes of the mountains and on the upper seaward slopes of the higher mountains to the east, as on the Amatole Mountains and on the Drakensberg escarpment in Natal. Montane forest occurs on the slopes of the higher mountains in northern Transvaal, above 1,400 m/4,500 ft, in the mist belt where most of the rain falls in summer. The mean temperature here is lower, and frosts may occur in winter.

In the forest of the southern coastal regions *Podocarpus falcatus* and *P. henkelii* are among the tallest trees, forming part of an upper canopy which is not continuous. In humid woods and thickets and along water-courses the blossom tree, *Virgilia divaricata*, is common, with *V. oroboïdes* as a pioneer species after fire, common on the drier slopes, as in the Knysna region of the south-eastern Cape. *Polygala myrtifolia* is found both in moist evergreen coastal forest and open grassy hillsides and sand dunes. The kaffirboom, *Erythrina caffra*, grows in the coastal forest and along stream-sides in the eastern Cape region, with other species such as *E. lysistemon* and *E. humeana* in the drier areas on the hills. Other species of the coastal forest and scrub include *Harpephyllum caffrum*, the red saffronwood (*Cassine crocea*), the bastard taaibos (*Allophyllus decipiens*) and the dune allophyllus (*A. natalensis*), the coast red milkwood (*Mimusops caffra* – a major constituent of dune vegetation, growing right down to the high-water mark) and the red milkwood (*M. obovata*) which grows in the evergreen coastal forest, the assegai tree (*Curtisia dentata*), the white milkwood (*Sideroxylon inerme*), *Akokanthera oblongifolia*, the amatungula (*Carissa macrocarpa*) and *C. bispinosa*, *Cordia caffra*, the puzzle bush (*Ehretia rigida*), and *Halleria lucida*. A common understorey tree in the evergreen coastal forest of the Knysna is *Gonioma kamassi*. The baboon grape, *Rhoicissus digitata*, is a plant of the coastal dunes and a common canopy climber in dry sand forest.

The Cape chestnut, *Calodendron capense*, and the kaffir plum, *Harpephyllum caffrum*, grow in kloofs and forests from the Cape to Natal, and over a similar geographical range *Crotalaria capensis*, the red beech (*Protorhus longifolia*), the silky bark (*Maytenus acuminata*), the kooboo berry (*Cassine aethiopica*) and the common saffronwood (*C. papillosa*), *Cassinopsis ilicifolia*, *Hippobromus pauciflorus*, the dogwood or shiny leaf (*Rhamnus prinoïdes*), the Cape plane (*Ochna arborea*) and the carnival bush (*O. serrulata*), the thorn pear (*Scolopia zeyheri*), *Schefflera umbellifera*, the parsley tree (*Heteromorpha arborescens*), *Myrsine africana*, the Cape beech (*Rapanea melanophloeos*), *Rothmannia capensis* and *Psychotria capensis* are among the trees and shrubs that grow at the forest edge and often in open woodland and bush as well. The wild peach, *Kiggelaria africana*, grows in evergreen forest and on mountain grasslands from the Cape to Transvaal.

Dombeya dregeana inhabits stony slopes at low altitudes, while *D. cymosa* is a plant of the coastal bush. Dombeyas are often known as Natal cherry trees, and several species, including *D. tiliacea* (*natalensis*) are widely grown in the subtropics. The hard pear, *Olinia ventosa*, ranges from the evergreen forest and coastal scrub to rocky hillsides in Cape province. One of the most widespread Cape shrubs is the African hemp, *Sparmannia africana*, a weed at the margins of the evergreen forest. *Eugenia capensis* grows in such varied habitats as coastal dune scrub, mangrove swamps, open woodland, evergreen forest and rocky mountain slopes. The Cape honeysuckle, *Tecomaria capensis*, grows over a wide range of altitudes at the forest margins and in bush and scrub, while *Bowkeria verticillata* grows only at mid to higher elevations at the forest margins and on stony hill slopes. At the margins of the coastal forest grows the wild pomegranate, *Burchellia bubalina*, which is also found in open bush veld and swampy places and in montane forest. *Pittosporum viridiflorum*, *Rhus chirindensis*, the common spike thorn (*Maytenus heterophylla*), the sand olive (*Dodonaea viscosa*), the blue bush or red star apple (*Diospyros lycioïdes*), *Akokanthera oppositifolia*, the white cat's-whiskers (*Clerodendrum glabrum*) and the blue cat's-whiskers (*C. myricoïdes*) grow in a range of habitats from scrub and riverine thickets to both deciduous woodland and evergreen forest, and over a wide range of altitudes in the southern and eastern Cape, Natal and Transvaal. The Lebombo wingnut, *Atalaya alata*, grows in coastal scrub thickets and at high altitude along rocky watercourses over a similar geographical range. The indaba tree, *Pappea capensis*, is widespread except in coastal western and southern Cape regions, in open woodland and on river margins.

In the eastern Cape the forest boerboom, *Schotia latifolia*, fringes the evergreen forest and is found in scrub vegetation, while in Transvaal it favours the dry bush veld; *S. brachypetala*, the tree fuchsia or parrot tree, also grows in scrub forest and dry grasslands in Transvaal and Natal and into Zimbabwe. *Buddleja auriculata* grows at forest margins in the eastern Cape, Natal and Transvaal; *B. saligna*, the olive buddleja or bastard olive, is more widespread in South Africa in a variety of habitats from the margins of the Knysna Forest of the Cape to the Kalahari thornveld, and the sage wood, *B. salviifolia*, is also widely distributed, mainly in disturbed habitats.

In the high wet forests and wet scrub, *Cunonia capensis* is abundant; at Knysna it is associated with *Platylophus trifoliatus* and the tree fern *Hemitelia capensis*, often forming an unbroken understorey, with moisture-loving ferns, filmy ferns and mosses on the ground. In these wet places epiphytes are common. On moist slopes *Widdringtonia nodiflora* is now rare, for accessible trees have been cut for furniture and panelling. A prevalent tree in the forest is the Knysna boxwood, *Gonioma kamassi*. The white gardenia, *G. thunbergia*, is a plant of the evergreen forest. The sneezewood, *Ptaeroxylon obliquum*, grows from the low altitude woodland and scrub forest to the evergreen montane forest in the mist belt, where it reaches its largest size. The common hard-leaf, *Phylica paniculata*, grows in high rainfall areas on rocky slopes and along stream banks and the flame combretum, *C. paniculatum* (*microphyllum*), grows at the margins of forest in high rainfall areas as well as along river banks, usually adopting a climbing habit. *Hibiscus diversifolius* also favours damp places along rivers and by lakes, as does the Cape bush willow, *Combretum caffrum*. The water berry, *Syzygium cordatum*, is always found near water, from the eastern Cape northwards to Mozambique, where it forms pure stands of swamp forest.

In the drier forest, *Olea capensis* is associated with the podocarps, with a shrub layer beneath and on the forest floor a variety of ferns, with *Moraea iridioïdes* and other non-woody species. The knobwood,

Zanthoxylum capense (?*Z. davyi*), inhabits dry woodland and extends also into the higher mist belt; its range is from the eastern Cape right up into the tropics. The poison apple, *Solanum aculeastrum*, is a plant of wooded grassland, and the red bitter apple (*S. giganteum*) grows on wooded mountain slopes, often in deep shade. There may be many climbers in the dry forest, but few epiphytes. Some of South Africa's climbers are known throughout the world where the climate is suitable for them: the Cape honeysuckle, *Podranea ricasoliana*, *Plumbago auriculata*, *Jasminum angulare*. *Clematis brachiata* is widespread in all provinces of South Africa, though rare in the south-western Cape.

As we have seen, the fynbos of the western Cape is rich in species of *Protea*, but others occur outside the Mediterranean-climate zones, among them *P. cynaroïdes*, a native of the mountains from Cape Peninsula eastwards, growing taller in the valleys and stunted on exposed flats and slopes; and *P. neriifolia*, which favours well-drained slopes and sandy flats but is to be found in a wide range of habitats. *Leucadendron* or silver trees are also found on the southern coast. The other great component of the fynbos is *Erica*, and species of Cape heath also extend eastwards in damp places from the coast to higher altitudes and on flats and stony, grassy slopes. One of the most widespread species is *E. cerinthoïdes*, which extends into the Transvaal; *E. caffra* and *E. caffrorum* grow in mountain ravines and cliffs, usually in damp sites.

Dry, sandy places are the common habitat of *Podalyria sericea* and of *Polygala virgata*, which like another plant of dry hillsides, *Sutherlandia frutescens*, is widespread in South Africa. The Natal bottlebrush, *Greyia sutherlandii*, grows on the crests of rocky ridges and on mountain slopes. Of the many species of *Aloe* native to southern Africa, some are from the eastern states, such as the widespread *A. arborescens* and *A. ferox* which grow in the eastern Cape, Orange Free State and Natal in scrub communities on sandy soils to the west of the forested regions, and *A. excelsa* from Transvaal and Mozambique. Another kind of scrub is characterized by *Widdringtonia juniperoïdes*, found at altitude in the Cedarberg mountains.

The trees of the higher forests include *Grewia occidentalis* (also found on the high veld), *Podalyria calyptrata* in the mountainous areas of the southern Cape, *Ocotea bullata* or stinkwood, and *Psoralea pinnata* or blue broom in damp places. In the Amatole mountains and in Natal grows the shrubby Cape figwort, *Phygelius capensis*, another species favouring wet slopes; it has a more southerly distribution than *P. aequalis*, which is usually found on rocky streambanks in full sun. The lion's-ear, *Leonotis ocymifolia* (*leonurus*), grows in the mist belt at the edge of woodlands in Natal, whereas in the Cape region it is found on flats and hillsides. In the damper parts of the mist belt forest the tree fern *Cyathea dregei* is common. Where light penetrates the canopy there is a layer of tall herbs such as *Hypoestis* species, *Impatiens capensis*, *Piper capense*, *Plectranthus* species and large ferns.

Among the trees of the subtropical eastern coastal forest and bush are *Ficus* species (including the common *F. natalensis*, a strangler fig), the Natal flame bush (*Alberta magna*), *Celtis africana*, *Beilschmiedia natalensis*, *Calpurnia aurea*, *Dalbergia armata*, the amatungula or Natal plum (*Carissa macrocarpa*), *Combretum kraussii*, *Ochna arborea* and *O. atropurpurea*, *Gardenia thunbergia*, *Bauhinia galpinii*, the honeysuckle trees (*Turrea* species), *Albizia gummifera*, *Protorhus longifolia*, *Brachylaena discolor*, *Sclerocarya caffra*, and *Trichilia emetica*, the Natal mahogany. They grow in a variety of habitats, including the evergreen forest itself as well as wooded ravines and the fringe forest along rivers. The African dog rose, *Xylotheca kraussiana*, is a plant of the coastal dunes and dune forest scrub. *Kraussia floribunda* grows in dune scrub, swamp forest and at woodland fringes in Natal and eastern Transvaal. The liana *Quisqualis parviflora* ranges from sea level to mid altitudes in Natal, in the evergreen forest and wooded ravines, and the tree strawberry (*Cephalanthus natalensis*), a liana in the montane forest but a scrambling shrub in open mountain grassland, is found in Natal and eastern Transvaal.

Mackaya (Asystasia) bella is a plant of the evergreen forest of Natal and eastern Transvaal, growing by streams, while *Bersama tysoniana* grows at the forest margins, and the red ivory, *Berchemia zeyheri*, favours open woodland and water-courses, while the pompon tree, *Dais cotinifolia*, and the lavender tree, *Heterophyxis natalensis*, range from the forest margin to the bush on steep, rocky hillsides. The curry bush, *Hypericum revolutum*, is a plant of high elevations in Natal and eastern Transvaal, growing in grassland, along streams, and at the margins of the evergreen forest. *Rawsonia lucida* is an understorey tree in the evergreen forest. The quinine tree, *Rauvolfia caffra*, is always found near ground water at the forest margin and along wooded stream banks.

Characteristic of the subtropical forest is the presence of large monocotyledons, such as *Dracaena hookeriana*, which grows in shady places in dry sour bush veld and dune forest undergrowth, as well as in mountain forests, and the palm *Phoenix reclinata*, which is widespread in coastal eastern South Africa and extends into the tropics. These and other monocots such as *Hyphaene crinita*, *Baphia racemosa* and

Strelitzia augusta give the name 'palm belt' to this vegetation. The palm-like cycads, species of *Encephalartos*, are found in varying habitats from hot, dry regions to sheltered mountain ravines in the eastern Cape. *Ensete ventricosum* is a plant of the high-rainfall forest, in ravines and at streamsides. The forest fever tree, *Anthocleista grandiflora*, grows in the forests of Transvaal, also in high rainfall areas.

Tree savannah is the dominant type of vegetation from the central part of Transvaal northwards; temperate savannah occupies the greater part of the coastal belt in the south-east, replaced by grasslands at higher altitudes and limited in the west by decreasing annual rainfall, about three-quarters of which falls in summer. The ground layer is dominated by grasses, with trees and shrubs of which acacias are the most common: *A. karroo*, *A. caffra* in the south-east Cape, and other species, with other thorny bushes such as *Zizyphys mucronatus* and *Gymnosporia buxifolia*, the kei apple (*Dovyalis caffra*) and species of *Cussonia*. Many of the plants of the drier parts of the warm temperate forests, such as *Harpephyllum*, also grow here, with aloes such as *A. ferox* amd tree-type euphorbias on rocky soils and *Encephalartos* species on steep slopes. Where the tree cover is relatively dense species of *Haemanthus*, *Sansevieria* and others are abundant.

In the bush veld of the northern part of the plateau in the Transvaal, the climate is modified by altitude so that night frosts in winter are not uncommon. Much of the vegetation is of the type described as small tree savannah, with an open to nearly continuous tree cover, its components varying according to soil. On deep soils *Acacia*, *Peltophorum* and others are widely separated; on rocky soils there is a close cover of bushy *Combretum zeyheri*. *Burkea* and *Terminalia* dominate on sands, *Combretum* on sandy loams, *Acacia* on black soils. On soils that are wet in summer *Spirostachys africanus* is dominant. On shallow soils over rock *Protea abyssinica*, *P. roupelliae* and *Faurea saligna* are often the only trees. *Aloe marlothii* is abundant on steep rocky slopes where it is not too dry.

BULBS AND PERENNIALS OF SOUTHERN AFRICA

As we have seen, many bulbous plants (using the term in the loose, horticultural sense) come from areas with dry summers; by holding nutrients in underground storage organs, these plants can endure the hot, dry season in a state of dormancy. Fewer bulbs come from areas with summer rainfall; among them are the many that grow in the eastern regions of South Africa, and here many monocots with fleshy but not bulbous roots, often with evergreen foliage, are also native.

The way in which climatic factors lead to different biorhythms is clearly seen in the two species of *Veltheimia*, *V. bracteata* from the coastal regions of the eastern Cape, which needs no resting period, and *V. capensis* from the western, summer-dry region.

The Scarborough lily, George lily or Knysna lily, *Cyrtanthus purpureus* (*C. elatus*, *Vallota speciosa*), is a native of the Knysna Forest in the south-east of Cape Province. *Cyrtanthus sanguineus*, the Ifafa lily, grows in damp grassland near the sea in Natal and East Cape, and *C. epiphyticus* in the moss on trees in the forest; *C. mackenii* var. *cooperi* grows along stream-sides in the eastern Cape. The blood lily, *Scadoxus multiflorus* ssp. *katherinae* (*Haemanthus katherinae*) grows in coastal forest in the eastern Cape and Natal, and the snake lilies, *Scadoxus puniceus* – which is summer growing – and *S. membranaceus*, extend from the southern Cape to Natal. The paintbrushes, evergreen *Haemanthus albiflos* and the winter-growing *H. coccineus*, are found in coastal bush and along shady river banks. The bush lily, *Clivia miniata*, favours sheltered shady ledges and ravines and moist forests, in coastal and inland eastern Cape Province, Natal and Transvaal. *Albuca nelsonii* is also a native of Natal, usually in shady places.

The Orange River lily, *Crinum bulbispermum*, extends from northern Namaqualand to the Transvaal and Natal, growing in wet areas. The Natal lily, *C. moorei*, also grows in wet, even swampy places; it has a more southerly distribution. Most nerines are summer-growing or evergreen, with a distribution in the eastern Cape, as *N. undulata* and *N. flexuosa*; *N. bowdenii* extends into Natal, growing in the Drakensberg on screes beneath cliffs and on ledges at altitudes of 3,000 m/ 10,000 ft or so; *N. filifolia* grows in moist open grass veld, its range extending northwards into Transvaal. The pineapple lilies, *Eucomis bicolor* and *E. comosa* (*punctata*), favour moist places – damp gullies, wet grassland or shaded rock crevices – at altitude in the eastern Cape region and Natal, while *E. autumnalis* (*E. undulata*) and *E. pallidiflora* are widespread in Natal from the coast to the Drakensberg, and also grow in Orange Free State and Transvaal.

The torch lilies are mainly from the eastern Cape and the Natal Drakensberg: *Kniphofia praecox* is from the southern Cape, *K. rooperi* from the eastern Cape, where it grows in marshy places in the open veld, and *K. caulescens* and *K. northiae* extend from the north-eastern Cape to the Drakensberg. The upland species *K. triangularis* grows in moist, peaty soils and among rocks in mountain grassland. The main distribution of the African lilies is also eastwards from the Cape peninsula to the mountains south of the Limpopo. The Cape species such as *Agapanthus praecox* are mainly evergreen, while those from Natal and the Transvaal, including *A. campanulatus* and *A. inapertus*, are summer-growing. *Tulbaghia violacea*, from the southern and eastern Cape, is evergreen.

The Berg lily, *Galtonia candicans*, grows on grassy hillsides, from south-eastern Transvaal through western Natal to the Drakensberg, disappearing at the point where the range bends sharply to face south-east and becomes much colder than the north-east facing slopes. Another middle-altitude species, *G. regalis*, grows on sandstone cliffs with *Agapanthus campanulatus* and *Gladiolus microcarpus*. At higher altitudes in Orange Free State and Lesotho grows *Galtonia viridiflora*, and at lower altitudes in marshy places, *G. princeps*. The kaffir lily, *Schizostylis coccinea*, grows in mountain areas beside streams or even in the water, its range from the eastern Cape to southern tropical Africa.

Some of South Africa's species of *Gladiolus* come from the summer rainfall areas, including *G. papilio*, which grows in damp, grassy places at middle altitudes in Transvaal and Natal, *G. cruentus* from cliff faces and stony, grassy places high in the Drakensberg, the large brown afrikaner (*G. grandis*) from sandy places on the southern coast, and *G. natalensis* (*G. primulinus*) or maid of the mist, which grows in the mist belt. Other South African irids with cormous roots include *Crocosmia aurea*, which grows at forest margins in the eastern Cape, Natal and the heights of Transvaal and tropical Africa, *C. pottsii* from stony or sandy grass veld in the eastern Cape, and *C. masoniorum* from Transkei.

Several watsonias grow in the summer-rainfall areas, *W. densiflora*, *W. fourcadei*, *W. pillansii*, *W. zeyheri* among them. *Moraea huttonii* and *M. spathulata* are evergreen species ranging from the eastern Cape to the Transvaal, and of the six species of *Dietes* five are South African, from the southern Cape eastwards (the sixth, *D. robinsoniana*, is from Lord Howe Island, New Zealand). *Aristea* is a genus mainly from southern Africa, with *A. ecklonii* ranging from the eastern Cape into tropical Africa, favouring damp places at the forest edge. Damp habitats along stream-banks are favoured by *Wachendorfia thyrsiflora*, and the arum lilies of the summer-rainfall areas also grow in damp places: among them are *Zantedeschia elliottiana*, the yellow arum from Natal, *Z. pentlandii* and *Z. rehmannii* from the Transvaal, and the wide-ranging *Z. albomaculata*, which extends into tropical Africa. The fully aquatic blue water lilies, *Nymphaea caerulea* and *N. capensis*, grow in pools and slow streams in Orange Free State, Natal, Transvaal and into tropical Africa.

Dierama pulcherrimum, the wand flower or angel's fishing rod, grows on grassy hillsides in damp places in the Amatole mountains, and *D. pendulum* on grassy flats and slopes in the eastern Cape and Natal; no dieramas are native to the summer-dry western Cape, and where their range extends northwards they are found only at altitude, in the cooler zones. *Anomatheca laxa* (*Lapeirousia laxa*, *L. cruenta*) is a small bulb from the coastal belt, from the eastern Cape to Mozambique, and into eastern Transvaal, while the little *Rhodohypoxis baurii* is from the Natal Drakensberg.

A South African genus which has transformed the face of northern temperate gardening is *Pelargonium*. The ivy-leaved geranium, *P. peltatum*, trails among shrubs and over rocks in the Amatole mountains, and *P. zonale* is found at the edge of forest and scrub, while of the several species with scented foliage, *P. graveolens* favours stony slopes facing away from the sun, and *P. capitatum*, from which oil of geranium is commercially extracted, grows on sand dunes and low hillsides near the sea. A genus more recently popular in the northern hemisphere is *Diascia*, of which *D. rigescens* and *D. vigilis* grow by water and at forest margins and in coastal grasslands, *D. anastrepta* in damp and partly shaded places at high altitudes, *D. fetcaniensis* in damp places, often heavily shaded, at the foot of cliffs or grassy banks as well as amid grass tussocks on exposed mountain tops, and *D. barbarae* in wet gravelly or silty places; *D. integerrima* is found in drier sites, such as the crevices of rock outcrops or on gritty slopes.

The bird-of-paradise, *Strelitzia reginae*, and the larger *S. nicolae*, are plants of the eastern coastal regions, the former commonly found in wet places, whereas *Sansevieria aethiopica* is a plant of dry regions in the semi-arid scrub of the eastern Cape. *Plectranthus saccatus* grows through bushes in the coastal forest. The climbing *Senecio mikanoïdes* and *S. tamoïdes* grow through bushes and trees at forest margins or in the bush veld of the eastern coastal belt. Two favourites of cold-climate greenhouses are the Cape primrose, *Streptocarpus*, which here grows in humusy soils, in sheltered places in the forest or on shady slopes at the forest edge, and *Begonia sutherlandii*, from damp places in open forest or among rocks.

10

The rhododendron heartlands of Asia

As we have seen, the effects on climate of increasing latitude and of increasing altitude are similar: the temperature falls, until at the permanent snow line, in any latitude, the climate resembles that of high latitudes, with long, cold winters and brief summers. The greatest extent of very high-altitude climates is found in Tibet and the great mountain ranges of the Himalayas, followed by the chain of mountains that runs from the north of North America to the southernmost tip of South America. In Africa only isolated peaks, Mount Kenya and Kilimanjaro and the Ruwenzori range, are high enough to have permanent snow, while in Europe, extending as it does through higher latitudes, the Alps are permanently snow-capped.

Much of southern Asia is influenced by the monsoon, the seasonal reversal of wind direction. The winds blow mainly off the ocean during the wet season, and off the land during the dry season. Between the plains, where a hot, dry season is followed by a hot, wet season, and the higher reaches of the mountains, lies a region where the heat is tempered by altitude to produce a climate where some rain falls all year round, with a peak during the July to October south-west monsoon, and where the winters are cool (becoming colder, of course, with increasing altitude) and the summers at intermediate altitudes are warm to cool.

Climates broadly of this nature are found in regions bordering the Himalayas – Sichuan (Szechwan) and Yunnan in south-western China,

245

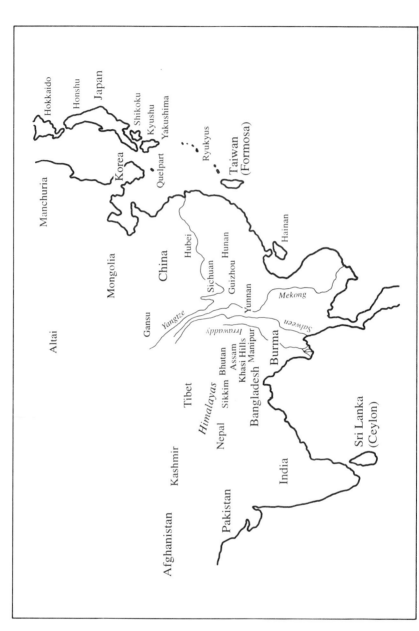

The rhododendron heartlands

south-east Tibet, upland Burma and Assam, Nepal, Bhutan and the tiny kingdom of Sikkim, and the high Himalayan foothills of northern India and Kashmir. Because the rain-laden monsoon winds blow from the east, the eastern Himalayas are wetter than the west, and the rainy season arrives earlier and lasts longer. The western Himalayas tend to have two precipitation peaks – July/August and January/April – resulting in heavy snowfalls, a lower winter snow line and a longer-lasting winter in Kashmir and western Nepal. In the foothills on the north bank of the Brahmaputra in Assam, and also in eastern Nepal, pre-monsoonal rain regularly falls in April/May.

The great barrier of the Himalayas acts as a rain screen, so that the climate of western China is comparatively dry and that of the Tibetan plateau very dry, while the uplands of Burma and Assam and other regions which feel the full impact of the monsoon are much wetter. Frank Kingdon Ward, who travelled extensively in the Sino-Himalayan region, wrote of the climate of northern Burma and south-eastern Tibet that 'For six months the passes through the mountains . . . away up at the sources of the Irrawaddy, are blocked by snow; for six months the mountains are swathed in impenetrable mists and drenched with rain.'

Japan's climate is softened by the surrounding ocean, but it too is dominated by the great seasonal wind reversal of the Asian monsoon, so that Japanese winters – except in the north, where heavy snowfalls are common – tend to be drier than the summers. Parts of central and southern Japan have two rainfall peaks – one in early summer and a second in late summer or autumn. In the south the winters are mild and almost subtropical. Japan is a mountainous country, and as elsewhere the temperature falls with increasing altitude. The mountains of northern Taiwan have a similar climate. Much of the flora of Japan and Taiwan has a close affinity with that of China and the Himalayas.

The type of vegetation that results from this high-rainfall climate is not far different from that of the warm temperate rain forests of south-eastern North America, lowland North Island, New Zealand, and parts of South America. However, the southern hemisphere flora in particular, as opposed to the vegetation type, is very different from that of the Asian rhododendron heartland. In the case of northern New Zealand, South America and south-eastern USA, the interaction of latitude and of oceanic air masses is the main climatic influence, whereas in the realm of the rhododendrons it is the interaction between altitude and the monsoon. It is the nature of the monsoon, again, which gives a type of climate and of vegetation in montane south Asia different from those of the tropical and equatorial uplands of Africa and of Central and South America.

Since the main influence on mean temperature in these mountainous regions is altitude rather than latitude, within a comparatively small distance the climate ranges from tropical and frost-free to snowbound. Even to the east of the Himalayas, in western China, much of the land is mountainous and there is, for example, a great difference between the fertile, well-watered plains of Sichuan province and the rugged, much less fertile, often arid mountains to the west and north of the province. In the higher ranges, and especially in the deeper gorges, the whole gamut of vegetation types can be seen within a few miles, from subtropical jungle through warm and cool temperate rain forest and rhododendron–conifer forest to subalpine meadow and high alpine scree. In this chapter neither subtropical jungle and warm-temperate rain forest species nor the very high-altitude plants of south and east Asia will feature, even though the boundaries between the different vegetation types are far from clearly defined; these plants are covered in Chapter 9 and Chapter 11.

The rhododendron heartland

The high slopes are often wreathed in mist, so that at all times the atmospheric humidity is high. In this climate, less pleasant for human beings than for plants, the majority of species of the great genus *Rhododendron* have evolved, together with many other beautiful things that have challenged and captivated generations of gardeners since the first plant hunters returned to Europe with their finds. Among them were nineteenth-century introductions such as *Rhododendron arboreum*, the lapageria-flowered *R. cinnabarinum*, introduced by Sir Joseph Hooker, and scarlet-flowered *R. barbatum*. More recently there have been George Forrest, who introduced many rhododendron and primula species, and much else besides; Ernest Wilson, for whom the genus *Sinowilsonia* was named; George Sherriff, who introduced the spectacular form of the blue poppy, *Meconopsis grandis*, which bears his collector's number GS600; Frank Kingdon Ward, who had an extraordinary eye for a garden-worthy plant; and many others.

Rhododendron arboreum, the first species to be introduced to the west from the Himalayas, has a wide range from Kashmir to Bhutan and is also found in the Khasi Hills of Assam, in upper Burma and in Sri Lanka. However, the true heartland of the genus, where the greatest density of species is found, is in the vast reaches of mountains and gorges bordering China, south-eastern Tibet and Upper Burma, forming the river basins and watersheds of the Salween, Mekong and Yangtze rivers: China's south-western province of Yunnan plus Sichuan to its north and western Hubei, with Upper Burma and Assam to its west, and the mountain kingdoms of Bhutan and Sikkim, in turn bordered on their west by Nepal, and to the north by Tibet. Not only rhododendrons but an astonishing array of other genera, woody and herbaceous, are native to these lands. There is a great variety of forest types, depending not only on altitude but also on aspect and situation. At the lowest levels in the foothills the forest type is subtropical; this chapter is concerned with the forests of higher elevations, the warm and cool temperate forests and the conifer and rhododendron forests. Apart from a few low-altitude species, rhododendrons first occur as isolated specimens or in small groups, in thickets and forests of mixed broad-leaved shrubs and trees; with increasing altitude they increase in numbers, to become dominant either as undergrowth in conifer forests or themselves forming thickets and forests.

The Himalayan temperate rain forest and its plants

The eastern Himalayas can be divided geographically into three zones: the foothills, rising from the plains to altitudes of 1,800–3,000 m/ 6,000–10,000 ft, covered on the outer slopes with dense subtropical evergreen rain forest below and semi-evergreen temperate rain forest at higher altitudes; secondly, the middle or inner ranges, rising to 4,500 m/15,000 ft, with intervening valleys as low as 1,500 m/5,000 ft. Drier than the foothills, the valleys are pine-forested, while the inner ranges are forested to about 3,800 m/12,500 ft with, successively, warm temperate, cool temperate and then conifer forests, with deciduous trees common in the semi-evergreen, cool temperate forests. The third zone is the crest or great snowy range, rising to 4,500–7,600 m/15,000–25,000 ft, with valleys down to 3,300 m/11,000 ft; conifer forest occurs at these lower elevations, but the vegetation is mainly alpine. North of the great snowy range is the Tibetan plateau, of which only the river gorge region of the south-east, marked by parallel or converging mountain ranges separated by deep gorges, is forest. The rivers that have so deeply scored their passage through the rock are the Tsangpo (called the Brahmaputra in Assam), the Mekong, the Salween, and the Yangtze.

Floristically, the mountains can also be divided into zones, which grade into each other more or less abruptly, are delineated more or less clearly by altitude, and are affected by aspect and local climates as we shall see in more detail. At the lowest levels, from the plains and lower river valleys to the foothills, is the cultivated zone, with a subtropical or warm temperate flora; next comes the rain forest belt, composed mainly of broad-leaved evergreens; higher again is the cool temperate belt, with deciduous trees and shrubs and many rhododendrons, especially in the higher reaches; this is succeeded by the temperate alpine belt, mainly moorland of small shrubs but with forest in sheltered places, mostly coniferous; above this again is the alpine belt, with its great diversity of meadow plants; and finally, on mountains high enough, between this and the limit of vegetation is the high alpine belt where little grows other than specialized cushion or rosette plants.

Rhododendrons are found over a wide altitudinal range, from *R. simsii* (an otherwise Japanese and Chinese coastal species) at 250–450 m/ 800–1,500 ft in Burma, through the upper forest where rhododendrons dominate, to the alpine zone above the tree line. In the lower ranges, however, rhododendrons are scarce in the warm temperate rain forest, coming into their own in the cool temperate rain forest. *Rhododendron arboreum* first appears at about 1,800 m/6,000 ft, its scarlet forms contrasting vividly with *Primula denticulata*, blue anemones, and species of *Roscoea*.

BHUTAN, SIKKIM AND NEPAL

In Bhutan, the temperate mixed forests of evergreen *Quercus semecarpifolia* and *Tsuga dumosa*, the hemlock of Bhutan, are the backdrop for *Rhododendron falconeri* growing with the tree-like *R. barbatum*, shrubby *R. keysii*, *Betula utilis* and magnolias: spring-flowering *M. campbellii* and summer-blooming *M. globosa*. The large-leaved *Rhododendron kesangiae*, which resembles *R. grande* except in flower colour, is found from central Bhutan eastwards, in the cool temperate forest. Other shrubs are *Skimmia laureola*, *Enkianthus deflexus*, *Gaultheria fragrantissima* and *Osmanthus suavis*. *Luculia grandiflora* grows at around 2,500 m/8,000 ft, and is likely to be more frost-resistant than *L. gratissima*. *Daphne bholua* is here at the eastern end of its range, and here too is the rare *D. ludlowii*, endemic to a single forest ridge in central Bhutan. A more familiar shrub is *Viburnum grandiflorum*.

Above the spruce and hemlock forest of Bhutan, in the almost continual mistiness of the montane cloud forest zone, is the moist, lichen-decked fir forest in which *Abies densa* is the dominant species. With it grow the ubiquitous *Rhododendron arboreum*, with large-leaved *R. hodgsonii* and others, and many ferns and small herbs in the mossy forest floor. In Sikkim, too, *R. arboreum* is abundant, with at higher elevations the big-leaved species *R. grande* and *R. falconeri*, with scarlet *R. barbatum*, *R. thomsonii*, *R. glaucum*, *R. wightii* and *R. cinnabarinum*.

The forest type found at the highest altitudes in Bhutan is composed of juniper scrub and scrubby thickets of rhododendron, virtually alone above the tree line but accompanied by a variety of genera below, at the edge of larch forest. *Rhododendron thomsonii* and *R. wallichii* are the dominant species in some areas and *R. flinckii* and *R. bhutanense* in others, with *R. campylocarpum*, *R. arboreum* and other species. With them grow species of willow and *Berberis*, *Cotoneaster* and *Sorbus*, birch and elder (*Sambucus*).

A similar range of species is found in Nepal as in Bhutan, in the cool temperate forest of *Quercus semecarpifolia* and *Q. lamellosa*, *Rhododendron arboreum*, *Betula utilis*, *Castanopsis* and *Symplocos*, with *Mahonia napaulensis* and *M. acanthifolia*, *Viburnum erubescens*, *Deutzia staminea* and climbers such as *Parthenocissus*, *Clematis montana* and *Schisandra grandiflora*. The forest is rich in mosses, ferns and orchids growing as epiphytes, with shrubs such as *Agapetes* (*Pentapterygium*) *serpens* and *Vaccinium nummularia* also epiphytic, indicating the high atmospheric moisture. In the mixed forest of *Quercus semecarpifolia*, *Rhododendron arboreum* and *Magnolia campbellii* grows *Hedychium densiflorum*; the shrubby understorey includes *Daphne bholua* and *Sarcococca hookeriana*. As the altitude increases *Rhododendron arboreum* becomes dominant; above 2,500 m/8,000 ft *R. barbatum* is abundant, this species and *R. campanulatum* marking the start of the subalpine zone. Above these altitudes too grow *Enkianthus deflexus* and *Skimmia laureola*, with the maple *Acer campbellii*. The bold-leaved *Populus jacquemontiana* and *Hydrangea robusta*, blue-fruited *Gaultheria semi-infera* and *Stachyurus himalaicus* with its catkin flowers also occur here.

At about 3,000 m/10,000 ft in Nepal, temperate deciduous trees become more abundant amid the still-dominant *Rhododendron arboreum*: the Himalayan whitebeam, *Sorbus cuspidata*, and the rowan *S. insignis*; *Acer sterculiaceum*, the Himalayan bird cherry, *Prunus cornuta*, evergreen shrubs such as *Pieris formosa* and *Osmanthus suavis*, and *Dichroa febrifuga*. *Abies spectabilis* also occurs amid the rhododendron forest, at the margins of which grows *Viburnum grandiflorum*; and in cool, damp glens, facing north, west or east, it grows with alpine birch and some-times with other conifers – *Picea smithiana*, *Pinus wallichiana* and others.

251

In the *P. wallichiana* zone grow *Incarvillea arguta* and *Colquhounia coccinea*.

The same species may be found in different habitats in different regions. Thus *Rhododendron thomsonii*, in Bhutan, favours waterlogged sites among thickets of bamboo, where it grows on tussocks; but in east Nepal it grows on the exposed tops of mountain ridges. The shrubby *Lyonia ovalifolia* occurs across a wide altitudinal range, from 800 m/2,600 ft where it is evergreen, up to 3,500 m/11,500 ft where it is deciduous. Forms of *Daphne bholua* from lower altitudes are generally evergreen, too, and less hardy than the deciduous forms from higher elevations. *Roscoea* species, members of the ginger family, grow in sun or shade, in moist or dry soils, in the leafy soil of the mixed broadleaved and coniferous forests or in rock crevices.

The region is rich in non-woody species, such as the climbing *Crawfurdia speciosa*, a member of the gentian family, and yellow-flowered *Dicentra scandens*. Several species of *Arisaema*, woodland plants enjoying the moist, leafy soil, push up their strange inflorescences followed by cylindrical clusters of red fruits. The giant lily, *Cardiocrinum*, *Cautleya* species (more ginger relatives) and orchids such as *Pleione humilis* grow on the forest floor beneath evergreen oak, maples and magnolias with an understorey of *Rhododendron arboreum*. Pleiones or Indian crocuses (which are neither solely Indian, nor crocuses) occur mainly in China and India with a few species in Nepal, Burma, Thailand, Taiwan and Laos. They are neither truly terrestrial nor properly epiphytic, growing on the deep litter at the edge of forests, and on moss- and debris-covered rocks, fallen tree trunks and stumps and the lowest branches of trees; their altitudinal range is from 1,000 m/3,300 ft – *P. formosana* in Taiwan – to 3,500 m/11,500 ft: *P. limprichtii* in Burma.

In eastern Nepal grows *Euphorbia schillingii*, a handsome spurge rather like *E. sikkimensis*; it is associated with the scrambling *Senecio scandens*, *Astilbe rivularis*, *Hedychium densiflorum*, *Cautleya spicata* and, among woody species, *Pieris formosa* and *Pinus wallichiana* as well as the inevitable *Rhododendron arboreum*; it favours rocky terrain. Nepal boasts several species of blue poppy (not all of them blue), including the noble *Meconopsis grandis* and, of course, *M. napaulensis*, which can be found with *Arisaema griffithii* and cardiocrinums in mixed forest with bamboo; they also inhabit open woodland, alpine meadows and rocky stream margins.

Everywhere in the rhododendron heartland the range of other genera and species is vast. In the foothills of southern Bhutan grow *Buddleja crispa*, *Lonicera quinquelocularis* and *Elaeagnus umbellata*. *Rhododendron virgatum* grows on steep banks at the edge of woodland of *R. grande*, *R. arboreum* and *R. maddenii*, with the yellow candelabra *Primula prolifera* in the valley bottoms. The rhododendron and conifer forests of Bhutan shelter some exquisite small plants, such as *Primula* species, and *Bryocarpum himalaicum* which looks just like a yellow soldanella in flower. The royal fern, *Osmunda regalis*, and other osmunda species grow in damp sites at the edge of *Pinus wallichiana* forests. With the interrupted fern, *Osmunda claytoniana*, grow *Euphorbia griffithii*, *Cardiocrinum giganteum* and *Trillium tschonoskii*.

ASSAM, MANIPUR AND BURMA

Some fine trees are native to these regions. On the Brahmaputra–Irrawaddy divide grows *Cornus chinensis*, like a very superior version of the European *C. mas* and a fine tree for regions where the frosts of winter are only moderate and the summers hot and damp. It ranges from Hupeh in China westwards to the eastern Himalayas. One of the loveliest trees of Upper Burma is Kingdon Ward's carmine cherry, *Prunus cerasoïdes rubea* (*P. puddum*), growing with *Rhododendron magnificum* in the region of the headwaters of the Irrawaddy and with *Pyrus pashia* in Ukhrul; it is found as far north as the regions to the north of the Tsangpo gorge.

The lower temperate rain forest of Manipur has many species of cherry, maple and oak, chestnut (*Castanopsis*), *Ilex*, and magnolias – *Magnolia* itself, and also *Manglietia* and *Michelia* – with the great climbing *Rosa gigantea*, *Buddleja macrostachya*, *B. paniculata* and *B. asiatica*, the no less fragrant *Elaeagnus umbellata* and *E. latifolia*, climbing *Holboellia latifolia* and *Rhododendron johnstoneanum* (section Maddenia). The carmine cherry grows with *Engelhardtia spicata*, Maddenia rhododendrons, *Cornus macrophylla*, *Symplocos*, *Ternstroemia japonica*, and many trees with bright spring foliage: *Cinnamomum*, *Ficus*, *Acer oblongum*, *Quercus serrata* and species of *Rhus*. *Lilium mackliniae* is found here, with *Iris kumaonensis* and hechychiums, especially *H. coronarium*.

The forests of Manipur are sharply stratified by altitude, and at increasing elevations the warm-temperate species yield to cool-temperate: *Rosa longicuspis*, *Clematis montana*, the bird cherry *Prunus nepalensis*, *Magnolia campbellii* and *Michelia manipurensis*, with *Sorbus insignis*, which usually starts life as an epiphyte. This rowan is also found in Bhutan, associated with *Magnolia campbellii* and *Acer campbellii*, *Skimmia multinervia*, *Daphne bholua*, *Betula utilis*, *Hydrangea heteromalla* and *Rhododendron arboreum*. Other plants that revel in the moist, temperate climate of upland Manipur, where the winter is short and the summers warm and perpetually wet, are ferns, *Agapetes* species, and orchids, but above all mosses.

Climbers are less common than epiphytes in the temperate rain forest, but among plants that have adapted to reach for the light by climbing through, rather than growing on, host trees, are species of *Schisandra* and *Clematis*, the most common genera, with *Actinidia*, *Lonicera*, *Hydrangea*, *Rosa*, *Holboellia*, *Akebia* and *Stauntonia*, and *Vitis*. Herbaceous plants are mainly small, and the undergrowth sparse, consisting of ferns, *Strobilanthes*, violets, begonias, oxalis, *Paris*, *Arisaema* species, orchids such as *Calanthe*, and *Cardiocrinum giganteum*.

The warm, wet summers and short, mild winters of the foothills of Assam and Upper Burma suit the deliciously fragrant rhododendrons of subsections Maddenia and Edgeworthia, the envy and despair of rhododendron buffs in Britain, where except in favoured localities the climate is just too severe for them, and they have to be grown under glass. These species belong above all to Burma and Assam, though some extend into western Yunnan where the flora, as far east as the Mekong, is fundamentally Indo-Himalayan rather than Chinese.

In Upper Burma, *Rhododendron simsii*, an azalea which is otherwise found only in Japan and in warm-temperate eastern China in coastal regions, appears as low as 240 m/800 ft. This and the wide-ranging *R. arboreum* apart, *R. notatum* and *R. dendricola* are among the first to make an appearance in the lower, warm-temperate forest. At progressively higher altitudes they are joined by species from the Vaccinioïdes section, as well as *R. chrysolepis*, *R. taggianum*, *R. lindleyi*, *R. edgeworthii*, *R. concinnoïdes* and *R. megeratum*. Other species, to be found growing as epiphytes, include *R. veitchianum* and *R. dalhousiae* (Maddenia), their hosts trees such as *Quercus glauca*. *Rhododendron lindleyi* grows high in the trees, *R. edgeworthii* more usually at the base of the trees or on rocks. The related *R. bullatum*, now sunk in *R. edgeworthii*, grows in open places whereas *R. edgeworthii* (in the narrow sense) is confined to heavily shaded forest. With these in the warm-temperate zone grows *Vaccinium gaultheriifolium*. In shady ravines *Rhododendron maddenii* can be found growing on the damp cliffs, with many species of fern – among them *Woodwardia unigemmata* and *Dryopteris wallichiana* – below. The giant fern *Gleichenia volubilis* carpets the floor of the oak forest with arisaemas such as *A. tortuosum* and *A. speciosum*, and hedychiums such as *H. gardnerianum*. The shrubby *Luculia gratissima* bears its large, pink flowers in autumn. Growing amid cultivated plants are *Edgeworthia gardneri*, *Buddleja asiatica*, and species of *Coriaria* and

Jasminum (*J. dispermum*, *J. subhumile*). *Rhododendron griffithianum*, a tree-like species, grows with *Albizia chinensis*, *Alcimandra* (*Michelia*) *cathcartii*, a magnolia relative, and *Agapetes* species, some of them, such as *A. serpens*, epiphytic and characterized by a swollen lignotuber. In the hot valley depths grows *Pinus bhutanica*, a five-needled pine.

Kingdon Ward described the climate of the temperate forest as one in which, but for the brief winter, 'the trees stand with their heads in a cool Turkish bath and their toes in a wet sponge'. In such conditions the big-leaved tree rhododendrons, often themselves hosting epiphytes, grow and spread their massive, leathery leaves: they belong in sections Grandia and Falconera and are represented by species such as *R. sinogrande*, *R. rex* and its subspecies *fictolacteum* and *arizelum*, and *R. macabeanum* from Manipur.

Overlapping with the big-leaved rhododendrons in Burma and Assam is the zone of the magnolias, *M. campbellii* and its eastern form ssp. *mollicomata*, *M. globosa* and *M. rostrata*. *Magnolia campbellii* ssp. *mollicomata* grows in wet places in the Delei valley with bamboos, while in the Seinghku valley it is accompanied by *Acer campbellii*, sword-leaved *A. wardii* and *A. sikkimense*, which is usually epiphytic in the wild, *Cinnamomum*, and *Magnolia rostrata*. The temperate rain forest, though it includes many deciduous species such as the maples, birch, magnolia, whitebeams, *Sorbus harrowiana*, *Bucklandia populnea*, and among shrubs *Enkianthus*, *Corylopsis*, *Viburnum*, *Heptapleurum* and *Gamblea ciliata*, is predominantly evergreen. As well as *Cinnamomum*, there are species of evergreen oak, *Ilex*, *Schima*, *Castanopsis*, *Illicium*, *Michelia*, and shrubs such as *Mahonia calamicaulis*, *Camellia tsaii* at the forest margins, and *Brassaiopsis speciosa*. Conifers include *Tsuga* (the only abundant conifer in the rain forest), *Podocarpus*, *Taxus wallichii*, and *Pinus wallichiana*, which at higher altitudes may form its own forest.

Above the upper limit of hill cultivation in Assam, rhododendrons and conifers gradually take over to exclude other trees; except on the lower hills, the whole sequence from subtropical valley jungle through temperate rain forest to rhododendron and conifer forests and finally alpine meadow can be seen. Altitude is only one factor; both the aspect and the nature of the surrounding vegetation also affect the range of various vegetation types. For example, although forests are found throughout the Himalayan region at around 2,000 m/7,000 ft, they will not everywhere be the same type of forest. To the south will be subtropical or warm-temperate jungle, to the north, the cool temperate rain forest extends to lower altitudes; jungle reaches higher in deep, damp gorges, the temperate forest pushes to lower altitudes from its stronghold on the high ranges. Where the forest faces due north, it is more luxuriant than on south-facing slopes; where there is less sun, the snow remains longer than where the warm air from the plains and the rays of the sun melt it away. On the steep north-facing slopes there may be a bare film of soil over the rock, yet the permanently moist atmosphere means that shallow-rooting rhododendrons never suffer from dryness. Small wonder that in less rain-drenched climates they need shade and shelter, and a loose, fluffy mulch to keep their fibrous roots cool in summer.

At higher altitudes in Burma and Assam is scattered forest of silver fir, spruce, juniper, larch and *Rhododendron rex* ssp. *arizelum*, with maples and, on the open slopes, rhododendron scrub of *R. chaetomallum* and *R. sanguineum*, and on broken ground a tanglewood of *Magnolia globosa*, *Viburnum wardii*, *Rhododendron neriiflorum* ssp. *euchaites*, and species of rose, berberis, enkianthus and cotoneaster. The mixed conifer forest of the Di Chu valley, where the humidity is slightly lower and the flora more akin to the dry ranges of southern Tibet, is decked with lichen, not moss; with the spruce and silver fir and *Tsuga* grow maples, oak, birch, and a range of shrubs such as *Rosa moyesii*, shrubby honey-suckles and rowans, *Philadelphus* and *Deutzia*, jasmine, *Euonymus*, *Ilex dipyrena*, and rhododendrons: *R. triflorum*, *R. megacalyx* and taller species of the Thomsonia section. Herbaceous plants include *Podo-phyllum*, *Rodgersia* and *Thalictrum* species, and *Primula chungensis* (which unlike other candelabra primulas is a woodland, not a meadow plant). The Mishmi valley also displays a vegetation typical of rather drier regions with *Pinus khasia*, oak, *Rosa bracteata*, *Ceratostigma griffithii*, and species of *Desmodium*, *Sophora* and *Ailanthus*. Manipur is home to the eponymous *Rhododendron manipurense*, *Lilium mackliniae*, *Primula capitata*, and species of mock orange (*Philadelphus*), *Deutzia* and honey-suckle.

On marshy meadows among bamboos and raspberry bushes, adjoin-ing rhododendron forest in northern Burma, *Primula dickeana* and cremanthodiums grow with the lovely *Nomocharis farreri*. Both *Primula alpicola luna* and the giant cowslip, *P. florindae*, grow at elevations some 450–600 m/1,500–2,000 ft below the zone of the alpine meadows pro-per, in south-eastern Tibetan grazing meadows; but *P. alpicola* var. *violacea* grows in the alpine meadows. Some of the loveliest of primulas are the petiolarids, most of which are forest plants, not alpine meadow species. As the monsoon rains abruptly end in late September, these primulas lose their large summer leaves, replacing them with tight rosettes of leaves which are often covered with farina, this presumably helping to prevent desiccation during the period until the return of the rains in early June. The flowers are borne in early April, giving the seeds time to ripen ahead of the rains.

Though much of Tibet is afflicted with a severe, cold-desert climate akin to that of Central Asia, south-eastern Tibet adjoins Assam and Upper Burma and receives the monsoon, resulting in very heavy summer rainfall and deep winter snowfalls, so that here too the mountain slopes are heavily forested. In the Tsangpo valley, above the gorge, the forest is composed of birch and *Quercus ilex*, while in the gorge, depending on the altitude, there is deciduous forest with *Magnolia rostrata* and *Acer campbellii*, larch, birch and bamboo, semi-deciduous oak and rhododendron forest or – in the upper reaches where the gorge is very deep and narrow – *Pinus wallichiana*; everywhere rhododendrons are to be found. In Pemako (which lies in the bend of the Tsangpo river, a remote and inaccessible area), the forest is dominated by *Tsuga* and rhododendrons, with *Magnolia globosa* and *Cotoneaster wardii*.

The river gorges and mountains of western China

The great rivers that burst through the mountain chains from south-eastern Tibet, carving their way seawards in great gorges and valleys, converge in north-western Sichuan, so close that from the Yangtze in the east to the Irrawaddy in the west is a mere 100 km/70 miles or so; they diverge again in western Yunnan. The region of convergence is the land of the blue poppy, *Meconopsis betonicifolia*, whose range extends from south-eastern Tibet and northern Burma eastwards to the ridges beyond the Yangtze, growing in alpine meadows and woodlands and on stream margins; on the bare mountains of Yunnan its place is taken by *M. speciosa*, which is far less adaptable to cultivation.

In the precipitous regions of the river gorges the collector George Forrest noted of species of rhododendron that, except for a few

such as *R. racemosum*, *R. lepidotum* and *R. decorum*, all are peculiarly local in their distribution, in latitudinal, longitudinal and altitudinal range. Only a few of the species found in the Yangtze basin are common in the areas drained by the Mekong or Salween, and vice versa. Many of the lateral spurs of the huge ranges separating those basins bear species indigenous to themselves alone.

257

In these regions the vegetation varies, sometimes quite abruptly, according to the variations of climate imposed by the topography; rich forests influenced by the south-west monsoon, generally on western exposures, may be separated by stretches of almost barren country.

Downstream from the convergence of the great rivers, the Yangtze makes a series of great angled bends and loops to run roughly eastwards across China, while the Mekong and the Salween pursue their southward course, the Mekong down to Cambodia and the China Sea, the Salween through Burma roughly parallel to the Irrawaddy, to emerge in the Gulf of Martaban. Each of the river valleys, and of the mountainous divides that separate them, has its own climatic quirks. The Mekong valley north of Yang-tsa is arid, and the middle Mekong is comparatively dry, these two zones separated by a rainy belt where the summer precipitation is heavy; the Salween has an arid and a wet zone separated by a very sharp line. The Salween–Mekong divide reaches high elevations, and here both the rainfall and the winter snowfall are heavy, but by the time the winds have crossed this high range they have shed their moisture, so the Mekong–Yangtze divide is barren scree and the snow line is much higher, whereas the Salween–Mekong watershed is clothed with forests and alpine meadows. The difference in climate is illustrated by *Meconopsis integrifolia*, which is abundant, to the point of colouring whole meadows, on the Mekong–Salween divide, but only sparsely represented on the dry Mekong–Yangtze ridge. The flora of the Mekong–Salween divide is essentially a summer flora, the snow falling in early October to put an end to flowering and fruiting, while that of the Mekong–Yangtze divide is chiefly an autumn flora.

Many fine plants have been introduced from these regions. *Rhododendron griersonianum* grows in open country in the upper Shweli valley on the Shweli–Salween divide on the borders of Yunnan and Burma, and *R. sinogrande* was introduced from the forests of the western flank of the Shweli–Salween divide; other large-leaved species from this region are *R. rex* ssp. *arizelum* and *R. basilicum*. *Rhododendron fulvum* was also introduced from here, but is widespread in Sichuan, Burma, Tibet and Assam as well as Yunnan. From the streams, marshy meadows and clay pastures of the region to the west of the Shweli, *Primula helodoxa* was introduced. *Rhododendron forrestii* and its creeping form *repens* were found on the Mekong–Salween divide. To these can be added snake-bark maples such as *Acer davidii*, widespread in mixed forests, and *A. forrestii* from the forests of shady valleys in the Lijiang Range; *Camellia reticulata* and *C. saluenensis*; *Stewartia pteropetiolata*

(*Hartia sinensis*) from open places in the Shweli valley and, at higher elevations, on the Shweli–Salween divide; *Syringa yunnanensis*, a shrub of open scrub and hillsides which also grows in oak and pine forests; *Osmanthus delavayi* and *O. forrestii* from wooded mountain slopes of Yunnan; *Jasminum polyanthum* from the regions to the west of the Shweli near the Burmese border; and *Sorbus harrowiana* (now considered to fall within *S. insignis*), a shrub in open rocky places and a tree in sheltered places.

In the mountains of north-western Sichuan grow many plants which are staples of the shrub and herbaceous borders of cool temperate gardens: *Buddleja davidii*, *Hydrangea villosa*, *Aruncus*, *Anemone vitifolia*, *Astilbe rivularis*, *Thalictrum delavayi*, monkshoods (*Aconitum* species), *Artemisia lactiflora* and *Rodgersia aesculifolia*. This is the home of the tea rose, of *Cornus controversa* (which like several dogwoods extends from the Himalayas through China to Japan) and *Rhus verniciflua*, and at higher elevations of *Rhododendron calophytum*, forming tall trees, with *Euptelea pleiosperma*, *Pterocarya hupehensis*, *Viburnum erubescens* var. *prattii*, *Magnolia nitida* and maples. *Arisaema candidissimum* grows on open rocky slopes and slate cliffs in the valleys of southern Sichuan.

The low, hot valleys of the Salween which lead up to the Yunnan plateau are characterized by a subtropical, Indo-Malayan forest flora, which yields at higher altitudes on the Mekong divide to a more typic-ally Chinese flora of *Rhododendron ciliicalyx*, *R. decorum* and *R. delavayi*, oak and pine. The beautiful *R. wardii* extends eastwards from south-eastern Tibet through Yunnan and Sichuan, growing among larch, oak, maple, fir and birch; to the east of the Lidang river it is replaced by *R. puralbum*. Where the pine-topped ridges and wide, cultivated valleys of Yunnan yield to the jagged limestone towers and crests are forests of rhododendrons and tall pines, *Rhododendron fortunei* in the more open pine forests and *R. racemosum* between the pines – it does not grow in the denser oak forests for, as George Forrest observed, 'it holds almost the same position on the mountains of western China as our heather does at home', but he also found it on clayey loam between forests of evergreen oak in drier places on clayey sandstone. In the pine and deciduous oak forest, open glades are carpeted with *Roscoea cautleyoïdes* and *R. purpurea*, *Cypripedium tibeticum*, *Stellera chamaejasme*, *Hemerocallis*, anemones and iris.

In marshy meadows there are great masses of *Primula sikkimensis*, *P. beesiana* and *P. bulleyana*, the second at lower elevations than *P. bulleyana*; the two have a preference for the same sort of habitat, but are not found in association. Other plants of wet sites are *P. poissonii*, marsh marigolds and *Cynoglossum*, with *Primula viallii*. *Rheum alexan-drae* grows in meadows and also at the margins of pools. In the drier meadows grow *Incarvillea grandiflora* and *I. lutea, Podophyllum, Mecon-opsis integrifolia, Iris chrysographes* and primulas, among them *P. secundi-flora, P. pseudosikkimensis*, and *P. wardii*, the Chinese equivalent of the Himalayan *P. involucrata*, with *Omphalogramma vinciflorum*. In the clay foothills, there are shady woods with a tall herbaceous understorey of *Astilbe, Rodgersia* and *Arisaema*. Above the meadows *Tsuga*, oak and birch fill the gullies. *Hemerocallis forrestii* grows on dry cliffs and ledges at mid altitudes in western Yunnan.

In the mountains east of the Yangtze bends, the growing season lasts eight months and is characterized by two main flowering peaks: spring, dependent on snow melt, with rhododendrons in April and May, blue poppies, and primulas in June–July; and an autumn season, stimulated by the first rains, when Campanulaceae, gentians and saxi-frages flower in September and October, from the second half of the rainy season to the onset of the cold, dry weather.

In ascending order, the vegetation here is pine forest, succeeded by forest of oak and *Picea*, and above this again the *Abies* and rhododen-dron forest. Rhododendrons, of course, are omnipresent: amid the pines grow *R. radinum, R. racemosum* and species of section Lapponica, on shaded cliffs, and *R. yunnanense* in open places. In the oak forest grow *R. heliolepis* and species of sections Cephalantha and Lapponica, with *R. oreotrephes* and *R. decorum* on open slopes and *R. setiferum* in drier places. The middle forest is also characterized by thickets of bamboo, and in places the floor is carpeted with *Androsace sarmentosa*. *Rhododendron wardii* and *R. puralbum, R. souliei* and *R. clementinae* are typical of the *Abies* zone, with *R. beesianum* almost making forests in itself, as does *R. traillianum*. On rocks by water, as well as on dry slopes, grows the fringe tree, *Chionanthus retusus*, and in open boggy places *Rhododendron hippophaëoïdes* thrives. On the open slopes above is rhododendron scrub of species from section Lapponica, with primulas – *P. szechuanica, P. sinopurpurea* and *P. sonchifolia* – in damp hollows, revelling in snowmelt and even flowering in the receding snow itself, when the temperature is just 0°C/32°F. Gaultherias, among them *G. forrestii* originally discovered on the eastern slopes of the Tali range in Yunnan, also grow in open scrub and among rocks, in moist places.

The montane forests of China

Some of the karst or limestone mountains of China, unlike the Himalayas, look quite unreal to western eyes; those Chinese landscape paintings with mountains as steep as pillars, and rocky crags that seem to float in the air above deep valleys, are not fantasy but a faithful representation of reality. Formations of this kind are found in Guizhou (Kweichou) province, bordered on the west by Yunnan and the north by Sichuan, in neighbouring Henan province, and in the 'stone forest' of western Yunnan. The highest peak of Guizhou, Fan Jin Shan, rises sheer from the valleys, the flora ranging from subtropical to cloud and rhododendron forest. The summit of Fan Jin Shan itself is above the tree line and is covered with dwarf bamboo, lilies and primulas.

This extraordinary landscape, where there is a high rainfall and a wealth of plant species, is part of the extensive mixed forest formation extending through the centre of China from the Pacific in the east to western Sichuan. Like the Himalayan foothills, it displays a great diversity of trees and shrubs, herbs and lilies. Here grow the golden larch, *Pseudolarix amabilis*, *Cryptomeria*, *Loropetalum*, *Poliothyrsis sinensis*, and *Rhododendron fortunei*, one of the best-known of Chinese species. The valleys shelter *Daphniphyllum*, hydrangeas, the Chinese tallow tree (*Sapium sebiferum*), *Celtis julianae*, *Meliosma veitchiorum*, *Cladrastis wilsonii*, *Acer davidii*, and several of China's monotypic trees, including *Idesia polycarpa* and *Emmenopterys henryi*, the latter sometimes festooned with climbing *Schizophragma integrifolium*. *Anemone hupehensis* and *Aconitum* flourish on the limestone hillsides. The range of this anemone overlaps with that of the more westerly, lower-altitude *A. vitifolia* and with that of the higher-altitude, higher-latitude *A. tomentosa*. Despite their reluctance to grow on lime soils in gardens, rhododendrons are frequently found on the limestone rocks of Yunnan, dominating for example the pure limestone range of Lijiang.

On Fan Jin Shan the dove or handkerchief tree, *Davidia*, grows in moist valley bottoms at altitudes where subtropical species yield to conifers and deciduous broad-leaved trees. There are rhododendrons, mahonias, stewartias, maples, alders, *Cephalotaxus* or Chinese yew, and a variety of fruiting trees and climbers; rowans such as *Sorbus hupehensis*, *Celastrus*, *Clerodendrum trichotomum*, *Euonymus hamiltonianus*. The understorey includes daphnes, ferns and *Sarcococca*. On the mist-wreathed, craggy submit are small rhododendrons, gesneriads and primulas, *Cardiocrinum*, hollies and the mountain's own silver fir, *Abies fanjinshanensis*.

261

Not all China's hills are karst types; one of the most famous of Chinese mountains, Emei Shan or Mt Omei in Sichuan, is a humpy beast with no peaks and no permanent snow. Made famous by Ernest Wilson, it is amazingly rich in species: three thousand or more. With annual precipitation averaging almost 1,940 mm/more than 76 in, it is well watered; the rain falls mainly between July and September, and the winter months are dry and cold. The plants of the foothills include *Pinus massoniana*, the southern red pine (which has a huge range, over ten or more provinces of China to Taiwan and northern Vietnam), *Quercus serrata*, *Cupressus funebris*, and *Alnus cremastogyne* along the stream-sides, with *Pterocarya stenoptera* and *Camptotheca acuminata*, giving way at about 900 m/3,000 ft to rainforest of *Cunninghamia lanceolata* and members of the Lauraceae such as *Persea* (*Machilus*), *Lindera* and *Litsea*, with several monotypic genera including *Tapiscia*, *Carrieria*, *Itoa*, *Emmenopterys* and *Idesia*. *Hedychium forrestii* grows near the base of the mountain, at the edge of woodland and along the ditches bordering cultivated fields.

The temperate flora, E. H. Wilson noted, is very aggressive, with species of *Viburnum*, *Malus*, *Rubus* and *Prunus*, *Cornus macrophylla* (with a native range from the Himalayas to Japan, this occurs in China south of the Yellow River and north of the subtropical coastal provinces), *Acer davidii* and *Betula luminifera* growing nearly down to the base of the mountain, where the climate would support a warm-temperate vegetation. At higher elevations the Lauraceae give way to evergreen oak and castanopsis, and higher still *Cunninghamia* yields to *Abies delavayi*, a wide-ranging, high mountain fir closely related to Forrest's *A. forrestii* and *A. georgei* from Yunnan, and adapted to long cold winters and short, cool, moist summers. With the fir grow occasional specimens of *Tsuga yunnanensis*, *Taxus cuspidata* var. *chinensis*, and on the summit *Juniperus squamata*. Autumn is bright with rowans (*Sorbus sargentiana* and others) and maples such as *Acer flabellatum* var. *yunnanense*; among them grow *Decaisnea fargesii*, mahonias including the recent introductions *M. confusa* and *M. gracilipes*, and the herbaceous berberid *Epimedium acuminatum*. Species of *Stachyurus* and *Rubus*, *Viburnum nervosum*, the fiercely-thorned *Rosa sericea* (*omeiensis*) var. *pteracantha*, are some of the plants both familiar and newly-introduced from Mt Omei that grace the gardens of the west.

Wa Shan is also clad with *Abies delavayi* and *Tsuga yunnanensis*, accompanied by *Juniperus formosa* and *Picea complanata*. Ernest Wilson found *Magnolia sinensis* growing at middle altitudes on Wa Shan, with broad-leaved deciduous trees and shrubs, rhododendrons and silver firs,

in moist woodland. As so often, rhododendrons are the main component of the forest, at their most abundant from 3,000 m/10,000 ft to
the summit, where they form almost a hundred per cent of the vegetation, though among *R. yanthinum* and others grow hydrangeas and
neillias, *Dipelta ventricosa*, *Enkianthus deflexus*, and much else, with *Rosa
sericea*, *Pieris* and *Gaultheria* species at the summit.

Many species are by no means confined to one small locality, as one
might conclude from reading only a single collector's field notes.
Magnolia sargentiana grows in thickets and moist woodlands to the west
of Wa Shan, and is found in similar habitats through much of Yunnan
and Sichuan. *Magnolia wilsonii* is a native of western Sichuan, growing
at forest margins and along mountain streams with deciduous broad-
leaved trees and shrubs, rhododendrons, silver fir, spruce and hemlock
fir. The warmer regions of Yunnan and Sichuan are the home of
Camellia saluenensis, which grows in a wide range of habitats from
scrub or open thickets, often on dry, stony or rocky hillsides but also
along streams, on cliffs and steep grassy slopes, to thickets in shady
gullies or in mixed and pine forest. The cooler, wetter sites suit *C.
pitardii*, while *C. reticulata* grows in scrub, thickets and open pine forests
at mid altitudes in Yunnan, and *C. cuspidata* has a more easterly
distribution in Sichuan and western Hubei, also in thickets and light
woodland. The wild form of *Rosa banksiae* is found at low altitudes
in the mountain ranges of western China, from Yunnan to Hubei.

HUBEI
The province of Hubei (Hupeh) reaches nothing like the elevations of
the mountains further to the west, and the flora of Yichang (Ichang)
on the Yangtze is essentially warm-temperate or even subtropical.
However, in the higher glens and gorges grow many plants familiar
to gardeners from temperate climates: *Rosa laevigata* in open places,
R. multiflora, *R. moschata* and *R. banksiae* on cliffs and growing into
tall trees; *Eriobotrya japonica*, the loquat; *Vitex negundo*, *Symplocos paniculata*, *Lagerstroemia indica*, *Deutzia discolor* and *D. schneideriana*, *Kolkwitzia amabilis* or beauty bush, *Jasminum floridum*, *Viburnum utile*, *Abelia
chinensis*, *Euonymus alatus*, *Hydrangea strigosa*, *H. sargentiana*, *Syringa
julianae* at woodland margins and *S. reflexa*, *Staphylea holocarpa*, *Itea
ilicifolia* with its creamy-green catkins, *Buddleja officinalis*, the tricky
lilac-flowered *Daphne genkwa*, and *Loropetalum chinense*. The popular
blue-flowered *Rhododendron augustinii* is at the eastern limit of its range
in Hubei; it extends as far west as Tibet. Familiar climbers include
Lonicera japonica, *Trachelospermum jasminoïdes*, *Clematis armandii*, *Vitis*

flexuosa, *Parthenocissus henryana*, *Wisteria sinensis* and *Dregea* (*Wattakaka*) *sinensis*.

Herbaceous plants cultivated in western gardens include *Anemone hupehensis*, *Iris japonica*, *Delphinium chinense*, *Platycodon grandiflora*, and *Hemerocallis fulva* and *H. lilio-asphodelus* (*H. flava*), the lemon lily. These two species of day lily grow in regions of China with very different climates, the first in regions of high rainfall, the lemon lily in dry regions at forest margins.

Hubei's trees are also well represented now in western gardens, with *Paulownia*, *Melia azedarach*, *Sapium sebiferum*, *Xylosma racemosum*, *Gleditsia sinensis*, *Toona* (*Cedrela*) *sinensis*, *Ailanthus glandulosa*, *Magnolia sprengeri* and the widespread *M. denudata*, and *Sophora japonica*, as well as many others, less familiar, from the warmer regions. More properly belonging to the cool-temperate flora are *Acer griseum* and the wide-ranging *Betula utilis* (which splitters class as *B. jacquemontii* in the western Himalayas and *B. albo-sinensis* in China). Near the summit of Hsan-lung Shan in north-western Hubei *Liriodendron chinense* is common in the woods, with *Viburnum plicatum*, *Styrax hemsleyana*, *Dipelta floribunda*, *Illicium henryi* growing on limestone cliffs, and the rare *Koelreuteria bipinnata*. Typical of the forests of Wan-tiao Shan are *Fagus sinensis*, the Chinese beech, with *Tetracentron sinense*, *Davidia involucrata*, cherry, rowan and wild pear, *Rhododendron sutchuenense*, *Viburnum plicatum* in shady places and *Rosa moschata* in the open, and *R. sericea* near the summit. Epimediums, corydalis and *Stylophorum* grow in the understorey. On the Hubei–Sichuan frontier, virgin forest of silver fir and birch grows with *Rhododendron fargesii*, *R. maculiferum*, *R. sutchuenense* and *R. adenopodum*; at lower elevations silver fir is replaced by hemlock spruce, with maples, *Davidia*, *Staphylea holocarpa*, *Aesculus wilsonii* (a close relative of the Indian horse chestnut, *A. indica*, from the north-eastern Himalayas), *Cladrastis sinensis* and *Pterostyrax*, as well as many of the shrubs already listed, and climbers such as *Lonicera tragophylla*, *Clematis montana*, *Schisandra*, *Holboellia*, and *Sinofranchetia chinensis*.

Plants of the drier regions from west to east

The drier regions, from Afghanistan and the western Himalayas to the inner valleys of Bhutan or the gorges of western and northern Sichuan, are home to a different vegetation. Afghanistan, indeed, has a more extreme continental climate, but some plants, among them the woodland *Syringa emodi*, have a range extending from subalpine Afghanistan to Kashmir and Kumaon. In the west, in Kashmir, there are also typically Iranian species, such as *Rosa foetida* and *R. ecae*, together with the Central Asian *R. beggeriana*. Well-known plants of the drier western regions of Nepal westwards in the temperate Himalayan zone include *Pyracantha crenulata*, *Deutzia staminea*, *Philadelphus coronarius*, *Spiraea canescens*, *Cotinus coggygria*, *Sophora mollis*, *Staphylea emodi*, *Rosa brunonii* and *R. webbiana*, *Abelia triflora*, *Jasminum humile*, *Colquhounia coccinea*, *Cornus capitata*, and species of *Elaeagnus*, *Berberis*, *Indigofera*, *Ligustrum* and *Buddleja*.

The chilghoza pine, *Pinus gerardiana*, is confined to the mountains of eastern Afghanistan, parts of Pakistan, and the dry inner valleys of the northern Himalayas. The Bhutan pine, *P. wallichiana*, is a major constituent of the mid to high altitude Himalayan forests, especially in the drier inner valleys. The Morinda or west Himalayan spruce, *Picea smithiana*, ranges from Afghanistan to central Nepal, occurring in mixed forests with *Abies pindrow*. This, the west Himalayan fir, is also found with *Pinus wallichiana* and *Betula utilis*, as well as in pure stands, mostly in the cooler, wetter valleys, at lower altitudes than *Abies spectabilis*, which grows where the winters are long and snow-bound.

The white-stemmed birch of the western region, once known as *Betula jacquemontii*, is now thought to be part of the *B. utilis* continuum reaching from Afghanistan to south-west China, showing its most obvious alteration in character at the point in central Nepal, at the gorge of the Kali Gandaki river, where the climate also changes most dramatically, between the monsoon-drenched southern subalpine flanks and the dry slopes within the rainshadow of the main mountain range. The birches of the wetter regions are dark-barked, those from the dry regions with higher light factors are white.

In the inner valleys of Bhutan is found a xerophytic type of forest with *Pinus wallichiana* growing with shrubs that include *Elaeagnus parvifolia* and *Hippophaë salicifolia*. With the pines, *Rhododendron triflorum* forms a subshrub below *R. arboreum*. Other species of the blue pine forest of Bhutan include *Acer campbellii*, *Malus sikkimensis*, *Schisandra grandiflora*, and *Cornus controversa*, with species of *Sorbus*, *Viburnum* and *Spiraea*. Here only the moister gullies offer a congenial home to the species of the montane cloud forest zone, the spruce *Picea spinulosa* and *Tsuga dumosa*, covered with epiphytes, including ferns.

Above Gulmarg in Kashmir, amid forests of *Picea smithiana*, are many flowers: *Rosa macrophylla* and *Paeonia emodi* at the forest margin, and in woodland glades *Morina coulteriana*. *Viburnum foetens* forms extensive stands in the open, or grows as an understorey to fir and spruce forests. Here too grow the Indian chestnut, *Aesculus indica*, and *Parrotiopsis jacquemontiana*. Above this zone, on the open plateau, grow *Fritillaria imperialis* and *F. roylei*, and meadows of *Euphorbia wallichii* and *Iris kumaonensis*, the turf between them spangled with alpine flowers: *Anemone obtusiloba*, gentians, and androsaces including *A. sarmentosa*, *A. sempervivoïdes* and *A. lanuginosa*.

CHINA'S ARID GORGES

The Sholo, a tributary of the Yangtze in western China, is characterized by dry, eroded gullies, flanked by pine forest and *Rhododendron radinum* with species of iris, and in the gullies themselves buddlejas and *Jasminum beesianum*. The arid gorge too is clad with pine forest, with shrubby bauhinias and oaks, cotoneaster, and climbing vines and clematis, and an understorey of lilies and hemerocallis. At Muli on the Lidang, in Sichuan, abrupt changes in the composition of the flora reflect the sensitivity of the vegetation to slight changes of shade, shelter and irrigation, in this rather dry climate. At the foot of the Muli cliff one passes from thickets of *Ceratostigma* and scented briar rose to *Cotoneaster*, *Berberis*, *Deutzia*, *Desmodium*, *Viburnum* and *Hypericum patulum*, tangled together with species of *Clematis* and *Codonopsis*, vines and *Leptocodon gracilis*, as Frank Kingdon Ward observed in his usual detailed way. On the higher slopes a transition zone of shrubby honeysuckles, daphne, berberis, juniper, cassiope and *Potentilla fruticosa* occurs between the forest of larch, silver fir and *Rhododendron traillianum* and *R. beesianum*, and the alpine turf where no woody plants grow.

The upper reaches of the gorges of northern and western Sichuan, dry and rocky in contrast to the lush subtropical lower valleys, are transformed for a spell in late spring from a semi-desert into 'a veritable fairyland', in the words of E. H. Wilson, when he discovered the regal lily (*Lilium regale*) perched on baking cliffs, with *Eremurus chinensis* and *Incarvillea arguta*. The hillsides are also home to roses, *Caryopteris incana*, buddlejas, *Neillia longiracemosa*, *Syringa*, *Ligustrum* and *Hypericum*. On open, west-facing slopes *Rosa soulieana*, *R. willmottiae*, *R. multibracteata* and *R. sericea* grow with *Lonicera deflexicalyx*, *Philadelphus purpurascens* and *Prunus serrula*. As in the valleys of the Lijiang range on the Sichuan–Yunnan border, the wayside slopes in Yunnan are decked with *Rosa longicuspis* and *Cornus capitata*, *Rosa multiflora* and *Hypericum patulum*, *Rhododendron decorum* and *R. delavayi*, lyonias, *Rosa sericea*, grey-leaved *Buddleja fallowiana*, firethorns (*Pyracantha* species), *Leyces-*

teria formosa, *Coriaria nepalensis*, *Elaeagnus* species, *Clematis chrysocoma* and the white-washed bramble, *Rubus biflorus*, and white-stemmed, glaucous-leaved *Berberis dictyophylla*, with other barberries, *Dipelta yunnanensis* and, thriving even in dry sites, *Rhododendron yunnanense*. On the drier valley slopes are deutzias and berberis and *Spiraea canescens*, rose species, *Clematis montana* and *C. rehderiana*, shrubby paeonies, and a variety of shrubby legumes of the genera *Indigofera*, *Desmodium*, *Caragana* and others, including *Desmodium praestans* in dry places at the margins of thickets. Herbaceous plants include *Primula cockburniana* and *Thalictrum dipterocarpum* growing in moist ditches, *Trollius yunnanensis* and *Rheum alexandrae* from moist, open, windswept meadows, *Iris kumaonensis*, and *Cynoglossum amabile*, found in both dry and moist pastures.

The lower meadows are home to a variety of small herbs, such as *Anemone demissa*, *Incarvillea mairei*, small irises (among them yellow *I. forrestii*), *Cypripedium* species and the daphne-relative *Stellera chamaejasme* var. *chrysantha*, and near the lower moraines *Hemerocallis forrestii*. A few bulbs grow in the meadows, *Fritillaria cirrhosa* among them. In the higher pastures and screes blue poppies (*Meconopsis horridula*) and their yellow relative *M. integrifolia* grow with *Clematis montana*, and in the wetter places primulas such as *P. secundiflora*; *P. forrestii* grows in drier places both in the lower and the higher meadows, often beneath a rocky overhang.

Also on the Yulong mountain of the Lijiang range in north-western Yunnan grow oaks, such as *Quercus pannosa* with gold-felted leaves, in spruce forest with the very widely-distributed *Buddleja asiatica*, here near the eastern extremity of its range, *Betula szechuanica*, *Schisandra rubriflora*, *Sorbus hupehensis* var. *obtusa* with its glaucous foliage and pink fruits, and *Litsea chunii*. The same mountain is home to *Acer forrestii*, *Paeonia delavayi*, *P. lutea* and *P. potaninii* (assuming these to be distinct species), *Photinia davidsoniae* and conifers including *Abies chensiensis* var. *salvensis*, *Picea brachytyla* var. *complanata* and *Larix potaninii*. The Lijiang spruce, *Picea likiangensis*, extends into Tibet and Sichuan as well as Yunnan. In the open forest of *Pinus densata*, and occasionally in bare, rocky places, grows the golden *Daphne aurantiaca*, with dwarf junipers, pleiones, slipper orchids and the prostrate *Rhododendron telmateium*.

Towards the north of Sichuan province the river gorges begin to yield to the high Tibetan plateau, with Gansu to the north and east and Tibet to the west. This great plain, surrounded by low rolling hills, is the home of the fabled scarlet poppywort, *Meconopsis punicea*, growing on the edge of woodland and among scrub, though always in the moister places, never on the really dry slopes. Among the plants of the scrub are *Spiraea* and *Lonicera*, *Potentilla* and shrubby roses, and even some rhododendrons: *R. przewalskii* and *R. sargentianum*. The herbaceous flora includes yellow *Cremanthodium*, blue delphiniums and gentians.

Japan

A great many plants that enrich western gardens were first introduced from Japan, but by no means all of them are actually Japanese native plants. Several bearing the specific epithet *japonicus/a/um* are natives of China, whence they were introduced to and cultivated in Japan and there first encountered by western botanists and plant hunters. Thus *Iris japonica*, *Kerria japonica*, *Aucuba japonica*, and *Eriobotrya japonica* are all, in fact, natives of western Hubei. The so-called Japanese anemones are all natives of the Himalayas and China, as we have seen. In their different ways, both the Chinese and the Japanese were gardeners centuries before Europeans progressed beyond the cultivation of plants for medicinal and economic purposes; in the case of some genera, such as *Hosta* and the flowering cherries, breeding and selection has so obscured the original species that virtually all the first introductions to reach the west were of garden forms.

However, some plants are rightly attributed to Japan. *Camellia japonica* is perhaps the most universally known; a native of near-coastal regions in southern Japan, it also grows wild in Korea and has long been cultivated in China. *Camellia sasanqua* is also Japanese, from woodlands, thickets and grassy slopes in the mountains of Kyushu. Like the camellias, *Pieris japonica* grows in the milder regions, but *Skimmia japonica* extends into the cooler zones. The flowering quince, *Chaenomeles japonica*, is a Japanese native from mountain woodlands, although the shrub that gardeners sometimes casually refer to as 'japonica' is the Chinese *C. speciosa*. The shrub or small tree usually called Japanese maple is *Acer palmatum*, which grows in the mountains except on Hokkaido, but also has a wide range in China and Korea; the full moon maple, *A. japonicum*, is also a mountain species, but confined to Japan. The Japanese witch hazel, *Hamamelis japonica*, occurs in mountain regions throughout Japan.

The familiar hydrangea, *H. macrophylla*, grown in mophead and lacecap forms, was originally a native of light woodlands in the coastal regions of central Japan. The smaller *H. involucrata* is Japanese too, while *H. serrata* occurs also in Korea. The climbing *H. anomala* ssp. *petiolaris* and related *Schizophragma hydrangeoïdes* grow in woods and thickets. Another great group of highly-bred garden plants associated with Japan is the flowering cherries, long the object of near-devotion by the Japanese people. They are probably derived from the Chinese *Prunus serrula* and the Japanese *P. jamasakura* (*serrula spontanea*). *Prunus incisa* is a shrubby species from Mt Fuji, and *P. sargentii* extends into Korea and Sakhalin. The Formosan cherry, *P. campanulata*, is native to southern Japan and Formosa.

It is not uncommon for Japanese plants to be found also in South Korea and Taiwan (Formosa), while others extend into China and even to the Himalayas. Thus *Stauntonia hexaphylla*, an evergreen climber related to the Chinese and Himalayan *Holboellia*, is found in Japan, South Korea, Taiwan and the Ryukyus, the string of islands between southern Japan and Taiwan; being so widespread, it is also variable. The katsura, *Cercidiphyllum japonicum*, also occurs in China. The Japanese honeysuckle, *Lonicera japonica*, extends into Korea and China, and *Viburnum plicatum* has a southerly distribution, growing in the thickets and woodlands of the mountains in Japan, Taiwan and China. In other genera, Japanese species are matched by allied Chinese species, as in *Callicarpa*, for example, with *C. japonica* and the Chinese *C. dichotoma* and *C. bodinieri*. Like China, Japan has its species of wisteria: *W. floribunda*, and *W. venusta*, which is known only from cultivated specimens. China's *Magnolia liliiflora* has long been cultivated in Japan, which has its own species: the very hardy *M. kobus* and the more southerly star magnolia, *M. stellata*, which grows in sphagnum bogs on the mountains of southern Honshu, with *Alnus hirsuta* and *Ilex crenata*; and *M. hypoleuca* (*obovata*), which occurs in mountain regions throughout Japan. *Magnolia salicifolia* grows in oak and beech forests at low to mid altitudes on Honshu, Shikoku and Kyushu. *Disanthus cercidifolius*, related to the witch hazels, is Japanese and Chinese, but the allied *Corylopsis* species are more regional, with *C. pauciflora* and others from Japan and the *C. sinensis* complex from China.

Many Japanese pines are also found elsewhere in the region. The Japanese cedar, *Cryptomeria japonica*, is properly a native of central China as well as of Japan. The Japanese red pine, *Pinus densiflora*, is widely distributed in Japan's three main islands, and also found in Korea and the Shandong peninsula of China. The Japanese white pine, *P. parviflora*, occurs throughout Japan, and on the Korean island of Ullung. However, the related *P. morrisonicola* or Taiwan white pine is found only in the mountains of Taiwan, particularly Mt Morrison, where the Taiwan fir, *Abies kawakamii*, also forms pure stands on steep northern exposures. This mountain also has its own spruce, *Picea morrisonicola*, the most southerly species of spruce; it forms pure forests in steep country. The Japanese black pine, *Pinus thunbergii*, is a maritime species from the three main islands, also occurring in South Korea.

One of the most striking of Japanese spruces is the tiger-tail spruce, *Picea polita*, a tree of the cool-temperate region of Honshu and the southern islands. Growing in boggy ground at altitudes from little above sea level to 1,600 m/5,300 ft, the Sakhalin spruce, *P. glehnii*, is found in Hokkaido, Honshu and south Sakhalin. The most important forest tree in Hokkaido is the Sakhalin fir, *Abies sachalinensis*. The Momi fir, *Abies firma*, is widely distributed from north to south in Japan, generally at the lower altitudes, sometimes forming pure stands in dry places and sometimes the dominant tree in woodland on blanket bogs. *Abies homolepis* is a mountain fir forming pure stands on the summits, and *A. mariesii* occurs on all the high mountains, while *A. veitchii* is restricted to the subalpine zone of Honshu. *Larix kaempferi*, the Japanese larch, occurs in the forests of central Honshu at mid elevations. The umbrella pine, *Sciadopitys verticillata*, is native to two small areas in central Honshu.

One of the few daphnes with yellow flowers is a Japanese native: *D. jezoensis*, which is summer deciduous and winter flowering (whereas the Chinese woodland species with yellow flowers, *D. giraldii*, is more conventionally winter deciduous, and flowers in late spring). In the mountains west of Izu grow *Enkianthus campanulatus* and *E. perulatus*. There are some rhododendrons among the plants of the uplands, *R. kaempferi* and *R. dauricum* among them; *R. mucronulatum* and the azalea *R. yedoense* are also found in Korea, on the mountain slopes. The probable parent of the Kurume azaleas, *R. obtusum*, may grow wild on the high mountains of Kyushu. Amid the moorland plants of Japan *Sorbus matsumurana* varies from tree stature to a low shrub, according to altitude and exposure.

In southern Japan, where the climate is warm-temperate, there are many broad-leaved evergreen woody plants in addition to the camellia: *Cinnamomum camphora*, *Cleyera japonica*, *Eurya japonica*, *Daphniphyllum macropodum*, *Trochodendron aralioïdes*, *Distylium japonicum*, *Fatsia japonica*, *Elaeagnus macrophylla*, *Ardisia crenata*, *Viburnum japonicum*, *Ligustrum japonicum*, the climbers *Kadsura japonica* and *Trachelospermum asiaticum* and *T. jasminoïdes*, and *Podocarpus macrophyllus* and *P. nagi*. The sacred bamboo, *Nandina domestica*, is also from the warmer southern half of Japan, where it grows in ravines and valleys in the mountains; it also occurs in southern China and India. *Michelia compressa* grows on steep, densely forested slopes of the mountains of southern Japan, Taiwan and the Ryukyus.

Cycas revoluta grows near the seashore; other near-coastal plants are *Rhaphiolepis umbellata*, *Eurya emarginata*, *Senecio scandens*. Between the dunes and the coniferous forests grow *Euonymus japonicus*, *Eurya emarginata*, *Hibiscus hamabo*, *Litsea japonica*, *Pittosporum tobira*, *Quercus phillyraeoïdes*, *Rosa wichuraiana* and *Ternstroemia gymnanthera*.

As we have already seen, Asiatic species are often echoed in North America by allied species. The snowbell, *Styrax japonica*, is found in Japan and Korea, but *S. obassia* is confined to Japan, while several species are natives of China; these Asiatic species find a counterpart in *S. americana* from the south-eastern United States. The camellia relatives *Stewartia* are Asiatic (for example, Japan's *S. pseudocamellia* and *S. serrata*, China's *S. sinensis*) and North American (*S. malacodendron* and others). The laurel family is well represented throughout the Far East; and in Japan and Korea, as well as China, several species of *Lindera* are found in the temperate regions, while the eastern United States has its own species in *L. benzoin*, the spice bush. The Japanese dogwood, *Cornus kousa*, has a counterpart in var. *chinensis* (which is found chiefly in Hubei, at the margins of woods and thickets), and is echoed across the Pacific in the western *C. nuttallii* and eastern *C. florida*.

JAPAN'S HERBACEOUS FLORA

Like its woody plants, the herbaceous flora of Japan bears many resemblances to that of North America. Early-flowering plants with underground storage organs, such as lilies, fritillaries, *Erythronium* species, arisaemas including the striking *A. sikokianum*, trilliums and helioniopsis, abound in the temperate deciduous woodland. In autumn there are fruits on the clintonias, *Disporum sessile*, *Ophiopogon japonicus* and *Streptopus streptopoïdes*. Hepaticas, *Corydalis ambigua*, shortias, and *Epigaea asiatica* favour open glades in the forest. In Japan's temperate regions a number of endemics occur in woodland regions: *Anemonopsis macrophylla*, *Deinanthe* species, *Glaucidium palmatum*, *Kirengeshoma palmata* and *Ranzania*.

In boggy places in the mountains of Honshu, *Gentiana makinoi* grows, while moisture also suits the tiny *Astilbe glaberrima* and *A. simplicifolia*, and *Tanakaea radicans*. *Iris laevigata* grows in wet places, as do *Primula japonica* from the hills and *P. sieboldii* from grassy lowland places, and *Ligularia stenocephala*. The gesneriad *Conandron ramondioïdes* occurs on wet rocky cliffs in the mountains, while *Lysionotus pauciflorus* is epiphytic in large trees in the mountains of the south. The Japanese shortias, *S. uniflora* and *S. soldanelloïdes*, grow in woods in low mountains, the latter also in more open places at altitude in southern Japan; their habitat is similar to that of *S. galacifolia* from eastern North America.

The toad lilies, species of *Tricyrtis*, are an Asiatic genus from Nepal eastwards, with the greatest number in Japan. Among Japanese species are the rare *T. macrantha* from a few ravines on the island of Shikoku, and *T. macranthopsis* which grows near waterfalls and on humid, shady, steep, rocky places in the mountains of Honshu; the woodland dwelling *T. flava* from eastern Kyushu and the mountain species *T. ohsumiensis*, also from Kyushu; the widespread Japanese and Chinese *T. latifolia*, a plant of the woods on the lower slopes of mountains; and the typical freckled toad lilies such as widespread *T. macropoda* and *T. hirta*; *T. formosana* (which now includes *T. stolonifera*) is a native of Taiwan, growing in moist shady places.

Although many hostas in cultivation derive from early introductions from Japanese gardens, the wild species from which those garden forms were developed grow on the hillsides and mountains of Japan, often in rocky or grassy places. Among them are *H. elata* and *H. sieboldiana*, which is also found on forest margins; *H. nakaiana* and *H. capitata* are also found in Korea, and both favour limestone. The related day lilies, *Hemerocallis*, are also represented in Japan, with *H. citrina* and the upland meadow species *H. esculenta*, while *H. thunbergii*, *H. dumortieri* and *H. middendorfii* extend from Japan into the Asian mainland. True lilies from Japan include *Lilium auratum* from the mountains of Honshu, *L. speciosum* and *L. japonicum* from southern Japan, and *L. longiflorum* from Okinawa Island in the Ryukyus south of the main islands.

11

Plants from high-altitude and subpolar regions

Above a certain altitude, and northwards (or southwards) of a certain latitude, the growing season is too short and the average temperature in summer too low for forests to exist. On mountains two further factors intervene to create microclimates where trees do not grow, even below the tree or timber line: snowfall and wind. Where snowfall is heavy, as for example in the Sierra Nevada and many of the lower mountains of New England, on the west and east respectively of North America, the snow may lie long on the ground, especially where the sun does not reach. Above the tree line this is likely to inhibit all plant growth, for the effective length of the summer will be reduced by the time the snow takes to melt. At lower altitudes, tree seedlings may be unable to establish where snow drifts and is slow to melt, resulting in open glades surrounded by forest.

Wind does not so much inhibit trees from growing at all as dwarf them, reducing them to gnarled and crooked shapes. This type of wind-dwarfed, high-altitude forest is called wind-timber or elfin forest; there are fine examples in the Rocky Mountains. At the extreme limit of tree growth the distorted trees are known as krummholz, which is also used as a synonym for elfin forest or elfinwood. On tropical mountains the upper limits of the forest often take the shape of wide reaches of dwarfed trees growing in a dense, interlaced mass, often covered with mosses and liverworts. These mossy forests, as they are called, are associated with

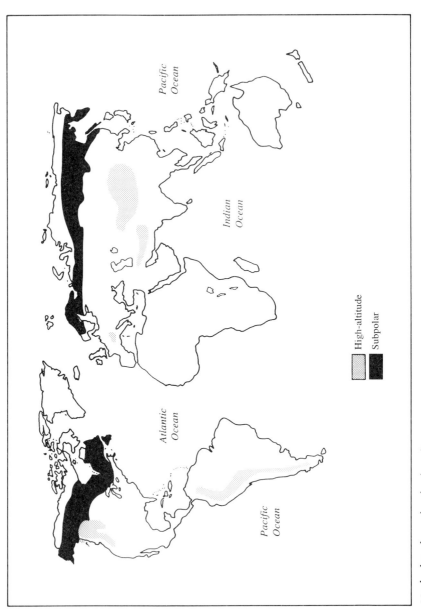

High-altitude and subpolar climates

high atmospheric humidity and exposure to wind rather than with temperature.

Although high-altitude and subpolar regions have in common a short growing season – too short or too cold to support trees – and a long, snowbound winter, there are significant differences between the two. Subpolar regions are characterized by low light intensity, varying from, in winter, perpetual night with at best a short period of twilight, to the long summer days when, while it never becomes fully dark, the sun is low even at midday. At high altitudes in the Alps, the Rockies and elsewhere in mid-latitude mountains, the annual variation in day length is not nearly so marked and solar radiation, both visible light and ultraviolet, is very intense, especially in summer, and the diurnal variation in temperature is greater than in arctic regions.

The typical alpine or arctic plant is a low, tufted perennial. Alpine plants tend to have deep-reaching root systems to search out all available moisture from the rocky clefts or screes where they are growing, whereas arctic plants are shallow-rooting because the permafrost below the thin upper layer of soil that thaws in summer is not favourable to deep, searching roots. Such woody plants as exist at high altitudes will be dwarf or creeping in habit. A little lower down the slopes, in open pastures or in clearings amid the trees, the vegetation becomes more lush; the meadows are spangled with flowers, and little bulbs make their appearance.

Gardeners who appreciate the challenge of growing alpine plants draw on the flora of many high-altitude regions: the Alps, the Pyrenees, the Apennines, the Carpathians, and the Balkan heights in Europe, the Urals and Altai Mountains, the Caucasian heights, the Cilician Taurus and the mountains of Iran, the Rocky Mountains and the Andes, the high Himalayas, and the Southern Alps of New Zealand. Plants of the high latitudes, some of which have a circumpolar distribution, are also found in lowland rock gardens where, like high alpines, they experience very different climatic conditions from those of their native lands.

Plants of the subpolar and cold-temperate northern regions

It is quite common for the same species to be found in the subpolar regions of North America and of Asia and in northern Europe, including the northerly regions of the British Isles. Among such are a number of dwarf shrubs in the heath family, most of them requiring damp, acid soil and coolth to do well in gardens. In the wild, members of the heath family prefer the more favourable, sheltered sites of the middle or low-arctic belts, those which are snow-covered in winter. Some are undemanding in a variety of garden climates, such as the red bearberry, *Arctostaphylos uva-ursi*, the cranberry, *Vaccinium oxycoccus*, and the cowberry, *V. vitis-idaea*. Like these, the bog rosemary, *Andromeda polifolia*, has a circumpolar distribution and is a rare native of the British Isles. Wild rosemary is the name given to *Ledum palustre*, which is closely related to the Labrador tea, *L. groenlandicum*. The Lapland rose-bay, *Rhododendron lapponicum*, grows in this soil, often over permafrost.

Another subarctic genus is *Loiseleuria*, which contains only one species, the mountain or creeping azalea, *L. procumbens*, a native of open places where it grows with other dwarf plants and mosses. *Arctous alpina* is another tiny plant of subarctic moist, peaty moorlands. The leatherleaf, *Chamaedaphne calyculata*, once known as *Cassandra*, is a larger shrub. Some *Cassiope* species have a circumpolar distribution; they include *C. tetragona*, which grows in the tundra, and its variety *saximontana* of the high northern Rockies, and *C. lycopodioïdes*. No less widespread is *Phyllodoce caerulea* or blue heath; it is found in Scotland but, paradoxically perhaps, the Japanese form seems easier to cultivate, in lowland British gardens at least. Both *P. empetriformis* and *P. glanduliflora* occur in western North America from Alaska to California, the latter often the dominant plant on high, open moorland.

The subarctic and mountain regions of North America are home to the creeping snowberry or ivory plum, *Chiogenes hispidula*. *Cassiope (Harrimanella) hypnoïdes* grows wild in subarctic Europe, on peaty banks with mosses and *Phyllodoce caerulea*, while *Cassiope stelleriana* extends from western North America to the Kuriles (Kuril Islands) and northern Japan, forming part of the turf on the tops of Japan's windswept mountains with *Loiseleuria*, *Bryanthus* and other ericaceous shrublets. Occasionally, a plant which occurs throughout the Arctic and north temperate regions is also found in the southern hemisphere. Thus *Empetrum hermaphroditum* not only inhabits windswept moors and mountains in the north but also extends into alpine zones of South America. It is allied to the better-known crowberry, *E. nigrum*, of northern high latitudes, and to the North American *E. atropurpureum* and South American *E. rubrum*. The range of *Diapensia lapponica* is similar to that of the crowberry. *Cornus suecica*, an even more modest version of the creeping dogwood (*C. canadensis*), also has a circumpolar distribution.

Avens, *Dryas octopetala*, is an arctic–alpine plant that may dominate dry, exposed, lichen-rich areas, growing even in the high-arctic belt, and purple saxifrage, *Saxifraga oppositifolia*, is also able to colonize exposed places in the arctic regions; it is found as far south as Italy, and from North America to the Himalayas. One of the original parents of the 'mossy saxifrage' hybrids of our gardens is *S. caespitosa*, a native of arctic Europe and North America, while another, the Dovedale moss, *S. hypnoïdes*, extends southwards from subarctic Europe. The harebell (Scotland's bluebell), *Campanula rotundifolia*, is widely distributed in the northern hemisphere in cool-temperate and subarctic regions. From eastern Siberia, Alaska and the Yukon comes *Douglasia ochotensis*, found on stony coasts and alpine slopes alike.

In damp depressions and along water-courses and lake margins in subarctic regions several dwarf willows grow, some of creeping habit such as *Salix herbacea*, *S. arbuscula* or *S. reticulata*, others more upright though still low-growing, among them the Lapland willow, *S. lapponum*, and the woolly willow, *S. lanata*. The dwarf birch, *Betula nana*, is another inhabitant of arctic scrub. The tiny bramble, *Rubus arcticus*, and the cloudberry, *R. chamaemorus*, are shrublets of the northern moors. In moist northern meadows of Europe grows the bird's-eye primrose, *Primula farinosa*. The twinflower, *Linnaea borealis*, is limited to the cooler regions of the northern hemisphere, where it grows in pine woods.

The alpine plants of Europe

For many non-gardeners, the plant that best conjures up images of the high alps is the edelweiss, *Leontopodium alpinum*. A truer challenge to the alpine gardener comes from *Eritrichium nanum*, which high in the Alps bears its forget-me-nots in abundance, and the high alpine buttercup, *Ranunculus glacialis*, is hardly easier. Also of the high alps are *Androsace alpina* and *A. helvetica*; from the Pyrenees come *A. pubescens* and *A. cylindrica*. Like *A. alpina* and unlike *A. helvetica*, *Campanula cenisia* and *C. excisa* are lime-haters. Calcifuge or calcicole, these are plants which grow in gritty, humusy screes, well supplied with snowmelt moisture in the growing season.

In the garden an imitation, as near as may be, of a mountain scree often provides the best home for alpines. Among those likely to need scree conditions are *Thlaspi rotundifolium*, *Petrocallis pyrenaica*, *Campanula allionii*, *Saxifrage burseriana*, which quickly suffers from sun-scorch and from dryness at the roots, *Potentilla nitida*, *Viola cenisia*, and *Dianthus alpinus*; *D. callizonus* from the Carpathians is similar.

Plants which grow in alpine rock clefts are often intolerant of winter wet in lowland gardens. They may form dense, compressed cushions, as in *Androsace vandellii*, *Saxifraga caesia*, *S. cochlearis* and *S. valdensis* of the Alpes Maritimes. Here too grow *Primula marginata*, and *P. allionii*, which is found in rock crevices in caves or beneath overhangs, or on rock faces in the open. The campanula-relative *Physoplexis comosa* (*Phyteuma comosum*) is another lime-lover. *Campanula raineri*, too, grows in limestone crevices in the Italian alps, but limestone is death to the almost legendary *Saxifraga florulenta*, crevice-dweller *par excellence*. This is one of a group of saxifrages that make rosettes of silvered, strap-shaped leaves – *S. cotyledon*, *S. paniculata* (*S. aizoön*) and the Pyrenean *S. longifolia* all belong here. One of the choicest of alpine shrubs, *Daphne petraea*, grows in limestone cliffs in the southern Alps.

Not all plants that grow at altitude are difficult, at least in the lowland rock gardens of Britain, even though instead of brilliant summer light and a snug blanket of snow in winter, they experience long, often overcast summer days and stop–go, damp winters. Among the more adaptable plants are some that are related to the tricky high-alpines, but that grow in less extreme conditions or are more widespread in nature, suggesting a greater innate adaptability: *Androsace carnea* and *A. villosa*, *Ranunculus montanus*, *Saxifraga marginata*, *Campanula cochlearifolia*. Given free drainage and a sunny spot, *Geranium argenteum* and the Pyrenean *G. cinereum*, *Potentilla cinerea* and *P. aurea*, *Primula auricula*, *Geum montanum* and, in stony soil, *G. reptans* all thrive, together with the silvery-leaved achilleas and artemisias, *Saponaria ocymoïdes* and *Silene acaulis*, and the Pyrenean *Lithodora oleifolia*. The alpine poppy, now said to belong in *Papaver nudicaule* (the Iceland poppy), seeds itself around freely in gritty soil.

Some mountain plants prefer cooler places, away from the sun. The gesneriads, *Ramonda myconi* from the Pyrenees and *R. nathaliae* and *Haberlea rhodopensis* from the Balkans, grow best in a vertical crevice in part or even full shade. The primula relative *Cortusa matthioli* appreciates light shade and cool, moist soil too, a recipe which also suits the tiny umbellifer *Hacquetia epipactis*, and *Geranium dalmaticum* from the northern Balkans. With added grit in a lime-free soil, *Saxifraga retusa* does well in light shade. A cool, gritty, leafy soil and protection from the ravages of slugs should ensure success with the soldanellas such as *S. minima*, *S. montana* and the Pyrenean *S. villosa*.

To the people who live in the Alps, the words *alpe* or *alpage* mean not the high, barren, snow-covered peaks but the meadows above the tree-line. These meadows are not lush pasturelands, but they are rich in flowering plants, and in their season few are more beautiful than the gentians: trumpet-flowered *G. angustifolia* and *G. alpina*, which grow in the western Alps, the related *G. clusii* from the eastern Alps and Carpathians, and the starry-flowered species typified by the spring gentian, *G. verna*. At least two species of *Androsace*, *A. chamaejasme* and *A. lactea*, grow in the alpine meadows, as do *Dianthus sylvestris* and *D. furcatus*. *Anemone baldensis* is a rare denizen of alpine meadows in the southern Alps; more widespread are the pasque flowers of the meadows, *Pulsatilla alpina* and *P. vernalis*. Composites such as *Arnica montana* and *Aster alpinus* are cheering, if not refined.

At lower altitudes still, below the tree-line, grow the plants of subalpine meadows and pastures: some are *Gentiana lutea* and the willow gentian, *G. asclepiadea*, *Veratrum album*, *Anemone narcissiflora*, *Aquilegia alpina*, St Bernard's lily (*Anthericum liliago*), *Doronicum* species, *Campanula patula*, *Eryngium alpinum* and the Pyrenean *E. bourgatii*, and the mountain knapweed (*Centaurea montana*); in damp places the globe flower, *Trollius europaeus*, is found.

The mountain pastures have their bulbs, too: as the snows recede crocuses come into flower, and later in the spring, here and there the fields are white with the poet's narcissus, *Narcissus poeticus*. The orange lily, *Lilium bulbiferum*, and the martagon lily flower in the meadows in early summer and are mown with the first cut of hay, but the poisonous *Colchicum autumnale* is avoided.

In woodland on the alpine slopes grows the alpen rose, *Rhododendron ferrugineum*, matched on limestone formations by *R. hirsutum*. *Clematis alpina* scrambles through low shrubs and over rocks. The little shrubby milkwort, *Polygala chamaebuxus*, enjoys the same lime-free soil as the alpen rose. Some of the choicest daphnes are alpine shrubs: *Daphne arbuscula*, from the Carpathian mountains, *D. alpina*, and *D. striata*, which is similar to the widespread *D. cneorum*. In the eastern Alps and the Dolomites *Rhodothamnus chamaecistus*, unusually for the heath family, grows on limestone soils.

The mountains of southern Europe and North Africa

Both Spain and parts of North Africa are mountainous regions – Spain, indeed, has the second highest average elevation of any European country, after Switzerland. The Balkan mountains extend southwards into Greece; they do not reach the heights of the Alps, but none the less many valuable alpine plants have originated in these more southerly mountains.

A number of the genera familiar to rock gardeners are represented in these regions: the crucifers *Arabis*, *Aubrieta* and *Alyssum*; *Dianthus*, and the related *Arenaria*; *Erysimum*; *Asperula*; *Globularia*; *Corydalis*; *Draba*; *Saxifraga*, including *S. paniculata* and several Porophyllums, better known as Kabschias; and the houseleeks, *Sempervivum* and *Jovibarba*.

Jankaea heldreichii, a gesneriad, grows on Mt Olympus and other Greek mountains. On Mt Olympus, too, grows the shrubby *Viola delphinantha*. The true, stemless *Anchusa caespitosa* is a native of high mountains of Crete. Greece has its campanulas, among them the crevice-dweller *Campanula oreadum* from Mt Olympus; the related *Edraianthus parnassicus* and other species grow throughout the Balkan heights, and *Erodium chrysanthum* is also from Mt Parnassus. Greece has its own soldanella, *S. pindicola*. The most alluring of the asperulas, *Asperula suberosa*, is Greek; other species are found in Spain, the Atlas mountains, the Pyrenees and the Alps. The rock cherry, *Prunus prostrata*, grows in mountainous regions in south-eastern Europe and the Mediterranean.

Campanula arvatica is a rock dweller from Spanish mountains, as are two species of *Arenaria*, *A. tetraquetra*, from the Sierras, and *A. erinacea*. *Convolvulus boissieri* is also from Spain, while *C. mauretanicus* is North African. In spring the flowers of *Ranunculus calandrinioïdes* open; this is a native of the Atlas mountains, as are the daisy-flowered *Anacyclus depressus* and *Asphodelus acaulis*. *Carduncellus* are diminutive thistles from the Mediterranean regions; *C. rhaponticoïdes* is found on the Atlas Mountains.

Alpine plants from Asia Minor and the Caucasus

Asia Minor or Anatolia, part of the Turkey of today, consists of a high plateau becoming more mountainous towards the east where it borders the former Soviet Union and Iran; it is enclosed by the Pontic ranges in the north and the Taurus and Anti-Taurus of Cilicia in the south. These mountains, together with isolated peaks such as Mt Ararat, rise to well over 3,000 m/10,000 ft and are often snow-capped throughout the year. Even the interior plateau experiences very cold winters, especially to the east, and the rainfall is low; the winter precipitation is mainly snow. The Caucasus mountains also experience cold spells and frequent low temperatures, both on the heights and in the deep, enclosed valleys.

One of the most challenging of alpine genera to those who would grow plants from high, dry regions in muggy lowland climates is

Dionysia, such as *D. aretioïdes* from the Elburz mountains of Iran. *Acantholimon glumaceum* is found on Mt Ararat and in Russia, and *A. venustum* in the Cilician Taurus; other species that form tight cushions are found in Cilicia and the Caucasus, as well as further west in Crete. From the mountains of Iran and the Caucasus comes *Gypsophila aretioïdes*, and from Turkish mountains *Linum aretioïdes*.

Several aethionemas come from the mountains of Asia Minor and Iran; one of the finest is *A. pulchellum*, now considered part of the more southerly *A. grandiflorum*. Another familiar cruciferous genus is *Arabis*, of which *A. androsacea* is a cushion species from the Cilician Taurus. *Alyssum montanum* extends as far east as the Caucasus. Several species of *Draba* in the same family are also native to the region, such as *D. acaulis* from the Cilician Taurus.

High in the Caucasus mountains, in cool, moist crevices, grows *Campanula petrophila*; another Caucasian is *C. imeritina*, as is *Saxifraga juniperifolia*. The miniature houseleek, *Sempervivum pumilum*, is a Caucasian native of which a richly-coloured form has been collected on Mt Elbruz, at 2,700 m/9,000 ft.

From the mountains of Turkey come two diminutive sages, *Salvia multicaulis* and *S. caespitosa*. and the Anatolian thymes, *Thymus cilicicus* and *T. neicefferi*. One of the most familiar of onosmas is from the Taurus mountains: *Onosma tauricum*; *O. albopilosum* is from the same region. Several species of origanum are natives of Asia Minor: among them *Origanum amanum* and *O. rotundifolium*. In gardens all these assort well with small silver-leaved plants such as *Tanacetum densum* ssp. *amani* from Asia Minor. *Geranium renardii* is a native of the Caucasus mountains, and the only hardy species of *Pelargonium*, *P. endlicherianum*, is a native of Asia Minor. *Gentiana gelida* belongs to the *septemfida* group, of which another native of Asia Minor is *G. freyniana*; *G. lagodechiana* is a Caucasian species in the same group. *G. septemfida* itself extends from the Caucasus through Asia Minor, Iran and Turkestan.

The autumn-flowering *Cyclamen cilicium* grows in pine woods in southern Turkey at altitudes of up to 2,000 m/6,700 ft, and the more widespread *C. coum*, which flowers very early in the year, is a native of beech or pine woods and scrub from sea level up to 2,000 m. The popular *C. hederifolium* is found as far west as southern France and as far east as Turkey, while the scented *C. pseudibericum* is from lower altitudes in beech and hornbeam or pine woods. The same leafy soil and cool position that suit these are also enjoyed by *Primula juliae*, a Caucasian species; it has married with the pale *P. vulgaris* of Europe to give a range of garden hybrids.

Plants of the high Himalayas

As we have seen, the mid-range slopes of the Himalayas and the mountains of China are home to many species of rhododendron, primula and blue poppy, as well as many other plants of outstanding garden value. Above the wooded slopes, and even at lower altitudes in the more rugged, drier regions, are grassy meadows, running into screes and moraines, rocky cliffs and finally the peaks capped with snow and ice. In general, the western Himalayas are drier than the east; locally the mountains of the east and of western China may also be arid and inhospitable.

Just as in the Alps and other mountain regions, the lower meadows are rich with flowering plants; many are familiar in gardens, but without doubt there remain plenty of good things still to be introduced to the west. Some of those that are already in cultivation have been noted in chapter 10. Here it is time to consider some of those from higher altitudes, plants more typical of the arctic–alpine flora.

The arctic cassiopes have their counterparts in the Sino-Himalayan region: *C. fastigiata* (with a range from south-east Tibet to Kashmir), *C. wardii*, which grows on screes and glacial gravel banks in south-east Tibet and Upper Burma, and *C. selaginoïdes* are among the Sino-Himalayan species, the latter growing amid dwarf rhododendrons in the temperate alpine belt. The circumpolar *Diapensia lapponica* has an Asiatic variant, *obovata*, but *D. himalaica* is found only in the Himalayas, as its name suggests, together with two other species.

The gentians of the Sino-Himalayan region vary from coarse meadow plants to the elusive and beautiful *Gentiana farreri*, introduced by Farrer himself and Purdom from the Da-Tung chain of the Kansu–Tibet region. Of the same nature as this are *G. sino-ornata*, introduced from moist pastures in north-west Yunnan, the Nepalese *G. ornata*, and Chinese *G. veitchiorum*. These and other gentians of the Ornata group are high alpines, spending six months of the year underground or under snow, emerging in July when the hot sun, warm rain and long daylight hours spur them into rapid growth to flower in autumn. In cultivation, the gentians from the drier regions are quite easy, while those from northern Burma, where the atmosphere is almost constantly wet, adapt less readily to drier climates. *Gentiana kurroo* comes from high altitudes in Kashmir and the north-western Himalayas and is reasonably adaptable to cultivation at lower elevations.

Many of the alpine genera that are found in Europe also occur in the Sino-Himalayan region. *Saxifraga andersonii* is a Porophyllum saxifrage from Nepal and *S. calcicola* is another, from north-western Yunnan, while *S. lilacina* has lent its lilac colouring to many fine Porophyllum hybrids. The saxifrage-like *Sedum oreadum* is a native of the Karakorum, and *S. primuloïdes* of Yunnan. There are *Androsace* species such as *A. lanuginosa*, *A. sarmentosa* (*A. primuloïdes*), *A. sempervivoïdes* from Tibet, and *A. villosa* var. *jacquemontii* (the Himalayan form of a species also found in Europe), or cushion plants typified by *A. muscoïdea*.

Some Asiatic potentillas are tricky in cultivation – *Potentilla biflora* from the Karakoram is one – but *P. cuneata* (*P. ambigua*) and *P. eriocarpa* are both easy. *Geranium farreri* is a plant of the screes high in the mountains of western China and Tibet; another Chinese species is *G. pylzowianum*. The Tibetan *Polygonatum hookeri* is quite unlike most Solomon's seals, with its stemless flowers.

The plant nicknamed the blue buttercup of Kashmir is a form of *Anemone obtusiloba*, with a high-alpine equivalent in *A. trulliifolia*; *A. rupicola* is widely distributed, and some forms, such as those of the Jade Dragon mountains, are highly desirable. *Caltha scaposa* is a tiny kingcup from Sikkim. Also related to buttercups are *Callianthemum farreri* and *C. cashmirianum*. The globe flowers of the Himalayas are mainly dwarfs – *T. pumilus* and *T. acaulis* – and *Delphinium muscosum*, from Bhutan, is similarly tiny compared with its big lowland relatives. On limestone cliffs in western China grows *Isopyrum thalictroïdes*. Still in the buttercup family is *Paraquilegia anemonoïdes*, which grows in vertical crevices; its range extends from Kashmir eastwards through the Himalayas.

The alpine aster has its counterparts in the Himalayas in such species as *A. likiangensis*, *A. farreri*, *A. heterochaeta*, *A. himalaicus*, *A. tibeticus* and others. More subtle in their appeal are the species of *Cremanthodium*, composites with nodding flower heads, among them *C. delavayi* and *C. reniforme*, *C. sheriffii* and *C. farreri*.

Not all Himalayan campanulas are worth growing, but *C. cashmeriana* is a pretty crevice-dweller. The related *Cyananthus* is a somewhat calcifuge genus; *C. incanus* is a plant of high alpine screes in north-western Sichuan, and *C. sheriffii* grows in high, arid regions in Tibet; it is trickier in captivity than *C. lobatus* or the Nepalese *C. microphyllus*. The genus *Omphalogramma* is closely related to *Primula*: *O. elegans* grows in peaty bogs in Tibet, and *O. minus* extends into Burma and Yunnan. Neither these nor any of the other species takes kindly to captivity, but *O. vinciflorum* is one of the least tricky.

The forget-me-not relative *Eritrichium canum* (*E. strictum*, *E. rupestre*) is from the mountains of Asia; it is marginally less tricky in captivity than *E. nanum* of the European Alps, but every bit as recalcitrant is *Myosotis hookeri*, which grows on the Mekong–Yangtze divide where limestone and porphyry meet: the forget-me-not hates lime, and equally hates growing at low altitudes. Other relatives include *Mertensia primuloïdes* and *Moltkia speciosa*, from Kashmir. There are several Himalayan corydalis, such as *C. cashmeriana*, *C. diphylla* and *C. crassifolia*. *Nepeta longibracteata* grows on stony Himalayan screes. The harebell poppy, *Meconopsis quintuplinervia*, is a plant of the alpine grasslands of north-eastern Tibet and eastwards to Kansu, in the drier regions.

THE RHODODENDRONS OF THE ALPINE REGIONS
The higher slopes are home to several small-growing and small-leaved rhododendron species, which are even to be found here and there on limestone formations, though in pockets of acid soil from which all free lime has been leached by the monsoon rains. These small rhododendrons are found on slopes fully exposed to wind and sun, conditions in which the smallest change of aspect or exposure leads to a change in the vegetation, a sensitivity almost entirely related to water demand and supply. In northern Yunnan and southern Tibet, to the north of the great snowy ranges, where the climate is drier than on the southern, monsoon-dominated face of the Himalayan range, the typical dwarf rhododendrons are those belonging in sections Cephalantha, Anthopogon and Lapponica. In north-western Yunnan the daphne-flowered *R. primuliflorum* grows in pockets of acid soil on limestone formations, and here too and in Sichuan (Szechwan) are found *R. intricatum*, *R. fastigiatum*, *R. russatum* and *R. impeditum*, all with blue-violet flowers. The suckering *R. pemakoense*, which bears large lilac-pink flowers on diminutive growths, is a native of Tibet, and *R. prostratum* is found in Yunnan, Sichuan and Tibet.

The wetter regions are congenial to the species of sections Neriiflora, Saluenensis and, again, Lapponica, among them *R. forrestii* Repens group, *R. calciphila*, *R. calostrotum*, *R. imperator*, *R. campylogynum* and its purple-belled Myrtilloides group, *R. saluenense*, *R. keleticum* and *R. sanguineum*. On the alpine slopes of Assam and Burma, above the tree-line, grow *R. patulum* and *R. pumilum*, with the creeping *R. forrestii*, dominating associations of shrublets in which are also species of berberis, willow, juniper and *Cassiope selaginoïdes*.

Though rhododendrons are so important a feature of the flora of the Sino-Himalayan region, other high-altitude shrublets are also valued by gardeners, among them *Daphne aurantiaca*, of which the dwarf var.

calcicola, very free with its bright yellow flowers, is found on the high cliffs of the Lijiang range of mountains of north-western Yunnan. Many shrubby gaultherias belong on the wooded lower slopes, but *G. thymifolia*, though not a high alpine in Himalayan terms, is a tiny spreader from the borders of Tibet and Upper Burma with large turquoise-blue fruits; hardly larger are the Himalayan *G. trichophylla* and *G. pyroloïdes*, with net-veined leaves; their flowers are borne in early April, giving the seeds time to ripen ahead of the rains.

PRIMULAS

Though in winter the atmospheric humidity of these regions is comparatively low, abundant moisture is to be found even during the dry season. Thus, on the south- and east-facing slopes forested by *Rhododendron arboreum*, which become quite warm and dry in clear weather, species such as *Primula irregularis* occur only by stream-sides; they become more common at higher altitudes, with *Rhododendron barbatum* and *R. campanulatum*. The popular *Primula gracilipes* is a plant of higher elevations and comparatively drier regions, but *P. aureata* is commonly found in wet places, even within reach of the spray and mist from waterfalls; these are likely to be snow-fed, however, so that the primulas would be drier in winter. The lilac-pink *P. edgeworthii* is typically a plant of the western Himalayas, where winter snow is heavier and more persistent than in Nepal. In its more easterly range it will be found on the colder slopes, again where *Rhododendron barbatum* and *R. campanulatum* grow.

High in the mountains of Yunnan, one of the first primulas to emerge as the snows recede is *Primula sonchifolia*, a Petiolarid that overwinters as resting buds. *Primula apoclita*, in the Muscarioïdes section, another high alpine from Yunnan and Tibet, is completely herbaceous; *P. bellidifolia*, in the same section, comes from alpine slopes in Sikkim. From western and central Nepal comes *P. reidii* var. *williamsii*, a Soldanelloïd species with wide, fragrant, lavender or white bells. Most Sikkimensis primulas inhabit moist alpine meadows, but *P. secundiflora*, with its one-sided head of dusky wine-red bells, was introduced from the glacial region of the Lijiang range of north-western Yunnan. Here too grows the yellow *P. forrestii*, with a range extending from the valleys to the heights, often sheltering from excess moisture beneath a rocky overhang; the same cliffs are home to purple *Roscoea humeana*. In the dry inner ranges of Tibet, Yunnan and Sichuan grow the dwarf, high alpine primulas of the Nivales section, all with violet or purple bells, while in the same region, lower down, grow taller alpine meadow species of the same section, such as *P. chionantha*, which is confined to the alpine meadows of north-west Yunnan; the medium-sized, large-flowered Nivales primulas such as *P. agleniana* are confined to the wet outer rim of mountains from the eastern Himalayas to Assam and Burma.

Mountain plants of Japan and Taiwan

All the islands of Japan are mountainous, particularly Honshu, the largest island, where the highest peaks such as Fujiyama rise to over 3,600 m/12,000 ft. The highest mountains in Hokkaido, the most northerly of the larger islands, and Honshu are snow-covered all year. Winter precipitation, as snow, is heavy on the west of northern Honshu and Hokkaido, and it is very cold. Taiwan (Formosa) is an island off the coast of China, mountainous and rugged; the highest peak rises to more than 4,000 m/13,000 ft, and the rainfall on the mountains is high because of the monsoon.

Where the Himalayas have dwarf rhododendrons and North America has cassiopes and phyllodoces, the mountain moorlands and windswept, rocky, mist-drenched summits of Japan are composed of a mixture of *Cassiope lycopodioïdes*, growing with the northern heath, *Arcterica nana*, and *Diapensia lapponica*. Other plants of the Japanese alpine moorlands are *Phyllodoce nipponica*, *P. aleutica* and *P. caerulea*, *Gaultheria miqueliana* and *Menziesia ciliicalyx* and *M. pentandra*. From the north (and also from Kamchatka) comes *Bryanthus gmelinii*, as diminutive as its pet name of mossflower suggests. Like the northern heath, *Vaccinium praestans* extends into north-east Asia as well as Japan. The high mountains of Hokkaido and Honshu are home to *Tripetaleia paniculata*, while *Tsusiophyllum tanakae* is a rare native of the mountains of Honshu. *Gentiana makinoi* grows in boggy places in the mountains of Honshu, and moisture also suits *Astilbe glaberrima* and *A. simplicifolia*. *Tanakaea radicans* resembles a small astilbe, and enjoys a cool moist site.

Wide carpets of *Geum pentapetalum* spread across the screes, and on screes and among rocks grows *Sedum cauticolum*. These and other genera in Japan's alpine flora are echoed by those of western North America; thus Japan has its own tiny *Aquilegia flabellata pumila* (*A. akitensis*, *A. japonica*), while *Campaula lasiocarpa* is also found in the Rocky Mountains of North America. Japan's alpine lyre flower is the tiny *Dicentra peregrina*.

North American alpine plants

The mountains of western North America are home to many fine alpine plants. Those of the northern Rockies are adapted to damp, cool conditions; among them is the avalanche lily, *Erythronium montanum*, which is found in subalpine and alpine forest and alpine meadows, flowering as the snows recede. The family Ericaceae is also well represented, chiefly in the north: *Cassiope mertensiana* extends from the Sierra Nevada of California northwards to the extreme west of the northern Rockies, and *C. tetragona* var. *saximontana* has a similar distribution. Like cassiopes, the phyllodoces occur both as isolated species, and as species with circumpolar distribution: *P. aleutica* in north-east Asia and western North America, *P. breweri* in moist places high in the mountains of California. *Kalmiopsis leachiana* is a rare native of the Siskiyou mountains of Oregon.

Several species of *Lewisia* grow in the more northerly ranges: *L. tweedyi*, from the Wenatchee mountains of Washington and the Walathina mountains of Canada, is one of the finest of the genus. Despite their specific names, both *L. columbianum* and *L. nevadensis* are widespread in their distribution, as are *L. cotyledon* with all its local variants, and the deciduous *L. rediviva*. *Spraguea*, to which belongs the pussy-paws, *S. umbellata* (*Calyptridium umbellatum*), and *Talinum* are two related genera.

South of the main habitat of the ericaceous shrublets grow *Petrophytum caespitosum* and *Kelseya uniflora*, which like *Petrophytum* is related to *Spiraea*; *Petrophytum hendersonii* is endemic to the Olympic Mountains of the State of Washington. The rare *Aquilegia jonesii* also grows in these parts; difficult to flower in cultivation, it is just as shy in the wild. From the Olympics come, too, the cut-leaved violas of the *Viola pedata* persuasion. The eritrichiums of the American north-west are less obdurate in captivity than the European *Eritrichium nanum*; high alpine species include *E. howardii*, *E. aretioïdes (E. elongatum)* and *E. argenteum*.

One of the most famous plants of the more southerly ranges (though it also grows further north) is *Boykinia (Telesonix) jamesii*, from Pike's Peak in Colorado; the southern Rockies are also home to *Erysimum nivale*. The San Francisco Peaks, the highest in Arizona, are the only mountains this far south to have an alpine tundra flora similar to that of the north. Alpine meadows here are dominated by *Geum rossii*, with *Phlox caespitosa*, *Erigeron simplex*, *Gentiana algida*, *Mertensia alpina*, *Dodecatheon radicatum*, *Silene acaulis*, *Eritrichium elongatum* and many other species. *Geum rossii* also grows in the drier rock fields, with *Primula parryi* and *Silene acaulis* again. In the south grow several species of *Lewisia*, such as the deciduous *L. brachycalyx*.

California's Sierra Nevada, where Mt Whitney is the highest peak in the USA outside Alaska, is home to *Ranunculus* (*Kumlenia*) *hystriculus*, which grows in rock crevices facing north, kept moist and cool by snow-melt in spring and summer-dormant to endure the heat of the dry season. *Mimulus tilingii* grows in rock crevices in damp places, with *Ranunculus eschscholzii* and *Dodecatheon alpinum*. On the dry slopes grows *Nama rothrockii*, and at highest altitudes the sky pilot, *Polemonium eximium*. Dwarf lupins such as *Lupinus breweri* and *L. lepidus* var. *lobbii* make wide mats in the more arid areas, as does *Antennaria rosea*. On the screes grow *Epilobium obcordatum* and *Primula suffrutescens*.

The mountain penstemons are popular and showy rock garden shrublets, among them *Penstemon newberryi* or pride of the mountain and *P. davidsonii*, natives of the Sierra Nevada, and *P. procerus*. Another genus from western North America popular in gardens is *Phlox*, with species such as *P. diffusa*, *P. subulata* and *P. douglasii* among many. *Eriogonum* species are common, and some – such as *E. acaule* and *E. ovalifolium* – are highly desirable. *Silene hookeri* and *S. suksdorfii*, *Sisyrinchium idahoense* (*S. macounii*), *Aster alpigenus*, *Erigeron aureus*, *E. nanus* and *E. flettii* from the Olympic Mountains – just three of many species from the western mountains – and a range of shooting stars (*Dodecatheon* species), from alpine pygmies such as *D. alpinum* and *D. frigidum* to the taller species of the lower slopes, are also popular with alpine-plant enthusiasts. The shooting stars, also called American cowslips, are primula relatives with reflexed, cyclamen-like petals; one of the most robust is *Dodecatheon jeffreyi*, which resembles the eastern *D. meadia*, and usually grows on wet ground, as do *D. pulchellum* and *D. dentatum*. Others, such as *D. clevelandii* and *D. hendersonii*, grow in drier places on the mountain slopes.

The mountains of the north-eastern United States and adjoining regions have their own alpine flora, closely allied to the tundra flora. Species such as the Lapland rosebay *Rhododendron lapponicum*, *Diapensia lapponica*, *Phyllodoce caerulea*, Labrador tea (*Ledum groenlandicum*), *Loiseleuria procumbens*, mountain cranberry (*Vaccinium vitis-idaea* var. *minus*), and moss plant (*Cassiope* [*Harrimanella*] *hypnoïdes*) grow on the heights, while the smallest of the kalmias, *Kalmia polifolia*, grows in swamps and boggy places; it occurs also in Newfoundland. Not all shrublets of these mountains are ericaceous: there are also bearberry willow (*Salix uva-ursi*) and arctic birches, with krummholz of *Picea mariana* and *Abies balsamea*. The mountain bluet, *Houstonia caerulea* var. *faxonorum*, and the mountain avens, *Geum peckii*, are endemic to the region, as is the rare *Potentilla robbinsiana*. *Silene acaulis* grows in a variety of habitats.

Andean alpines

The great mountain chain of the Cordillera de los Andes runs the length of South America, a distance of 7,500 km/4,700 miles, the highest peak over 7,000 m/23,000 ft. The Andes have a typical mountain climate, except that apart from the southern ranges the precipitation is low and the snowline correspondingly high (as much as 6,000 m/20,000 ft). The high, dry screes give way on the east to desert, while on the west, only towards the south of Chile is the precipitation high. In the far south the climate even at sea level is harsh, and alpine-tundra plants may be found at all altitudes. Almost everywhere the plants grow in fast-draining scree or volcanic debris, and are exposed to strong winds – thus *Oreopolus glacialis* (*O. citrinus*, *Cruckshanksia glacialis*), which is found at sea levels in Magellan and also in the screes above the tree line in the Argentine Andes, with *Ranunculus semiverticillatus*, cushion-forming erigerons, *Perezia* species, *Calandrinia* species, *Adesmia glomerula* ssp. *glomerula* and *A. parvifolia*, *Geranium sessiliflorum* and *Azorella trifurcata*; *Oreopolus macrantha* also grows on alpine scree beds in Patagonia. Typical of the Andean mountain flora are the rosulate violas such as *Viola cotyledon* and *V. volcanica*, with their sedum-like rosettes. The composite *Nassauvia* species are squatty, often heath-like little plants, and *Werneria* is another Andean genus in Compositae. Several small *Calceolaria* species, such as *C. darwinii*, grow at or near sea level, but *C. lagunae-blancae* is a crevice-lover from higher altitudes.

In the shelter of rocks where rivulets bring some moisture, *Ourisia* species grow: *O. suaveolens* (*O. fragrans*) and *O. racemosa*. Here too grows *Empetrum rubrum*, one of a very few species found in both northern and southern alpine-tundra, *Euphrasia chrysantha*, *Sisyrinchium filifolium*, *Caltha appendiculata* and *Cardamine glacialis*.

Not all Andean or southern alpine-tundra plants are as obdurate in cultivation as the rosulate violas, or the choice little species of *Tropaeolum*: several *Oxalis* species are easy, such as *O. adenophylla* and *O. magellanica*, *O. enneaphylla* from the Falkland Islands and *O. laciniata* from Patagonia, while some, again – such as *O. lobata* and cushion-forming *O. microphylla* – are more tricky.

The alpines of New Zealand, Tasmania and Australia

Above the bush line in the southern alps of New Zealand grow cushion plants and those that make low tuffets of growth, with dwarf shrublets. The high-altitude plants of the antipodes have evolved along the same lines as those from the northern hemisphere, alhough the genera, and more particularly the species, to which they belong are often endemic to the region: it is estimated that no less than three quarters of New Zealand's species are endemic, nearly half of them in the South Island. Climatically, much of New Zealand is similar to the British Isles; but New Zealand is separated from the nearest continent by over 1,500 km/1,000 miles of deep water, while the British islands are continental islands, separated from the European mainland by a shallow and narrow strip of water comparatively recently.

Both North and South Islands of New Zealand are mountainous, with the highest peaks in the southern alps of the west coast of South Island, where Mt Cook rises to over 3,700 m/12,000 ft; there are extensive snowfields and glaciers, and precipitation is heavy on the west of the island. Australia's mountains run along the east coast, and are highest on the border between New South Wales and Victoria in the south, where the Snowy Mountains include Australia's highest peak (2,225 m/7,300 ft). There is fairly heavy snowfall during winter, but it does not lie all year; the winds blowing off the Pacific make this the wettest part of the continent.

Though they belong to well-known families, *Celmisia* (Compositae) and *Aciphylla* (Umbelliferae) are not known outside the antipodes. The aciphyllas have stiff leaves tipped with very sharp points. The celmisias range from tiny, often silvery-hairy or white-woolly plants, such as *C. argentea* or the needle-leaved *C. sessiliflora*, to *C. spectabilis*. *Celmisia viscosa* seems impervious to searing winds on exposed slopes, where it grows with *Phyllachne colensoi*, *Raoulia subsericea*, and *Aciphylla hectori*. Other associates on the high slopes may include *Dracophyllum longifolium* and *D. uniflorum*, and gentians such as *G. divisa* and *G. corymbifera*. Both species of *Leucogynes*, *L. grandiceps* and *L. leontopodium*, are as white-woolly as the name of the second, recalling the edelweiss of the European Alps, suggests.

The 'vegetable sheep', *Raoulia mammillaris*, forms large whitish mounds suggesting a recumbent sheep, growing with other high-altitude plants such as *Aciphylla monroi* and *Epilobium pycnostachyum*. *Raoulia bryoïdes*, *R. eximia* and *R. buchananii* are similar hummocks, and *R. haastii* often grows in rock crevices, along with *Leptinella atrata*, and the tiny grasses *Poa colensoi* and *P. buchananii*. Easier in lowland gardens are the carpeting raoulias such as *R. australis*, *R. hookeri*, and *R. tenuicaulis*. *Haastia pulvinaris*, which makes a tight, woolly hummock, is as tricky in captivity as the vegetable sheep. The genus *Chionohebe*, alpine cushion plants endemic to New Zealand, used to be more descriptively called *Pygmaea*; *Chionohebe pulvinaris* grows with *Celmisia laricifolia*, and a little lower down the slopes occurs *Donatia novae-zelandiae*, a hard cushion spreading over rocks. The related *Forstera sedifolia* is a trailing sub-shrub from subalpine regions, and another relation is *Oreostylidium subulatum*. *Scleranthus biflorus* is found also in Tasmania. One of the most recalcitrant of New Zealand alpines is the penwiper plant of high screes, *Notothlaspi rosulatum*, a crucifer with symmetrical, flat rosettes of grey, felted leaves.

New Zealand has several alpine *Epilobium* species, including *E. crassum*, *E. glabellum* and the fast-creeping *E. nummularifolium*. The little creepers now in *Lobelia* were formerly separated as *Pratia*: *Lobelia linnaeoïdes*, *L. angulata*, *L. treadwellii* and others. The mimulus-relatives of New Zealand, *Mazus pumilio* and *M. radicans*, make prostrate mats. New Zealand's campanulas belong to the genus *Wahlenbergia*.

More than one species of *Leptinella* (formerly *Cotula*) makes a flat carpet of fern-like leaves: *L. squalida* and *L. atrata* ssp. *luteola*. Other plants of upland slopes and open places are *Jovellana sinclairii*, and *Acaena* species with their ferny leaves and burr-like heads, such as *A. microphylla*; *A. adscendens* is also found in the Falkland Islands.

New Zealand's gentians are white-flowered, not blue; they include *Gentiana saxosa* and *G. bellidifolia*, which favours damp places where the miniature kingcup, *Caltha obtusa*, also grows, and *Geum uniflorum* prefers damp places too. On the screes of New Zealand's mountains grow *Myosotis colensoi* and *M. pulvinaris*. The flat rosettes of *Geranium sessiliflorum* and its var. *nigricans* are supported by a long tap-root. The New Zealand ourisias, *O. macrocarpa* and *O. macrophylla* among them, can be found among cool, damp rocks with companions such as *Lobelia angulata* and *Celmisia glandulosa* on the mountain slopes.

The buttercups of New Zealand are a varied lot, including small species such as *Ranunculus haastii*, and the noble, tall *R. lyallii*. Both *R. crithmifolius* and *R. chordorhizos* live on sandstone or gritstone screes where they are camouflaged by their mottled, greyish leaves. New Zealand's gunneras, unlike the massive *Gunnera chilensis* of South America, are miniatures: *G. hamiltonii* and *G. prorepens*. Another little carpeter that likes moist places is *Hydrocotyle moschata*.

The daphne relatives of New Zealand include *Drapetes lyallii*, a cushion plant, *D. dieffenbachii, Pimelea prostrata (P. coarctata)*, and *P. buxifolia*. The New Zealand brooms have dwarf representatives in *Carmichaelia enysii* and *C. monroi*. Both are leafless, with the flattened stems typical of the genus.

The shrubby veronicas of New Zealand which are now classed as *Hebe* range from tall and tender shrubs to tiny alpine shrublets. Some of these have whipcord stems, such as *H. epacridea* and *H. tetrasticha*; others are more conventional in aspect. The parahebes are looser in growth and their flowers are individually larger, like a veronica's: *Parahebe catarractae* is prostrate, and *P. bidwillii* is a carpeter. Some of the antipodean helichrysums have whipcord stems, too, silvered or white-felted – *Helichrysum selago, H. coralloïdes* – but *H. bellidioïdes* is a little mat with white everlasting daisies.

The heath-like *Leocopogon ericoïdes* varies from dwarf to tall, and *L. (Cyathodes) fraseri* is almost prostrate, while among shrublets still classed as *Cyathodes* are *C. empetrifolia* and *C. juniperina*, which at altitude forms a dwarf shrub; *C. colensoi* is now called *Styphelia colensoi*. Also related is *Pentachondra pumila*, which is found in New Zealand, Tasmania and Australia.

The Swan River daisy of western Australia has its counterparts on the eastern heights, with *Brachycome rigidula, B. tadgellii (B. nivalis var. alpina)* and others, dwarf tufted plants. *Montia australasica*, also from Australian mountains, is a semi-succulent related to *Lewisia*. *Herpolirion novae-zelandiae*, in the lily family, ranges over the mountains of Australia, Tasmania and New Zealand. A small kingcup from the Australian mountains, *Caltha introloba*, departs from the family tradition of yellow flowers; it may be white, lilac-blue or purple.

The windswept heights of Tasmania's mountains are also home to some members of the family Proteaceae, among them *Bellendena montana, Orites revoluta* and *O. acicularis*, with the prostrate *Leptospermum humifusum, Richea sprengelioïdes* and *R. scoparia, Exocarpos strictus, Hakea lissosperma*, and species of *Melicytus, Cyathodes* and *Tasmannia*; few of these are thought of as frost-resistant, yet the summits are snow-covered in winter. Three dwarf conifers that occur at high altitude are *Diselma archeri, Microcachrys tetragona*, the strawberry pine, and *Microstrobus niphophilus*. Higher still, the vegetation is composed of very dwarf shrubs and cushion plants: *Donatia novae-zelandiae, Abrotanella forsterioïdes, Pterygopappus lawrencii* and *Dracophyllum minimum*. *Epacris serpyllifolia*, its windward growth buds killed, quickly assumes an asymmetrical outline.

12

Plants of the tropics

Tropical climates are of two main kinds: the equatorial, where the weather is hot and wet all year round, and tropical climates with a distinct wet and dry season, which occur roughly between 5° and 15°, north and south of the equator. Typically, these regions experience a combination of heat, rainfall and high humidity during the period of high sun. In parts of south and south-east Asia, the division between the wet and dry seasons is very marked; these regions are described as having a tropical monsoon climate.

Equatorial climates occur within about 5° of latitude either side of the equator, in the eastern parts of Central America, the western coastal regions of Columbia and Ecuador, the Amazon basin and the eastern coastal regions of Brazil, equatorial west and central Africa, Malaysia and Indonesia, the southern Philippines, and most of New Guinea. The mountains of New Guinea are high enough for the tropical climate of that large island to be much modified at altitude; the highest peak, in the west, is permanently snow-covered, although it is almost on the equator. The precipitation is very high in the mountains, and thick, cold mists or, on calm and cloudless nights, freezing temperatures are not unknown.

Lowland Mexico, the western regions of Central America, much of Columbia and Venezuela, and the Brazilian plateau and east coast, have a tropical climate. In Africa this type of climate extends almost across the country in the tropics from the west coast, crossing the equatorial

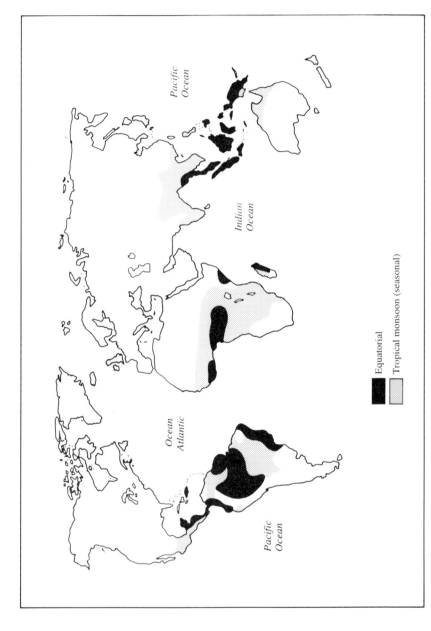

Equatorial and tropical climates

Pacific
Ocean

Indian
Ocean

Ocean
Atlantic

Pacific
Ocean

■ Equatorial

▨ Tropical monsoon (seasonal)

zone and extending throughout the southern tropics to coastal Mozambique. Madagascar also has a tropical climate – wet virtually all year round in the eastern half by virtue of the trade winds, which are forced upwards by the steep eastern escarpment – as do the southern part of New Guinea and northern Australia, comprising coastal Queensland and the Northern Territory. Except for the Rajasthan desert and the Himalayan regions, the whole of the Indian subcontinent has a tropical monsoon climate, which extends into lowland Burma, Thailand, Cambodia and Vietnam, southern China, and the northern Philippines.

The climate of islands such as Hawaii, the Maldive Islands, the Seychelles, Mauritius and Réunion, and the islands of the western and south Pacific is modified by the ocean so that temperature and humidity vary little from month to month. Many of these islands are mountainous, and both temperature and rainfall are modified by altitude. Some mountain slopes on the island of Hawaii, for example, are among the wettest regions of the world, with annual rainfall of over 10,000 mm/400 in.

Tropical upland climates are characterized by wide diurnal but little seasonal variation in temperature. Above the *tierra fria* zone on the Andean plateau of Bolivia and Peru, at altitudes in excess of 3,000 m/ 10,000 ft, is the *altiplano* or *paramo*, which experiences an extreme tropical upland climate with rather low rainfall, mostly falling during the summer months; at these elevations night frosts are frequent in the dry winter.

The Kenya highlands in Africa, which straddle the equator, also experience little variation in temperature season by season; there is a double rainfall peak, in March to May and again in November to December, with intervening drier seasons. The sunniest time of year is from December to March; the cloudiest from June to September, when there is frequent drizzle, though little heavy rain, and the nights are chilly. At higher elevations on Mount Elgon and Mount Kenya frosts may occur. To the north of Kenya, much of Ethiopia has a tropical climate modified by altitude, with warm but rarely very high temperatures and most of the rain falling between April and September. This monsoon period is associated with a change in wind direction from the north-easterlies of the dry season to the westerly or south-westerly winds of the rains.

Tropical rain forests

In the tropical and equatorial lowlands, wherever the rainfall is both heavy and well distributed, the climax vegetation is tropical rain forest. Other terms that have been used are bush or jungle; however, with increasing environmental concern, the term tropical rain forest has become widely known. Some destruction is wrought by fire, some by hurricanes or tornadoes, but in regions of such wet, hot climates it is only where the ground is permanently swampy or on young volcanic lava soils that forest is absent – with one massive exception: mankind has destroyed huge reaches of tropical rain forest, and is still doing so at a rate that is almost beyond imagining. Much of the damage has been caused by the shifting cultivation widely practised in the tropics by indigenous peoples – only in tropical India and the lowlands of Java have sedentary systems of cultivation been developed. Shifting cultivation involves felling a patch of forest, burning the trees and then planting crops. The soil fertility is rapidly depleted; it may only be possible to take one crop before the plot is abandoned. If the clearance is of jungle on steep slopes, the shallow-rooted crops cannot hold the soil, and erosion adds to the havoc. Without trees to hold the soil and soak up the rain, the risk of floods increases dramatically. With world population multiplying, the destruction caused by shifting cultivation accelerates.

The spread of western civilization to the tropics brought a new threat, plantation agriculture: the cultivation of rubber, coffee, cocoa and other export crops. Theoretically intended to be permanent, plantation agriculture has in fact proved little more so than shifting cultivation, and old plantations of even long-lived crops such as coffee or rubber are soon overtaken by second-growth vegetation.

Despite man's assault on these forests, they still encircle the globe in an almost continuous belt unevenly bisected by the equator; more land in the northern than in the southern hemisphere is covered by tropical rain forest, which is interrupted by mountain ranges and plateaux and the climatic variations resulting from these and other topographical factors. The largest continuous tropical rain forest is in the Amazon basin, extending westwards to the lower slopes of the Andes, northwards to the Guiana highlands, and southwards into the Gran Chaco. There is also a band of forest along eastern Central America extending into the Yucatan peninsula and along the Gulf coast of southern Mexico and the chain of the Antilles; another narrow belt on the Pacific side of the Andes in the extreme north-west of South America, in Columbia and Ecuador; and a belt on the east coast of Brazil.

Another tropical rain forest formation is in Africa, with the largest area in the Congo basin, extending westwards into Gabon and Cameroon, with a narrow strip further west running parallel to the Gulf of Guinea coast, from Nigeria to Liberia, interrupted by a band of dry climate reaching to the coast; there is none in East Africa east of the Rift Valley. Rain forest is also the natural climax vegetation in the islands of the Indian Ocean – the Seychelles, Réunion, Mauritius and the east coast of Madagascar – though little remains.

In the orient, tropical rain forest is the climax vegetation in south-western Sri Lanka and the Western Ghats, a strip along the west coast of India, in the eastern Himalayan lowlands, the Khasi Hills, lowland Assam and Burma; in parts of Thailand and Vietnam; in the Malay Peninsula and Archipelago, Indonesia and the Philippines to New Guinea; as a narrow strip along the northern part of Australia's east coast lowlands; and in the islands of the west Pacific. The largest continuous areas of rain forest in this Indo-Malayan formation are in the Malay Peninsula, Sumatra and Borneo and in New Guinea.

Each of these three regions, the American, the African and the Indo-Malayan, has its own species, few of which are found elsewhere; indeed, many genera and even families are peculiar to just one region. However, structurally and developmentally the three forest formations are very similar, and they show parallel responses to different climates and soils. In the strict sense, the term tropical rain forest means only the non-seasonal forest of the wet tropics and equatorial zones, not tropical monsoon evergreen forests with a marked dry season, and still less the semi-deciduous savannah forest and thorn forest. Sometimes the less luxuriant evergreen forest at low and mid altitude on tropical mountains is also called rain forest.

Tropical rain forest is evergreen, moisture-dependent, composed of tall trees (30 m/100 ft or more in height) with many thick-stemmed lianas and woody and herbaceous epiphytes. The great majority of the plants in the forest are trees; most of the climbers and many of the epiphytes are also woody. The undergrowth, except in clearings and by rivers where there is more light, is not dense, consisting mainly of sapling trees and shrubs and young climbers; the light level in the interior is subdued but sunlight-speckled. The forest is usually multi-layered, with two or even three tree storeys plus a shrubby and a herbaceous layer. The ground is covered with only a thin layer of litter or none at all, for in the hot, wet climate decomposition is extremely rapid and nutrients are quickly recycled.

Compared with temperate forests, the tropical rain forest is extraordinarily diverse, with many more species per hectare, usually with many co-dominants and only very rarely with one or two species dominant. In each of the main geographical divisions of the rain forest, however, there are some communities in which a single species is dominant; this may occur where soil or topography are only marginally favourable to tropical rain forest. It is quite common, however, to find 'family dominance' – for example, Dipterocarpaceae in the lowland forests of Indo-Malaya. No temperate plant communities, except perhaps in the South African and Australian sclerophyll scrub, can compare in diversity with the tropical rain forest, especially in the Indo-Malayan formation.

The majority of the typically tall trees of the tropical rain forest average 46–55 m/150–180 ft, with some reaching 60 m/200 ft and occasional specimens nearly 92 m/300 ft (they cannot compare, however, with the tallest and bulkiest specimens of temperate-zone trees – for example, *Sequoia sempervirens* has been recorded at over 110 m/360 ft, and *Eucalyptus regnans* almost as tall). They have straight, slender trunks, not branching until near the top, with the base often widely buttressed, a characteristic very rare in temperate forest trees; they have thin, smooth bark, large, leathery, dull green leaves all of more or less the same oval, untoothed outline with just a few trees bearing compound leaves, and their flowers are almost always inconspicuous. The only distinctively different trees are palms, *Dracaena* and *Pandanus*, but they are not common (indeed, do not stand out and are often entirely absent).

Most of the climbers are woody lianas, with very long, thick stems; some cling, but most climb like cables or hang down in festoons. Climbing palms or rattans are particularly abundant in the forests of Malaysia and in the rain forests of Queensland, Australia, where they are known as lawyer vines. Some of the many epiphytes are mosses and other lower plants, but there are also many ferns, orchids and flowering plants. In South America, epiphytic bromeliads are particularly common, but they occur nowhere else, while epiphytic asclepiads are found only in the eastern tropics. Tropical America has many epiphytic cacti but there is only one genus outside the Americas, *Rhipsalis*, occurring in tropical Africa, the Mascarene Islands and Sri Lanka. Tree-top epiphytes are often shrubby; stranglers, mainly *Ficus* species but also some *Schefflera* and *Clusia*, such as *C. grandiflora* and *C. major* (*rosea*), the autograph tree or balsam apple, with *Coussapoa* and *Posqueria* in South America and some species of *Metrosideros*, also start life as high-level epiphytes. Some plants are partially epiphytic; many Araceae, for example, send roots down to the ground but never become self-supporting as the stranglers often do.

The trees of secondary have several different characteristics from those of primary rain forest. They are almost all intolerant of shade; they grow very fast; have soft-textured and lightweight wood (balsa, *Ochroma* species, are an example of secondary forest species in tropical America); they are short-lived; and they have efficient means of seed dispersal, either by wind or by animals and birds. They originally evolved to take advantage of small and often temporary habitats such as the clearings left by the death of a large tree, or river-banks, but since mankind began felling the rain forests, secondary forest trees have been able to establish themselves in abandoned plots as well. Thus secondary forest species would always have been present in small numbers in primary forest, but are much more abundant in the vegetation that develops in the wake of primary forest destruction.

Secondary forest itself is also different in character from primary forest. Except in the earliest stages, it is very irregular, with a haphazard distribution of lianas and dense undergrowth among stands of trees with little undergrowth. These stands are often composed of one or a few species, all of the same age, and there are often very few species in secondary forest compared with the great diversity of primary forest. Furthermore, secondary forest is often composed of introduced cultivated species which have become naturalized, or species accidentally introduced from elsewhere.

Monsoon, savannah and thorn forest

In contrast to the tropical evergreen forest, monsoon forest is often leafless during the dry season; and the trees are usually less tall. There are many lianas and herbaceous epiphytes but few woody epiphytes. In drier climates, again, low open forest or savannah forest occurs: it is park-like, with dry-season deciduous or, rarely, evergreen tree species, smaller than those of the monsoon forest. There are few shrubs, lianas or epiphytes, but a rich herbaceous, especially grassy, flora. As its name implies, thorn forest has many thorny species; it favours drier sites than savannah forest, and is much poorer in grasses, but richer in shrubs and lianas.

The combined influence of climate and soil determines which type of forest develops. The evergreen rain forest centred on Singapore divides the seasonal monsoon forest of south-east Asia. There may be belts of evergreen forest amid savannah country, growing along water-courses and river valleys where there is always moisture available to sustain the trees through the dry season. Fire may also be a factor that helps to determine the type of vegetation; lowland tropical grasslands and open savannahs may be the result of fires inhibiting tree growth, rather than of a climate too dry for forest. Human activity may also produce savannah, which if left undisturbed would revert to forest. Savannahs are sometimes classified according to which factor (soil, climate, or other) is the major influence inhibiting the development of forest.

The natural vegetation of tropical Burma has remained relatively undisturbed by human activities or by fire, and here it has been possible to identify a gradual transition from evergreen forest at one extreme to semi-desert at the other, corresponding to the increase in length and severity of the dry season. The drier the climate, the more marked the differences in vegetation on different soil types. In tropical Africa west of the Cameroons there are well-defined zones of vegetation running roughly parallel to the coast and the equator, from the wet coastal belt with a short dry season and year-round high atmospheric humidity, supporting tall evergreen forest, to the arid climate of the interior with strongly differentiated seasons, of which the most extreme result is the Sahara desert. Between the two extremes are, from wettest to driest, savannah woodland, open savannah with a mixture of small-leaved thorny species and thornless broad-leaved species, and the very open vegetation of the Sahel zone, dominated by spiny trees such as *Acacia*. Similar transitions have been studied in South America.

Tropical Mexico, Central and South America

In tropical Mexico and Central America, together with the adjacent regions of northern South America, there are several types of vegetation; in Guatemala, for example, no fewer than twelve climatic divisions and corresponding vegetation types and flora have been identified. Tropical broad-leaved forest occurs in lowland regions with seasonal rains. Here typical trees are mahogany (*Swietenia macrophylla*), breadnut

(*Brosimum alicastrum*), chicle (*Manilkara achras* [*Achras sapota*]), climbing *Ficus* species and epiphytes. Just below the pine–oak forest in Mexico and Central America is a belt of mainly drought-deciduous trees, with a few evergreen shrubs such as *Duranta repens*, occupying the foothills on the Pacific slopes and a small strip above the coastal plains of the Gulf. The annual rainfall is moderate (600–1,500 mm/24–60 in), falling mainly in summer; periods of up to eight months without rain are not unknown. The trees lose their leaves at the end of the drought, and many flower on the bare branches – among them *Bombax palmeri* from the Pacific slopes and *B. ellipticum* from both the Atlantic and Pacific slopes, *Ceiba aesculifolia*, the golden trumpet tree (*Tabebuia chrysantha*), *T. palmeri* and *Plumeria rubra* var. *acutifolia*.

The forest consists of three layers, the tallest composed of trees such as *Conzattia sericea*, the kapok tree (*Ceiba acuminata*), *Lysiloma watsonii*, and, in the south, *Bucida*, *Lonchocarpus* and *Bursera simaruba*. Other large trees include *Tabebuia* (*Cybistax*) *donnell-smithii*, *Bombax palmeri* or silk cotton tree, *Hymenaea courbaril*, and *Cordia dodecandra*. The majority of trees are shorter, and form the middle layer: among these are *Tabebuia rosea* (*pentaphylla*), *Guazuma ulmifolia*, which often grows with the morning glory tree, *Ipomoea arborescens*, or forms secondary growth in clearings and along stream-banks, *Oreopanax peltatus*, *Heliocarpus tomentosus* and *Pithecellobium*. Unusually, *Jacquinia pungens* is a small understorey tree that is deciduous in the rainy season; leafing in the dry season, it is able to photosynthesize, flower and fruit with the increased sunlight that reaches it through the bare canopy above. Along stream-banks and where ground-water is available, trees from the wetter regions are common.

There is a layer of smaller trees such as the madre de cacao or quick stick (*Gliricidia sepium*), *Alvaradoa amorphoïdes* or pinkwing, the anatto or lipstick tree (*Bixa orellana*), and shrubs such as *Cassia biflora*, the white popinac (*Leucaena glauca* [*leucocephala*]), and *Xylosma flexuosum*. Wet places are favoured by the palo de agua, *Astianthus viminalis*, and by *Piper aduncum* and *P. auritum*, which grow in moist thickets. A common thicket tree is the tropical blueberry, *Comostegia xalapensis*, growing with *Abutilon notolophium*, palo granizo (*Harpalyce arborescens*) and sangre de toro (*Hamelia patens* [*erecta*]). *Pisonia capitata* also forms dense thickets, or develops into a liana. There are many other lianas in the forest, among them *Solandra maxima*, the copa de oro or gold chalice vine, *Combretum farinosum*, *Senecio confusus*, the blood trumpet vine (*Phaedranthus* [*Distictis*] *buccinatorius*), the queen's wreath or coral vine (*Antigonon leptopus*), climbing morning glories and the stinging

Cnidoscolus (Jatropha) urens. The Spanish shawl, *Heterocentron (Heeria)* *elegans*, climbs or sprawls in the shade of the trees.

THE DRIER REGIONS

Inland arid areas, with high temperatures and low humidity, are the habitat of *Tecoma stans*, coca (*Erythroxylon fiscelense*), Manila tamarind (*Pithecellobium [Inga] dulce*), calabash tree (*Crescentia alata*), wild cotton (*Cochlospermum vitifolium*), *Plumeria rubra* in among scrub and cacti and *Petraea volubilis* in thickets and dry forest. *Wigandia kunthii* is a pioneer in disturbed ground, as it might be where new roads are cut, and among wayside plants is *Zinnia elegans*. At higher altitudes inland, where there is a marked dry season, drifts of *Tagetes* colour the roadsides, with *Tithonia*, *Dahlia*, acacias, *Wigandia* and the retama, *Cassia indecora*.

TROPICAL EVERGREEN FOREST

In the high rainfall areas of Mexico tropical evergreen forest grows at low elevations, at its most luxuriant very like rain forest with huge evergreen, large-leaved trees, massive lianas, and epiphytic orchids and bromeliads. Among the tallest, emergent trees of the evergreen forest are caoba or mahogany (*Swietenia macrophylla*), *Terminalia obovata*, and *Aspidosperma megalocarpum*. Comparatively few dominant trees form the main canopy, chicle or sapodilla (*Manilkara achras*), cacao (*Theobroma cacao*) and *Brosimum alicastrum* among them. A lower layer again includes *Cecropia mexicana* and *Calophyllum brasiliense*, and the understorey is formed of various *Trichilia* species. The parlour palm, *Chamaedorea elegans* (*Neanthe bella*), grows among understorey plants of the evergreen forest of southern Mexico and Guatemala. The balm tree, *Myroxylon (Toluifera) balsamum* is widespread in Central America and Mexico, and *Inga spuria* grows along water-courses.

Among dominant trees of the tropical evergreen forest in the regions of Central and South America where the rainfall is slightly less are *Ficus* species, *Cedrela mexicana*, *Apeiba*, *Lonchocarpus longistylis* and the silver tree or trumpet tree, *Cecropia peltata*. Some canopy species such as the kapok tree, *Ceiba pentandra*, and *Tabebuia guyacana* are deciduous for a few months and flower prodigiously during that time. Smaller trees and shrubs include the guava (*Psidium guajava*), a pantropical species, the yellow oleander or lucky nut (*Thevetia peruviana [neriifolia]*), the candlestick senna (*Cassia alata*), *Cephaelis tomentosa*, the rouge-puff or Panama flame (*Brownea macrophylla*), *Erythrina coralloïdes*, *Bocconia frutescens*, *Rondeletia cordata* and *Cestrum fasciculatum*. Mexico has many cestrums, including the familiar *C. elegans* and the queen of the night, *C. nocturnum*, which grows in warm valleys; *C. aurantiacum* is from humid, shady places on the Pacific slopes in Guatemala.

There are many lianas in the tropical evergreen forest, among them aroids such as *Anthurium xanthosomifolium*, *Monstera deliciosa*, *Philodendron* species such as *P. radiatum* and the widespread *P. scandens* or sweetheart vine, and *Syngonium podophyllum* (*Nephthytis afzelii*), the arrowhead vine. Other climbers include *Bomarea* species, *Rhodochiton atrosanguineum*, *Agdestis clematidea*, *Wigandia caracasana* and the climbing dahlia, *Hidalgoa ternata*. Stranglers, some of them *Clusia* species but most of them figs (*Ficus*), are common. Epiphytic ferns, orchids, bromeliads (species of *Guzmannia*, *Tillandsia*, *Vriesea*, *Aechmea*, *Nidularium* and *Billbergia*) and gesneriads (*Episcia* species among them) and even cacti inhabit the branches or the mossy trunks of canopy trees. At ground level the macaw flower, *Heliconia bihai* (*distans*), and the parrot flower, *H. psittacorum*, grow in wet, shady places and *H. latispatha* in clearings or in open places by rivers, where *Calliandra subnervosa* and *Dichorisandra reginae* also grow. Other ground plants of the tropical evergreen forest are tree and other ferns, *Selaginella* species, *Fittonia argyroneura*, the ginger relative *Renealmia, Eucharis, Maranta* and *Calathea*. The gum tree, *Castilla elastica,* is common in clearings, as is *Tibouchina spathulata.*

Aroids grow in every level of the rain forest in the American tropics, many of them epiphytic (in contrast to the Old World, where the majority of terrestrial aroids grow). Of New World species that are terrestrial or lithophytic, some *Anthurium* species grow on rocks by stream-sides, others – such as the heart-leaved *A. clarinervium* – on limestone outcrops. Most *Spathiphyllum* species grow deep in the forests, in damp places and along water-courses. The dumb canes, species of *Dieffenbachia*, also grow along streams and trails in the rain forest. *Anthurium andreanum*, the wax flower, is a scandent epiphyte from the wet montane forest in Ecuador and southern Columbia, occurring between the altitudes of 400–1,300 m/1,300–4,300 ft, while the clump-forming epiphytic *A. scherzerianum* is found between 1,300–2,100 m/4,300–7,000 ft. The bird's nest, *A. superbum*, is an example of a species adapted to a dry season; it grows in seasonally flooded forest in Ecuador.

The cactus family, with one exception, the genus *Rhipsalis*, is confined to the Americas; many of them are adapted to very dry conditions, but some come from wetter, rain forest areas. Many of these are epiphytes, growing in small pockets of humus on the branches and trunks of trees, along with orchids and bromeliads; the atmosphere is generally humid and the plants are shaded from direct sunlight by the tree canopy overhead. One group of these epiphytic cacti, containing such familiar genera as *Epiphyllum* and *Selenicereus*, originates in Central America; the second group is South American and is equally familiar through the genus *Schlumbergera*, the Christmas cacti, and *Rhipsalidopsis*, the Easter cacti, as well as *Rhipsalis*. One of the most distinct of the first group is the Mexican *Epiphyllum chrysocardium*, a native of the tropical rain forests with, like many of this group, nocturnal flowers. The most famous of the night-flowering cacti is *Selenicereus grandiflorus*; this and other species are climbing, or climbing with aerial roots.

ORNAMENTALS OF THE CARIBBEAN AND VENEZUELA

The Caribbean region, including the regions of tropical America that border the Caribbean sea, are rich in showy species, some of them widespread, others endemic to one island or another. Despite the moderating influence of the Caribbean sea that surrounds them, several different types of climax vegetation developed on the islands, from rain forest on the wetter east coasts and slopes to dry scrub on the drier west and south, and montane forest on the heights. Bordering the Caribbean on the south, northern Venezuela and Colombia also have a range of vegetation types: wet and dry forest, *matorrales* and savannah, as well as the montane vegetation of the *paramo*. There is not space here to mention more than a few of the many species of the region: frangipani (*Plumeria alba*), pink poui (*Tabebuia rosea*) and yellow poui (*T. serratifolia*), which grows on sandy ridge tops and hillsides in the interior forest, the West Indian cedar (*Cedrela odorata*), the allspice (*Pimenta dioica*) from wooded hills and upland pastures, *Ipomoea horsfalliae* twining through thickets and woodlands, the shaving brush tree (*Pseudobombax ellipticum*), the climbing red hot poker (*Norantea guianensis* [*brasiliensis*]) of Trinidad's forests, the rose of Venezuela (*Brownea ariza* [*grandiceps*]), the wild cacao (*Pachira insignis*), the swamp immortelle (*Erythrina glauca*) and *E. berteroana*, the silver chalice (*Solandra grandiflora* [*nidita*]) and the copa de leche (*S. longiflora*), the tomatillo (*Solanum seaforthianum*), the golden trumpet (*Allamanda cathartica*), the morning glory (*Ipomoea purpurea*), a beautiful weed of fields and plantations, *Securidaca* (*Polygala*) *diversifolia* from sheltered gullies, and *Jacaranda filicifolia*. The geiger tree, *Cordia sebestana*, grows on dry sandy cays and islands from southern Florida and the Bahamas to the northern coast of South America, and the shrubby *C. boissieri* has a similar range. The pride of Barbados or red bird of paradise, *Caesalpinia pulcherrima*, is a plant of dry open scrub. The Cuban royal palm, *Roystonea regia (Oreodoxa regia)*, grows in lowland swampy areas and rain forest, or along streams, often near the sea. In the wet lowlands there are often freshwater swamp forests, with some tree species forming nearly pure stands: *Mora oleifera*, *Pterocarpus officinalis*, cativo (*Prioria copaifera*) and oré (*Campnosperma panamensis*), which has a restricted range in Panama, Costa Rica and Nicaragua. In Costa Rica, *Manicaria saccifera* grows in interior swamps.

The shampoo ginger, *Costus spicatus*, grows in the rain forest or shady secondary forests of the Caribbean islands, and the wild plantain, *Heliconia caribaea*, in clearings and at forest margins, in wet places. The Indian shot, *Canna indica*, is a West Indies native commonly growing in secondary vegetation, and now widely cultivated in the tropics, subtropics and temperate regions.

The northern coastal range of Venezuela is covered with dense forest, in which there are many epiphytic orchids and bromeliads, with ferns, aroids and calatheas at ground level. *Euterpe* palms grow on the summit. Above Caracas the mountains rise to the height of the *paramo* zone, with Ericaceae and tree espeletias. Below these heights grows the rose of the Andes, *Bejaria glauca*. In the drier regions the vegetation ranges from savannah to dry tropical woodland, with *Tabebuia chrysantha*, and *Cereus* and *Pereskia guamacho*.

The South American tropics

The range of vegetation types in the South American tropics is considerable. The Amazon basin, with its wet equatorial climate, is largely composed of tropical rain forest, interspersed to the north of the Amazon with open areas of savannah or *campos* and merging in the south into the *campo* of the Mato Grosso. The vegetation of much of the rest of Brazil, especially the Planalto Central, is known as *cerrado* – a woody, open vegetation with a herbaceous layer, and riverine forest along the banks of the Amazon tributaries. There are traces remaining of the strip of tropical forest along the Atlantic coast of Brazil, and in the north-east an arid region of *caatinga* (described in Chapter 8) and on the coast, between the *caatinga* and the equatorial forest, a region dominated by palms – the *palmares*. The savannahs of Venezuela and eastern Colombia and the flat coastal plains are known as *llanos*. The heights of Guyana are similar to the *cerrado*, with a very rich flora abundant in endemics. There is extensive virgin forest still on steep slopes of the westerly Perija range of Venezuela. Outside the equatorial forest zone there is a distinct dry season and a season of heavy rain during which the ground in low-lying regions is often marshy.

THE FORESTS OF TROPICAL SOUTH AMERICA

The wet forests of Brazil fall into three main types; those on the higher ground, those which are seasonally flooded, known as *varzea*, and the *igapo* or flood forest, almost permanently inundated. There is also tropical rain forest in Guyana and Surinam, southern and eastern Venezuela, the Amazon tributary regions of Colombia, Peru, Ecuador and Bolivia. The principal trees are mahogany (*Swietenia macrophylla*), *Calophyllum brasiliense*, kapok tree (*Ceiba pentandra*), cannonball tree (*Couropita guianensis*), and rabo de arara (*Warszewiczia coccinea*). Emergents include *Manilkara achras* and *Bertholletia excelsa*. In the secondary forest grow *Cecropia*, *Inga* and *Jacaranda* species, and in the transition to *cerrado* rubber tree (*Hevea brasiliensis*) is common, with *Copaifera* species and palms such as *Euterpe oleracea*. Trees typical of the *cerrado* include *Cochlospermum* species, *Anacardium occidentale* and *Tabebuia caraiba*.

Several of these species occur in the *varzea*: *Bertholletia*, *Ceiba pentandra*, *Hevea brasiliensis*, with *Hura crepitans* and *Carapa guianensis*. The blue ginger, *Dichorisandra thyrsiflora*, is often found in wet places and along river-banks, as are *Tabebuia incana* and *T. serratifolia*. In the flood forest of the Amazon and Orinoco deltas grow *Bombax aquaticum*, *Triplaris surinamensis* and many palms, and it is also the habitat of the giant water lily, *Victoria amazonica*. Palms are dominant in the vegetation known as *palmares*: *Copernicia cerifera* forms pure stands in plains and flood valleys of the northern *caatinga* area, and yolillo palm (*Raphia taedigera*) grows along slow-moving rivers and in seasonal inland swamps. Fan palms form extensive groves or *palmares* of *Sabal mexicana*; the cohune palm, *Orbignya* (*Attalea*) *cohune* also grows in savannah regions.

COASTAL FOREST AND MANGROVE

The Surinam cherry or pitanga, *Eugenia* (*Syzygium*) *uniflora*, is a maritime species favouring damp sandy soils at the edge of the forest. Where forest yields to the rocky sea-shore *Solandra scandens* grows, with begonias, orchids, anthuriums, gesneriads and *Rhipsalis*. Typical of the secondary forest along the Atlantic coast are species of *Cassia*, *Cecropia* and *Tibouchina*, the palm *Euterpe edulis* and bamboos. Along the coasts coconuts (*Cocos nucifera*) grow, and on sandy sea-shores the sea grape, *Coccoloba uvifera*. There are mangrove woodlands of red mangrove (*Rhizophora mangle*), *Avicennia nitida* and *Laguncularia* along the shoreline, often in distinct zones according to salinity, with button tree (*Conocarpus erectus*) and marsh plants such as *Pachira aquatica*, the wild cocoa or zapote de agua. The mangrove forests extend well inland on deltas and rivers on the Pacific coast, but only a short distance along rivers on the Caribbean coast where there are lower tidal fluctuations, more freshwater flow and a less marked dry season.

SAVANNAH AND MONSOON FOREST
Where the rainfall is distinctly seasonal, tropical deciduous or monsoon forest forms. In the transition forest there are more deciduous trees than in the largely evergreen rain forest, while in the monsoon forest drought-deciduous trees are the norm. Dominant trees include *Cahycophyllum multiflorum*, *Anadenanthera colubrina*, *Astronium urundeuva*, and *Phyllostylon rhamnoidea*. Bignonia relatives (species of *Jacaranda*, *Tecoma* and *Tabebuia*) form sizeable trees; one of the most familiar in cultivation is *Tabebuia argentea*, the golden bell. The secondary canopy is formed of *Patagonula americana*, *Saccelium lanceolatum*, *Cordia trichostoma*, *Brunfelsia hopeana*, *Amburana ceazensia*, *Pseudobombax argentinum* and *Pterogyne nitens*.

The *llanos* of the Orinoco basin, the Brazilian *campos* and the *parque mesapotámica* of northern Argentina and Uruguay are all savannah formations, flanked to the north and south by tropical deciduous forest which also occurs in patches in the savannah itself. The vegetation is coarse tropical grasses and scattered trees. Dominant among the latter in the savannah are *Crescentia alata*, *Byrsonima crassifolia*, *Curatella americana*, *Hura polyandra* and *Acacia pennatula*, with islands of forest which include *Licania arborea*, *Hymenaea courbaril*, *Bursera simaruba* and *Andira inermis*. *Ficus* species follow the water-courses. The lignum vitae, *Guaiacum officinale*, grows in coppices, scrublands and savannah, generally near the coast. In some places the only tree is the palmetto, *Sabal mexicana*, which can resist long periods of drought.

From Panama to Bolivia and eastwards to the coast of Brazil, where there is a distinct dry season, the tuberous aroid *Caladium bicolor* grows in grassy places, often on sandy soil. In Bahia state, in eastern Brazil south of the Amazon basin, the interior is quite arid, with seven months or more of drought each year. The soil is thin, supporting a scrub vegetation with orchids, bromeliads, cacti, and aroids such as *Anthurium affine* and *Philodendron saxicolum*.

Where the monsoon forest merges into the thorn forest of the Chaco, there are two types of transition forest: one dominated by *Zizyphus mistol*, and another, where the rainfall is slightly higher, dominated either by *Calycophyllum multiflorum* or by *Tipuana tipu* and *Enterolobium*. There are many lianas in this transition forest.

WIDELY DISTRIBUTED SPECIES OF TROPICAL AMERICA

A number of well-known species are very widely distributed in tropical America and many are cultivated almost everwhere in the tropics, while several are grown as house plants or for summer bedding in cool temperate zones. Among those that may be encountered anywhere in the tropics are the rain tree, *Samanea (Pithecellobium) saman*, *Jacaranda mimosifolia*, the star apple (*Chrysophyllum cainito*), *Thevetia peruviana*, *Heliconia bihai*, *Duranta plumieri* and the ginger *Renealmia cernua*. *Sinningia speciosa*, the gloxinia, is a popular greenhouse plant in cold regions; it originates in rocky places in Brazil's forests. *Canna glauca* is widespread throughout the tropics of the New World, usually in marshy places, wet ditches and lake shores.

In addition to those such as rubber and cacao already mentioned, several species grown for their economic value originate in tropical America, and are widely cultivated in other tropical countries: the custard apple (*Annona squamosa*) and the sour sop (*A. muricata*), the cashew (*Anacardium officinale*), the Brazilian strawberry guava (*Psidium cattleyanum*), the papaya (*Carica papaya*). As well as these there are trees grown in Brazil for their timber, such as rosewood (*Aniba duckei*), tornillo (*Cedrelinga catenaeformis*), setico (*Cecropia setico*), *Copaifera multijuga*. The Brazil nut, *Bertholletia excelsa*, grows wild in the jungle where all the nuts are currently harvested, but the palm heart is taken from palms grown in plantations, *Euterpe precatoria*.

Tropical Africa

The northern coastal and lowland regions of South Africa have an almost tropical climate; the neighbouring countries of Mozambique and landlocked Zimbabwe, with Zambia and Malawi to the north, adjoining Tanzania which extends to the coast, all have a tropical climate, modified by altitude to warm-temperate or cooler in the highlands. Kenya, Uganda, Zaire and the countries of central Africa are equatorial countries; the climate in these lands is modified by a variety of local features including altitude.

In the low-altitude northern regions of South Africa and the adjoining countries of Mozambique and Zimbabwe is the low veld, the vegetation between the less elevated country in the Transvaal and the Lebombo Mountains, extending to the Limpopo River and up the Limpopo valley until the climate becomes too dry to sustain it, and south into some of the deeper valleys in northern Natal. The summers are hot, the winters frost-free, and the rainfall – occurring mainly in the summer – is moderate. In the regions of lowest elevation the typical vegetation is deciduous tree savannah, open woodland of smallish trees of varying heights with an undergrowth of tall grass. On the better soils there are also scattered or clumped shrubs, some of which are evergreen.

On deeper soils where the rainfall is adequate the most common trees are *Adina galpinii*, species of *Albizia*, *Combretum* and *Commiphora*, *Lonchocarpus capassa*, *Sterculia murex*, *Terminalia sericea* and, as a local dominant, *Acacia nigrescens*. In slightly drier regions the cover is more open, and as well as *Terminalia sericea* and species of *Commiphora*, other species such as the African wattle (*Peltophorum africanum*) and *Securidaca longipedunculata* are abundant; acacias are less prominent and there are few shrubs. On dry rocky outcrops the proteaceous evergreen *Faurea saligna* and *F. speciosa* are abundant, along with *Commiphora* and *Combretum*, *Aloe marlothii* and succulent tree euphorbias such as *E. ingens* and *E. cooperi*.

In damp places the vegetation is more luxuriant, of course, though the dambos, waterlogged in summer, are generally treeless; there may be the odd *Ficus* or *Bauhinia* in these wet sites. Where the drainage is better the fever tree, *Acacia xanthophloea*, is locally dominant; other acacias, such as *A. campylacantha* and *A. dulcis*, grow along rivers and by permanent water, usually forming a thin fringe along the river-banks. The fan palm, *Hyphaene ventricosa*, is locally common. The most common evergreen trees are Natal mahogany (*Trichilia emetica*) and *Kigelia pinnata*, the semi-evergreen sausage tree, with *Ficus* species. In lower rainfall areas on poor, shallow soils, one species above all is dominant, *Copaifera mopane*.

VALLEY AND RIVERSIDE COMMUNITIES
On the higher ground below the mountains the rainfall is generally higher and there are more evergreen or near-evergreen trees, widely separated or forming small groups. The most abundant of the larger evergreen trees are *Parinarium mobola* and *Ficus* species, with the water berry, *Syzygium cordatum*, and *Trichilia emetica* in the valleys. Smaller,

deciduous trees include *Combretum*, *Cussonia* and *Erythrina* species, *Terminalia sericea*, and an understorey of *Cassia* species and *Bauhinia thonningii*. In the valleys with the *Syzygium* grow *Acacia campylacantha*, *A. woodii* and *Albizia* species, so that these valley communities are transitional to the riverside forest. Here, along river channels and gorges, the trees are taller and form a closed canopy, with evergreens nearest the rivers and deciduous trees further away. Climbers festoon the trees, and there is a shrubby layer beneath the trees, including *Phoenix reclinata*. The ground level is covered by ferns and tall herbs rather than grasses.

On the steeper valley sides away from the river this riverside forest yields to deciduous forest, which grows close to the mountains and on the foothills, where the rainfall is heavier and the climate moister than that of the deciduous-tree savannah. Here, only in ravines or on very wet slopes are the trees evergreen or semi-evergreen. There is a broken understorey of small trees and shrubs, and a ground layer of tall grasses and herbs; low climbers sprawl among the shrubs. The most abundant trees are *Pterocarpus angolensis* and the ubiquitous *Terminalia sericea*, with *Acacia nigrescens*, *Albizia discolor*, *Combretum* species, *Peltophorum africanum* and others. On the wetter slopes *Syzygium cordatum*, *Trichilia emetica*, *Ficus*, *Albizia* and *Acacia woodii* grow, as they do along the rivers. On drier west-facing slopes the most abundant trees may be *Schotia transvaalensis* and *Pterocarpus rotundifolius*. In the deeper valleys in northern Natal similar communities develop, with an abundance of the succulent *Euphorbia tirucallii*.

In the hot, dry Limpopo valley, there are few or no trees; instead, there are shrubs or low-branching small trees, and a continuous bush layer. The most common of the woody plants is *Copaifera mopane*, with scattered baobabs (*Adansonia digitata*), and occasional small trees of *Boscia* and *Commiphora*. On rocky koppies the *Copaifera* are replaced by *Acacia litakunensis*, species of *Commiphora*, *Securidaca* and *Combretum*, and *Euphorbia cooperi*. Along streamsides in this hot, dry region some trees grow, among them *Acacia woodii* and *Combretum erythrophyllum*; *Hyphaene natalensis* occurs locally. The impala lily, *Adenium obesum*, is a plant of hot dry regions in the low veld, among rocks and in sandy woodland, in northern Natal and Mozambique.

THE SAVANNAH AND WOODLANDS

The East African savannah extends from northern Transvaal to Sudan and Ethiopia, and where the amount or distribution of rainfall is adequate open woodlands or even forest can be found. Some of the species of East Africa are *Bauhinia galpinii*, a plant of woodland and thicket habitats; *Erythrina abyssinica*, a characteristic tree of open savannah and of patches of forest; the sneezewood, *Ptaeroxylon obliquum*; *Galpinia transvaalica*, which grows in medium- to low-altitude woodland; *Combretum zeyheri*, another plant of open woodland but also found on rocky hillsides and along rivers; *Mimusops zeyheri*, from low altitudes with adequate rainfall on rocky, wooded hillsides, and at the margins of evergreen forest; *Gardenia volkensii*, which extends across tropical southern Africa in woodland; and the forest fever tree, *Anthocleista grandiflora*, a characteristic tree of the high rainfall forest at medium to low altitudes. The powder puff tree, *Barringtonia racemosa*, grows on the banks of rivers, in fresh-water swamps, and even in the less saline areas of mangroves, in coastal Natal and Mozambique; true mangroves of the region are *Avicennia marina*, *Rhizophora*, and *Brugniera*. At mid altitudes crinums grow in damp places that become dry in winter, and *Nymphaea caerulea* grows in still pools. The East African doum palm, *Hyphaene coriacea*, grows in the hot, dry regions, often where the drainage is poor.

Cussonia arborea, the octopus cabbage tree which is so widely seen in Africa, grows in tropical southern regions in *Brachystegia* woodland among rocks. The most widespread *Brachystegia* in Zimbabwe and Mozambique, dominant over much of its range, is the msasa, *B. spiciformis*; also prominent are *Julbernardia* species. Along rivers the bush willows, *Combretum molle* and *C. erythrophyllum*, are widely distributed throughout Zimbabwe. *Azanza garckeana*, the snot apple, and *Dombeya rotundifolia*, the wild pear, are scattered throughout woodland over a wide range of altitudes in northern Transvaal and into Zimbabwe, and another widespread tree in tropical southern Africa is *Ficus thonningii*.

By comparison with the East African savannahs and forests, the savannah of the more westerly regions encircling the forests of the Congo and Niger is not rich in species. The most conspicuous plants are acacias, grasses and palms: *Acacia senegal*, the doum palm (*Hyphaene thebaica*), *Phoenix reclinata*. North-east Africa has provided *Coffea arabica*, and here too, as in the savannah of tropical Africa, grow acacias, euphorbias and aloes.

One of the most striking trees of tropical Africa is the African tulip tree, *Spathodea campanulata*, now widely cultivated in the tropics. The bean tree, *Markhamia acuminata*, and the golden bean tree, *M. obtusifolia*, are widely distributed in tropical southern Africa at low to medium altitudes, growing at the margins of forests or in riverine

311

fringe forest, while the pink jacaranda, *Stereospermum kunthianum*, belongs to the eastern regions where it grows on rocky hillsides and in open woodland. Dry to moist woodland in the eastern tropical regions is the habitat also of yet another trumpet-vine relative, *Fernandoa magnifica*. *Kigelia africana*, the sausage tree, grows in open woodland and riversides at low altitude only, and *Sericanthe andongensis* is found on wooded hills and stream-banks among rocks in Zimbabwe. The large pink gardenia, *G. imperialis*, grows not only along rivers in the fringe forest but also in swampy regions, in Mozambique. In hot dry woodland and on rocky slopes at low altitude the wild coffee, *Coffea racemosa*, grows.

RAIN FOREST
The high rainfall at higher altitudes in East Africa supports a type of rain forest, with species such as *Albizia gummifera*, *Faurea forficuliflora*, *Khaya nyasica*, *Ficus chirindensis*, *Fernandoa magnifica* and *Terminalia stuhlmannii*. The climbing campanulas, *Canarina eminii* and *C. abyssinica*, come from the wet forests of East Africa. The equatorial rain forest region of West Africa has a rich flora which has given us two important economic plants, *Coffea liberica* and *Elaeis guineensis*, the oil palm; and timber trees such as *Khaya senegalensis*. Cultivated species from the region include the ashanti blood (*Mussaenda erythrophylla*) from the wet forests of the Congo, the African nutmeg (*Monodora myristica*) and the bleeding heart vine (*Clerodendron thomsonae*); *C. splendens* grows in deciduous and secondary forest and around abandoned farmsteads from Senegal to Angola and the Congo.

Madagascar

This great island lying off the coast of Africa in the Indian Ocean is not of Asia nor of Africa. There is a high proportion of endemic species in Madagascar, many of them related to African species, though there are also plants with affinities to both Asiatic and Pacific floras. Comparatively few of them are grown in gardens, though at least one, the poinciana or gul mohr from the drier west of Madagascar (*Delonix regia*), grows in climates as diverse as near-desert Karachi and humid, steamy Florida, and *Stephanotis floribunda* and *Buddleja* (*Nicodemia*) *madagascariensis* are popular greenhouse plants in cold climates. In the drier regions the vegetation is dry deciduous forest with several species of baobab (*Adansonia*), or thorn forest with species of *Euphorbia* and

Pachypodium, a bottle-tree *Delonix*, and other spiny species. Also from Madagascar are the African mallow (*Dombeya wallichii*), *Ixora odorata*, the rubber vine (*Cryptostegia grandiflora*), the monkey hairbrush bush (*Combretum coccineum*), *Dracaena marginata*, the screw pine (*Pandanus utilis*), the bamboo palm (*Chrysalidopsis lutescens*), the triangle palm (*Neodypsis decaryi*), a fan palm – *Medemia* (*Bismarckia*) *nobilis* – and the raffia palm (*Raphia roffia*), *Colvillea racemosa*, the palm-like travellers' tree *Ravenala madagascariensis*, the crown of thorns *Euphorbia milii*, and *Kalanchoë blossfeldiana*. The best-known orchid of Madagascar is *Angraecum sesquipedale*, epiphytic in the forest in the lighter, sunnier places.

Two palms often cultivated in warm climates are natives of the Mascarenes (Mauritius, Réunion and associated islands): the bottle palm, *Hyophorbe lagenicaulis*, and the blue latan palm, *Latanea loddigesii*. The climate of these small volcanic islands in the Indian Ocean is tropical oceanic, with warm but seldom excessively hot temperatures all year round and rainfall in every month, though concentrated in the period of high sun. As in Madagascar, the rainfall is heaviest on south and south-east coasts exposed to the trade winds.

The Indian subcontinent and mainland south-east Asia

The more fertile parts of India have been densely habited, and intensively cultivated, for millennia, so that there is little of the original vegetation left and it is not always easy to be sure whether a given species is indigenous or introduced. Many trees have long been cultivated for their medicinal qualities, for culinary purposes, or for their fragrance.

Evergreen trees of the Indo-Malayan region include the weeping fig (*Ficus benjamina*) and the rubber tree (*F. elastica*), the jack fruit (*Artocarpus heterophyllus*), the mango (*Mangifera indica*), cinnamon (*Cinnamomum zeylanicum*), the jambolan plum (*Syzygium cumini* [*Eugenia jambolana*]) and the rose apple (*S. jambos*), the ylang-ylang (*Caranga odorata*), the kassod (*Cassia siamea*), the karnikar (*Pterospermum heterophyllum*), the mulsari (*Mimusops elengi*) and *Amherstia nobilis*, exceedingly rare in the wild but widely cultivated. The asoka (*Saraca indica*) and the elephant apple (*Dillenia indica*) grow along streams or in the shade of evergreen forests, ranging from the Khasi Hills and Upper Burma to Sri Lanka and Malaysia. *Michelia champaca*, several Lauraceae (*Litsea* and *Cinnamomum* species), and *Syzygium* species, grow above a lower storey of the orange jessamine or satinwood, *Murraya paniculata* (*exotica*), *Micromelum integerrimum*, araliads, *Phlogocanthus thyrsiflorus* and *Eranthemum pulchellum* (*venosum*), the blue sage. Among the evergreens there are often some deciduous trees, for example *Toona ciliata* (*Cedrela toona*), *Acrocarpus fraxinifolius*, and species of *Albizia*.

In northern India (United Provinces, Bihar) and in the band of lowland in southern Nepal the vegetation is tropical, with very small pockets of monsoonal tropical evergreen forest in shady gullies and damp places below 900 m/3,000 ft, while on the foothills the plants are typical of subtropical to warm temperate climates. The lowland terai, part of the Gangetic plain, is little forested, mainly in western Nepal where water is too scarce for cultivation. On the foothills and the *dun* valleys, broad and gently sloping, the forest is mainly deciduous or semi-deciduous. Though much of the forest has been felled, some of the original sal forest (*Shorea robusta*) remains, with *Acacia catechu* or shisham (*Dalbergia sissoo*) along rivers and water-courses, sal forest on the higher ground and, on the terraces between, a range of mostly deciduous trees flowering at the end of the dry season: the red silk cotton tree or simul, *Bombax* (*Salmalia*) *malabaricum*, *Holoptelea integrifolia*, *Schleichera trijuga*, *Ehretia laevis*, *Trewia nudiflora*, *Garuga pinnata*, and near the water *Syzygium cumini*. Sal is widespread in northern India and the sub-Himalayan zone. Other species of the sal forest are *Terminalia* species, *Adina cordifolia*, *Lagerstroemia parviflora*, the dhobi nut or bibba (*Semecarpus anacardium*) and the karmal (*Dillenia pentagyna*), which also grows in the deciduous forests of peninsular India. The climber *Beaumontia grandiflora* reaches to the tops of the tallest trees. A common scandent shrub in the foothills is *Holmskioldia sanguinea*.

India's trees and climbers

Among familiar deciduous trees of India are *Careya arborea*, *Erythropsis colorata*, *Sterculia guttata*, *Wrightia tomentosa*, *Ficus glomerata* and *F. hispida*, the sacred barna (*Crataeva nurvala*) and the spider tree or gold and silver tree (*C. religiosa*), *Bombax* (*Salmalia*) *insigne*, the margosa or neem tree (*Azadirachta indica*), the Indian laburnum (*Cassia fistula* [*excelsa*]), the semi-evergreen soap nut or arita (*Sapindus laurifolius*), the red sandalwood or coralwood (*Adenanthera pavonina*), the hog plum (*Chaerospondias axillaris*), the pharral or tree of Damocles (*Oroxylum indicum*), the flame of the forest (*Butea monosperma*), the yellow silk cotton tree (*Cochlospermum religiosum*) of dry, hot hillsides, and *Moringa oleifera*. Well-known climbers of the monsoon regions include the sky flower (*Thunbergia grandiflora*) and the Mysore trumpet vine (*T. mysorensis*), and the candy corn vine, *Wagatea spicata*.

The semi-evergreen monsoon dry forest of southern India and the monsoon regions of Burma and the dry lowlands of Sri Lanka is composed of some of these species, to which can be added satinwood (*Chloroxylon swietenia*), longan (*Dimocarpus* [*Euphoria, Nephelium*] *longana*), palu or raujana (*Mimusops* [*Manilkara*] *hexandra*), Ceylon ironwood (*Mesua ferrea*), and the asupala, *Polyalthia longifolia*, native of the drier east of Sri Lanka by rivers, in open places and near the sea. The niroli or fern tree (*Filicium decipiens*), a native of Sri Lanka and of Malabar, is more commonly found in the western wet regions of Sri Lanka, where *Harpullia arborea* and *Randia uliginosa* also grow.

The mota-bondara or queen crape myrtle, *Lagerstroemia speciosa* (*flos-reginae*), which grows along rivers and in swamps, *Bombax malabaricum*, *Ixora coccinea*, *Firmiana colorata*, the crown flower (*Calotropis gigantea*), and the Burmese rosewood (*Pterocarpus indicus*) are among the species that extend from India through Burma and Malaya to China, and the sebesten (*Cordia myxa*) is found in all these regions and in the Philippines. Deciduous, thorny species characteristic of the drier regions include *Zizyphus jujuba*, *Vangueria spinosa*, and the Bengal quince or bael fruit (*Aegle marmelos*).

The white silk cotton tree (*Ceiba pentandra*), already encountered in South America, is also widely distributed from Sri Lanka to the Malay Peninsula, and *Sterculia foetida* occurs in eastern tropical Africa, northern Australia and Sri Lanka, as well as in western and southern India and Burma. The white gul mohr, *Delonix elata*, which grows wild in Abyssinia and Arabia, may also be a native of the drier regions of India, and *Tecomella* (*Bignonia*, *Tecoma*) *undulata* grows in the drier regions of the Punjab and Rajputana, Baluchistan and Arabia. *Erythrina fusca* ranges from Bengal and the plains of lower Burma to Sri Lanka, the Malay archipelago and Polynesia, and the copper pod or yellow poinciana, *Peltophorum pterocarpum* (*roxburghii, inerme, ferrugineum*) and the epiphytic *Fagraea berteriana* have a more southerly distribution, even into northern Australia.

THE MONSOON FOREST OF BURMA

Lowland Burma is wet in the west and south, with heavy rainfall and a short dry season, but the central Irrawaddy basin is known as the dry belt; the much lower rainfall here mostly falls in very heavy bursts during the wet season, which is measured in days rather than weeks, the rest of the year being almost wholly dry. In the wettest regions of Burma the rain forest is dominated by members of the family Dipterocarpaceae, while in regions where the dry season is more marked monsoon forest species occur. One of the typical trees of the monsoon forest is teak, *Tectona grandis*, which cannot be successfully grown in the rain forest, with several species of bamboo in the understorey of teak forest. Other trees typical of the tropical Burmese flora are *Albizia lebbek*, the pink orchid tree (*Bauhinia monandra*) and *Lagerstroemia floribunda*, together with the Rangoon creeper, *Quisqualis indica*. In the dry belt *Acacia catechu* forms low scrub, and on alkaline soils there are thorny euphorbias and occasional *Bombax insigne*. *Cassia renigera* is a native of the dry regions of Upper Burma.

THE MALAY PENNINSULA AND ARCHIPELAGO
The Malay peninsula, to the north of a line across its narrow, waisted central regions, has a monsoonal climate similar to that of Thailand, while to the south the rainfall is virtually non-seasonal. In these southerly, wetter regions the original climax vegetation is five-layered tropical rain forest, with mangroves on the coast. Where the virgin forest has been destroyed by slash-and-burn cultivation secondary forest or *belukar* (a Malay word) with far fewer species has developed. In the great chain of islands that stretches between mainland Asia and Australia, from west of the Malay peninsula to the Solomon Islands, including the large islands of Sumatra and Java in the west, Borneo, and New Guinea in the east, the numerous islands of the Philippines and the Moluccas, and the Celebes, the climate is basically equatorial, with more or less non-seasonal rainfall. The south-east monsoon, however, passing over the hot, dry continent of Australia, affects the southerly islands of Timor and the Lesser Sunda islands, Bali and part of eastern Java, where there is a marked dry season and the climax vegetation is thorn forest, deciduous in the dry season, with palms and bamboos. This is in contrast to the tropical rain forest which represents the climax vegetation elsewhere in the archipelago. The vegetation of Timor is typically open woodland of eucalypts, sandalwood and acacia, with grasses.

Several species native to Burma and the Malay peninsula and archipelago, long since introduced to India, have more recently become widely cultivated in tropical regions: the padank, *Pterocarpus indicus*, a common roadside tree; the pink shower, *Cassia javanica*, and the pink and white shower, *C. nodosa*; the cork tree, *Millingtonia hortensis*;

Bauhinia purpurea and the phanera, *B. corymbosa*, from the hills of Malaysia and southern China; the white champac, *Michelia alba*; the dwarf date palm, *Phoenix roebelenii*; *Congea tomentosa*, the pink shower orchid; and possibly *Aleurites moluccana*, the candlenut tree. The betel, *Areca catechu*, is widely cultivated for its nuts, chewed alone or with *pan* leaf (*Piper betle*). The palmyra, *Borassus flabellifer*, from which jaggery (palm sugar) is obtained, is both wild and widely cultivated, especially in coastal regions.

Ornamental species from the archipelago that are widely cultivated in the tropics or in glasshouses range from the croton (*Codiaeum variegatum*), the Sumatran *Ixora duffii*, the virgin's tree (*Mussaenda philippica*) and the clerodendrons – *C. macrostegium* from the Philippines and *C. speciosissimum*, the glory bower, from Java – to the climbing green jade vine, *Strongylodon macrobotrys*, which grows in damp, forested ravines along streams in the Philippines, and *Mucuna bennettii*, another climber from the wet forests of Malaysia and the East Indies. The plant that perhaps best symbolizes tropical islands for gardeners and non-gardeners alike is the hibiscus. *Hibiscus rosa-sinensis* has been grown in Asia and south Indian Ocean islands since before recorded history, and was probably brought to the islands of the south Pacific during the Polynesian migrations; it is so ancient that its actual origin is unknown, and indeed it may be a hybrid with blood of *H. schizopetalus* from the African east coast, *H. liliiflorus* from Mauritius and other species, perhaps even from Hawaii.

Though many of the same tropical fruits are cultivated in the islands of the Malay archipelago as in mainland Asia, others are typical of the region: the mangosteen (*Garcinia mangostana*), the rambutan (*Nephelium lappaceum*), the durian (*Durio zibethinus*, a large forest tree), the bilimbi (*Averrhoa bilimbi*), the Malay apple or pomerac (*Syzygium malaccense*). The clove, *S. aromaticum*, grows in deep, well-drained loamy soils. The jaggery palm, *Caryota urens*, provides palm sugar and sago, and more than one species of sago 'palm', cycads such as *Metroxylon laeve* and *M. rumphii*, yield a starchy pith from which sago is also prepared. A famous Malay dessert, gula malacca, is also known as three palms pudding, as it is made from sago, coconut and jaggery or palm sugar.

Palms of the region – and there are many – include the gregarious *Livistona rotundifolia*, the talipot (*Corypha umbraculifera*), which grows in open country, and forest species such as *Veitchia merrilii* and the fishtail palm, *Caryota cumingii* from the Philippines, both occurring over an altitudinal range from sea level to the cloud forests of the mountains. The wanga palm, *Pigafetta filaris*, is found in the high rainfall areas of the Celebes and Moluccas, but not in forest; it grows above all in newly disturbed ground.

COASTAL PLANTS OF THE MALAY ARCHIPELAGO AND PACIFIC ISLANDS

There is a remarkably uniform coastal flora ranging from East Africa and Madagascar, through southern Asia, Malaysia, Micronesia and Polynesia to the Marquesas islands and Hawaii in the tropical north Pacific. The damper regions just inland are favoured by trees such as *Barringtonia speciosa* and *B. racemosa*, *Calophyllum inophyllum*, the Bengal almond (*Terminalia catappa*), *Sterculia foetida*, and the beefwood, *Casuarina equisetifolia*, which often forms pure stands as narrow strips of forest fringing sandy beaches. *Erythrina indica*, the Indian coral tree, is a deciduous, thorny species from coastal forests with a range from India to Polynesia, and *E. variegata* ranges from the coasts of East Africa and Madagascar through India, Indochina and Malesia to northern Australia and Polynesia. The coconut palm, *Cocos nucifera*, is ubiquitous but probably always planted.

One of the most common of smaller strand trees or shrubs on both sandy and rocky shores is the screw pine, *Pandanus tectorius* (*odoratissimus*), which often forms dense thickets. *Cycas circinalis* is more local in distribution. Other small trees that are very common are bhendi (*Thespesia populnea*), *Cerbera manghas* and *Hibiscus tiliaceus*, which is usually found just inland from the beach but sometimes forming dense thickets further inland still. *Dodonaea viscosa*, which grows as far afield as New Zealand, is another common species. The karanj, *Pongamia glabra*, is widespread in tidal forest. *Messerschmidia* (*Tournefortia*) *argentea* grows only on sandy beaches, not inland. Creepers, both woody and herbaceous, and other non-woody plants, often cover extensive stretches of beach, among them the pan-tropical *Ipomoea pes-caprae* and *Scaevola sericea*. Just inland from the beaches, in thickets, there are vines of the periwinkle and milkweed families (Apocynaceae and Asclepiadaceae) and semi-epiphytes such as *Hoya* and *Dischidia*, with the loofah (*Luffa cylindrica*) and the moonflower (*Ipomoea alba* [*I. bona-nox*, *Calonyction aculeatum*]). *Catharanthus* (*Vinca*) *rosea* or Madagascar periwinkle may have originated in the Caribbean, but is fully naturalized on the beaches of the archipelago and the Pacific islands.

Everywhere in the tropics, but particularly in the Malaysian region, mangrove forests are typical of coastal waters. The characteristic genus is *Rhizophora*, though other genera are also present. Secondary mangrove species growing on the landward side include *Heritiera littoralis* and halophytic ferns. Between the mangrove forests and the upland forests yet another range of plants have found a niche, including *Caesalpinia nuga*, the bagnit vine (*Tristellateia australasiae*), and the nipa palm (*Nipa fruticans*). In wet regions the mangrove trees are host to epiphytes, among them ferns such as *Asplenium nidus*, the bird's-nest fern.

SECONDARY FOREST AND GRASSLANDS IN MALAYSIA AND PACIFIC ISLANDS
Much of Malaysia and the larger islands such as Fiji and Samoa is characterized by secondary forest. Though there are fewer species than primary forest, there are none the less several worthy of mention: species of *Litsea*, *Ficus*, *Antidesma* and *Cordia*; *Kleinhovia hospita*; and the candlenut tree (*Aleurites moluccana*). The secondary forest is dense and jungly in the regions of high rainfall; where this is lower, or where grass fires are common, the forest is more open and park-like, with a grassy cover between the trees.

PLANTS OF THE INDO-MALAYAN TROPICAL RAIN FOREST
The dominant trees in the primary forests of Indo-Malaya belong to the family Dipterocarpaceae, so that these forests are often called dipterocarp forests. Many species, both woody and non-woody, are endemic to these forests, and the following is the briefest account of a few.

Where tropical rain forest survives there is an understorey of tree ferns, Musaceae, Zingiberaceae, aroids, begonias (often growing in rocky places) and Melastomataceae such as the so-called Malaysian orchid of the Philippines, *Medinella magnifica*. There are many epiphytic orchids, some – *Coelogyne* and *Phalaenopsis* species and *Vanda lowii* especially – with showy flowers. The slipper orchids (*Paphiopedilum*), which are confined in China to the tropical provinces of the south, are also represented in Vietnam, Thailand, Burma and Malaya. Some grow in rocky places, in crevices and hollows, others – for example, *Paphiopedilum micranthum* – in wet forests and on shady stream banks. In the cloud forests of higher altitudes there is an abundance of epiphytic ferns, mosses and lichens. On the mountain tops the pitcher plants, *Nepenthes*, grow as epiphytes or terrestrials. Typical of the rain forests are the climbing rattan palms, species of *Calamus*, which are also represented in the tropical forests of Queensland, north-eastern Australia, by *C. australis*, the lawyer cane. Here and there are also thickets of *Pandanus*; otherwise the forest interior is relatively open, except along river banks.

Some of Asia's aroids are well known in cultivation. The dieffen-bachia-like *Aglaonema* species are all Asiatic, some terrestrial and some lithophytic: *A. modestum*, extending from southern China to south-east Asia, and *A. commutatum* and *A. crispum*, natives of the Philippines. Another terrestrial or lithophytic genus of aroids is *Alocasia*, including the very striking *A. cuprea*; some species grow in the rugged, steep mountains of south-east Asia. The climbing *Scindapsus pictus* occurs in the rain forests of the region. *Epipremnum aureum* (*Scindapsus aureus*), the golden philodendron, is also a native of south-east Asia. The arborescent *Alocasia macrorrhiza* has been introduced all through the tropics as a food crop. Indeed, the oldest cultivated crop in the world is an aroid, taro (*Colocasia esculenta*), grown in subtropical and tropical Asia for more than 10,000 years, antedating even rice.

Another group of non-woody plants from tropical Asia widely cultivated in frost-free regions are the gingers: the hidden lily (*Curcuma cocana*) and *Kaempferia galidgesii* from the tropical rain forests, the crape ginger, *Costus speciosus*, the Malesian torch ginger, *Nicolaia elatior* (*Phaeomerea speciosa*), and the red ginger, *Alpinia purpurata*. The culinary ginger, *Zingiber officinale*, is so widespread in cultivation that its country of origin is unknown; the family also provides turmeric (*Curcuma longa*), cardamom (*Elettaria cardamomum*) and other spices.

Islands of the Pacific Basin

The mountainous, volcanic islands – Fiji, Samoa, Hawaii, Tahiti and the Marquesas, as well as other smaller groups – are generally forested; most of the plants are related to those of Malaysia, though there are some endemic species allied to those of the tropical regions bordering the western Pacific. Malaysian genera of which there are many species in mainland Asia and the archipelago are represented by far fewer in the high Pacific islands: *Elaeocarpus*, *Ficus*, *Syzygium*, *Calophyllum*, *Medinella*, *Antidesma*, *Sterculia*, and orchids such as *Dendrobium*, all show this attenuation of species. As regards the vegetation, there are both primary and secondary forests on the high islands, the result here, as in Malaysia, of slash-and-burn cultivation.

Hawaii is the most isolated of what plant geographers call floristic regions, and has a very high proportion of endemic species – over ninety per cent. However, the centuries of isolation that enabled these species to evolve have ended, and introduced species have largely displaced the natural vegetation. Even before the arrival of Captain Cook and the *Resolution* initiated the modern history of the Hawaiian islands, there had been earlier discoveries: the population Captain Cook found there originated from the seafaring immigrants from the Marquesas and Tahiti, about one thousand to 1,500 years ago. They and their animals had a considerable influence on the native flora, eliminating much of the dryland and mixed mesic forests that originally covered much of the leeward side of the islands, and introducing many alien species such as the breadfruit (*Artocarpus altilis*), coconut, taro (*Colocasia esculenta*), yam (*Dioscorea* spp.), sweet potato (*Ipomoea batatas*), sugar cane (*Saccharum officinarum*) and banana (*Musa acuminata* hybrids). Today there are just a few patches of natural dry lowland forest left.

Around the coasts, especially to the south and west, strand and coastal vegetation, mainly composed now of alien species such as *Leucaena leucocephala* and *Casuarina equisitifolia*, give way to dryland forest and scrub, also primarily on the leeward side. Hawaii's curious lobelioids, belonging to six endemic genera as well as to *Lobelia* itself, occur in the dry forest, this too now populated mainly by aggressive alien species. The richest vegetation is that of the mixed mesic forest, though very little remains. Two of the most common trees are koa (*Acacia koa*) and ohia lehua (*Metrosideros polymorphus*); there are also species of *Antidesma*, *Pittosporum*, *Santalum*, *Psychotria* and others. In Hawaii as elsewhere, many introduced species have become serious weeds, such as *Passiflora mollissima*. In the regions of high rainfall rain forest is the climax vegetation, dominated again by *Metrosideros polymorphus* and *Acacia koa*, with an understorey that includes tree ferns (*Cibotium splendens* and *C. chamissoi*). Epiphytes abound, above all ferns and mosses, but also flowering plants such as the ieie, *Freycinetia arborea*.

The ohia lehua has the ability to grow in almost every habitat save the very dry or very high; it even colonizes recent lava. (A related species of Samoa and south-east Polynesia is *Metrosideros collina*.) On the lava fields and alpine deserts grow the silverswords, *Argyroxiphium* species; some silverswords are found in the bogs that form in level montane areas of high rainfall and impeded drainage, where the most prominent plants are *Vaccinium* species and the ubiquitous ohia lehua.

Another type of island is the coral island, generally associated with atolls; their surface is barely above sea level, except for a few that have become raised – these are known as *makatea*. The native vegetation of the coral islands is generally very poor in species, and though the islands are widely separated, the flora of one is much the same as another.

321

TROPICAL AUSTRALIA AND NEW GUINEA

Although the eucalyptus is thought of as typically Australian, one species, *E. deglupta*, extends into parts of New Guinea, Celebes, the Moluccas and as far as Mindanao in the Philippines: other eucalyptus grow in the islands closest to Australia and are dominant in the driest parts of New Guinea. In northern and north-eastern coastal Australia, and inland in the north where the rainfall exceeds 500 mm/20 in per year, the climate supports a tropical vegetation adapted to a distinct dry season. In the coastal north-east there is a narrow strip of tropical rain forest, with trees displaying some of the typical features such as cauliflory, in which the flowers emerge direct from the trunk and branches (*Syzygium cormiflorum*, *S. moorei* and *Archidendron lucyi*), or brightly-coloured new leaves. The rain forest is rich in epiphytes, among them the bird's-nest fern (*Asplenium nidus*), *Platycerium bifurcatum* and *P. superbum*, and lianas. The dominant palms of Australia's tropical swamp forest are *Hydriastele* and *Licuala* species. Although both Indo-Malayan and Australasian genera and species are found in the Australian tropics, on the whole they occur separately, being characteristic of different environmental conditions.

Plants typical of the brush or jungle, as it is often called in Australia, which extends down the east coast from Cape York to Cape Otway, are the coachwood (*Ceratopetalum apetalum*), *Doryphora sassafras*, *Ficus* species, brush box (*Lophostemon confertus*), *Toona australis*, *Brachychiton acerifolius*, rosewood (*Synoum* species), the gold blossom tree (*Barklya syringifolia*), the firewheel tree (*Stenocarpus sinuatus*), *Oreocallis pinnata*, *Castanospermum australe*, *Schefflera actinophylla*, and the lilly pillies (species of *Acmena* and *Syzygium*). Many of these extend into sub-tropical climatic regions. The ivory curl, *Buckinghamia celsissima*, grows in deep, well-drained soils in the rain forest, in the coastal ranges of northern Queensland, and *Lomatia fraxinifolia* also grows at altitude in the rain forest. The Queensland nut, *Macadamia integrifolia*, is a lowland rain forest species, often growing on slopes in rocky soils, in southern Queensland. The Queensland kauri, *Agathis robusta*, grows in dense rain forest in the far north and on Fraser Island. The Queensland lily, *Eurycles cunninghamii*, grows on river banks in the Araucariae forest, in leaf mould among rocks.

In the drier regions where rain forest is absent grows *Banksia dentata*, often found in seasonally wet sandy flats or savannah woodland. *Acacia holosericea* extends across northern Australia from tropical Queensland to Western Australia, growing on creek banks and well-drained hillsides; similar habitats suit the zigzag wattle, *A. macradenia*, which only occurs in Queensland; *A. simsii* is a coastal species from sandy or gravelly soils, also found in New Guinea. The palm *Archontophoenix alexandrae* is a coastal species, but the king palm, *A. cunninghamiana*, grows in the rain forest.

In southern New Guinea around Port Moresby the climate is monsoonal, like that of much of northern Australia. Here grow several species of eucalyptus, including *E. papuana* and *E. deglupta*, with *Casuarina equisetifolia* along the shores. The cajeput, *Melaleuca quinquenervia*, is also found here. With increased rainfall in the foothills from about 300 m/1,000 ft, primary rain forest remains extensive. Among the species from the forest that are well known in cultivation are the bignonia relative *Deplanchea tetraphylla*, the liana *Mucuna novoguineensis*, the flame of the forest, which grows by rain forest streams and on riverbanks in secondary forest, the gingers *Riedelia* and the giant spiral ginger, *Tapeinochilus ananassae*, and the caricature plant, *Graptophyllum pictum*. Less familiar is the liana *Macropsychanthus lauterbachii*, which grows with *Mucuna*.

Tropical uplands

In the tropics as in the temperate zones, vegetation changes with increasing altitude. On a typical forested tropical mountain, the tropical rain forest of the lowlands gives way to shorter-growing, simpler evergreen communities and the tropical flora yields to a montane flora in which the genera and even species are temperate; these higher-altitude communities have been described as submontane rain forest and montane rain forest, to distinguish them from the temperate rain forest outside the tropics. On exposed ridges and isolated peaks is the type of vegetation called mossy forest or elfin forest, with stunted, twisted trees covered in epiphytes, above all liverworts and mosses. The high ranges of New Guinea exceed the tree-line and are capped by alpine plants and even permanent snow.

Much of the Indo-Malayan and the Australasian rain forest area is mountainous, though most of the mountains do not reach the climatic tree limit. In the Malaysian mountains the lowland rain forest and submontane rain forest species belong to Indo-Malayan genera, but in the montane forest among the Indo-Malayan genera there are many Australasians, such as *Leptospermum*, *Tristania*, *Phyllocladus*, as well as north-temperate genera. In the Malay peninsula the lowland, hill and high hill tropical rain forest is composed above all of dipterocarps, chiefly *Shorea* species, each zone with its characteristic species. Above these are two montane zones, one dominated by Lauraceae and Fagaceae, with many oaks (*Quercus* and *Lithocarpus* species), and the other markedly ericaceous, with *Pieris*, *Vaccinium* and *Rhododendron*. In both dipterocarp and lower montane forest there are many palms, of different types in each: the lower montane forest is characterized by species of *Areca*, *Calamus*, *Caryota*, *Livistona* and others. In north-east Thailand above the zone of the montane rain forest there are rhododendrons such as *R. lyi*, *Schima wallichii*, *Michelia kerrii*, evergreen oaks, *Castanopsis*, *Pinus khasia*, *Agapetes hosseana*, *Mahonia siamensis* and *Camellia oleifera*. On shady slopes *Rhododendron veitchianum* grows as an epiphyte. A similar transition from dipterocarp to lower montane forest with Lauraceae and oaks occurs in the islands of the archipelago. In Java above the level of the tropical rain forest the commonest trees are oaks, *Castanopsis* species, *Litsea javanica* and *Podocarpus imbricatus*; as elsewhere, the upper montane zone is characterized by *Vaccinium* species, with *Schima wallichii* ssp. *noronhae*. In the Philippines there is a gradual transition from lowland dipterocarp rain forest to a montane community with *Quercus* and *Neolitsea* species, many epiphytes and climbers, and a ground storey of ferns and herbaceous plants. The mossy forest is composed of species of *Cyathea* and *Astronia*.

In the rain forest of the foothills of Papua New Guinea in the east (300–1,650 m/1,000–5,500 ft), there are many ferns and lianas, and fewer epiphytes than in the lowlands. From 1,650 m the cloud belt begins and the forest is an oak–conifer association, with *Quercus*, *Araucaria cunninghamii*, *Podocarpus* and *Phyllocladus*, ferns and mosses. Above this again is mossy forest, with heavy growths of liverworts and mosses in the perpetual dampness and mist. One of the trees of the montane forest of New Guinea is *Nothofagus grandis*, a host to epiphytic rhododendrons such as *R. konori*. There are many other rhododendron species on the island, both epiphytic and terrestrial. Species of the ericaceous genus *Dimorphanthera* may be epiphytic or terrestrial shrubs or tall lianas, varying according to habitat: *D. amoena*, for example, is a liana in montane forest and a pendent shrub in subalpine areas. *Dimorphanthera kempteriana* is a long-stemmed shrub or a large liana, terrestrial or epiphytic, climbing by means of adventitious roots in dense forest with *Agathis*, *Castanopsis* and *Nothofagus*. Other genera of the higher altitudes are *Syzygium*, *Leea*, *Rhodomyrtus* and *Vaccinium*. On the higher ridges there are coniferous forests of *Dacrydium* and *Afrocarpus*, with *Nothofagus nobilis*. In the 'frost grasslands', basins where cold air accumulates to produce temperatures sufficiently low (though not freezing) to prevent the growth of native trees, the most prominent woody plant is a tree fern, *Cyathea atrax*, with lower shrubs and ground plants around including *Gaultheria mundula* and *Gunnera papuana*.

Most of the high African mountains are in regions of relatively dry climate, so that their lower slopes are covered with savannah and other vegetation types adapted to a marked dry season. Where the rain forest does approach the mountains it is succeeded by a transition zone and then by a montane rain forest zone where there are many epiphytes but few or no lianas, and a dense shrub layer. One of the conifers of this zone is *Afrocarpus* (*Podocarpus*) *usambarensis*, and in the Usambara mountains there are forests of *Juniperus procera*. In ravines tree ferns are often associated with *Ensete edule*. In the Kenya uplands grows *Crotalaria agatiflora*, of which there are at least two races, one growing at high altitude where the rainfall is ample, at the edges of grassy glades or in mixed forest, and another of medium-altitude grasslands and bush. The black-eyed Susan, *Thunbergia alata*, also favours the wetter regions at higher altitudes, growing in bushlands and thickets. In the upland rain forests, in gullies, by river banks and waterfalls, grows *Impatiens tinctoria*, a tuberous perennial, one of several species that grow in the African mountains. Above the montane rain forest is a characteristic bamboo zone on most of the higher East African mountains. Above this again are Ericaceae, mainly arborescent *Erica* and *Philippia*. Finally there is the alpine zone with its tree-like senecios, tall columnar lobelias and Ericaceae, adapted to extreme diurnal temperature variations.

In South America, the Amazonian forest extends westwards to the foothills of the Andes. The tropical rain forest of the foothills, known as *montaña*, is very like that of the Amazon lowlands, but at about 1,500 m/5,000 ft it gives way to a quite different type of vegetation. First comes the transitional *medio yungas* and then the *ceja de la montaña*. Above this again is the open *paramo* or steppe, with Ericaceae and arborescent composites, species of *Espeletia*, very like the tree senecios of the African mountains, and like them adapted to extreme diurnal variations in temperature. In the *medio yungas* zone the cinchona forests grow, and there are *Chusquea* species and tree ferns. The *yungas* extend southwards into northern Argentina – the Tucumán–Bolivian forest. From the foothills of the Andes in Colombia, Ecuador and Bolivia come plants such as the mountain immortelle (*Espeletia poeppigiana*). The *ceja de la montaña* forests are elfin forests. In the zone of 'permanent spring' at about 2,000 m/6,600 ft there are tacsonia types of *Passiflora* scrambling over the bushes, and echeverias growing in grassland; in the equatorial regions of Ecuador there is cloud forest at about 2,500 m/8,000 ft, with silver trees (*Cecropia* species). The Andean heights are often very arid, and plants such as *Puya raimondii* are to be found at 4,000 m/13,200 ft in the Andes of Bolivia and Peru.

In the West Indies the tropical rain forest first yields on the slopes to a forest type very like that of the lowlands, except that the trees are smaller and generally lack the typical tropical rain forest features of buttressing and cauliflory. There are few lianas or epiphytes. Above this in a few limited regions is montane rain forest with an abundance of lianas and epiphytes, and a lower layer of palms and tree ferns.

Glossary

boreal forest: mainly coniferous forest of high northern latitudes, also known as northern coniferous forest or subarctic forest (see also taiga)

calcicole: lime-dwelling

cauliflory: in tropical rain-forest trees, the formation of flowers on old, bare wood of the trunk and branches

climax vegetation: the relatively stable plant community which represents the most advanced stage of development in a given climatic region or on a particular soil type

cloud forest: montane (q.v.) forest that is frequently or permanently shrouded in mist

dambo: in South Africa, almost treeless stretches of grassland along flat valleys and drainage channels, waterlogged during the wet season

ecotypes: distinct races within a single species, genetically adapted to cope with local environmental conditions

endemic: occurring naturally only in one region

edaphic: pertaining to the soil

epiphytic: growing on other plants

fellfields: regions at high altitude or latitude where only a sparse and discontinuous vegetation grows

floristic region: a region in which the collectivity of plant species constitutes a distinct whole, for example the grasslands (prairies and plains) of North America

halophytic: tolerant of extremely saline soils

kloof: in South Africa, a deep, narrow valley or ravine

kop, koppie: in South Africa, a small hill

laterite: the soil typical of high rainfall tropical areas, characterized by leaching and loss of siliceous minerals and retention of iron and aluminium oxides, giving a characteristic red colour; laterite soils absorb water easily, and are low in humus and in available mineral nutrients

lithophytic: growing on rocks

mallee: multi-stemmed *Eucalyptus* species with lignotuber or woody swelling at the base of the trunk, from which new growths are formed after the topgrowth is killed by fire; the maquis-like vegetation dominated by such species

mesophytic: adapted to climates where moisture is usually neither deficient nor excessive

montane: of or growing on mountains or mountain slopes, generally referring to the zone extending from the foothills to the lower altitudinal limit of the subalpine zone

pocosin: low, wooded swampy ground

sclerophyll: evergreen tree or shrub with small, hard, often thick and leathery leaves

sclerophyll forest: vegetation of sclerophyllous trees and shrubs: 'wet' sclerophyll forest, formed in regions where there is a permanent supply of soil moisture, is a tall open forest of more than two layers; 'dry' sclerophyll forest is less tall, composed of two layers only – small trees and shrubs

taiga: the northernmost, open, park-like areas of the boreal forest

vegetation: the type of plant community – forest, grassland, etc. – of a given region

vlei: in South Africa, a shallow pool, or low-lying ground under shallow water in the rainy season

xerophytic: adapted to dry or arid climates

Bibliography

Anon: *Vegetation Map of South America*, Unesco, 1981

Anon: *Libro del árbol*, Buenos Aires, 1975

Adamson, R. S.: *Vegetation of South Africa*, British Empire Vegetation Committee, London, 1938

Alpine Garden Society: Quarterly Bulletins

Alzugaray, D. & C. (eds): *Flora Brasileira*, Três Livros e Fascículos, São Paulo, 1984

Atkinson, B. W. & Gadd, Alan: *A Modern Guide to Forecasting Weather*, Mitchell Beazley, 1986

Barbour, M. G. & Billings, W. D. (eds): *North American Terrestrial Vegetation*, Cambridge University Press, 1988

Barbour, M. G., Burk, J. H. and Pitts, W. D.: *Terrestrial Plant Ecology*, Benjamin Cummings, 1980

Batten, Auriol & Bokelmann, Hertha: *Wild Flowers of the Eastern Cape*, Books of Africa, 1966

Blatter, E. & Millard, W. S.: *Some Beautiful Indian Trees*, Bombay Natural History Society, 2nd edn (rev. W. T. Stearn), 1954

Blombery, A. & Rodd, T.: *Palms*, Angus & Robertson, 1982

Bond, P. & Goldblatt, P.: *Plants of the Cape Flora*, Journal of South African Botany Supplement Vol. 13, 1984

Bor, N. L. & Raizada, M. B.: *Some Beautiful Indian Climbers and Shrubs*, Bombay Natural History Society, 1954

Bown, D.: *Aroids*, Century, 1988

Bramwell, D. & Z.: *Wild Flowers of the Canary Islands*, Stanley Thomas, 1974

Brandis, D.: *Indian Trees*, Archibald Constable, 1906

BIBLIOGRAPHY

Chandler, T. J.: *Modern Meteorology and Climatology*, 2nd edn, Thomas Nelson & Sons, 1981

Chang Hung Ta & Bartholomew, B.: *Camellias*, Timber Press, 1984

Chickering, C. Rogers: *Flowers of Guatemala*, University of Oklahoma Press, 1973

Chodat, R. & Vischer, W.: *La Végétation du Paraguay*, Geneva, 1916

Cochrane, G. R. et al (eds): *Flowers and Plants of Victoria*, Reed, 1968

Collinson, A. S.: *Introduction to World Vegetation*, George Allen & Unwin, 1977

Du Plessis, N. & Duncan, G.: *Bulbous Plants of Southern Africa*, Tafelberg, 1989

Eley, Charles: *Twentieth Century Gardening*, Country Life, 1939

Elliott, W. Rodger & Jones, D. L.: *Encyclopaedia of Australian Plants*, Vols 1–4, Lothian, revised edn 1983

Ericksson, R. et al (eds): *Flowers and Plants of Western Australia*, Reed, 1973

File, Dick: *Weather Watch*, Fourth Estate, 1990

Fortune, Robert: *Three Years' Wanderings in China*, John Murray, 1847

Gardiner, Jim: *Magnolias – their care and cultivation*, Cassell, 1989

Gentry, H. S.: *Rio Mayo Plants*, Carnegie Institute, 1942

Gleason, Henry A. & Cronquist, Arthur: *The Natural Geography of Plants*, Columbia University Press, 1964

Munz, P. A.: *A Californian Flora*, University of California Press, 1939

Padilla, V.: *Bromeliads*, Crown, 1975

Palgrave, K. C.: *Trees of Southern Africa*, C. Struik, Cape Town, 1983

Pearce, E. A. & Smith, C. G.: *The World Weather Guide*, 2nd edn, Hutchinson, 1990

Pearson, S. & A.: *Rainforest Plants of Eastern Australia*, Kangaroo Press, 1992

Pesman, M. W.: *Meet Flora Mexicana*, Dale S. King, 1962

Polunin, Nicholas: *Introduction to Plant Geography*, Longmans, 1960

Ragonese, A. E.: *Vegetación y Ganadería en la República Argentina*, Colleccion cientifica del I.N.T.A., Buenos Aires, 1967

Richards, P. W.: *The Tropical Rain Forest*, Cambridge University Press, 1964

Royal Horticultural Society's Journal (now *The Garden*)

——— *New RHS Dictionary of Gardening*, 1992

——— *The Plantsman*

Sabuco, John J.: *The Best of the Hardiest*, 3rd edn, Plantsmen's Publications, 1990

Salisbury, E. J.: *The Living Garden*, G. Bell & Sons, 1935

Salmon, J. T.: *The Native Trees of New Zealand*, Reed, 1980

Schell, R.: *La Flore et la Végétation de l'Amérique Tropicale*, Masson, 1987

Sealy, R.: *A Revision of the Genus Camellia*, Royal Horticultural Society, 1958

Searle, S. A. & Smith, L. P.: *Weatherwise Gardening*, Blandford Press, 1958

Simmons, M.: *Acacias of Australia*, Nelson, 1981

Simonds, Calvin: *The Weather-wise Gardener*, Rodale Press, 1983

Smith-Dodsworth, John C.: *New Zealand Native Shrubs and Climbers*, David Bateman, 1991

Sohmer, S. H. & Gustafson, R.: *Plants and Flowers of Hawaii*, University of Hawaii Press, 1987

Stainton, J. D. A.: *Forests of Nepal*, John Murray, 1972

Taylor, J.: *Plants for Dry Gardens*, Frances Lincoln, 1993 (US: *Drought Tolerant Plants*, Prentiss Hall, 1993; Australia: *The Dry Garden*, Lothian, 1993)

—— *The Milder Garden*, J. M. Dent, 1990

Thomas, Arthur: *Gardening in Hot Countries*, Faber & Faber, 1965

Uhl, N. W. & Dransfield, J.: *Genera Palmarum*, L. H. Bailey Hortorum & International Palm Society/Allen Press, 1987

Urban, O.: *Plantas Endemicas de Chile*, Concepción, 1934

Verdoorn, F. (ed.): *Plants and Plant Science in Latin America*, Chronica Botanica, 1945

Vince-Prue, Daphne: *Photoperiodism in Plants*, McGraw Hill, 1975

Walker, J. & Hanly, G.: *The Subtropical Garden*, Godwit Press, 1992

Wallace, A. R.: *The Malay Archipelago*, Macmillan, 1902

Ward, F. Kingdon: *The Land of the Blue Poppy*, Cambridge University Press, 1913

—— *From China to Hkamti Long*, Edward Arnold, 1924

—— *The Romance of Plant Hunting*, Edward Arnold, 1924

—— *The Riddle of the Tsangpo Gorges*, Edward Arnold, 1926

—— *Plant Hunting on the Edge of the World*, Victor Gollancz, 1930

—— *A Plant Hunter in Tibet*, Jonathan Cape, 1934

—— *Plant Hunter's Paradise*, Jonathan Cape, 1937

—— *Assam Adventure*, Jonathan Cape, 1941

—— *Burma's Icy Mountains*, Jonathan Cape, 1949

—— *Plant Hunter in Manipur*, Jonathan Cape, 1952

—— *Return to the Irrawaddy*, Andrew Melrose, 1956

—— *Pilgrimage for Plants*, George G. Harrop 1960

Wettstein, R. R. v.: *Aspectos da Vegetação do Sul do Brasil*, University of São Paolo, 1904 (trs. 1970)

Wilson, E. H.: *A Naturalist in Western China*, Methuen, 1913

Winter, E. J.: *Water, Soil and the Plant*, Macmillan, 1976

Woodward, F. I.: *Climate & Plant Distribution*, Cambridge University Press, 1987

Worrell, E. & Sourry, L.: *Trees of the Australian Bush*, Angus & Robertson, 1968

Wrigley, J. W.: *Australian Native Plants*, Collins, 3rd edn, 1988

—— *Banksias, Waratahs and Grevilleas*, Collins, 1988

Index

INDEX

340

342

INDEX

343

INDEX

Hypocalymma angustifolium, 178; *H. cordifolium*,
181; *H. myrtifolium*, 181; *H. robustum*, 178; *H. speciosum*, 181
Hypoestis, 240
hyssop, 164

Iberian peninsula, 166
ice: hailstones, 109–10; precipitation, 110
ice age, 209
Idesia, 262; *I. polycarpa*, 261
ieie, 321
Ilex, 167, 221, 253, 255; *I. aquifolium*, 35, 158; *I. argentina*, 229; *I. cassine*, 222; *I. coriacea*, 222; *I. crenata*, 269; *I. decidua*, 221; *I. dipyrena*, 256; *I. doniana*, 214; *I. glabra*, 23, 219, 222; *I. opaca*, 221; *I. paraguariensis*, 228; *I. perado* ssp. *platyphylla*, 168; *I. verticillata*, 221; *I. vomitoria*, 219, 220
Illicium, 255; *I. floridanum*, 220; *I. henryi*, 264; *I. religiosum*, 217
illyarrie, 183
Impatiens, 214; *I. capensis*, 240; *I. tinctoria*, 325
Incarvillea, 266; *I. arguta*, 252; *I. grandiflora*, 260; *I. lutea*, 260; *I. mairei*, 267
incense plant, 231
incense tree, 217
indaba tree, 238
India, 252, 271; coastal flora, 318; monsoon, 87, 247; Mughal gardens, 14; rainfall, 107; subtropical climate, 211, 214; tropical climate, 15, 295, 313–15; tropical rain forests, 296, 297
Indian bean tree, 149
Indian crocus, 252
Indian Ocean, 40, 105, 211, 297, 312, 313, 317
Indian poke, 150
Indian shot, 30, 305
indigo, false, 148
Indigofera, 205, 265, 267
Indo-Malaya, 298, 313; tropical rain forest, 319–20
Indochina, 318
Indonesia, 232, 293, 297
Inga, 306; *I. dulce* see *Pithecellobium dulce*; *I. spuria*, 302
Ingram, Collingwood ('Cherry'), 17
inkberry, 23
Inula magnifica, 161
Iochroma grandiflora, 198, 227
Ipomoea, 204, 227; *I. alba*, 318; *I. arborescens*, 194, 196, 301; *I. batatas*, 321; *I. coccinea* see *Quamoclit coccinea*; *I. horsfalliae*, 304; *I. learii*, 228; *I. nil*, 34, 35; *I. pes-caprae*, 318; *I. purpurea*, 304; *I.p.* 'Heavenly Blue', 34
Iran, 161, 208, 275, 281
Ireland, 90
Iris, 131, 173, 259, 266; *I. caucasica*, 208; *I. chrysographes*, 260; *I. cristata*, 151; *I. douglasii*, 172; *I. ensata*, 157; *I.* 'Florentina', 166; *I. foetidissima*, 144; *I. forrestii*, 267; *I. histrio*, 166; *I. innominata*, 172; *I. japonica*, 264, 268; *I. kumaonensis*, 253, 266, 267; *I. lacustris*, 151; *I. laevigata*, 77, 157, 271; *I. pseudacorus*, 77, 144; *I. setosa*, 157; *I.*

sibirica, 147, 161; *I. spuria*, 143; *I. tenax*, 126; *I. tingitana*, 167; *I. unguicularis*, 167
iris: bearded, 145, 166; Dutch, 167; lake, 151; snake's head, 166; water, 157; widow, 166
iron, sulphate of, 71
iron plant, 204
ironbark, red, 206
ironwood, 149, 194, 195, 214, 221; Ceylon, 315; desert, 191
Irrawaddy River, 214, 247, 253, 257, 258, 315–16
irrigation, 74–6, *112*
island climates, 123–44
Isocoma, 193
Isophysis tasmanica, 134
Isoplexis canariensis, 168; *I. sceptrum*, 168
Isopogon, 179, 181; *I. anemonifolius*, 233; *I. anethifolius*, 233; *I. ceratophyllus*, 185; *I. cuneatus*, 180; *I. formosus*, 180; *I. latifolius*, 181; *I. teretifolius*, 182
Isopyrum thalicroides, 283
Isotoma axillaris, 185
Israel, 116
Italy, 116, 162, 166, 277, 278
Itea ilicifolia, 263; *I. virginica*, 221
Itoa, 262
ivory, red, 240
ivory curl, 322
ivory plum, 276
ivy, 37, 158
Ixerba brexioïdes, 137
Ixia, 176; *I. campanulata*, 176; *I. viridiflora*, 176
ixia: green, 176; red, 176
Ixora coccinea, 315; *I. duffii*, 317; *I. odorata*, 313
Izu, 270

Jacaranda, 12, 13, 306, 307; *J. filicifolia*, 304; *J. mimosifolia*, 308
jacaranda, pink, 312
Jacarctica dodecaphylla, 227
jack fruit, 313
Jack-in-the-green, 142
Jack-in-the-pulpit, 151
jackfruit, 15
Jacksonia, 183
Jacobinia ovata, 194
Jacquinia pungens, 196, 301
Jade Dragon mountains, 283
jam tree, 183
Jamaica cherry, 15
jambhool, 15
jambolan plum, 313
Jambosa jambos see *Syzygium jambos*
Jankaea heldreichii, 280
Japan: continental climate, 152, 153, 154, 155, 156, 157; droughts, 113; herbaceous flora, 271–2; monsoon, 247; mountain plants, 286; rainfall, 145; rhododendron heartland, 268–72; warm-temperate and subtropical climate, 209, 211–12, 217–18
Japan pepper, 153
jarrah, 43, 178, 179, 181